Public International Law Textbook

15th edition

Edited by Robert M MacLean

LLB, Dip LP, LLM

HLT Publications

HLT PUBLICATIONS
200 Greyhound Road, London W14 9RY

First published 1979
15th edition 1993

© The HLT Group Ltd 1993

ISBN 0 7510 0315 8

British Library Cataloguing-in-Publication.
A CIP Catalogue record for this book is
available from the British Library.

Acknowledgement
The publishers and author would like to
thank the Incorporated Council of Law
Reporting for England and Wales for kind
permission to reproduce extracts from the
Weekly Law Reports.

Printed and bound in Great Britain

Contents

Preface

HLT Textbooks are written specifically for students. Whatever their course, they will find our books clear and concise, providing comprehensive and up-to-date coverage. Written by specialists in their field, our textbooks are reviewed and updated on an annual basis.

This textbook is intended for those studying Public International Law at undergraduate level. It embraces all the principal topics found in the syllabus of university and polytechnic courses on this subject. Although the textbook stands as a work of its own, it is best employed when supplemented by the *Public International Law Casebook*, which has been written as a companion text.

This edition of the *Public International Law Textbook* takes into account the most current developments in the field of international law. From the United Kingdom courts, the decision in *Republic of Somalia* v *Woodhouse Drake and Carey (Suisse) SA* relating to the recognition of governments has been included. This decision is a landmark case in the jurisprudence of the UK courts towards the problem of recognising the standing of foreign governments.

Similarly the decision in *Wahda Bank* v *Arab Bank* provides an insight into the British courts' policy towards the effect of international sanctions on private contracts.

The International Court has also been quite active. It has rendered important decisions in the *Lockerbie Case* (interim measures of protection), *El Salvador* v *Honduras* (delimitation of land, island and maritime frontiers), the *Certain Phosphate Lands in Nauru Case* (time bar and limitation in international actions) and the *Guinea-Bissau* v *Senegal* case (appeal to the International Court of arbitral awards).

Also in this edition, we have given consideration to the controversial decision of the US Supreme Court in *United States* v *Alvarez-Machain*, in which the Supreme Court held that American courts had jurisdiction to try foreign nationals seized by US agents from foreign countries.

This edition takes into account the developments in the law occurring prior to 30 March 1993.

Table of Cases

Table of Statutes

Table of Treaties.

Including Covenants, Treaties, Conventions, ICJ Statute and UN Charter.

Table of Documents – Agreements, Declarations, Resolutions, etc

1

Introduction

1.1 The historical development of international law

1.2 The nature of public international law

1.1 The historical development of international law

The development of international law is uniquely and indissolubly linked with the emergence of the nation State, and the accompanying decline of the imperial order. Yet it is to the imperial order that international law owes a rich intellectual legacy, notably the Ius Gentium of Roman Law. The Ius Gentium was the common universal law based on the doctrine of the universal law of nature; the significance of this concept lay in the fact that although it was shared by all nations it did not connote a common jurisdiction. The Ius Gentium also served the Christian notion of a universal order underlying Christendom and so it survived the dark ages and into the middle ages. Until the Renaissance, the idea of empire remained the principal concept of political science.

Intellectually, the imperial concept was strongly questioned by many of the great thinkers in the sixteenth century. Both Bodin and Hobbes saw the authority of the sovereign as the best guarantee of the well being of the subject by protecting him from the evil of civil strife. Thus the concept of sovereignty emerged.

Sovereignty has separate but related connotations. It places the supreme power within the State, but since all States are equally sovereign, sovereignty also conveys the idea of independence. The claim of a State to be sovereign does not mean that the power of the State is subject to no limitations. The obvious limitation is territorial: any State is finite and has necessary boundaries. Beyond the scope of its boundaries, where its writ does not run, the independence of each State presupposes that of the others. Sovereignty as a concept is decisive in distinguishing Europe from the rest of the world. In the East the decline of empire spelt anarchy and a power vacuum which led to colonial subjugation. In the West power was devolved to States, content simply to rule themselves rather than to succeed to the imperial mantle. This growing relationship between sovereign States provides the customary source for international law.

The origin of the international community is commonly traced back to the Peace Treaty of Westphalia (1648) which brought to an end the Thirty Years War in

1

Europe. While the identification of one particular date belies the fact that relations between communities had from time immemorial been conducted on a formal footing which exhibited many of the characteristics of law (eg the conduct of diplomatic relations or the conclusion of treaties of alliance), the Peace of Westphalia signalled the development in Europe of the sovereign nation State independent of the church. While Europe, prior to the Peace of Westphalia, had been dominated by two competing power structures – the Catholic Church and ecclesiastical law on the one side and the Holy Roman Empire and Imperial law on the other – the end of the Thirty Years War saw first acceptance of the notion of a secular State with sovereign rights. As Professor Cassese has put it:

> ' ... the Peace of Westphalia testified to the rapid decline of the Church ... and to the de facto disintegration of the Empire; by the same token it recorded the birth of an international system based on a plurality of independent states, recognising no superior authority over them'.

The intellectual origins of international law run concurrently with the development of sovereignty. The two leading figures in the field were Hugo Grotius and Gentillus. The former is commonly spoken of as 'the father of international law' and published *De Jure Belli ac Pacis* in 1625. The latter was an Italian law professor, an adviser of governments and a practitioner of international law. It is essential to understand that these two academics were theologians by training and looked to the middle ages for their ideas. They recognised and feared the new edifice of the nation State and sought to discipline this new phenomenon by recourse to the Ius Gentium of Rome. It has been argued that the contribution of Grotius to the development of modern international law has been overstated. The substantive matters of international law were hardly touched by him and derived from municipal law analogies. Treaties were considered on par with contract. The rules governing the acquisition and loss of territory derived from Roman law and were not markedly different from municipal law. Put simply, this thesis maintains that international law was municipal law writ large.

However, there is one area where this thesis breaks down. The boundaries of nations do not move as the boundaries of private estates do when fortunes of families wax and wane. Even in the middle ages territorial sovereignty was something more than real property. Thus, one must recognise that the State is the political expression of a community based on land, and there is a distinct element of command behind the transfer of land and changes in boundaries. It is in the idea that the transfer of land means more than property, and approximates to the right to govern a sub-community, that the term of the doctrine of self-determination lies.

To examine Grotius and other Renaissance lawyers for the intellectual origins of international law is to misread the Renaissance mind. During this period a vast mass of literature was produced on methods of preserving peace. This literature articulates many of the assumptions upon which the lawyers wrote and throws much light on the origins of the discipline. Some of the better known examples of this writing were

Sir Thomas More's *Utopia*, Dante's *De Monarchia* and Sully's *The Grand Design of Henry IV*. The common assumption shared by the authors was the containment and directive of political power. The *Grand Design* explained the division of Europe on equitable principles designed to ensure a balance of power. The ideas in the literature are in opposition to the growing nation State and are sustained by the medieval idea of empire. It is through this parallel system that modern Europe inherited from medieval Europe a conception counter-balancing the doctrine of sovereignty.

Later, the principles came to be known as the public law of Europe – a description apt in that it assigns it a legal as opposed to political nomenclature but unhappy in that it suggests it has only a regional rather than a universal application.

It must be recognised that these ideas predate the system by several centuries. The notions of 'neutrality' and a 'permanent diplomatic mission' did not develop until the eighteenth century. After the Napoleonic wars, the Congress of Vienna saw the first major summit meeting to organise peace by the Major Powers. A series of international treaties established the neutrality of Switzerland (1815) and of Belgium (1831); laid down general rules for the navigation of rivers (1815), and specific regulations for the Rhine; codified law relating to maritime warfare (Declaration of Paris 1856). During this period State practice produced the framework for modern international law dealing with recognition of States, which achieved prominence in the attitudes of Great Britain and the USA to the independence of Greece. Rules governing State responsibility also developed. The present century has witnessed efforts to limit or abolish war as an instrument of national policy (Kellogg-Briand Pact, 1928). Thus, the concept was formed and the foundations of modern international law were laid.

1.2 The nature of public international law

Is international law, law?

The standard question is whether international law is law at all. This question may be examined at two levels:

Firstly: people believe that States have little respect for international law and have no incentive to comply with it in the absence of world government. This belief springs firstly from the common misconception that international law is broken with impunity. But the same could be said of any legal system. In English criminal law, where prosecutions are brought by the police, around 60 per cent of crimes known to the police are never solved, and there must be a larger number which are never reported in the first place. The breaches of international law are more spectacular than the comparatively staid law of international co-operation. Secondly, people imagine that international disputes are not necessarily governed by international law, just as disputes between individuals are not necessarily governed by national law.

Secondly: does international law conform to a proper legal system? This question has suffered from the Austinian fallacy. John Austin, the nineteenth century positivist, argued that international law is not really law because it has no sovereign. He defined laws 'properly so called' as commands of a sovereign. A sovereign he defined as a person who received the habitual obedience of the members of an independent political society and who, in turn, did not owe such obedience to any person. Rules of international law did not qualify as rules of positive law by this test and not being commands of any sort were placed in the category of laws 'improperly so called'.

The reply of any international lawyer would be to ask what legal system does conform to Austin's concept. In the USA the separation of powers does not admit a single sovereign; and in the UK the legislature is not the only source of law-making. His criticism of international law is largely based on his peculiar conception of law. But it must be conceded that his definition of law does not invalidate his criticism and he does expose one problem which constitutes the crisis of contemporary international law; the lack of effective enforcement mechanisms.

Professor Hart's reply to Austin does not answer this problem. He argues that international law is law, but in a primitive form. His conception of law includes primary and secondary rules: the primary rules impose duties and the secondary rules are the rules of adjudication. Hart concludes that a system largely reliant on primary rules can constitute a legal system.

It is of interest to examine international law secondary rules with reference to those of a municipal system.

Rules of change
Every legal system needs rules of change. Laws are not fixed and immutable: they are shaped and moulded to meet the changing needs of society. In municipal law change is largely effected through legislation.

It has been argued that treaties are the closest analogy to legislation in international law: they are a flexible and precise mechanism for effecting government's policy. However, it has also been argued that treaties are more akin to contract than legislation – a source of obligation rather than law. If a treaty is viewed as a bargain concluded between parties then it is apparent that parties are more concerned with their own self-interest rather than with the 'general good' so characteristic of legislation.

The proposition that treaties are consensual obligations gives rise to the following results:

1. States are not bound unless they consent to them;
2. governments may be in a position to pick and choose parts of a treaty to obey;
3. States are empowered to opt out of the process at any time.

If the analogy between treaties and legislation is in doubt, then what about the role of custom in international law? The common factor it shares with legislation is that all parties are bound, regardless of consent. This argument, however, overlooks the fact that consent permits a general practice to crystallise and become custom. States pursue a practice because they wish to do so. Moreover, dissent, even if not major, can mean that customary international law will not bind the dissenting State. The proponents of custom as international legislation can reply with the example of new States. They are automatically bound by laws they never consented to. However, the trend is against implied consent. The Latin American States for example rejected the rules regarding the continental shelf and in practice it is irrelevant that such rejection is technically illegal.

Adjudication

In contrast to adjudication in municipal law, there is no obligation upon States to appear before the International Court of Justice (ICJ) at the Hague unless the parties have consented in advance. However, while consent is still integral to the process of international adjudication, its limiting effect is increasingly subject to review as more mechanisms for dispute settlement *require* consent to be granted as a prerequisite for the operation of the system concerned.

Machinery for enforcement

In municipal systems the machinery for enforcement is centralised in the governmental authority. In international law it is of necessity decentralised, since the subjects of international law are sovereign States.

Professor Kelsen has argued that international law does have machinery for enforcement. Traditionally, in a decentralised society enforcement of laws is accomplished through self-help. The legal order leaves enforcement to the individuals injured by the delict or illegality. He states: 'Although in this case the individuals appear to take the law into their own hands, they may nevertheless be considered as acting as organs of the community.'

Kelsen's argument is not without a historical attraction. Until recently the use of force did constitute a recognised method of enforcing international law. However, the use of force, except in self-defence, is now illegal. The problem therefore arises as to what to put in place of self-help as a means of enforcement.

It was widely thought that the Charter of the United Nations would provide a substitute, particularly by means of provisions which enable collective action to be taken against an aggressor or State committing a breach of the peace. This approach however is to misunderstand the ambit of the Charter's provisions. It is not against law breaking in the generic sense, but against particular law breaking that takes the form of an act of aggression or a breach of peace. Moreover, even when a clear act of aggression has been committed the Security Council has until recently been reluctant to exercise its powers, with the veto symbolic of the East-West conflict in the Security Council.

But if the United Nations sanctions were of little practical importance and remain unproven, the sanctions the law of co-operation can provide may be more effective. Professor Friedmann has argued that States who wilfully fail to discharge their obligations to international institutions can be excluded from the benefits. The World Bank, for example, withheld a loan to Tanzania on the ground that Tanzania had nationalised UK property in a unfair and discriminatory manner.

Having examined the inadequacies of international law's secondary rules, Hart's contention that it conforms to a legal system is not entirely convincing. Austin's view that international law is similar to positive morality may therefore be closer to the truth. The flaw in such an argument, however, is that States do in practice distinguish between moral and legal obligations.

The fact that States do distinguish between these respective obligations is evidenced in the following instances.

When a non-legal rule is turned into a legal rule it acquires a vigour it never had before. An immoral or discourteous act is regarded in a worse light if it is illegal as well. Argentina reacted sharply to the Israeli abduction of Eichmann from Argentina, not out of any regard for Eichmann, but because such an abduction constituted an infringement of Argentina's rights under international law. A sphere of influence is also buttressed if put on a legal basis. The USA has promised by treaty to protect Europe and so America is more likely to honour her promise.

When a non-legal rule is turned into a legal rule, arguments about its scope take on a new dimension. Lawyers are trained not only to know the law when the law is clear, but also how to argue a case when the law is not clear, how to interpret or distinguish previous authorities, how to make use of analogies, etc.

Legal argument is a distinctive form of argument. The applicability of legal argument to particular rules is both a consequence and proof of the legal nature of those rules; to argue about the rules of morality or etiquette as one would rules of law is clearly absurd. As Hart has said:

> 'What predominates in the arguments, often technical, which states address to each other over disputed matters of international law, are references to precedents, treaties and juristic writings; often no mention is made of moral right or wrong ... Hence the claim that the Peking Government has or has not the right under international law to expel the Nationalist Forces from Formosa, is very different from the question whether this is fair, just, or a morally good or bad thing to do, and is backed by characteristically different arguments.'

If the contention that States do distinguish in practice between a moral and a legal obligation – giving aid to the Third World and adhering to the rules of a shipping convention – then it is possible to state that international law exists because it is perceived to exist.

Situations to which international law is relevant

If it is accepted that international law does exist, what form does it take? It is suggested that international law is relevant at three separate levels in international relations: the level of co-operations; co-existence; and conflict.

Co-operation

States are naturally interdependent in many ways and international law facilitates co-operation. States have a common interest in an international postal system, stamping out disease by means of common rules as to vaccination. These are areas where action on an international scale is essential, and in general, States obey these rules of international law.

Co-existence

States have to co-exist with one another and a means of doing this is to define their relationships in treaties and other consensual obligations. At this level, Professor Schwarzenberger has argued, obedience is high and the law is generally effective. Several reasons have been suggested for this fidelity. The concept of reciprocity plays an important part in State thinking. Since international relations is uniquely concerned with the actions of States, a gain in foreign policy is only considered as a gain in relation to other States. Thus, if State A nationalises assets of State B, State B might nationalise assets of State A, or State B might use force in retaliation. There is both medium- and long-term thinking involved. The former is illustrated by an example of a State thinking of extending its territorial waters, but not doing so because it may encourage other States to do the same. In the long term all States have an interest in international stability, so there is an incentive not to rock the boat excessively.

An important psychological reason for compliance with international law may also be that all foreign offices have a legal department with international lawyers. These lawyers are generally trained initially as municipal lawyers and as a consequence they support a legal approach and observe legal niceties. Moreover, they are supported in this by bureaucrats, who out of basic inertia, like to comply with rules.

Conflict

The role of international law is confined to two main functions: (1) the technical rules of conduct, (2) keeping the breach to the minimum.

For example, many of the rules of warfare exist in an unwritten form but some of the rules are embodied in international conventions, particularly the Hague and Geneva Conventions. All these rules are included in manuals of military law for use by commanders in the field.

The impact of breach is in many cases psychological. States will try to keep violations of international law to the minimum. A good example of this psychological impact is evinced in the US blockade of Cuba. In the Suez Crises, Sir Patrick Dean, the Foreign Office legal adviser, and the Lord Chancellor were consulted throughout.

2

The Sources of International Law

2.1 Introduction

2.2 Treaties

2.3 Custom

2.4 The relationship between treaties and custom

2.5 General principles of law

2.6 Judicial decisions

2.7 The writings of publicists

2.8 Other sources of international law

2.1 Introduction

When referring to sources of international law, international lawyers usually begin by reference to Article 38 of the Statute of the International Court of Justice (ICJ). This provision, adopted from the same article in the Statute of the Permanent Court of International Justice (PCIJ) which operated under the League of Nations system, is frequently regarded as enumerating *all* the sources of international law. While there is little doubt that Article 38(1) does embody the most important sources of law, it is increasingly becoming the case that international lawyers will have regard to instruments and principles that do not fit comfortably into this structure. General Assembly resolutions, international trade practice, treaties not yet in force and principles of equity widely drawn are becoming increasingly important additional sources of law. It remains the case, however, that any examination of the sources of international law must begin with an assessment of the provisions of Article 38(1) of the State of the ICJ.

Article 38(1) of the Statute of the ICJ provides:

The Court, whose function is to decide in accordance with international law such disputes as are submitted to it, shall apply:

1. international conventions, whether general or particular, establishing rules expressly recognised by the contesting States:
2. international custom, as evidence of a general practice accepted as law;
3. the general principles of law recognised by civilised nations;
4. judicial decisions and the teachings of the most highly qualified publicists of the various nations, as subsidiary means for the determination of rules of law.

Does Article 38(1) create a hierarchy of sources?

The sources enumerated in Article 38(1) are not stated to represent a hierarchy but they do represent an order of importance which in practice the Court may be expected to observe.

For example: if there is a dispute between State A and State B, the first point an international tribunal will examine will be the treaty governing the particular relationship breached, and if there is no treaty then custom will be examined. But it is possible that neither treaty nor custom may be apparent for the international tribunal to base its decision upon. In such a situation an international tribunal will have recourse to the general principles of international law recognised by civilised nations. But if the conventions, practices and principles are not clear from evidences of the behaviour of States, the tribunal may resort to judicial decisions and teachings of the most highly qualified publicists of the various nations as a subsidiary means for the determination of the rules of law.

The distinction between 'formal' and 'material' sources

Salmond explains the distinction in the following terms:

> 'A formal source is that from which a rule of law derives its force and validity ... The material sources, on the other hand, are those from which is derived the matter, not the validity of the law. The material source supplies the substance of the rule to which the formal source gives the force and nature of law.'

For example, a rule will be legally binding if it meets the requirements of a custom, which is a formal source of international law, and its substance will be indicated by State practice, which is the material source of the custom.

2.2 Treaties

Treaties represent a source of international law, the importance of which is ever increasing.

The effect of a treaty on the formation of rules of international law depends upon the nature of the treaty concerned. In this respect a distinction is sometimes made between law-making treaties, ie those treaties which lay down rules of general or universal applications, and treaty contracts, eg a treaty entered into between two or only a few States, dealing with a particular matter concerning those States exclusively. While this distinction may be helpful in distinguishing treaties – usually multilateral – which are general in nature and which establish common principles of law, from those – usually bilateral – which focus more on the regulation of particular conduct (eg trade), it is important to bear in mind that a treaty of whatever kind is a direct source of obligation for the parties. The binding force of a treaty comes from the consent of the parties, *not* from the subject-matter or form of the treaty.

Law-making treaties

Since the middle of the nineteenth century there has been a great development of law-making treaties primarily due to the inadequacy of custom in meeting the demands of States for rules regulating the industrial and economic changes which have taken place.

These treaties deal with a wide range of activities. For example, the Red Cross Conventions, the protection of submarine cables, the suppression of the slave trade, international waterways, the pacific settlement of international dispute, the control of narcotics, nationality and statelessness.

These are all matters which called urgently for international statute law and where it would have been impossible to rely on the eventual emergence of customary rules.

Treaty contracts

Treaty contracts, unlike law-making treaties, are usually concerned to regulate a narrow area of practice between two States (eg trade agreements). Such treaties may lead to the formation of general international law through the operation of the principle governing the development of customary rules.

1. A series of treaties laying down a similar rule may produce a principle of customary international law to the same effect.
2. A rule contained in a treaty originally concluded between a limited number of parties may subsequently be accepted or imitated as a general rule.
3. A treaty may have evidentiary value as to the existence of a rule which has crystallised into law by an independent process of development.

The essential characteristics of treaties

The essential characteristic of a treaty as a source of law is that it becomes binding on the parties to the treaties by virtue of their consent. While there may be limited circumstances in which a treaty may create rights or duties for third States (see Articles 34–37, Vienna Convention on the Law of Treaties, 1969), it remains the case that a treaty, *qua* treaty, will only be binding as between its parties.

While treaties will, in most cases, be written instruments concluded between States, the term applies equally to unwritten agreements and to agreements between States and international organisations (eg the Convention on the Privileges and Immunities of the United Nations of 1946) and between international organisations. Agreements between States and private parties, while exhibiting many of the characteristics of treaties, and frequently subject to the same rules of interpretation, are generally described by some other terms, eg concessions.

Many treaties, particularly those of a multilateral nature designed to establish general rules of common application, exhibit a mixture of 'legislative' characteristics. There may, for example, be provisions which purport to *codify* existing rules of customary law, eg Article 55 of the 1982 Law of the Sea Convention which provides for the recognition of the Exclusive Economic Zone. Equally, a treaty provision may *crystallise* a developing rule of law, firmly establishing on a legal footing a situation which had hitherto been part of the practice of a limited number of states, eg the 1958 Convention on the Continental Shelf which placed on a legal footing the practice that had developed amongst some States since 1945 to claim an area of sea-bed off their coast. Finally, treaty provisions may *generate* rules of law independently of the previous practice of States, eg Article 2(4) of the United Nations Charter which prohibits the threat or use of force on international relations.

2.3 Custom

The ICJ in the *Asylum Case: Columbia* v *Peru* (1950) described custom as a 'constant and uniform usage, accepted as law', ie those areas of State practice which arise as a result of a belief by States that they are obliged by law to act in the manner described.

Evidence of custom

Brownlie lists the following in a non-exhaustive list of the material sources of custom: diplomatic correspondence, policy statements, press releases, the opinions of official legal advisers, official manuals on legal questions (eg manuals of military law), executive decisions and practices, orders to naval forces etc, comments by governments on drafts produced by the International Law Commission, State legislation, international and national judicial decisions, recitals in treaties and other international instruments, a pattern of treaties in the same form, the practices of international organs, and resolutions relating to legal questions in the United Nations General Assembly.

General and regional customs

Custom may be either general or regional. General customs are those customary rules binding upon the international community as a whole. Local or regional customs are those applicable to a group of States or just two States in their relations *inter se*.

In the *Right of Passage Case: Portugal* v *India* (1960) the ICJ accepted the argument that a rule of regional custom existed between India and Portugal. The Court said:

'With regard to Portugal's claim of a right of passage as formulated by it on the basis of local custom, it is objected on behalf of India that no local custom could be established between only two States. It is difficult to see why the number of States between which a local custom may be established on the basis of long practice must necessarily be larger than two. The Court sees no reason why long continued practice between two States accepted by them as regulating their relations should not form the basis of mutual rights and obligations between the two States'.

Local customs may supplement or derogate from general customary international law.

The elements of custom

As indicated above, the ICJ in the *Asylum Case* described custom as a constant and uniform usage, accepted as law. The Court did not, however, go on to describe what degree of uniformity of practice and over what duration would be sufficient for the practice to meet the requirement of 'constant and uniform'. Nor did the Court give any indication as to the evidence that would be required before a constant and uniform practice would become a rule of customary law. For example, there is probably a constant and uniform practice to salute the ranking officers in the armed forces of another friendly State. However, it is unlikely that this practice would be regarded as a rule of law. It is rather a rule of comity. In determining which examples of practice are to be regarded as embodying rules of law it is important, therefore, to determine whether that practice is 'accepted as law' by the State carrying out the act. That is, State practice will only be transformed into customary law when the State concerned is conducting itself in the belief that the action is required by law. This element of subjective intention can, however, be extremely difficult to ascertain in practice.

Following the *Asylum Case*, four questions remained for consideration:

1. What duration of practice is required?
2. How uniform and consistent must the practice be to give rise to a rule of law?
3. How is the Court to determine the subjective element in practice, ie an acceptance that the practice is based on law?
4. How general must the practice be in order to bind third States?

Duration of the practice

The jurisprudence of the ICJ indicates that no particular duration is required for practice to become law provided that the consistency and generality of a practice are proved.

In the *North Sea Continental Shelf Cases* (1969) it was recognised that there is no precise length of time during which a practice must exist; simply that it must be followed long enough to show that the other requirements of a custom are satisfied:

> 'Although the passage of only a short period of time is not necessarily, or of itself, a bar to the formation of a new rule of customary international law on the basis of what was originally a purely conventional rule, an indispensable requirement would be that within the period in question, short though it might be, State practice, including that of States whose interests are specially affected, should have been both extensive and virtually uniform in the sense of the provision invoked – and should moreover have occurred in such a way as to show a general recognition that a rule of law or legal obligation is involved.'

Uniformity and consistency of the practice

It is clear that major inconsistencies in practice will prevent the creation of a rule of customary international law. In the *Asylum Case* the ICJ noted that:

> 'The facts brought to the knowledge of the Court disclose so much uncertainty and contradiction, so much fluctuation and discrepancy in the exercise of diplomatic asylum and in the official views expressed on different occasions; there has been so much inconsistency in the rapid succession of conventions on asylum, ratified by some States and rejected by others, and the practice has been so much influenced by considerations of political expediency in the various cases, that it is not possible to discern in all this any constant and uniform usage, accepted as law...'

However, complete uniformity is not required and minor inconsistencies will not prevent the creation of a customary rule provided that there is substantial uniformity. In the *North Sea Continental Shelf Cases*, the Court noted only that State practice should be 'both extensive and virtually uniform'. This question of the uniformity and consistency of practice was returned to by the Court in the *Nicaragua Case* (*Nicaragua v US; Merits*, 1986) where the ICJ indicated that it was not necessary that all State practice be rigorously consistent in order to establish a rule of custom. It would suffice that conduct *in general* was consistent with the rule and that instances of practice inconsistent with the rule be treated as breaches of that rule rather than as recognition of a new rule.

Acceptance of the practice as law – *opinio juris et necessitatis*

To assume the status of customary international law the rule in question must be regarded by States as being binding in law, ie that they are under a legal obligation to obey it.

In this way customary rules of international law may be distinguished from rules of international comity which are simply based upon a consistent practice of States not accompanied by any feeling of legal obligations, eg the saluting by a ship at sea of another ship flying a different flag.

The distinction between those international rules which create a legal obligation and those which simply permit a State to act in a certain way was illustrated in the *Lotus Case: France v Turkey* (1927).

The question before the Court was whether Turkey had the jurisdiction to try the French officer of a French merchant ship which had, through his alleged negligence, collided with a Turkish merchant ship on the high seas, causing loss of life.

Turkey argued before the Court that in the absence of a rule to the contrary, there was a permissive rule empowering her to try the officer. France, however, argued that there was a customary rule imposing a duty on Turkey not to try the officer as previous practice showed that 'questions of jurisdiction in collision cases ... are but rarely encountered in the practice of criminal courts ... in practice prosecutions only occur before the Courts of the State whose flag is flown'.

The Court rejected the French argument. 'Even if the rarity of the judicial decisions to be found among the reported cases were sufficient to prove in point of fact the circumstances alleged by the Agent for the French Government, it would merely show that States had often, in practice, abstained from instituting criminal proceedings, and not that they recognised themselves as being obliged to do so; for only if such abstention were based on their being conscious of having a duty to abstain would it be possible to speak of an international custom. The alleged fact does not allow one to infer that States have been conscious of having such a duty ...'

Can opinio juris *or intention be presumed from the general practice of States or must it be strictly proved?* In the *North Sea Continental Shelf Cases* the ICJ required that *opinio juris* be strictly proved:

> 'Not only must the acts concerned amount to a settled practice, but they must also be such, or be carried out in such a way, as to be evidence of a belief that this practice is rendered obligatory by the existence of a rule of law requiring it. The need for such a belief, ie the existence of a subjective element, is implicit in the very notion of the *opinio juris sive necessitatis*. The States concerned must therefore feel that they are conforming to what amounts to a legal obligation. The frequency, or even habitual character of the acts is not in itself enough. There are many international acts, eg in the field of ceremonial and protocol, which are performed almost invariably, but which are motivated only by considerations of courtesy, convenience or tradition, and not by any sense of legal duty.'

A number of the dissenting judges, however, took issue with this strict requirement. Judge Sorenson, echoing comments made years earlier by Sir Hersch Lanterpacht, argued that because of the difficulty in establishing *opinio juris*, uniform conduct should be taken as implying the requisite intention unless the contrary was established. Judge Tanaka, in contrast, proposed that *opinio juris* be inferred from evidence of a need for that rule in the international community. In the *Nicaragua Case*, the majority of the Court accepted that, in cases where a rule of customary law existed alongside a rule of treaty law with similar content, *opinio juris* could be deduced by examining the attitude of the parties to the particular convention. This approach has, however, come in for widespread criticism on the grounds that it confuses two different sources of obligation – a treaty, binding because of the express consent of the parties, and custom, which only becomes law when practice and intention are separately proved. Given the practical difficulties in establishing *opinio juris*, however, it seems likely that the Court will place increasing emphasis on determining the extent of the practice and will be ready to infer *opinio juris* from those examples of practice that confirm that the actions in issue are not merely casual acts or acts dictated by international comity.

Generality of the practice

The recognition of a particular rule as a rule of international law by a large number of States raises a presumption that the rule is generally recognised. Such a rule will be binding on States generally and an individual State may only oppose its application by showing that it has persistently objected to the rule from the date of its first formulation.

In the *Anglo-Norwegian Fisheries Case* (1951), for example, the Court, rejecting the UK argument that the 10 mile closing line for bays was a rule of customary international law, went on to observe that even if it had acquired the status of a rule of customary international law '[i]n any event the ... rule would appear to be inapplicable as against Norway, in as much as she has *always opposed* any attempt to apply it to the Norwegian coast'.

However, universality is not required to *create* a customary rule and it will be sufficient if the practice has been followed by a small number of States provided that there is no practice conflicting with that rule. Therefore, rules of customary law can exist which are not binding on all States: the practice may be limited to a small group of States, or a State may contract out of a custom in the process of formulation.

In the *Asylum Case*, the ICJ stated:

'The Columbian Government has finally invoked "American international law in general" ... it has relied on an alleged regional or local custom particular to Latin American States.

The Party which relies on a custom of this kind must prove that this custom is established in such a manner that it has become binding on the other Party. The Columbian Government must prove that the rule invoked by it is in accordance with a constant and uniform usage practised by the States in question, and that this usage is the expression of a right appertaining to the State granting asylum and a duty incumbent on the territorial State. This follows from Article 38 of the Statute of the Court, which refers to international custom "as evidence of a general practice accepted as law".'

The Court having commented on the uncertainties and contradictions disclosed by the practice of the States concerned continued:

'The Court cannot therefore find that the Columbian Government has proved the existence of such a custom. But even if it could be supposed that such a custom existed between certain Latin American States only, it could not be invoked against Peru which, far from having by its attitude adhered to it, has, on the contrary, repudiated it by refraining from ratifying the Montevideo Conventions of 1933 and 1939, which were the first to include a rule concerning the qualification of the offence in matters of diplomatic asylum.'

2.4 The relationship between treaties and custom

As indicated above, treaty provisions will frequently have a close relationship with custom. This relationship flows in both directions: treaties may give rise to rules of custom and treaties may reflect pre-existing or evolving rules of custom. In the *North Sea Continental Shelf Cases* the argument advanced on behalf of Denmark and the Netherlands was that, even though Germany was *not* party to the Geneva Convention on the Continental Shelf and was not, therefore, bound by Article 6 of that Convention in respect of the delimitation of the shelf, that a rule of customary law of similar content had developed since the adoption of the Convention.

The Court accepted that a norm-creating provision in a treaty could indeed generate a rule of customary law which would become binding on third parties. However, it indicated that this process is not to be lightly inferred. The Court continued to lay down a number of conditions that would have to be satisfied before the process could be accepted:

1. the provision should be of a fundamentally norm-creating character;
2. while a very widespread and representative participation in the Convention would suffice, such participation must include those States whose interests would be specially affected by the provision in question. A treaty rule could not become binding on third parties as a rule of custom if those third parties had not shown their consent to the rule;
3. within the period of time since the adoption of the Convention, State practice, including that of States whose interests are specially affected, must have been both extensive and virtually uniform.

In other words, for a treaty provision to become binding as a rule of customary international law, the party invoking the rule must be in a position to show that the rule meets all the general requirements for the creation of customary law.

This approach by the Court was further advanced by Judge Arechaga who suggested that a treaty may reflect custom in one of three ways:

1. it may be *declarative* of custom, ie it may *codify* a pre-existing rule of customary law;
2. it may *crystallise* a rule of custom in *statu nascendi*, ie in the process of development;
3. it may serve to *generate* a rule of custom in the future; ie a treaty rule may come to be accepted as a rule of custom.

The process of concluding a treaty will of itself have important consequences for the content of the rule of custom. In the first case above, for example, it is likely that the process of codification will alter the content of the customary rule. The very act of putting down in words what had hitherto been a flexible, unwritten rule will exert an influence on the content of that rule. Equally, the process of interpreting and amending a rule of treaty law will be different from that relating to custom. The fact that a treaty purports to codify custom does not mean, therefore, that the content of the rule will remain the same.

In the second case – that of crystallisation – the act of concluding the treaty may be an important example of State practice. The treaty-making process, with its detailed discussions on the content of the rule and inevitable compromises between Parties, may see the content of the emerging rule change. The objective of certainty in the treaty provisions may thus be achieved at the expense of the flexibility of the rule of custom.

The argument in the *North Sea Continental Shelf Cases* discussed above provides an example of generative treaty provisions. A more recent example arose in the context of the *Nicaragua Case*. In that case the ICJ accepted that Article 2(4) of the United Nations Charter – a treaty provision prohibiting the threat or use of force – had, together with other instruments such as General Assembly resolutions, the effect of generating a rule of customary law of similar content to Article 2(4) which existed side-by-side with the treaty provisions.

The relationship of treaty law to customary law is important in one other respect. In the event of a conflict between a rule of treaty and a rule of custom which rule prevails? While it nevertheless is generally accepted that Article 38(1) of the Statute does not create a strict hierarchy of sources of law, it is possible to discern a number of principles and propositions relating to the hierarchy of sources:

1. general rules of interpretation apply; eg the principles of *lex posterior* – a new treaty replaces an old treaty (see Article 30, Vienna Convention on the Law of Treaties, 1969) – and *lex specialis* – a special rule prevails over a general rule – will be relevant in the event of conflicting treaty provisions;
2. the *North Atlantic Fisheries Case* (1910) establishes the principle that developments in customary law will not relieve a state of its obligations under treaty;
3. Article 103 of the UN Charter provides that the Charter is to prevail over any inconsistent treaty obligations. A number of commentators have suggested that this provision would apply equally to inconsistent customary law;
4. perhaps the clearest proposition is that to be found in Articles 53 and 64 of the Vienna Convention on the Laws of Treaties of 1969 which provides that a treaty that is in conflict with a rule of *jus cogens* – *peremptory verus* of international law – will be void. In such circumstances, therefore, rules of custom will prevail over inconsistent treaty provisions.

These propositions not withstanding, the better view is probably that whether the Court will apply a rule of custom or conflicting rule of treaty law will depend largely on the circumstances of the case in issue.

2.5 General principles of law

Article 38(1)(c) of the Statute of the ICJ refers to 'the general principles of law recognised by civilised nations'. Sir Hersch Lauterpacht noted that this provision was first introduced into the Statute of the PCIJ by the Commission of Jurists charged with drawing it up in order to avoid the problem of 'non-liquet' – the argument that a court could not decide a matter because there was no law on the subject. If there is no treaty relevant to the dispute, or if there is no rule of customary international law that can be applied, the Court is directed to apply general principles of law.

The meaning and scope of the phrase

There is little agreement as to the precise significance of the phrase.

In the course of discussion by the Advisory Committee of Jurists on Article 38(1)(c) Lord Phillimore, the author of that provision, stated that:

> 'The general principles referred to ... were those which were accepted by all nations in *foro domestico*, such as certain principles of procedure, the principle of good faith, and the principle of *res judicata*, etc.'

Oppenheim states that: 'The intention is to authorise the Court to apply the general principles of municipal jurisprudence, in particular of private law, in so far as they are applicable to relations of State.'

In this way private law, being in general more developed than international law, has provided a reserve store of legal principles upon which international law can draw. The inclusion of Article 38(1)(c) has therefore been seen as a rejection of the positivist doctrine, according to which international law consists solely of rules to which States have given their consent, and as affirming the naturalist doctrine whereby if there appeared to be a gap in the rules of international law recourse could be had to general principles of law, ie to natural law. For example, the writers of the seventeenth and eighteenth centuries, when dealing with questions as to the acquisition of territory, turned for assistance to the rules of Roman private law.

The difficulty in evaluating the role of these general principles, however, is that Article 38(1)(c) does not make clear if it is referring to general principles of international law recognised by civilised nations or general principles of law in the broadest sense, including principles of private law which have their counterpart in most developed legal systems.

References by international tribunals to general principles of law

It is difficult to establish the precise extent to which general principles have been used by international tribunals as specific reference to such sources is rarely made in their judgments. However, some references do exist. For example: In the *Chorzow Factory Case* (1927) the Permanent Court of International Justice stated that: 'the Court observes that it is a principle of international law, and even a general concept of law, that any breach of an engagement involves an obligation to make reparation'.

In the *Eastern Carelia Case* (1923) the Court referred to the independence of States as being a 'fundamental principle of international law'.

Examples of municipal principles of law adopted by international tribunals

Res judicata: *United Nations Administrative Tribunal Case* (1973)
The ICJ referred to the 'well established and generally recognised principle of law (that) a judgment rendered by a judicial body is *res judicata* and has binding force between the parties to the dispute'.

Estoppel: *Temple Case* (1962)
The ICJ was asked to rule that Cambodia and not Thailand, had sovereignty over the Temple of Preah Vihear. In 1904 the boundary between Cambodia (then a French protectorate) and Thailand (then Siam) was determined by a treaty between France and Siam under which a map was prepared which placed the Temple in Cambodia. The Siamese received and accepted the map without protest and in 1930 a Siamese Prince actually paid a State visit to the disputed area where he was officially received by the French authorities.

The Court with reference to these facts stated that:

> 'Even if there were any doubt as to Siam's acceptance of the map in 1908, and hence of the frontier indicated thereon, the Court would consider, in the light of the subsequent course of events, that Thailand is now precluded by her conduct from asserting that she did not accept it.'

Circumstantial evidence: *Corfu Channel Case*: *United Kingdom* v *Albania* (1949)
The ICJ remarked that 'this indirect evidence is admitted in all systems of law, and its use is recognised by international decisions'.

Other examples of municipal principles adopted by international tribunals include prescription; the rule that no man may be judge in his own suit, etc.

The application by international tribunals of general principles

As the afore-going illustrates, international tribunals have not been slow in having recourse to general principles of law in the absence of other rules of international law or in order to complement their application. There remains, however, the question of the manner in which these rules are applied. Are they, for example, imparted into international law directly from one or other municipal legal system? This issue was addressed by Lord McNair in his Separate Opinion in the *South West Africa Case* (1950) in which South Africa's obligations under the mandate were considered. Drawing analogies with the municipal concept of a trust, McNair, however, indicated that international law would not import 'lock, stock and barrel' principles found in municipal legal systems. It was rather a question of finding legal principles appropriate to the case in issue and to apply them in a manner consistent with international law.

A similar approach has more recently been adopted by the European Court of Justice (ECJ) in its protection of fundamental rights within the Community legal order. The Treaty of Rome provides no explicit protection for fundamental human rights. In many cases, however, fundamental rights are safeguarded by the laws and constitutions of the Member States. In *Internationale Handelsgesellschaft* (1970) the ECJ confirmed that fundamental rights formed part of the general principles of law protected by the Court. While, however, the protection of these rights may be inspired by the constitutional traditions of the Member States, the application of these principles must be ensured within the framework, and according to the objectives, of the Community.

Apart from the manner of application of general principles, the question also arises as to the ambit of the search before a principle can be applied as a general principle of law. Would it be sufficient, for example, that a principle was found in one municipal legal system? If not, how common must be the principle to be accorded the status of a general principle? The better view seems to be that there is no hard and fast rule on the matter. Much will depend on the nature of the case before the Court, the parties to the case and any special agreement concluded giving the Court or tribunal jurisdiction. In the *LIAMCO Case* (1977), for example, the arbitration agreement provided that the tribunal should apply principles common to Libyan law and international law and, failing this, general principles of law. Arbitrator Mahmassani, in applying this clause, looked at principles of law found in common law and Arab legal systems.

2.6 Judicial decisions

Article 38(1)(d) of the Statute of the ICJ directs the Court to apply:

'... subject to the provisions of Article 59, judicial decisions ... as subsidiary means for the determination of rules of law'.

Article 59 of the Statute of the Court provides that:

'The decision of the Court has no binding force except between the parties and in respect of that particular case.'

There is, therefore, no binding authority of precedent in international law and international court and tribunal cases do not make law. Judicial decisions are not, therefore, strictly speaking a formal source of law.

It can be argued, however, that if an international tribunal is unable to discover an existing treaty or customary rule relevant to a dispute, any rule which the tribunal adopts in deciding the case will, in theory at least, form a new rule of international law. The question is whether the new rule is a rule of customary law or whether the tribunal's decision may itself, be regarded as a source of international law.

Examples of 'law making' by international tribunals

Several decisions of the ICJ have introduced innovations into international law which have subsequently won general acceptance.

Anglo-Norwegian Fisheries Case (1951)

Norway had promulgated a series of decrees claiming as the baseline of Norwegian territorial waters the general line of the Skjaergaard – a series of islands and rocks stretching along Norway's north-western coast, often at considerable distance from the mainland. As a result a large area of what was formerly high seas became enclosed as Norwegian national waters and closed to British fishing.

The UK contested the legality of Norway's acts before the ICJ. The Court held that the method of baselines employed by Norway was not contrary to international law given, *inter alia*, the special geographical facts involved and the economic interests peculiar to the region.

The Court in effect, therefore, created a new rule of international law for the delimitation of the territorial sea in those parts of the world where peculiar geographical and economic factors are present.

Reparations Case (1949)

The ICJ was asked to advise whether the United Nations had the right to present a claim on the international plane against a State for injuries suffered by United Nations officials in the performance of their duties. The Court decided that the United Nations could claim damages under international law against a State responsible for injuries suffered by its officials.

The Court's decision that such a power could be implied from the express functions entrusted to the Organisation was clearly an extension of the rights of the Organisation as laid down in the Charter and thus created a new principle in international law.

Judicial precedent and the Statute of the Court

Article 59 of the Statute was intended to prevent the Court from establishing a binding system of judicial precedent.

In the *German Interests in Polish Upper Silesia Case* (1926) the Court stated that:

> 'The object of (Article 59) is simply to prevent legal principles accepted by the Court in a particular case from being binding on other States or in other disputes.'

In its practices the Court has, however, of necessity followed previous decisions in the interests of judicial consistency, and has where necessary distinguished its previous decisions from the case actually being heard.

Interpretation of Peace Treaties Case (*1950*). The General Assembly of the United Nations requested an advisory opinion regarding the interpretation of the peace treaties with Bulgaria, Hungary and Rumania. The three States refused to take part in the proceedings before the Court and it was argued that, following the *Eastern Carelia Case*, the Court should decline to give an advisory opinion. In the *Eastern Carelia Case* the Court had held it to be a fundamental principle that a State could not, without its consent, be forced to submit its dispute to arbitration or judicial settlement.

The Court in rejecting this argument said:

'Article 65 of the Statute is permissive. It gives the Court the power to examine whether the circumstances of the case are of such a character as should lead it to decide to answer the Request. In the opinion of the Court, the circumstances of the present case are profoundly different from those which were before the Permanent Court of International Justice in the *Eastern Carelia Case* (Advisory Opinion No. 5), when that Court declined to give an Opinion because it found the question put to it was directly related to the main point of dispute actually pending between two States, so that answering the question would be substantially equivalent to deciding the dispute between the parties, and that at the same time it raised a question of fact which could not be elucidated without hearing both parties.

... the present Request for an Opinion is solely concerned with the applicability to certain disputes of the procedure for settlement instituted by the Peace Treaties, and it is justifiable to conclude that it in no way touches the merits of those disputes.'

Decisions of national courts

Article 38(1)(d) of the Statute of the Court is not confined to international decisions. Although not in the same category as international courts and tribunals, the decisions of municipal courts do have some evidential value. It should also be noted that decisions of municipal courts will also form part of the practice of a state for the purposes of deciding on rules of custom.

Municipal decisions may also be important sources of material on sovereign and diplomatic immunity and the laws of prize.

2.7 The writings of publicists

Article 38(1)(d) directs the Court to apply:

'The teachings of the most highly qualified publicists of the various nations, as subsidiary means for the determination of rules of law.'

Although this source only constitutes evidence of customary law, learned writings can also play a subsidiary role in developing new rules of law.

The contributions of writers such as Grotius, Bynkershoek and Vattel were very important to the formulation and development of international law, and writers of general works, such as Oppenheim, Hall, Hyde, Guggenheim and Rousseau, have international reputations. Although it is sometimes argued that some writers reflect national and other prejudices, their opinions are used widely by legal advisers to States, arbitral tribunals and courts. Their value has been described as follows:

'International law is part of our law, and must be ascertained and administered by the courts of justice of appropriate jurisdiction, as often as questions of right depending upon it are duly presented for their determination. For this purpose, where there is no treaty, and no controlling executive or legislative act or judicial decision, resort must be had to the customs and usages of civilised nations; and as evidence of these, to the works of jurists and commentators who by years of labour, research, and experience have made themselves peculiarly well acquainted with the subjects of which they treat. Such works are resorted to by judicial tribunals, not for the speculations of their authors concerning what the law ought to be, but for trustworthy evidence of what the law really is.'

2.8 Other sources of international law

As indicated at the outset, the sources of law enumerated in Article 38(1) of the Statute are often regarded as comprising the sum of the traditional sources of international law. Increasingly, however, this approach is subject to limitation as international courts and tribunals look to additional sources to give them guidance on the law. Many of these 'new' sources may be squeezed within existing headings. Given the evolution of international law and the changes taking place in international society it may, however, be more sensible to look to such sources as additional sources of law. The most important of these sources of law are as follows:

General Assembly resolutions (GAR) and resolutions of other international organisations

There is often confusion in the approach by many writers to the question of whether GAR constitute a source of international law. Under the provisions of the Charter the majority of such resolutions have no direct legal affect (unlike decisions of the Security Council which, under Article 25, are to be binding). However, it is clear that some resolutions embody a clear consensus of the international community. Other resolutions may be very significant in influencing the development of international law and practice.

Attempt is often made to fit GAR into the parameters of either treaty or custom. Clearly, such resolutions do not conform to the formal requirements of a treaty and it may perhaps be unrealistic to apply treaty rules on interpretation, amendment etc, to them. Equally, GAR do not on their face meet the requirements laid down for customary law – constant and uniform usage accepted as law. The compromise is generally to regard GAR – and resolutions of other international bodies – as evidence of customary law. The weight of the evidence would be determined by considering all the relevant factors surrounding the adoption of the resolution in question – the degree of support for the resolution; whether or not that support was widespread amongst ideologically or politically divided groups; the intention of States in voting for the resolution as illustrated by the debates; the form of words used, etc. This approach was adopted by arbitrator Dupuy in the *Texaco* (1977) arbitration in which he considered the legal effect of two General Assembly resolutions: GAR 1803 (1962) on the Permanent Sovereignty over Natural Resources and GAR 3281 (1974), the Charter of Economic Rights and Duties of States.

Although GAR 3281 was adopted twelve years after GAR 1803 with very strong support from developing states – 120 votes in favour, 6 against (Belgium, Denmark, FRG, Luxembourg, UK and USA) and 10 abstentions – Dupuy concluded that it was GAR 1803 that reflected existing customary law. The reasoning behind this was that GAR 1803 had achieved wide support from both the capital importing (developing) States and capital exporting (Western) States. GAR 1803 was therefore illustrative of a broad consensus between the groups likely to be affected by its provisions. In contrast, GAR 3281 had received virtually no support from capital exporting States. To be regarded as evidencing customary law, a resolution must be seen to have gathered support from a broad cross-section of the international community.

A recent example in which resolutions of the General Assembly were held to be reflective of customary international law arose in the *Nicaragua Case* (1986). In that case the majority of the Court considered that GAR 2625 (1970) on Principles of International Law Concerning Friendly Relations and Co-operation Among States was illustrative of customary law. While there is little dispute about the relative importance of this resolution or about the broad measure of support it achieved (it was adopted by consensus), some commentators have voiced concern at the manner in which the Court accepted that the resolution could be evidence of both State practice *and opinio juris* for the purposes of establishing custom. Any acceptance of this dual characteristic of such resolutions would have the effect of elevating GAR to a form of 'instant custom'. This approach remains highly controversial.

Equity

Equity is most frequently regarded as coming within the concept of general principles of law discussed above. Certainly, this will be true in many respects as has been illustrated in the context of the doctrine of estoppel and good faith generally (see Chapter 14). It is clear, however, that international tribunals have resorted to equity or equitable principles quite apart from general principles derived from municipal law. Perhaps the best example of this wider definition of equity is to be found in the concept of 'relevant circumstances' employed by the Court in cases of maritime delimitation. Resort to equity in these circumstances may be more easily assimilated with resort to principles of fairness and justice. It is nevertheless important to stress that equity in this context remains an element of a *legal* decision. It must be contrasted with the *ex aequo et bono* provision in Article 38(2) of the Statute. In the *Gulf of Maine Case* (1982) the Court held that while the latter would permit a Court or tribunal to examine socio-economic and political considerations, equity as a component of a legal decision would involve the Court in taking a decision on the basis of legal reasoning.

Other sources of law may include:

Treaties not yet in force. While the provisions of a treaty not yet in force will not be binding qua treaty provisions they may be persuasive as between those States that have signed and ratified the treaty. Note also that Article 18, Vienna Convention on the Law of Treaties, 1969, imposes a positive obligation on a state that has indicated its consent to be barred from defeating the object and purposes of the treaty.

Draft treaties and texts adopted by the International Law Commission. While such 'sources' of law are often regarded as writings of publicists, the significance of such attempts at the codification or development of international law require, perhaps, that they be considered as an independent 'source' or evidence of law.

International trade practice and usages. A number of commentators have suggested that there is a developing body of *lex mercatoria* which may be applied by international courts and tribunals in the case of disputes involving questions of international trade.

3

International Law and Municipal Law

1.1 Introduction

1.2 The relationship between international law and municipal law

1.3 The application of municipal law before international tribunals

1.4 The application of international law in UK courts

1.5 Conclusion

3.1 Introduction

The relationship between international law and municipal law gives rise to two main problems:

Firstly, the theoretical question as to whether international law and municipal law are a part of a universal legal order (monist doctrine) or whether they form two distinct systems of law (dualist doctrine).

Secondly, the situation where there exists a conflict between the rules of international law and the rules of municipal law:

1. before an international tribunal,
2. before a municipal court.

3.2 The relationship between international law and municipal law

The question of the relationship of international law to municipal law is of more than just academic interest. As well as the jurisprudential questions relating to the relationship of the two systems of law (eg whether they form part of one all-embracing legal system but with different spheres of operation or whether they form two distinct systems) it will frequently be important to determine the scope of the application of rules of international law before domestic tribunals and vice versa. So, for example, it is important to be able to determine the scope of the application of the European Convention on Human Rights in English law in order to be able to

26

determine whether or not it is possible to found a claim for breach of the Convention before English courts. At the *jurisprudential level*, the relationship of international law to municipal law has been cast in terms of the monist/dualist debate. At the level of the *practical application* of international law before UK courts, this debate is cast in terms of the incorporation/transformation debate. While these debates are important, it is in the nature of things that they focus on general issues. The actual relationship of international law to English law can only be properly understood by examining the jurisprudence of English law on the questions of the application of treaties, custom and other sources of international law in English courts.

Dualism

Dualist doctrine is closely connected with positive doctrine and considers international law and municipal law to be two separate legal orders existing independently of one another. It is based on the view that international law is the law applicable between sovereign States and that municipal law applies within a State to regulate the activities of its citizens. On this basis, neither legal system has the power to create or alter rules of the other.

Where there is a conflict between international law and municipal law, municipal courts following the dualist doctrine would give precedence to municipal law.

Monism

Monism considers international law and municipal law to be both part of the same legal order and emphasises the supremacy of international law even within the municipal sphere. It is supported by the naturalist doctrine that authority and legal duty are both subject to the universality of natural law.

Advocates of the doctrine, such as the late Sir Hersch Lauterpacht considered a supreme universal law a more trustworthy repository of civilised values than the municipal law of the nation States and thus better able to give effect to the protection of international human rights.

The Fitzmaurice Doctrine

Sir Gerald Fitzmaurice sought to overcome the conflict between the monist and dualist schools by challenging their common premiss that there exists a common field in which the two legal orders both simultaneously have their spheres of activity.

He argued that the two systems do not come into conflict as systems since they operate in different spheres, each being supreme in its own field. Formally, therefore, international and domestic law as systems can never come into conflict.

There may, however, occur a conflict of obligations, or an inability on the part of the State on the domestic plane to act in a manner required by international law. In such cases if nothing can be or is done to deal with the matter, it does not invalidate the local law, but the State will, on the international plane, have committed a breach of its international law obligations for which it will be internationally responsible.

On a practical level, whether or not the municipal courts follow the monist, dualist or Fitzmaurice approach to the relationship of international law and municipal law will be determined by the constitutional law of the State concerned. Thus, the constitutions of many of the civil law States of Continental Europe provide expressly that customary international law is to be regarded as part of the domestic law of the State concerned. So, for example, Article 10 of the Italian constitution provides that 'Italian law shall be on conformity with the generally recognised rules of international law.'

Common law traditions have also largely accepted this principle in the case of customary international law. In the UK, for example, the accepted view is still probably that customary law forms part of the law of the land to be applied by English courts unless it is in conflict with a provision of statute.

As with customary law, the reception of treaty law into domestic law will be determined by the constitutional traditions of the state concerned. Once again, many of the civil law States of Continental Europe accept as a general premise that treaties may be directly applicable by the courts of that State. The approach of common law systems is frequently more confusing. In the USA, for example, a treaty may only be ratified with the approval of two-thirds of the Senate (unlike the UK where no parliamentary involvement is required for the conclusion of a treaty). Although the Constitution provides that treaties shall be the 'supreme law of the land', US courts have since developed the distinction between 'self-executing' and 'non-self-executing' treaties. Thus, self-executing treaties, which confer certain rights upon citizens, rather than being primarily a 'compact between independent Nations', will be applied by US courts in the same way as with Federal laws. Not so the case with respect to non-self-executing treaties. Whether or not a treaty should be regarded as self-executing is, however, frequently a matter of debate.

In the UK, as is discussed below, constitutional convention dictates that only treaties that have been incorporated into domestic law by Act of Parliament may be given effect by UK courts. In the last analysis, therefore, the relationship between international law and municipal law at the level of municipal courts, is determined by the municipal law of the State concerned.

3.3 The application of municipal law before international tribunals

There is ample judicial and arbitral authority for the rule that a State cannot rely upon the provisions or deficiencies of its municipal law to avoid its obligations under international law.

Alabama Claims Arbitration (1872)

During the American Civil War, a number of ships were built in England for private buyers. The vessels were unarmed when they left England but it was generally known that they were to be fitted out as warships by the Confederates in order to attack Union shipping. These raiders caused considerable damage to American shipping. The USA sought to make Great Britain liable for these losses on the basis that she had breached her obligations as a neutral during the War in contravention of the 'Three Rules of Washington'.

Great Britain argued *inter alia* that under English law as it then stood, it had not been possible to prevent the sailing of vessels constructed under private contracts.

In rejecting the British argument the arbitrators had no hesitation in upholding the supremacy of international law:

'... the government of Her Britannic Majesty cannot justify itself for a failure in due diligence on the plea of insufficiency of the legal means of action which it possessed. ... It is plain that to satisfy the exigency of due diligence, and to escape liability, a neutral government must take care ... that its municipal law shall prohibit acts contravening neutrality.'

Polish Nationals in Danzig Case *(1931)*

In the *Polish Nationals in Danzig Case* (1931) the Permanent Court of International Justice stated that:

'It should ... be observed that ... a State cannot adduce as against another State its own constitution with a view to evading obligations incumbent upon it under international law or treaties in force. Applying these principles to the present case, it results that the question of the treatment of Polish nationals or other Persons of Polish origin or speech must be settled exclusively on the basis of the rules of international law and the treaty provisions in force between Poland and Danzig.'

UN Headquarters Agreement Case *(1988)*

Most recently, the principle of international law that international law prevails over municipal law was reaffirmed by the ICJ in its Advisory Opinion in the *UN Headquarters Agreement Case* (1988).

The principle of primacy of international law over municipal law before international tribunals applies to all aspects of a States municipal law, to its constitutional provisions, its ordinary legislation and to the decisions of its courts.

The validity of conflicting laws

The conflict between a State's municipal law and its international obligations does not necessarily affect the validity of that law on the municipal plane. Thus a municipal act contrary to international law may be internally recognised as valid but other States will be under no duty to recognise its external effects.

3.4 The application of international law in UK courts

Customary international law as part of English law

Can English law have regard to rules of customary international law? In the event of a conflict, which rule prevails? Two approaches are in evidence here: the *doctrine of transformation*, ie that customary international law only forms part of English law to the extent that it has been made part of English law by Act of Parliament, judicial decision or established usage; and the *doctrine of incorporation*, ie that rules of customary international law are automatically part of English law as long as they are not inconsistent with Acts of Parliament or authoritative judicial decision.

The doctrine of incorporation

The traditional rule is that, provided they are not inconsistent with Acts of Parliament or prior authoritative judicial decisions, rules of customary international law automatically form part of English law.

The doctrine of incorporation is supported by a long line of authority.

In *Buvot* v *Barbuit* (1737) Lord Chancellor Talbot declared: 'That the law of nations, in its full extent was part of the law of England'.

Holdsworth described the approach of the English courts as follows:

> 'It would, I think, have been admitted that, if a Statute or a rule of the common law conflicted with a rule of international law, an English judge must decide in accordance with the statute or the rule of common law. But, if English law was silent, it was the opinion of both Lord Mansfield and Blackstone that a settled rule of international law must be considered to be part of English law, and enforced as such.'

The doctrine of transformation

It has been argued by some writers that in some cases decided since 1876, the doctrine of incorporation has been displaced by that of transformation, ie customary international law forms a part of the law of England only in so far as it has been accepted and made part of the law of England by Act of Parliament, judicial decision, or established usage.

In *R* v *Keyn* (1876) the *Franconia*, a German ship, collided with the *Strathclyde*, a British ship in British territorial waters. The defendant, the German captain of the *Franconia*, was prosecuted for the manslaughter of a passenger on board the *Strathclyde* who was drowned as a result of the collision. The defendant was found guilty. However the question whether an English court had jurisdiction to try the case was reserved for the Court of Crown Cases Reserved which decided by seven votes to six that it did not.

The majority was of opinion that the English court did not have jurisdiction in the absence of an Act of Parliament granting such jurisdiction. This decision has been interpreted as supporting the 'transformation' approach and as displacing the doctrine of incorporation.

However *Keyn* remains an ambiguous precedent, the true *ratio decidendi* being difficult to establish from among the eleven different judgments delivered.

Lauterpacht, commenting on the case observed:

'... it cannot be said that this judgment amounts to a rejection of the rule that international law is a part of the law of England. Writers seem to forget that the main issue of the controversy in the case was not the question whether a rule of international law can be enforced without an Act of Parliament; what was in dispute was the existence and the extent of a rule of international law relating to jurisdiction in territorial waters.'

In *West Rand Central Gold Mining Co* v *R* (1905) Lord Alverstone CJ in an obiter statement while appearing to support the principle of transformation, noted that:

'It is quite true that whatever has received the common consent of civilised nations must have received the assent of our country, and that to which we have assented along with other nations in general may properly be called international law, and as such will be acknowledged and applied by our municipal tribunals'.

However, these words would seem to rest on an assumption that the doctrine of incorporation holds good. Indeed, Oppenheim regards the case as 'a reaffirmation of the classical doctrine', ie of incorporation.

In *Mortensen* v *Peters* (1906), Court of Judiciary, Scotland, the judgment of Lord Dunedin, Lord Justice-General contains the following dictum:

'It is a trite observation that there is no such thing as a standard of international law extraneous to the domestic law of a kingdom, to which appeal may be made. International law, so far as this Court is concerned, is the body of doctrine ... which has been adopted and made a part of the law of Scotland.'

This statement is understood to be in favour of the transformation doctrine.

A remark made by Lord Justice Atkin in *Commercial and Estates Company of Egypt* v *Board of Trade* (1925) is also regarded as supporting the doctrine of transformation:

'International Law as such can confer no rights cognisable in the municipal courts. It is only in so far as the rules of International Law are recognised as included in the rules of municipal law that they are allowed in municipal courts to give rise to rights and obligations.'

In *Chung Chi Cheung* v *The King* (1939) Lord Atkin, delivering the opinion of the Privy Council, stated:

'It must always be remembered that, so far, at any rate, as the Courts of this Country are concerned, international law has no validity, save in so far as its principles are accepted and adopted by our own domestic law. There is no external power that imposes its rule upon our own code of substantive law or procedure.

The Courts acknowledge the existence of a body of rules which nations accept amongst themselves. On any judicial issue they seek to ascertain what the relevant rule is, and having found it, they will treat it as incorporated into the domestic law, so far as it is not inconsistent with rules enacted by statutes or finally declared by their tribunals.'

Lord Denning MR followed the transformation approach of Lord Atkin in the case of *Thakrar* v *Secretary of State for the Home Office* (1974).

The current approach

Three years after his decision in *Thakrar*, Lord Denning reversed his views on the relationship between customary international law and English law. In *Trendtex Trading Corporation* v *Central Bank of Nigeria* (1977) he put the argument in these terms:

> 'A fundamental question arises for decision: what is the place of international law in our English law? One school of thought holds to the doctrine of incorporation. It says that the rules of international law are incorporated into English law automatically and considered to be part of English law unless they are in conflict with an Act of Parliament. The other school of thought holds to the doctrine of transformation. It says that the rules of international law are not to be considered as part of English law except in so far as they have been already adopted and made part of our law by the decisions of the judges, or by Act of Parliament, or long established custom. The difference is vital when you are faced with a change in the rules of international law. Under the doctrine of incorporation, when the rules of international law change, our English law changes with them. But, under the doctrine of transformation, the English law does not change. It is bound by precedent.
>
> As between these two schools of thought, I now believe that the doctrine of incorporation is correct. Otherwise I do not see that our courts could ever recognise or change on the rules of international law'.

Since *Trendtex* it has been generally accepted that, in so far as customary international law is concerned, the doctrine of incorporation applies. Some doubt has, however, recently been cast on this view following the decision by the House of Lords in the *International Tin Council Cases* (1989). Although the issue directly in point was not one of customary law, the dismissal by the Lords of a subsidiary argument involving recourse to custom, with reference that custom was a 'rule of construction', has led some commentators to remark that English law has reverted to a strongly dualist approach. Given the complexity of the litigation and the fact that a rule of customary law was not directly in issue, the better view is probably that the decisions of the Lords on the *International Tin Council Cases* do not radically alter the situation one way or another. In so far as custom is concerned, it probably remains correct to say that the prevailing doctrine is that of incorporation.

Situations in which English courts cannot apply customary international law

If there is a conflict between customary international law and an Act of Parliament, the Act of Parliament prevails

In *Mortensen* v *Peters* (1906) the appellant was a Dane and the master of a Norwegian ship. He was convicted by a Scottish court of otter trawling contrary to a by-law issued by The Fishery Board for Scotland. He argued that the by-law was in contravention of a rule of international law limiting territorial waters to bays and estuaries of no greater breadth of 10 miles.

His appeal against conviction was dismissed unanimously by a full bench of 12 judges. The Lord Justice-General, Lord Dunedin said:

'In this Court we have nothing to do with the question of whether the Legislature has or has not done what foreign powers may consider a usurpation in a question with them. Neither are we a tribunal sitting to decide whether an Act of the Legislature is *ultra vires* as in contravention of generally acknowledged principles of international law. For us an Act of Parliament duly passed by Lords and Commons and assented to by the King is supreme, and we are bound to give effect to its terms.'

Where such matters as the status of a foreign State or government, or the existence of a state of war, are in issue

English courts accept a certificate signed by the Foreign Secretary as being conclusive of such questions. The determination in the Foreign Office Certificate is treated by the courts as conclusive and therefore no independent judicial determination will be entered into by the courts.

The 'Act of State' doctrine

Under English constitutional law an alien injured abroad by an act authorised or subsequently ratified by the Crown has no remedy in the English courts.

Treaty rules and their relation to English law

In the UK, the conclusion and ratification of treaties are within the prerogative of the Crown. Parliament has no part in this process. If the courts could apply treaties in municipal law, the Crown would be in a position of being able to alter English law without parliamentary consent. To forestall this, treaties are only part of English law if an enabling Act of Parliament has been passed.

In *The Parlement Belge* (1878–79) Sir Robert Phillimore reaffirmed in that part of the first instance decision which still stands that the Crown, by entering into a treaty cannot alter the law of England.

If such an Act is not passed by Parliament, the treaty is nevertheless still binding on the UK from the international point of view.

There is a distinction, therefore, between the effects of a treaty in international law and the effects of a treaty in municipal law. The treaty is effective in international law when ratified by the Crown. But if the treaty alters the law of England it has no effects in municipal law until an Act of Parliament is passed giving it effect.

The general rule that an English court may not look at an unincorporated treaty has been confirmed by a number of recent decisions. In the *International Tin Council Cases* (1989) the House of Lords confirmed the rule that an English court could not examine the International Tin Agreements to establish the liability or otherwise of Member States of the International Tin Council. This rule has since been strictly interpreted by the Court of Appeal in *Arab Monetary Fund* v *Hashim* (1990) where they held that the decision by the House of Lords in the *International Tin Council Cases* precluded the court from having reference to and applying the provisions of a treaty establishing the Arab Monetary Fund. In this case, the Arab Monetary Fund had legal personality, owned assets and conducted business in the UK. The UK was not a party to the treaty of establishment. However, owing to the English constitutional rule requiring transformation in respect of treaties, the court held that they could not have regard to the treaty. Each of the three Lord Justices of Appeal however remarked on the obvious injustice of the result, indicating that it was up to Parliament to legislate to change the matter.

Treaties and the interpretation of statutes in the UK

It is a general principle of British constitutional law that in the case of a conflict statute prevails over treaty.

However, as a rule of construction where domestic legislation is passed to give effect to an international convention, there is a presumption that Parliament intended to fulfil its international obligations.

In *Salomon* v *Commissioners of Customs and Excise* (1967) a provision of a statute being ambiguous, the court had to consider whether recourse could be had to a treaty, which the provision was intended to implement, to interpret the provision.

Diplock LJ stated:

'... if the terms of the legislation are not clear but are reasonably capable of more than one meaning, the treaty itself becomes relevant, for there is a *prima facie* presumption that Parliament does not intend to act in breach of international law, including therein specific treaty obligations; and if one of the meanings which can reasonably be ascribed to the legislation is consonant with the treaty obligations and another or others are not, the meaning which is consonant is to be preferred'.

Lord Diplock went on to hold that provided there is cogent extrinsic evidence that the statute was intended to give effect to a particular international convention, then that convention may be consulted as an aid to interpretation of the statute.

In *R* v *Chief Immigration Officer, ex parte Bibi* (1976) the point at issue was whether Immigration Rules made under the Immigration Act 1971 should be interpreted and applied by immigration officers in accordance with the right to family life in Article 8 of the European Convention on Human Rights.

Lord Denning MR stated:

'The position as I understand it is that if there is any ambiguity in our statutes, or uncertainty in our law, then these Courts can look to the Convention as an aid to clear up the ambiguity and uncertainty, seeking always to bring them into harmony with it. Furthermore, when Parliament is enacting a Statute, or the Secretary of State is framing rules, the Courts will assume that they had regard to the provisions of the Convention, and intended to make the enactment accord with the Convention: and will interpret them accordingly. But I would dispute altogether that the Convention is part of our law. Treaties and declarations do not become part of our law until they are made law by Parliament.'

This rule of construction does not, however, extend to the interpretation of subordinate legislation. In *R* v *Secretary of State for the Home Department, ex parte*

Brind (1990) the Court of Appeal refused to apply this principle in an application by a number of journalists for judicial review of the right of the Home Secretary to issue directives to broadcasting authorities prohibiting the broadcast of statements by proscribed terrorist organisations in Northern Ireland. The applicants contended that the directives were unlawful because they violated Article 10 of the European Convention on Human Rights, which provides that the right to freedom of expression includes the freedom 'to receive and impart information and ideas without interference by public authorities'. According to the applicants, the Home Secretary was obliged to exercise his powers in a manner consistent with the European Convention.

While the court was prepared to acknowledge the existence of a presumption that statutes and primary legislation should be interpreted in a manner consistent with the international obligations of the UK, it was not prepared to accept that this principle extended to the interpretation of secondary legislation or executive action. The court held that, where Parliament has delegated subordinate legislative powers to ministers or other functionaries, it has enacted the primary legislation in full knowledge of the obligations of the UK. Parliament has therefore had an opportunity to draft the primary legislation in light of the obligations of the UK and if no express reference was made in the delegation to the terms of an international agreement, no such restraints could be imposed on the discretion of the Minister exercising the power.

The court therefore concluded that an extension of this principle of construction to subordinate legislation would involve 'imputing to Parliament an intention to import international conventions into domestic law by the back door, when it has quite clearly refrained from doing so by the front door'.

The principal exception to the rule that the courts will not give direct effect to international treaties is, of course, the treaties establishing the European Community. The three original constitutional agreements – the European Coal and Steel Community Treaty, the European Economic Community Treaty and the EURATOM Treaty – together with the various treaties amending these agreements may have direct effect in the law of the UK, given the existence of certain conditions.

Provisions of the Community treaties may be given direct effect in the UK notwithstanding that there has been no implementing legislation passed to give effect to them. This became evident after the House of Lords rendered its judgment in *R v Secretary of State for Transport, ex parte Factortame (No 1)* [1989] 2 WLR 997.

In this case the House of Lords had to consider whether the Merchant Shipping Act 1988 was superseded by, *inter alia*, Article 5 of the EEC Treaty. The court fully embraced the principle of the direct effect of provisions of the EEC Treaty and Lord Bridge of Harwich commented:

> 'Directly enforceable Community rights are part of the legal heritage of every citizen of a Member State of the EEC. They arise from the Treaty itself and not from any judgment of the ECJ declaring their existence. Such rights are automatically available and must be given unrestricted retroactive effect.'

Once the principle of the direct effect of Community treaties is accepted, the next question that arises is which type of law prevails in the event of conflict – a provision of the Community treaties or an Act of Parliament? This question was also settled as part of the *Factortame* saga.

The House of Lords referred the question of supremacy to the European Court which replied that the Community treaties prevailed over an Act of the British Parliament. Once the House of Lords had received the decision of the ECJ on this point, it was obliged to apply it to the facts of the case before it. In *R* v *Secretary of State for Transport, ex parte Factortame (No 2)* [1990] 3 WLR 818, again Lord Bridge delivered the leading opinion. In explaining the modification of the doctrine of parliamentary sovereignty in the case of Community treaty provisions, Lord Bridge observed by way of obiter:

> '[W]hatever limitation of its sovereignty Parliament accepted when it enacted the European Communities Act 1972 was entirely voluntary. Under the terms of the Act of 1972 it has always been clear that it was the duty of a United Kingdom Court, when delivering final judgment, to override any rule of national law found to be in conflict with any directly enforceable rule of Community law'.

3.5 Conclusion

The discussion above illustrates the different approach adopted by English courts to the application of customary international law and treaty law in UK courts. The reasoning behind this approach is clear enough – that, as Parliament had no part in the conclusion of treaties, treaties should not create legal obligations within the UK. However, given the discussion above (in Chapter 2) on the relationship between treaty and custom, the question to be asked is whether this distinction is warranted. After all, the fact that the UK is party to a treaty will be important evidence of State practice when determining whether or not the rule embodied in that treaty is part of customary international law. If the rule in question is indeed part of customary law, English courts – under the doctrine of incorporation – will be in a position to apply the rule whether or not the treaty in question has been transformed into UK law. In many cases, therefore, the strict rule against unincorporated treaties may be bypassed. It may well be the case, therefore, that the approach of English courts to the application of international law will have to undergo further refinement.

4

International Personality

4.1 Introduction

The conferment of legal personality is an acknowledgement of capacity on the part of an entity to exercise certain rights and be subject to certain duties under a particular system of law.

In municipal law the individual human being is the typical subject of the law. Under international law, however, the State is the typical legal subject. It alone has capacity to make claims on the international plane in respect of breaches of international law, capacity to make treaties and other binding international agreements, and enjoys privileges and immunities from national jurisdiction. Other entities may only be considered as the subjects of international law in so far as they can enter into international legal relations.

Thus, the traditional view was that only States are subjects of international law. They alone are capable of possessing international rights and duties and they alone have the capacity to maintain those rights by bringing international claims. However, following the establishment of the United Nations and the resulting proliferation of international organisations it is now increasingly recognised that international law is no longer exclusively limited to the rights and duties of States. It is now beyond contention that international organisations can have a measure of international personality. Increasingly, also, there is a trend towards accepting that private persons – whether legal or natural – may have limited international personality for the purposes of carrying out a limited category of transactions.

In spite of these modern developments, however, States remain the primary subjects of international law. The reasoning underlying the primacy of the State has been stated by Professor Friedman as follows:

'The basic reason for this position is, of course, that the world is to-day organised on the basis of the co-existence of States, and that fundamental change will take place only through State action, whether affirmative or negative. The States are the repositories of legitimated authority over peoples and territories. It is only in terms of State powers, prerogatives, jurisdictional limits and law making capabilities that territorial limits and jurisdiction, responsibility for official actions, and a host of other questions of co-existence between nations can be determined ... this basic primacy of the State as a subject of international relations and law would be substantially affected, and eventually superseded, only if national entities, as political and legal systems, were absorbed in a world State.'

4.2 The State as an international person

Legal criteria of Statehood

Article 1 of the Montevideo Convention on Rights and Duties of States 1933 provides:

'The State as a person of international law should possess the following qualifications:
a) a permanent population;
b) a defined territory;
c) government; and
d) capacity to enter into relations with other States.'

The Montevideo Convention has traditionally been accepted as reflecting generally the requirements of statehood under customary international law.

Population

The requirement of 'a permanent population' connotes a stable community. There is no minimum population requirement: Nauru, for example, has a population of fewer than 10,000 inhabitants. The fact that an element of the population is nomadic will not of itself affect the existence of a State.

Defined territory

There is no limit to the size of a State's territory. The Vatican City, for example, comprises a mere 100 acres. There is no requirement that the frontiers of the State be fully defined and undisputed, either at the time it comes into being or subsequently. The State of Israel was admitted to the United Nations in 1949, though the final delimitation of its boundaries had not yet been settled. Many of the States created after 1918 were recognised by the Allied Powers although their boundaries were only drawn up in the subsequent peace treaties.

What matters is the effective establishment of a political community.

In *Deutsche Continental Gas-Gesellschaft* v *Polish State* (1929–30) the German-Polish Mixed Arbitral Tribunal said: 'In order to say that a State exists and can be recognised as such ... it is enough that ... (its) territory has a sufficient consistency, even though its boundaries have not yet been accurately delimited.'

Government

In order for a territory to be considered as a State, it must have a government of its own and not be subject to the control of another State. However, once it has been established, the absence of governmental authority does not affect the existing State's right to be considered as a State. 'States have frequently survived protracted periods of non-government, civil war, anarchy and hostile occupation.'

State practice, for example, during the Spanish Civil War, suggests that the requirement for a 'stable political organisation' in control of the territory of a State does not apply during a civil war after a State has become established.

Capacity to enter into relations with other States

This is the requirement of independence of States. In order to conduct relations with other States, a State must be legally independent from the authority of any other State.

As Lauterpacht said:

'The first condition of Statehood is that there must exist a government actually independent of that of any other State ... If a community, after having detached itself from the parent State, were to become, legally or actually, a satellite of another State, it would not be fulfilling the primary conditions of independence and would not accordingly be entitled to recognition as a State.'

The case of Manchuria: Manchuria was conquered by the Japanese in 1931 and in 1932 the Japanese recognised the province as the new independent State of Manchukuo. The League of Nations sent the Lytton Commission to Manchukuo to observe the situation. It reported:

'In the Government of Manchukuo Japanese officials are prominent and Japanese advisers are attached to all important Departments. Although the Premier and his Ministers are all Chinese, the heads of the various Boards of General Affairs, which, in the organisation of the new State, exercise the greatest measure of actual power, are Japanese. At first they were designated as advisers, but recently those holding the most important posts have been made full Government officials on the same basis as the Chinese'.

In the light of the Lytton Report the League adopted a principle of non-recognition of Manchukuo. It was not an independent State but a mere 'puppet' of the Japanese.

Other requirements of Statehood

A number of writers have more recently challenged these traditional requirements of Statehood and have proposed that a State's willingness to observe international law or the legality of the circumstances in which it was established should be taken into account. These arguments, ultimately, also become bound up with the question of the role of recognition in determining Statehood (see Chapter 5). Commentators such as Professor Dugard, for example, have taken the view that the international community is entitled to deny recognition – and hence personality – to entities purporting to be States that came into existence in conflict with a rule of *jus cogens* (a basic norm of international law). The operation of this approach can be seen to great effect in the case of the South African homelands of Transkei, Ciskei, Bophutatswana and Venda. In each case it was arguable that the homeland in question satisfied the traditional requirements of Statehood set out in the Montevideo Convention. However, the emergence of these 'States' in conflict with basic principles of human rights led the Security Council to call upon all States to refrain from recognising the homelands in question. This non-recognition effectively acted to deny to these entities personality under international law.

4.3 Non-self-governing territories

These comprise territories, protectorates, trusteeship territories, principalities and various colonies which have restricted powers of control over their foreign relations.

Colonies

Under the traditional rules of international law colonies were not regarded as possessing international personality. The exercise of their international relations was under the effective control of the Colonial Power. However, colonies in the process of becoming independent may have limited capacity to enter into international relations. For instance before its independence the British Colony of Singapore was authorised to enter into commercial treaties and join international organisations, subject to the veto of the UK.

Until recently it was contended by the Colonial Powers that the administration of such colonies was a matter exclusively within their own domestic jurisdiction and, therefore, not subject to interference by the United Nations. It is now recognised, however, that the emergence of the principle of self-determination overrides any plea of domestic jurisdiction and may give colonial and other non-independent territories a measure of international personality.

Protected territories

Protectorates

In the nineteenth century it was the practice of certain European States to create 'protectorates' over certain primitive areas of Africa and Asia by entering into treaties of protection with the local rulers. The effect of such agreements was that, while the local ruler retained control of his territory's internal affairs, foreign relations were placed exclusively in the hands of the protecting power. Examples in British Africa included Northern Rhodesia and Nyasaland.

Such protectorates did not have international personality before the 'protectorate' was created and therefore international personality only came about when the protectorate began to operate on the international plane. Once the protecting power was removed the protectorate would become a State in its own right.

The example of Kuwait: Kuwait became a British protectorate in 1899. It was gradually given responsibility for its own international relations and this position was formally recognised by the UK in 1961. But Kuwait had already achieved Statehood independently of formal recognition by the UK. Edward Heath speaking in the House of Commons in 1961 stated the position as follows:

> 'For some time past the State of Kuwait has possessed entire responsibility for the conduct of its own international relations, and, with the full support of Her Majesty's Government, Kuwait has already joined a number of international organisations as an independent Sovereign State.'

Protected States

Protected States are those States which possessed international personality but subsequently surrendered their international competence to one or more protecting States. It would appear that such protected States retain their original personalities as States in international law notwithstanding any subsequent treaty of protection.

Rights of Nationals of the United States in Morocco Case (1952). Under the Treaty of Fez 1912 Morocco made an arrangement of a contractual nature whereby France undertook to exercise certain sovereign powers in the name of and on behalf of Morocco, and, in principle, all of the international relations of Morocco. The ICJ held that Morocco, even under the protectorate, had retained its personality as a State in international law.

Mandates and trusteeship territories

Mandates

The Mandate System was established under the Covenant of the League of Nations to provide for the administration of:

> 'Those colonies and territories which as a consequence of the late war have ceased to be under the sovereignty of the States which formerly governed them and which are inhabited by people not yet able to stand by themselves under the strenuous conditions of the modern world.'

They were divided into three categories 'according to the stage of their development'.

Class A: comprised communities, which were formerly part of the Turkish Empire – Iraq, Palestine and Transjordan, Syria and Lebanon. These territories were sufficiently advanced for their independence to be provisionally recognised subject to the administrative advice and assistance of the Mandatory until such time as they are able to stand alone.

Class B: comprised those people still at a stage where the Mandatory must be responsible for the administration of the territory. They comprised: British and French Cameroons, Ruanda-Urundi, Tanganyika, British and French Togoland.

Class C: comprised territories 'which owing to the sparseness of their population, or their small size, or their remoteness from the centres of civilisation, or their geographical contiguity to the territory of the Mandatory' were 'best administered under the laws of the Mandatory as integral portions of its territory, subject to the safeguards ... in the interests of the indigenous population'. They comprised: Nauru, New Guinea, Pacific Islands north of the Equator, South West Africa, Western Samoa.

Trusteeship system

When the United Nations replaced the League of Nations after the Second World War the system of mandates was replaced by a trusteeship system.

Article 77(1) of the Charter of the United Nations provides:

'The trusteeship system shall apply to such territories in the following categories as may be placed thereunder by means of trusteeship agreements:

a) territories now held under mandate;

b) territories which may be detached from enemy States as a result of of the Second World War; and

c) territories voluntarily placed under the system by States responsible for their administration.'

The object of the system is to enable dependent territories to proceed peaceably to self-government under the guarantee of international supervision.

International status of mandates and trusteeship territories

The traditional view of mandates and trusteeship territories was that, as long as they subsisted in respect of a particular territory, that territory could not be regarded as having international personality.

In the *International Status of South West Africa Case* (1950) the ICJ stated in its Advisory Opinion that under the system 'the doctrine of sovereignty' had no application: sovereignty was in abeyance until 'the inhabitants of the Territory obtain recognition as an independent State'.

With regard to the actual status of the people inhabiting such territories Judge Ammoun stated in the *Namibia Case (1971):*

'Namibia, even at the periods when it had been reduced to the status of a German Colony or was subject to the South African Mandate, possessed a legal personality which was denied it only by the law now obsolete ... It nevertheless constituted a subject of law ... possessing national sovereignty but lacking the exercise thereof ... sovereignty ... did not cease to belong to the people subject to mandate. It had simply, for a time, been rendered inarticulate and deprived of freedom of expression.'

Although the Mandate System no longer applies to any territory and the United Nations Trusteeship System is now applicable only to a number of Pacific Islands, the history of the system does show that such non-self-governing territories cannot be regarded as attaining full legal personality until independence is achieved.

Liberation movements

In practice liberation movements and other belligerent insurgent bodies within a State may enter into legal relations and conclude valid internationally recognised agreements with States and other insurgent bodies.

Sir Gerald Fitzmaurice attributed treaty making capacity to:

'... para-Statal entities recognised as possessing a definite if limited form of international personality, for example, insurgent communities recognised as having belligerent status – *de facto* authorities in control of specific territory'.

[handwritten: ANC In South Africa?]

Federations

The usual practice under a federation is for governmental responsibility to be divided between the federal authority and the constituent member States of the federation. Thus it will be the federal State which has exclusive competence in foreign affairs while the constituent member States concern themselves solely with internal domestic matters. Consequently, only the federal State is regarded as a State under international law.

[handwritten: USA = federal State]

However, there are some federal constitutions which give member States of the federation a limited capacity to enter into international relations. In the normal case, the member State is simply acting as a delegate of the federal State. But such a situation may create separate personality in international law.

For example, in 1944 the Constitution of the USSR was amended to allow the Ukrainian SSR and Byelorussian SSR, both of which are member States of the USSR to conclude treaties on their own behalf and become members of the United Nations alongside USSR.

4.4 International organisations

An international organisation is an organisation set up by agreement between two or more States. There are now well over 100 public international organisations in existence most of which have been created since 1945. They range from organisations of universal membership and general competence, such as the United Nations, to regional organisations with specialised functions such as NATO.

The leading judicial authority on the personality of international organisations is contained in the Advisory Opinion of the ICJ in the *Reparation for Injuries Suffered in the Service of the United Nations Case (1949)*.

On 17 September 1948, Count Bernadotte, a Swedish national, was killed, allegedly by a private band of terrorists, in the City of Jerusalem which was then under Israeli possession. Count Bernadotte was the Chief United Nations Truce Negotiator for the area. The United Nations considered that Israel had been negligent in failing to prevent or punish the murderers and wished to make a claim for compensation under international law. The United Nations General Assembly sought the advice of the ICJ as to whether the United Nations had the legal capacity to make such a claim. The question put to the Court was:

> 'In the event of an agent of the United Nations in the performance of his duties suffering injury in circumstances involving the responsibility of a State, has the United Nations, as an organisation, the capacity to bring an international claim against the responsible *de jure* or *de facto* government with a view to obtaining the reparation due in respect of the damage caused (a) to the United Nations, (b) to the victim or to persons entitled through him?'

The Court answered this question in the affirmative:

> 'In the opinion of the Court, the Organisation was intended to exercise and enjoy, and is in fact exercising and enjoying, functions and rights which can only be explained on the basis of the possession of a large measure of international personality and the capacity to operate upon an international plane. It is at present the supreme type of international organisation, and it could not carry out the intentions of its founders if it was devoid of international personality ...
>
> Accordingly, the Court has come to the conclusion that the Organisation is an international person. That is not the same thing as saying that it is a State, which it certainly is not, or that its legal personality and rights and duties are the same as those of a State. Still less is it the same thing as saying that it is a 'super-State', whatever that expression may mean. It does not even imply that all its rights and duties must be upon the international plane, any more than all the rights and duties of a State must be upon that plane. What it does mean is that it is a subject of international law and capable of possessing international rights and duties, and that it has capacity to maintain its rights by bringing international claims.'

It must be remembered, however, that when States create an international organisation they set it up for specific purposes and in this respect legal personality must be treated as being relative to those purposes. As the Court said:

> 'Whereas a State possesses the totality of international rights and duties recognised by international law, the rights and duties of an entity such as the Organisation must depend upon its purposes and functions as specified or implied in its constituent documents and developed in practice.'

The practical question must, therefore, always remain: has this particular organisation the legal competence to do this particular act?

Such competence may be implied:

> 'Under international law, the Organisation must be deemed to have those powers which, though not expressly provided in the Charter, are conferred upon it by necessary implication as being essential to the performance of its duties.'

In some cases an international organisation may be expressly prohibited from operating on the international plane.

Thus, Article 4 of the Statute of the International Hydrographic Bureau provides:

> 'The Bureau is a purely consultative agency: it has no authority over the hydrographic offices of Member States ... The Bureau shall not be concerned with matters involving questions of international policy.'

Usually, however, the question whether an international organisation possesses international personality can only be answered by examining its functions and powers expressly conferred by, or to be implied from, its constitution. Relevant factors may include:

Status under municipal law

Many treaties setting up international organisations provide for the enjoyment of legal personality under the municipal laws of its member States.

For example, Article 104 of the Charter of the United Nations provides:

> 'The Organisation shall enjoy in the territory of each of its Members such legal capacity as may be necessary for the exercise of its functions and the fulfilment of its purposes.'

It is doubtful that international personality can be deduced from such a grant of municipal personality although some writers have argued that the granting of such immunities may be a recognition of that status.

Treaty making power

The most important attribute of international personality is the power to make treaties. Treaty making power is strong evidence of international personality.

Under Article 43 of the Charter of the United Nations, for example, the United Nations is empowered to make certain treaties with Member States.

International claims

If the constitution of the organisation provides for the settlement of disputes by arbitration or other international adjudication this may be of relevance in deciding its status, the power to present claims on the international plane being one of the basic rights of international personality.

General powers

It is apparent from the *Reparations Case* that the whole powers of the organisation must be considered. These will therefore include those implied powers which must be conferred on an organisation in order for it to perform the duties required under its constitution.

Recognition

If international personality is conferred on the organisation, either expressly or impliedly, then by signing the constitution of the organisation its members will have effectively recognised the independent international status of the organisation.

UN

But what will be the effect of this international status as regards non-members of the organisation? One of the issues before the Court in the *Reparations Case* was whether the United Nations had the capacity to bring an international claim against a non-Member State. The Court said:

'Fifty States, representing the vast majority of the members of the international community, had the power, in conformity with international law, to bring into being an entity possessing objective international personality, and not merely personality recognised by them alone'.

The personality of international organisations in national law has become an issue of increasingly important concern. States possess a number of rights and duties under UK law, including the right of immunity from legal proceedings and the right to bring actions in the domestic courts. Until recently, it was not clear whether international organisations could exercise the same rights and duties. The position was substantially clarified in the leading case, *Arab Monetary Fund v Hashim and Ors (No 3) (1990)*. The AMF was established by an international agreement among 20 Arab States and the Palestine Liberation Organisation. Article 2 of the agreement conferred the organisation with 'independent juridical personality' which included the rights to own, contract and litigate. The headquarters of the organisation was in Abu Dhabi, and in 1977 the United Arab Emirates passed legislation incorporating the treaty into its national law, thereby conferring legal personality on the organisation in the law of the United Arab Emirates.

Hashim, a former director-general of the Organisation, was alleged to have absconded with approximately US$50 million in assets belonging to the Fund. In 1988, Hashim was found resident in the UK and the Fund raised an action against Hashim, and a number of banks which had allegedly assisted in laundering a substantial part of the embezzled proceeds, for recovery of the stolen money. The defendants argued that the plaintiff possessed no legal personality, being an international organisation established under a treaty to which the UK was not a party, and therefore had no standing to bring the action.

The Court made a number of interesting statements concerning the legal personality of international organisations in English law. Most importantly, it held that the UK was not obliged to recognise an entity created by a treaty to which it was not a party. But, the fact that the British Government has not accorded recognition to an international organisation was not necessarily a bar to it having legal personality in English law. However, ultimately the Court held that Fund could not have legal personality in English law unless the treaty creating it had been incorporated into English law. In the past, incorporation of international organisations had been achieved by means of Orders-in-Council which establish the rights and duties to the particular entity in domestic law. The Fund therefore had no legal existence in English law.

The action was, however, allowed, not on the ground that the AMF possessed legal personality, but by virtue of the conflict of laws principle that entities which possess legal personality in foreign systems of domestic law are entitled to raise actions by virtue of their status as foreign juridical entities.

4.5 The position of the individual

Traditionally, States have been regarded as the only subjects of international law and the individual has remained an object of the law. However, there has been a growing tendency to admit that individuals may have some degree of international personality. Such personality is, however, invariably strictly limited. International law is nevertheless increasingly conferring direct rights and duties upon individuals.

The Nuremberg Tribunal held that the individual is responsible for war crimes, crimes against peace and crimes against humanity:

> 'It was submitted that international law is concerned with the actions of sovereign States, and provides no punishment for individuals; and further, that where the act in question is an act of State, those who carry it out are not personally responsible but are protected by the doctrine of the sovereignty of the State. In the opinion of the Tribunal, both these submissions must be rejected. That international law imposes duties and liabilities upon individuals as upon States has long been recognised ... Crimes against international law are committed by men, not by abstract entities, and only by punishing individuals who commit such crimes can the provisions of international law be enforced.'

There have also been mounting pressures for full access by individuals to international tribunals. This pressure has developed from two sources: access to tribunals in the case of human right abuses and access to tribunals in the case of trade and investment disputes. While some inroads are being made it nevertheless remains within the power of the sovereign States to block the access of the individual to certain international tribunals and to continue to assert the traditional rule of nationality of claims.

Some treaties have, nevertheless, conferred procedural capacity upon the individual.

The Treaty of Versailles

This Treaty, together with several other peace treaties concluded after the First World War, conferred upon individual citizens of the victorious Powers the right to submit to the various Mixed Arbitral Tribunals established for the purpose, claims against the governments and nationals of the defeated Central Powers.

The European Convention on Human Rights

Under Article 25 of the European Convention of Human Rights, provides that a party to the Convention may grant individual petitioners *locus standi* before the Commission.

The Court of Justice of the European Communities

Individuals and corporations may appeal directly to the ECJ in matters arising from the application and interpretation of the treaties and secondary legislation of the European Communities.

Quite apart from individual access in the case of human rights abuses, a number of international treaties have provided for States to recognise the international personality of individuals in the case of trade or investment disputes. These treaties were originally agreed in order to encourage foreign investment in developing States by assuring the investors concerned that they would have access to an international tribunal in the event of their investment being interfered with by the host State. The best-known of these treaties is the Washington Convention of 1965 establishing the International Centre for the Settlement of Investment Disputes between States and Nationals of other States (ICSID). The inclusion of ICSID arbitration clauses has been instrumental in encouraging investment into States party to the Convention.

5

Recognition

5.1 Introduction

5.2 Recognition in international law

5.3 Recognition in municipal law

5.1 Introduction

The international community is in a process of continuous change and new situations are constantly arising which affect the legal relations between States. Territorial changes may take place. New States are established. Revolutions occur sweeping aside existing governments and replacing them with new regimes. The question arises as to the legal consequences flowing from these new factual situations. Does the new entity thus created automatically acquire legal status on the international plane, or does such status depend upon subsequent recognition by the other members of the international community?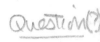

In State practice the birth of a new State, the establishment of a new government and a territorial change are in general recognised by another State. However, it can also happen that a State may expressly withhold recognition. The considerations which determine whether a State will accord or withhold recognition are in many cases of a political nature. Recognition is for many States an instrument of foreign policy, a means of expressing either approval or disapproval of the new situation. Recognition is therefore the process whereby a State acknowledges its approval of the change that has occurred. Recognition has effects in both international and municipal law.

Recognition is therefore important for two main reasons: firstly, at the level of international law it *may* tell us something about the status of the entity, eg whether or not it has international personality. Secondly, at the level of municipal law, it will usually only be entities that are recognised that will be accorded rights and have obligations under the law concerned.

5.2 Recognition in international law

Recognition is the willingness to deal with the new State as a member of the international community, or with the new government as the representative of the State.

The act of recognition

Recognition is a matter of intention and may be express or implied. The act of recognition may be effected expressly, by a formal announcement or by a bilateral treaty of recognition, or, in some circumstances, impliedly through any act indicating an intention to effect recognition.

Express recognition

A formal announcement may take the form of a public statement, a congratulatory message on attainment of independence or a simple diplomatic note delivered to the party recognised.

Express recognition may also be granted by a bi-lateral treaty formally regulating the relations between the two States. This has been the method usually employed by the UK when establishing the independence of its colonial or other dependent territories. An example is the treaty between the UK Government and the Provisional Government of Burma of 17 October 1947. By this treaty the UK recognised 'the Republic of the Union of Burma as a fully independent sovereign State'.

Implied recognition

It is possible under certain circumstances for recognition to be implied from the conduct of one State towards another. It has been stated, however, that 'to bring about recognition by implication the act must be an unequivocal one and of such a character as clearly to indicate that recognition was intended or is inescapable'. Implied recognition thus has a very narrow application.

Lauterpacht was of the opinion that, in the case of recognition of States, only the 'conclusion of a bi-lateral treaty regulating comprehensively the relations between the two States, the formal initiation of diplomatic relations and, probably, the issue of consular exequaturs' would justify the implication of recognition.

There must be a clear intention to recognise. State practice shows that recognition is not implied:

1. by the fact that a State has become party to a multilateral treaty to which an unrecognised State was already a party;
2. by the fact that a State remains a party to a multilateral treaty after an unrecognised State becomes a party;
3. by the establishment of unofficial representations;
4. by exchange of trade missions with an unrecognised State;
5. by the presentation of an international claim against, or by payment of compensation to an unrecognised State;
6. by entering into negotiations with an unrecognised State;

   For example, at the Geneva Conference on Korea and Indo-China the US Government entered into negotiations with the Communist Chinese for the release of captured American airmen. The US delegation stated:

[handwritten margin note: basically must be express.]

'The United States Government has made the decision to authorise informal United States participation in this meeting because of its obligations to protect the welfare of its citizens ... United States participation in these conversations in no way implies United States accordance of any measure of diplomatic recognition to the Red Chinese regime.'

(In practice many States may have to negotiate with unrecognised regimes. To avoid embarrassment such negotiations will usually take place in secret.)

7. by the admission of the unrecognised State to an international organisation, in respect of those States opposing the admission;

8. by the presence of the State at an international conference in which the unrecognised State participates.

Collective recognition

Collective recognition may arise in two contexts: in situations where recognition is accorded collectively by a group of states (eg following a peace treaty) and in the case of the admission of an entity to membership of the United Nations. Of these, the latter situation is both more controversial and more important.

Article 4(2) of the United Nations Charter provides that 'the admission of any ... State to membership in the United Nations will be effected by a decision of the General Assembly upon the recommendation of the Security Council'. While it is clear that non-admission does not act as an effective denial of the Statehood of the entity concerned and that admission to membership does not establish that the entity has been recognised in so far as the bilateral relationship between the entity and each existing member is concerned, it is evident from State practice that admission to membership will be prima facie evidence of Statehood.

The effects of recognition in international law

There is a profound doctrinal controversy regarding the legal effects of recognition. On the one hand proponents of the *constitutive theory* argue that a State does not exist for the purposes of international law until it is recognised by the international community. On the other hand, proponents of the *declaratory theory* advocate that the existence of a State is only a question of fact. Recognition is therefore merely an acknowledgement of that fact and has no independent legal effect.

Constitutive theory

According to the constitutive theory a State may possess all the formal attributes and qualifications of Statehood but unless or until recognition is accorded there will be no international personality. Recognition is a necessary condition for the 'constitution' of the State.

Fitzmaurice illustrates the theory as follows:

'Does the new State join a club, to which it must be duly elected or is it born into an international family? The constitutive view reflects the first of these attitudes. One must be elected, and can be black-balled.'

A modern example is the German Democratic Republic which was not recognised by the Western Powers until 1973. This subsequent recognition had a constitutive effect as far as the Western Powers were concerned and converted the Republic from an illegal Soviet 'puppet regime' into a State with full international rights and obligations. A more recent example relates to the non-recognition of the four South African homelands of Transkei, Ciskei, Bophutatswana and Venda. Although it is arguable that in some cases these entities will have satisfied the formal criteria of Statehood – particularly in the case of the Transkei – the failure by any State other than South Africa to recognise them has effectively deprived these entities of personality under international law.

Despite its appeal in cases such as the South African homelands, there are several defects inherent in the constitutive theory:

1. New States are without rights and obligations under international law until recognised.
2. State practice shows that recognition is primarily a political act on the part of the States. Why should the legal status of an entity be dependent upon the performance of such a political act?
3. State practice shows that it may not be possible to ignore completely an unrecognised entity. For instance while the USA did not recognise Communist China, it nevertheless had to enter into negotiations with it on several occasions and thereby acknowledge its existence.
4. How many members of the international community must recognise the new entity?
5. Is existence relative only to those States which do extend recognition?

Declaratory theory

The declaratory theory states that recognition is a mere formality serving no legal purpose. States exist as a matter of fact and the granting of recognition is merely an acknowledgement of that fact. Thus the position of an entity under international law stems from its actual control over territory and not from its recognition or non-recognition by the members of the international community.

In the *Tinoco Arbitration – Great Britain v Costa Rica* (1923) Tinoco ousted the Government of Costa Rica by force. In 1919 Tinoco was ousted in his turn and the new Government repudiated certain obligations undertaken by the Tinoco Government towards British nationals. In the course of ruling upon the claims brought by Great Britain on the basis of these obligations, the arbitrator discussed the question of recognition:

'I must hold that from the evidence ... the Tinoco Government was an actual sovereign Government. But it is urged that many leading Powers refused to recognise the Tinoco Government, and that recognition by other nations is the chief and best evidence of the birth, existence and continuity of succession of a Government. Undoubtedly recognition by other Powers is an important evidential factor in establishing proof of the existence of a Government in the society of nations ... The non-recognition by other nations of a

Government claiming to be a national personality, is usually control entitling it by international law to be classed as such. But when recognition *vel non* of a Government is by such nations determined by inquiry, not into its *de facto* sovereignty and complete governmental control, but into its illegitimacy or irregularity of origin, their non-recognition loses something of evidential weight on the issue with which those applying the rules of international law are alone concerned. What is true of the non-recognition of the United States in its bearing upon the existence of a *de facto* Government under Tinoco for 30 months is probably in a measure true of the non-recognition by her Allies in the European War. Such non-recognition for any reason, however, cannot outweigh the evidence disclosed by this record before me as to the *de facto* character of Tinoco's Government, according to the standard set by international law'.

Although the *Tinoco Case* was concerned with the recognition of a Government, this reasoning applies equally to States.

In *Deutsche Continental Gas-Gesellschaft v Polish State* (1929–30) it was stated:

'... according to the opinion rightly admitted by the great majority of writers on international law, the recognition of a State is not constitutive but merely declaratory. The State exists by itself (*par lui meme*) and the recognition is nothing else than a declaration of this existence, recognised by the State from which it emanates.'

The objection to the declaratory theory is that it reduces recognition to an empty formality. The fact that a State possesses the attributes of Statehood is no guarantee that it will discharge its obligations under international law.

Recognition of States

Even if a particular entity has the factual requirements of Statehood – territory, population and government – it will not qualify as a State in the absence of recognition as a State by the international community.

Is there a duty of recognition?
Lauterpacht takes the view that once the factual characteristics of Statehood exist there is a legal duty to accord recognition to the new State:

'To recognise a political community as a State is to declare that it fulfils the conditions of Statehood as required by international law. If these conditions are present, the existing States are under a duty to grant recognition. In the absence of an international organ competent to ascertain and authoritatively to declare the presence of requirements of full international personality, States already established fulfil that function in their capacity as organs of international law. In thus acting they administer the law of nations. This legal rule signifies that in granting or withholding recognition States do not claim and are not entitled to serve exclusively the interests of their national policy and convenience regardless of the principles of international law in the matter. Although recognition is thus declaratory of an existing fact, such declaration, made in the impartial fulfilment of a legal duty, is constitutive, as between the recognising State and the community so recognised, of international rights and duties associated with full Statehood. Prior to recognition such rights and obligations exist only to the extent to which they have been expressly conceded or legitimately asserted, by reference to compelling rules of humanity and justice, either by the existing members of international society or by the people claiming recognition.'

The political nature of recognition

Usually, however, the decision whether to grant or withhold recognition will be based on political expediency. Inevitably, therefore, there will arise situations in which an entity is recognised as a State by some members of the international community, but denied recognition by others. Two examples illustrate the point:

Manchukuo. Manchukuo was recognised by El Salvador, Germany, Hungary, Italy and Japan. Other States, including the USA and those of the League of Nations denied recognition on the grounds that Manchukuo was a puppet State of the Japanese seized from China by illegal force.

The German Democratic Republic (East Germany). East Germany was denied recognition by the Western Powers for many years on the grounds that it was a mere dependent territory of the USSR and not a sovereign independent State. The UK did not recognise the German Democratic Republic until February 1973.

Thus it can be argued that those who advocate that there is a legal duty to recognise new States fail to take account of State practice and the inconsistency of recognition.

Yugoslavia. The State of Yugoslavia originally consisted of six republics – Slovenia, Croatia, Serbia, Bosnia-Hercegovina, Montenegro and Macedonia – and two autonomous regions – Kosova and Vojvodina. After declarations of independence from Slovenia and Croatia on 25 June 1991, civil conflict broke out between the forces of the central Government and those of the provisional Slovenian and Croatian Governments.

The problem was perceived by the USA as a mainly European issue and the European Community took the lead in trying to resolve the conflict through diplomacy and other peaceful means. By December 1991 it had become clear that a peaceful settlement was unlikely as the rival republics persistently failed to agree the terms of a constitutional settlement.

On 16 December 1991, the European Community announced that it would extend recognition as sovereign states to those former republics which gave assurances that five conditions would be respected. These conditions were:

1. continued respect for the UN Charter and the Helsinki Final Act, particularly with respect to the rule of law, democracy and respect for human rights;
2. guarantees for the rights of ethnic and national groups and minorities in accordance with the commitments given within the framework of the CSCE system;
3. respect for the inviolability of all frontiers which were only to be altered by peaceful means and with mutual agreement;
4. acceptance of all international obligations concerning non-discrimination and nuclear non-proliferation, as well as security and regional stability; and
5. undertakings to settle peaceable all questions concerning state succession and regional disputes.

The Community also affirmed that it would not recognise any entity as a State if it came into existence as a result of aggression.

Recognition was extended by the Community to Slovenia and Croatia on 15 January 1992, and to Bosnia-Hercegovina on 6 April 1992, after receiving the appropriate undertakings were received from these republics.

Quite clearly the European Community used the device of recognition as a political tool to extract these commitments from the former republics of Yugoslavia, which confirms the political nature of recognition. The policy adopted was one of conditional recognition whereby the Community withheld recognition pending political undertakings relating to security in the region.

It is unclear whether the European Community will retain this doctrine of conditional recognition or whether the circumstances of this particular case were unique. However, by acting in unison at the Community level, a number of Member States have significantly altered their own national policies towards the recognition of States.

Recognition of governments

A distinction has traditionally been drawn between the recognition of States and the recognition of governments. The practical reasoning behind this distinction was to permit the recognising State to withhold recognition from the authorities in control of the entity in question, on the grounds of its failure to comply with some requirement of international law, while continuing to recognise the entity itself – ie the abstract concept of, for example, the State of Costa Rica – for the purposes of membership of the international community. As will be immediately apparent, this distinction is bound to introduce a measure of confusion into the law on recognition, particularly so as the non-recognition of governments has been almost exclusively dominated by political considerations. As will be discussed below, the effects in *municipal law* of the non-recognition of a State or of its government is the same save in the case where there is more than one authority requesting recognition as the government of the entity concerned.

Much of the evolution of State practice on the question of recognition of governments is due to the confusion that the doctrine has engendered in this area of the law.

General State practice

State practice suggests that there is no legal duty upon States to extend recognition to new governments. Examples include the non-recognition by the USA and the Allied Powers of the Tinoco Regime that ruled Costa Rica between 1917 and 1919. The Soviet Government which came to power in Russia in 1919 was not recognised by Great Britain until 1921 and by the USA until 1933. It was only recently that the US extended recognition to the Communist regime ruling China. As a US Department of State spokesman said in 1958:

'The United States Government has been criticised for its failure to recognise the Chinese Communist regime, some commentators taking the view that, since the Communist regime controls the great mass of mainland China as well as its 600 million inhabitants, the United States must accord recognition. It is the view of the United States Government that international law does not require one government to accord diplomatic recognition to another government. It is our view that the matter of diplomatic recognition is one solely to be determined as the national interest dictates, and in this case on an examination of all facets of the subject the United States Government believes that it would be contrary to our national interest to accord recognition.'

The Estrada Doctrine

If non-recognition can be an expression of disapproval of a new government then it can be argued that recognition may be interpreted as implying approval of the new government even in cases where no such approval was intended. To avoid such misunderstandings some States have adopted the policy of never recognising governments, but instead of granting or withholding recognition only in respect of States. This doctrine originated in Mexico and has been adopted by several other States.

British practice

Generally, the policy of the UK has been to follow the Lauterpacht doctrine and to accept that there is a duty to recognise entities which fulfilled the factual requirements of Statehood or government.

In 1951 the then Foreign Secretary, Herbert Morrison, speaking in the House of Commons, stated the British position as follows:

'The question of the recognition of a State or Government should be distinguished from the question of entering into diplomatic relations with it, which is entirely discretionary. On the other hand, it is international law which defines the conditions under which a Government should be recognised *de jure* or *de facto* and it is a matter of judgment in each particular case whether a regime fulfils the conditions. The conditions under international law for the recognition of a new regime as the *de facto* Government of a State are that the new regime has, in fact, effective control over most of the State's territory and that this control seems likely to continue. The conditions for the recognition of a new regime as the *de jure* Government of a State are that new regime should not merely have effective control over most of the States territory, but that it should, in fact, be firmly established. His Majesty's Government consider that recognition should be accorded when the conditions specified by international law are, in fact, fulfilled and that recognition should be be given when these conditions are not fulfilled. The recognition of a Government *de jure* or *de facto* should not depend on whether the character of the regime is such as to command His Majesty's Government's approval.'

The requirement of *de facto* control is illustrated by the attitude of the UK Government towards the Kadar Government established in Hungary after the 1956 uprising. The Under Secretary of State for Foreign Affairs said:

'Her Majesty's Government have never taken any special step to recognise the Kadar Government. ... They have ... continued to maintain a diplomatic mission there and to accept a Hungarian Mission in London. Generally speaking, Her Majesty's Government's policy in the matter of recognition of Governments is to face facts and acknowledge *de facto* a Government which has effective control of the territory within its jurisdiction, and of the inhabitants within that territory. Such *de facto* recognition does not constitute a judgment on the legality of the Government concerned; still less does it imply approval of it.'

However, notwithstanding this purported *de facto* control approach of the British Government there have been exceptions where the UK has refused to recognise certain States even though there can be no doubt about their *de facto* status. The UK, for instance, does not recognise North Korea as a State even though it is a Democratic Republic with its own government exercising legislative and administrative control over a defined territory.

In order to avoid some of the confusion that has arisen as a result of these exceptional cases where the UK has refused to grant recognition to an authority whose *de jure* status is in doubt, the Foreign Secretary, in April 1980, announced that the UK would no longer formally extend recognition to governments.

The terms of the Foreign Secretary's statement was as follows:

'Where an unconstitutional change of regime takes place in a recognised State, Governments of other States must necessarily consider what dealings, if any, they should have with the new regime, and whether and to what extent it qualifies to be treated as the Government of the State concerned. Many of our partners and allies take the position that they do not recognise Governments and that therefore no question of recognition arises in such cases. By contrast, the policy of successive British Governments has been that we should make and announce a decision formally "recognising" the new Government.

This practice has sometimes been misunderstood, and, despite explanations to the contrary, our "recognition" interpreted as implying approval. For example, in circumstances where there may be legitimate public concern about the violation of human rights by the new regime ... It has not sufficed to say that an announcement of "recognition" is simply a neutral formality.

We have therefore concluded that there are practical advantages in following the policy of many other countries in not according recognition to Governments. Like them, we shall continue to decide the nature of our dealings with regimes which come to power unconstitutionally in the light of our assessment of whether they are able ... to exercise effective control of the territory of the State concerned, and seem likely to continue to do so.'

While the precise implications of this statement are open to debate, the doctrine would seem to substitute implied recognition for express recognition, ie the recognition is not announced expressly, but can be implied from any dealings between the governments. (See further *GUR Corp* under section 5.3 (below).

US practice regarding recognition

US practice differs from that of the UK in a number of important respects.

Recognition as a diplomatic weapon. The USA has openly used recognition or the withholding of recognition as a diplomatic weapon in the conduct of international relations. This political aspect of recognition was emphasised by Senator Austin in the United Nations Security Council in respect of US recognition of Israel in 1948:

'I should regard it as highly improper for me to admit that any country on earth can question the sovereignty of the United States of America in the exercise of that high political act of recognition of the *de facto* status of a State. Moreover, I would not admit here, by implication or by direct answer, that there exists a tribunal of justice or of any other kind, anywhere, that can pass judgement upon the legality or the validity of that act of my country.'

Current US practice: (1) recognition of States. In 1973 the US Department of State issued the following instructions on the recognition of States in relation to the recognition of the former Portuguese African colony of Guinea-Bissau:

'The United States Government has traditionally looked to the establishment of certain facts before it has extended recognition to a new State. These facts include the effective control over a clearly defined territory and population; an organised governmental administration of that territory; and a capacity to act effectively to conduct foreign relations and to fulfil international obligations. In Africa these factual criteria have generally been met in the past, following a peaceful transition to independence from colonial status through an agreement between the colonial power and representatives of the people of the territory concerned. Under international law, however, even if the above factual criteria are present, a State is not obliged to recognise another entity as a State.'

Current US practice: (2) recognition of governments. Regarding the US attitude to the Communist Chinese Government the US Department of State mentioned three factors it considered as significant when deciding whether to extend recognition: (1) whether the government in question is in control of a certain territory; (2) whether the government reflects the will of the nation substantially declared; (3) whether the government is prepared to honour its international obligations. Regarding the latter, it was declared:

'... there is no doubt, in view of flagrant past treaty violations and violations of the United Nations Charter and violations of international law and in view of statements made by the Chinese Communist regime about disregarding pre-existing treaties, that the Chinese Communist regime is not prepared to honour its international obligations ... the Chinese Communists are not entitled to recognition.'

Current US practice: (3) quasi-diplomatic relations with unrecognised entities. The US Government is prepared to engage in quasi-diplomatic relations with unrecognised States and governments if it is in the USA's interest to do so. Again with respect to Communist China:

'... our failure to recognise the Chinese Communist regime has not meant that we refuse to deal with them where it is essential to our purposes and inures to our benefit. Thus we are at present carrying on conversations in Warsaw as we have carried on conversations in Geneva; we dealt with them in the Korean armistice negotiations; we dealt with them with respect to the ceasefire in Indo-China; and we are prepared to deal with them whenever we believe it to be in the interests of the United States to do so.'

De jure *and* de facto *recognition*

The terms '*de jure*' and '*de facto*' recognition have traditionally been applied to recognition of governments. The terms reflect the quality of the government rather than that of the act of recognition. Thus, it would be recognition of a government as a *de jure* or *de facto* government.

In the UK, the 1980 Statement and the change in UK practice regarding recognition of governments has all but made this aspect of recognition irrelevant. There are, however, many examples from pre-1980 practice which were based on this distinction between de jure and de facto authority.

In particular two situations stand out where a distinction of this nature has been made:

Where a *de facto* authority is exercising the powers of government in an area under the nominal control of the existing *de jure* government of a State

In *Luther* v *Sagor* (1921) Banks LJ described the distinction as follows:

> 'A *de jure* Government is one which in the opinion of the person using the phrase ought to possess the powers of sovereignty, though at the time it may be deprived of them. A *de facto* Government is one which is really in possession of them, although the possession may be wrongful or precarious.'

For example, in 1936, after the invasion of Abyssinia by Italy, Emperor Haile Selassie continued for two years to be recognised by the British Government as the *de jure* Government of Abyssinia.

Where the *de jure* government has ceased to exist and the recognised *de facto* authority is the only government of the State, but *de jure* recognition is withheld because of doubts as to the regime's degree of permanence, or as a sign of disapproval

For example, in the case of Abyssinia, although Haile Selassie was recognised as the *de jure* government, *de facto* recognition was extended to the Italian regime following its occupation.

De facto recognition has been used by the UK as an expression of disapproval and has also been employed where the original *de jure* government has ceased to exist.

For instance, Latvia, Lithuania and Estonia were independent States which were occupied by the Russians and incorporated into the USSR in 1940.

In 1967 the Foreign Secretary stated: 'Her Majesty's Government recognise that Latvia, Lithuania and Estonia have been incorporated *de facto* into the Soviet Union but have not recognised this *de jure*.'

The doctrine of non-recognition

The withholding of recognition from new governments or States has often been used as a mark of disapproval or as a protest against some international illegality perpetrated by or on behalf of the new regime.

Basis of the doctrine

Non-recognition has traditionally been based on two considerations: (1) that the entity concerned does not satisfy the formal criteria for independence, or (2) that the non-recognising State is unwilling, usually for political reasons, to have normal relations with the State concerned. More recently, a number of writers have argued that a doctrine of collective non-recognition should apply in circumstances in which the entity in question has come into being in conflict with a rule of *jus cogens*. So, for example, it has been argued that a breach of basic norms of human rights or of the principle of self-determination should operate to preclude States from recognising the entity in question. As might have been expected, this argument has found support in the context of the claim to independence and Statehood of the South African homelands.

The origins of the doctrine of non-recognition

Following the Japanese invasion of Manchuria and the establishment of the puppet State of Manchukuo, American Secretary of State Stimson announced that the USA would not recognise such situations brought about by aggression:

> '... the American Government deems it to be its duty to notify both the Imperial Japanese Government and the Government of the Chinese Republic that it cannot admit the legality of any situation *de facto* nor does it intend to recognise any treaty or agreement entered into between those Governments ... which may impair the treaty rights of the United States ... including those which relate to the sovereignty, the independence, or the territorial and administrative integrity of the Republic of China ... and that it does not intend to recognise any situation, treaty or agreement which may be brought about by means contrary to the ... Pact of Paris'. (This policy became known as the *Stimson doctrine*.)

This approach by the USA found support in the League of Nations. In 1932 the Assembly of the League of Nations passed a resolution stating that:

> '... it is incumbent upon the members of the League of Nations not to recognise any situation, treaty or agreement which may be brought about by means contrary to the Covenant of the League of Nations or to the Pact of Paris'.

However, the principle of non-recognition was not applied with any degree of uniformity or consistency. The Italian invasion of Abyssinia in 1936 was generally recognised and some governments accepted German control of Austria in 1938 and of Czechoslovakia in 1939.

Even prior to the Stimson doctrine and the development of collective non-recognition under the aegis of the League, writers have argued that the doctrine of non-recognition can be traced to the Pact of Paris 1928 which condemned recourse to war for the solution of international controversies, and renounced war as an instrument of national policy.

This in turn can be traced back to Article 10 of the Covenant of the League of Nations which provided that:

> 'Members of the League undertake to respect and preserve as against external aggression the territorial integrity and existing political independence of all members of the League.'

More recently, Article 2(4) of the Charter of the United Nations provides:

'All members shall refrain in their international relations from the threat or use of force against the territorial integrity or political independence of any State, or in any other manner inconsistent with the Purposes of the United Nations.'

On the basis of this provision, any territorial or other changes brought about in breach of Article 2(4) of the Charter of the United Nations, would, in theory at least, be subject to the doctrine of non-recognition by the other members of the international community.

United Nations practice on non-recognition

United Nations practice suggests that the Security Council, using its powers under Article 25 of the Charter, may impose a duty of non-recognition on the part of Member States of the United Nations Organisation.

In the case of Rhodesia, for example, following the Unilateral Declaration of Independence by the Smith regime in 1965 the Security Council passed a number of resolutions calling on all States not to recognise the illegal regime. A similar situation arose in respect of South Africa's continued presence in Namibia.

In 1970 the Security Council of the United Nations declaring the presence of South Africa in South West Africa to be illegal called upon 'all States particularly those which have economic and other interests in Namibia, to refrain from any dealings with the Government of South Africa'.

The ICJ in its advisory opinion in the *Namibia Case (1971)* considered this declaration by the Security Council to be binding on all Member States of the United Nations:

'Member States, in compliance with the duty of non-recognition imposed (by the resolution), are under obligation to abstain from sending diplomatic or special missions to South Africa including in their jurisdiction the Territory of Namibia, to abstain from sending consular agents to Namibia and to withdraw any such agents already there. They should also make it clear to the South African authorities that the maintenance of diplomatic or consular relations with South Africa does not imply any recognition of its authority with regard to Namibia.'

United Nations practice on non-recognition has also seen developments in the form of General Assembly resolutions. Following the declaration of independence of the South African homeland of the Transkei in 1976, the General Assembly passed a resolution by 134 votes to 0 with 1 abstention calling upon:

'... all Governments to deny any form of recognition to the so-called Independent Transkei and to refrain from having any dealings with the so-called Independent Transkei'.

Following the declaration of independence of the Ciskei in 1981 the Security Council called upon all States to withhold recognition to the so-called independent homelands of South Africa.

The doctrine of collective non-recognition has found expression in a number of other situations. Following the Turkish invasion of Northern Cyprus in 1975 and the subsequent declaration of the Turkish Republic of Northern Cyprus in 1983, the Security Council passed a resolution calling on all States to refrain from recognising the new entity of TRNC. The Security Council had by Resolution 662 called upon all States to refrain from recognising the Iraqi annexation of Kuwait and the establishment of an Iraqi-backed administration in the territory.

Withdrawal of recognition

De facto recognition is, by its very nature, conditional upon the continued factual existence of the entity recognised. If it ceases to exist, then recognition no longer applies.

De jure recognition on the other hand cannot be withdrawn unless there is a fundamental change affecting the status of the entity recognised. Until this change is acknowledged by the recognising State, *de jure* recognition will remain with the original entity. For instance, the UK refused to acknowledge the incorporation of the former independent States of Latvia, Lithuania and Estonia into the USSR and continues to accept the diplomatic agents of these States as accredited representatives of a *de jure* sovereign.

Once the successor entity is acknowledged, however, then, as with the case of Abyssinia in 1936–8, *de jure* recognition will be withdrawn from the former regime and conferred instead upon the successor regime which will thereby supplant the former *de jure* authorities.

Severance of diplomatic relations does not constitute withdrawal of recognition.

Conditional recognition

The granting of recognition may be made conditional upon the performance by the entity of some specified act. For example, the UK granted recognition to the Provisional Governments of Poland and Czechoslovakia during the Second World War on the condition that they agreed to hold free elections after the liberation of their countries from German occupation.

Premature recognition

It is generally accepted that the recognition of rebels, governments, or States before they have established permanent control over the territory of the established government is illegal. Likewise the premature withdrawal of recognition from the established government in such cases is also considered to be illegal.

Recognition and the United Nations

Admission to membership of the United Nations is *prima facie* evidence of Statehood. While admission to membership will entail the recognition of the international personality of the State concerned it is generally accepted that it will not involve the recognition, on a bi-lateral level, of the State as regards the individual members of the United Nations.

The importance of this principle is illustrated by the case of Israel, a Member of the United Nations but one which is denied recognition as a State by the majority of Arab State Members of the Organisation. This notwithstanding, the United Nations considers both Israel and her Arab neighbours, as Members of the Organisation, to be bound by and recognise each others' rights and duties under the Charter of the United Nations in their dealings with each other.

5.3 Recognition in municipal law

International lawyers frequently draw a distinction between the effects of recognition in municipal law in the case of States or governments. In general, there is little merit in making this distinction for a number of reasons. Firstly, it will often be difficult in practice to distinguish between non-recognition of States and governments at the international level. For example, was the non-recognition by the UK of the Soviet Union prior to 1924 a failure to recognise the Soviet State or the Soviet Government? Similarly, was the non-recognition of the Smith regime in Rhodesia post-UDI in 1965 a refusal to recognise an illegal government or a withholding of recognition from the Rhodesian State? At first sight these questions may appear straightforward. In truth, though, they are more complex.

Secondly, the distinction between non-recognition of States and governments *for the purposes of municipal law* is seldom significant because the effect of non-recognitions *in either case* will invariably be the same. Thus, it will make little difference whether entity 'X' or its government is not recognised. In either case, 'X' will not be entitled to claim sovereign immunity before English courts or to sue in this country. The reasons why non-recognition will have the same effect in the case of a State or its government is that a State is invariably represented on the international plain by its government. The importance of this relationship draws attention, therefore, to the one set of circumstances when it will be important to distinguish between non-recognition of a State or its government for the purposes of municipal law, ie when the State in question remains recognised while the authority in *control* of the State is an illegal authority with which the third State has had no dealings. Such a situation has arisen recently following the Iraqi invasion of Kuwait. While it was clear that the State of Kuwait remained a recognised entity, it was equally apparent that the Iraqi-imposed administration was not recognised. At one level, therefore, the non-recognition of the illegal administration was fatal to the international standing of the State. However, attempts were made by the deposed but still recognised and legitimate government of Kuwait to retain a measure of international personality to act on behalf of the State on the international level was successful. In these circumstances (ie where there are competing authorities in respect of the same State) it will be important to distinguish between the non-recognition of a State or of its government.

Recognition of States in English law

Generally, English courts will not recognise a foreign State unless the Foreign Office certifies that it has been recognised by the British Government.

Effects of recognition in English law

A recognised State has sovereign immunity and cannot be sued in the English courts without its consent

In *Duff Development Company v Kelantan* (1924) The House of Lords had to decide whether Kelantan, a State in the Malay Peninsula then under the protection of Great Britain, was an independent State so that it could claim State immunity in the English courts. The Under Secretary of State for the Colonies submitted a letter stating: 'Kelantan is an independent State in the Malay Peninsula ... His Majesty the King does not exercise or claim any rights of sovereignty or jurisdiction over Kelantan.'

This Colonial Office statement was accepted as binding by the court, Lord Dave said: 'it is the duty of the Court to accept the statement of the Secretary of State thus clearly and positively made as conclusive upon the point'.

An unrecognised State cannot sue in an English court

An unrecognised State is not recognised for purposes of conflict of laws

It is a rule of English conflict of laws that in cases of dispute over title to property, English courts will apply the *lex situs*, ie the laws of the State where the property is situated. In *Carl Zeiss Stiftung v Rayner and Keeler Ltd* (1967) the court had to consider the validity of title to property based upon legislative and administrative acts of the German Democratic Republic. At the time of the case, the German Democratic Republic was not recognised by the British Government who considered East Germany as being under the *de jure* control of the USSR.

The Court of Appeal therefore refused to apply East German law. Diplock LJ said that where English rules of private international law made reference to a foreign system of law, that law would only be regarded as effective in so far as it was:

'... made by or under the authority of those persons who are recognised by the Government of the United Kingdom as being the sovereign Government of the place where the thing happens'.

The correctness of this decision notwithstanding, the consequences of the application of this rule of law could potentially be very harsh. As in *Adams v Adams* (1970), where the UK courts refused to recognise a divorce granted by the Rhodesian courts, this strict conflicts approach could lead to hardship in the day-to-day transactions of ordinary people.

With this in mind the House of Lords reversed the decision of the Court of Appeal in *Carl Zeiss*. Two approaches to the problem of the non-recognition of East

Germany were in evidence in their Lordships' decision. In the first place Lord Wilberforce indicated that, non-recognition notwithstanding, English courts should in some circumstances recognise the administrative acts of a non-recognised State. These comments pre-empted those of Lord Denning in *Hesperides Hotels* (1977) (see below). Secondly, and the approach preferred by the majority of the Lords, was for the court to rely on a legal fiction. Thus, the Lords accepted that the East German Government was an administration or subordinate authority controlled by the Soviet Union. As the Soviet Union was recognised by the UK Government, the English courts could grant recognition to the acts of its local authority, normally the East German Government.

It was therefore possible for the House to accept the acts of the unrecognised German Democratic Republic as being those of a subordinate authority of the USSR.

Lord Reid explained the effect of a strict application of the rule:

'We must not only disregard all new laws and decrees made by the German Democratic Republic or its Government, but we must also disregard all executive and judicial acts done by persons appointed by that Government because we must regard this appointment as invalid. The results of that would be far reaching. Trade with the Eastern Zone of Germany is not discouraged, but the incorporation of every company in East Germany under any new law made by the German Democratic Republic or by the official act of any official appointed by its Government would have to be regarded as a nullity so that any such company could neither sue nor be sued in this country. Any civil marriage under any such new law or owing its validity to the act of any such official would also have to be treated as a nullity so that we should have to regard the children as illegitimate; and the same would apply to divorces and all manner of judicial decisions whether in family or commercial questions. That would affect not only the status of persons formerly domiciled in East Germany but also property in this country the devolution of which depended on East German law.'

Although the strict application of the rule that non-recognition equals non-existence, was avoided by the House of Lords on the particular facts of the *Carl Zeiss Case*, nevertheless it may have effect in respect of other unrecognised States which may be called in question before the English courts.

The possibility of the strict applications of the rule has attracted a great deal of criticism.

In *Hesperides Hotels* v *Aegean Holidays Ltd* (1977) the plaintiff, a Greek Cypriot, owned two hotels which, following the Turkish invasion of 1974, were being run by Turkish Cypriots with the approval of the Turkish Cypriot administration which now governed the part of Cyprus in which the hotels were located. The Court of Appeal rejected the plaintiffs action in trespass for lack of jurisdiction on the basis of English conflict of laws rules. The UK continues to recognise the pre-invasion Government of Cyprus as the *de jure* Government of the whole of Cyprus and does not recognise the Turkish administration *de jure* or *de facto*. Lord Denning stated, obiter:

'If it were necessary to (do so) ... I would unhesitatingly hold that the Courts of this country can recognise the laws or acts of a body which is in effective control of a territory even though it has not been recognised by Her Majesty's Government *de jure* or *de facto*:

at any rate, in regard to the laws which regulate the day to day affairs of the people, such as their marriages, their divorces, their leases, their occupations, and so forth; and furthermore that the Courts can receive evidence of the state of affairs so as to see whether the body is in effective control or not.'

Recognition of governments in English law

In the past the English courts applied the same reasoning to the recognition of governments as they did to the recognition of States. The Foreign Office certificate of recognition being evidence of the government's existence.

If a government was not recognised, it was not entitled to sovereign immunity

A plea of immunity can be raised by an authority recognised as being in *de facto* control of territory, even if the proceedings are brought by the *de jure* sovereign.

The *Arantzazu Mendi* (1939) case arose out of the Spanish Civil War. In June 1937, shortly before the Basque region of Spain fell to the Nationalist insurgents, the Spanish Republican Government issued a decree requisitioning all ships registered in Bilbao, including the *Arantzazu Mendi* owned by the respondent Spanish company and which was at sea when the decree was issued. In March 1938 the Nationalist Government issued a decree requisitioning ships registered in Bilbao. The respondent company did not oppose this second requisition and agreed to hold the ship, then in the Port of London, for the Nationalists. The Republican Government then issued a writ for possession of the *Arantzazu Mendi* on the basis of its 1937 decree. The Nationalist Government sought to have the writ set aside on the ground that it impleaded a sovereign State.

On the question whether the Nationalist Government of Spain was a sovereign State the judge at first instance directed a letter to be written to the Secretary of State for Foreign Affairs as to the status of the Nationalist Authorities. In reply it was stated that His Majesty's Government recognises Spain as a sovereign State and recognises the Government of the Spanish Republic as the only *de jure* Government of Spain or any part of it. The reply also stated that:

'5. His Majesty's Government recognises the Nationalist Government as a Government which at present exercises de facto administrative control over the larger portion of Spain.
6. His Majesty's Government recognises that the Nationalist Government now exercises effective administrative control over all the Basque Provinces of Spain.
7. His Majesty's Government have not accorded any other recognition to the Nationalist Government.
8. The Nationalist Government is not a Government subordinated to any other Government in Spain.
9. The question whether the Nationalist Government is to be regarded as that of a foreign Sovereign State appears to be a question of law to be answered in the light of the preceding statements and having regard to the particular issue with respect to which the question is raised.'

The court held that the Foreign Office letter established that the Nationalist Government of Spain at the date of the writ was a foreign sovereign State and could not be impleaded. Lord Atkin stated:

> '... this letter appears to me to dispose of the controversy. By "exercising *de facto* administrative control" or "exercising effective administrative control", I understand exercising all functions of a Sovereign Government, ie maintaining law and order, instituting and maintaining acts of justice, adopting or imposing laws regulating the relations of the inhabitants of the territory to one another and to the Government ... That the decree, therefore, emanated from the Sovereign in that territory there can be no doubt. There is ample authority for the proposition that there is no difference for the present purposes between a recognition of a State *de facto* as opposed to *de jure*. All the reasons for immunity which are the basis of the doctrine in international law as incorporated into our law exist'.

If a government was not recognised it could not sue or be sued in an English court

In *City of Berne* v *Bank of England* (1804) it was held that an unrecognised government has no *locus standi* in English courts.

The question of the *locus standi* of an unrecognised government has arisen more recently before the English courts. In *GUR Corp* v *Trust Bank of Africa Ltd* (1986) the question in issue was whether the Government of the Republic of the Ciskei could be joined to the proceedings as third party. In the Queen's Bench Division Steyn J, after receiving a certificate from the Foreign Office indicating that

> 'Her Majesty's Government does not recognise the "Republic of Ciskei" as an independent sovereign state, either *de jure* or *de facto*, and does not have any dealings with the "Government of the Republic of Ciskei" ',

held that the Government of the Republic of Ciskei had no *locus standi* before English courts.

The case did not end there. On appeal, Counsel for the Trust Bank, which sought to have the Government of the Ciskei joined as third party, successfully argued, on the precedent of *Carl Zeiss*, that the Government of the Republic of Ciskei was 'a subordinate body set up by the Republic of South Africa to act on its behalf' and that, as such, it had *locus standi* before the courts of the UK.

The effect of this decision is to avoid, by the use of a legal fiction, doing an injustice to private parties in the conduct of their day-to-day activities.

If a government was not recognised its laws were not applied in English courts

In *Luther* v *Sagor* (1921) (First Instance), the defendant company purchased in 1920 a quantity of timber from the then recently constituted Soviet Government of Russia. The plaintiff Russian company claimed title to the timber on the ground that it had come from a factory in Russia that had been owned by it before being nationalised by the Soviet Government in 1919. The plaintiff argued, *inter alia*, that the decree should not be recognised by the English court because the Soviet Government had not been recognised by Great Britain. Roche J held:

'If a foreign Government, or its sovereignty, is not recognised by the Government of this country the Courts of this country either cannot, or at least need not, or ought not, to take notice of, or recognise such foreign Government or its sovereignty ... I am not satisfied that His Majesty's Government has recognised the Soviet Government as the Government of a Russian Federative Republic or of any Sovereign State or power. I therefore am unable to recognise it, or to hold it has sovereignty, or is able by decree to deprive the plaintiff company of its property.'

(On appeal this decision in favour of the plaintiff was reversed in the light of the intervening recognition of the Soviet Government by the British Government. This recognition was held to be retroactive and dated back to the actual coming into being of the recognised entity, which in this particular case was when the Soviets seized power in 1917. The decree confiscating the timber could therefore be recognised.

However, in the Court of Appeal, Banks LJ stated that so far as the first instance decision was concerned: 'Upon the evidence which was before the learned judge I think that his decision was quite right'.)

If a government was not recognised it was not entitled to the property of the State which it claimed to govern

Haile Selassie v Cable and Wireless Limited (No 2) (1939). In 1935 Italy invaded Abyssinia and formally annexed the territory on 9 May 1936. Prior to the invasion the plaintiff had made a contract with the defendants for the transmission of wireless messages between Abyssinia and Great Britain. In 1937 the plaintiff commenced proceedings to recover money due under the contract. At this time the plaintiff was still recognised by Great Britain as the *de jure* sovereign although Italy was recognised as the *de facto* government.

The question before the court was stated as follows:

'Does the fact that the Italian Government has been and is recognised by the British Government as the *de facto* Government of Ethiopia vest in the Italian Government the right to sue for and obtain judgment in an English court for a debt formerly due to and recoverable by the plaintiff as the sovereign authority of Ethiopia, the debt being due to the plaintiff as Emperor of Ethiopia and the British Government recognising the plaintiff as the *de jure* Emperor of Ethiopia?'

At first instance Bennett J held that the plaintiff had not been divested of the right to sue for the debt in spite of the fact that the British Government recognised the Italian Government as the *de facto* government of virtually the whole of Abyssinia.

The defendants had relied *inter alia* on *Luther v Sagor* to establish the exclusive power of the *de facto* government. The learned judge distinguished the case, saying:

'I think the only point established by (*Luther v Sagor*) is that where the Government of this country has recognised that some foreign Government is *de facto* governing some foreign territory, the law of England will regard the acts of *de facto* Government in that territory as valid and treat them with all the respect due to the acts of a duly recognised foreign Sovereign State. It is clear I think that the acts so treated are acts in relation to persons or property in the territory which the authority is recognised as governing in fact.

It was not suggested in that case nor was anything said in it which supports the view that on or in consequence of such recognition a title to property in this country vests in the de facto Government and that a title vested in a displaced Government is divested ... The present case is not concerned with the validity of acts in relation to person or property in Ethopia. It is concerned with the title to a chose in action – a debt, recoverable in England.'

While an appeal by the defendants was pending the British Government recognised the King of Italy as *de jure* Emperor of Ethiopia.

Sir Wilfrid Greene MR stated:

'It is not disputed that in the Courts of this country, His Majesty the King of Italy as Emperor of Abyssinia is entitled by succession to the public property of the State of Abyssinia and the late Emperor of Abyssinia's title thereto is no longer recognised as existent ... that right of succession is to be dated back at any rate to the date when the *de facto* recognition of the King of Italy as the *de facto* Sovereign of Abyssinia took place ... in December 1936 ... Now that being so the title of the plaintiff to sue is necessarily displaced.'

The question of claim to property also arose more recently in *Republic of Somalia* v *Woodhouse Drake and Carey (Suisse) SA* [1992] 3 WLR 744. In this case, the incumbent Government of Somalia purchased a cargo of rice for delivery at the port of Mogadishu. However, prior to delivery, the Government was overthrown and a Provisional Government established. In the meantime, the cargo was not delivered to its port of destination due to fighting.

The Provisional Government of Somalia raised an action for recovery of the price of the undelivered goods and the court had to consider whether the Provisional Government had standing to bring the action.

Hobhouse J examined four criteria in order to decide whether the plaintiffs existed as the Government of the State of Somalia:

1. whether the plaintiffs' were the constitutional government of the State;
2. the degree, nature and stability of administrative control, if any, that the plaintiffs maintained over the territory of the State;
3. whether Her Majesty's Government had any dealings with the Provisional Government and, if so, what were the nature and extent of those dealings; and
4. the extent of the international recognition afforded by the world community as the Government of the State.

The evidence submitted by the Provisional Government of Somalia failed to satisfy these criteria and the claim to the price of the consignment was rejected.

The withdrawal of *de jure* recognition and the retrospective effect of the granting of *de jure* recognition to the successor, did not affect the validity of the transactions already completed by the previous sovereign

In *Gdynia Amerika Linie* v *Boguslawski* (1953) the Government of National Unity in Lublin became *de facto* Government of Poland on 28 June 1945, and at midnight 5–6 July 1945, the British Government accorded *de jure* recognition to this

Government. Before this the Polish Government-in-Exile in London had been recognised *de jure* by Great Britain. The question at issue was whether the *de jure* recognition of the Government of National Unity of 5–6 July had retroactive effect on the validity of acts done by the Government-in-Exile in London, in respect of the Polish merchant marine fleet and personnel under its control.

The Foreign Office certificate stated that the question of the retroactive effect of recognition of a government was a question of law to be decided by the courts. Their Lordships were unanimous in upholding the validity of the actions of the Government-in-Exile. Although the recognition of the Government of National Unity in Lublin might be retroactive in its effect so far as Poland was concerned where the Government had effective control, it could not apply retroactively to events over which it had no control, such as the actions taken in London prior to midnight 5–6 July by the Government-in-Exile.

In *Civil Air Transport Inc* v *Central Air Transport Corpn* (1953) (Privy Council) Viscount Simon stated: 'Primarily ... retroactivity or recognition operates to validate acts of a *de facto* Government which has subsequently become the new *de jure* Government and not to invalidate acts of the previous *de jure* Government'

Recognition of governments in English law and the 1980 Statement on UK policy

The decision of the British Government in April 1980 to abandon the practice of expressly recognising foreign governments has introduced an element of uncertainty into this particular area of the law.

In the House of Lords in May 1980, the Foreign Secretary, Lord Carrington, was asked:

'How in future, for the purposes of legal proceedings, it may be ascertained whether, on a particular date, Her Majesty's Government regarded a new regime as the Government of the State concerned.'

The Foreign Secretary replied:

'In future cases where a new regime comes to power unconstitutionally our attitude to the question whether it qualifies to be treated as a Government will be left to be inferred from the nature of the dealings, if any, which we may have with it, and in particular on whether we are dealing with it on a normal Government-to-Government basis.'

Possible problems in the implementation of the new policy

The abandonment of express recognition of foreign governments may give rise to several problems for the judges when deciding whether an entity qualifies to be treated as a government.

1. The Foreign Office may not make available to the judges details of its dealings with the foreign government.

2. If such details are made available it may be difficult for the judges, in the absence of diplomatic experience, to infer from the nature of those dealings whether or not the foreign government qualifies to be treated as a government.

3. If a government is in firm control of a State, it may be unjust to refuse to apply its laws in an English court solely because the British Government refuses to have dealings with it.

4. The extent of a government's control over its territory, and not the extent of its dealings with the British Government, remains the best test of its international status.

5. If the courts were to adopt the control test and the Foreign Office refused to provide the judges with details of a particular government's control over its territory, the judges may have difficulty in deciding whether such control does in fact exist.

6

Sovereignty and Equality of States

6.1 The doctrine of equality of States

6.2 Domestic jurisdiction

6.1 The doctrine of equality of States

The doctrine of equality of States was introduced into the theory of international law by the naturalist writers. Wolff stated:

'By nature all nations are equal the one to the other. For nations are considered as individual free persons living in a state of nature. Therefore, since by nature all men are equal, all nations too are by nature equal the one to the other.'

The doctrine recognises that all States are equal in law despite their obvious inequalities in other respects: inequality of size, wealth, population, strength or degree of civilisation. This principle of sovereign equality of States has found expression in the Charter of the United Nations, Article 2(1) of which states: 'The Organisation is based on the principle of the sovereign equality of all its Members.'

The conceptual problem of equality

The doctrine of equality may become seriously misleading. It cannot for instance mean that all States have equal rights, and the legal notion of equality must therefore be limited in practical terms. The need for international co-operation in such areas as international peace and security and in economic and social matters has led States to accept limitations upon their national equality in relation to other States. For instance, politically the Great Powers have always exercised a primacy among States. Today this is illustrated by the Security Council of the United Nations in which certain States are given both permanent membership and a privileged voting position.

Sovereign equality or independence?

The better view today, therefore, is that the doctrine of sovereign equality of States is more accurately described as the independence of States. It has been suggested that it is difficult to find any consequence flowing from the doctrine of sovereign equality which does not equally flow from, and is not better explained by, the fact that States are independent.

Legal consequences of sovereign equality or independence

Certain practical consequences flow from this legal equality or independence of States:

Each State has a *prima facie* exclusive jurisdiction over a territory and the permanent population living there

States have a duty of non-intervention in the area of exclusive jurisdiction of other States:

1. no State can claim jurisdiction over another;
2. the courts of one State do not as a rule question the validity of the official acts of another State in so far as these acts purport to take effect within the latter's jurisdiction;
3. municipal courts will not exercise jurisdiction over a foreign sovereign in his public capacity.

Membership of international organisations is not obligatory, but as regards States members of such organisations:

1. when a question arises which has to be settled by consent, every State has a right to a vote and to one vote only;
2. the vote of the weakest State has as much weight as the vote of the most powerful.

Jurisdiction of international tribunals depends on the consent of the parties
In the *Eastern Carelia Case* (1923), the Permanent Court of International Justice stated that it is: 'well established in international law that no State can, without its consent be compelled to submit its disputes with other States either to mediation or to arbitration, or to any other kind of pacific settlement'.

These principles were restated by the United Nations Special Committee on Principles of International Law Concerning Peaceful Relations and Co-operation among States in 1964:

'All States enjoy sovereign equality. As subjects of international law they have equal rights and duties.
a) States are juridically equal;
b) each State enjoys the rights inherent in full sovereignty;
c) each State has the duty to respect the personality of other States;
d) the territorial integrity and political independence of the State are inviolable;
e) each State has the right freely to choose and develop its political, social, economic and cultural systems;

f) each State has the duty to comply fully and in good faith with its international obligations, and to live in peace with other States.'

6.2 Domestic jurisdiction

One important consequence of the doctrine of sovereign equality of States is the principle that certain matters are within the exclusive competence of States and are not subject to international obligations. Thus, for example, such matters as the granting of nationality and a State's treatment of its own nationals within its territory are not subject to interference by other States or international organisations.

The principle is expressly stated in the Charter of the United Nations, Article 2(7) of which provides:

'Nothing contained in the present Charter shall authorise the United Nations to intervene in matters which are essentially within the domestic jurisdiction of any State or shall require the Members to submit such matters to settlement under the present Charter; but this principle shall not prejudice the application of enforcement measures under Chapter VII.'

In practice Article 2(7) has been given a narrow interpretation by the organs of the United Nations. They have claimed the inherent power to determine their own competence and therefore to undertake preliminary investigations to ascertain whether a particular matter is 'essentially within the domestic jurisdiction of any State'.

In practice the organs have taken action on a wide range of topics, despite protests from the States concerned that such matters were wholly within their domestic jurisdiction. These include such matters as human rights violations, the principle of self-determination and colonialism. The organs have expressed the view that if a matter is contrary to the purposes and principles of the Charter of the United Nations, or if it endangers international peace and security, then their competence to deal with the matter overrides any plea of domestic jurisdiction under Article 2(7).

7

Territorial Sovereignty

7.1 Introduction

The occupation of territory and the exclusive exercise of jurisdiction therein is one of the essential elements of State sovereignty.

Territorial sovereignty was described in the *Island of Palmas Arbitration* (1928) as being: 'the right to exercise therein, to the exclusion of any other State, the functions of a Sovereign'.

The concept of territory

The territory of a State is the foundation of its factual existence and the basis for the exercise of its legal powers. The territory of a State comprises all land areas, including

75

subterranean areas, waters, including national rivers, lakes, the territorial sea appurtenant to the land and the sea-bed and subsoil of the territorial sea and the airspace over the land and the territorial sea. Territorial sovereignty may be exercised over various geographical features analogous to land territory including islands, islets, rocks and reefs.

Other forms of territorial sovereignty

It is sometimes said that territorial sovereignty is indivisible, but there have been numerous instances in international practice both of division of sovereignty and of distribution of the components of sovereignty.

Titular, residual and distributed sovereignty

No territory, unless it be *terra nullius,* is without sovereignty and some entity must be isolated as sovereign. The entity which has the ultimate capacity of disposing of the territory may be said to possess 'titular' or 'residual' sovereignty: the entity which exercises plenary power over the territory but lacks the capacity of ultimate disposal may be said to possess 'effective' sovereignty. The two together, residual and effective powers, make up the totality of sovereignty.

Similarly, two or more entities may exercise divided functions, and this may give rise to either dual, divided or distributed sovereignty depending upon whether the actors must act jointly or may act separately within defined spheres of competence.

Residual sovereignty

Oppenheim describes this form of sovereignty as 'nominal'. It occurs when a grantor cedes the administrative competence of a territory to a foreign power by treaty during a time of peace. Thus Japan placed the Ryukya Islands under US administration under Article 3 of the Treaty of Peace 1951, while retaining residual sovereignty in the islands.

Condominia

Oppenheim describes this as follows: 'In the case of a piece of territory consisting of land or water under the joint tenancy of two or more States, these several States exercising sovereignty conjointly over it, and over the individuals living therein.'

The best example was the Anglo-French Condominium of the New Hebrides constituted in 1906. This arrangement was said to create: 'a region of joint influence ... each of the two Powers retaining sovereignty over its nationals ... and neither exercising a separate authority over the group'.

Indeterminate sovereignty

It may be that a piece of territory which is not a *res nullius* nevertheless has no determinate sovereign. It would apply for instance in a situation where a sovereign has renounced his sovereignty and the coming into being of an interregnum with disposition postponed until a certain condition is fulfilled. An example is that of Japan's renunciation of any right to Formosa and the subsequent dispute as to recognition between the Communist and Nationalist Chinese Governments.

Terminable and reversionary sovereignty

Territorial sovereignty may be defeasible by operation of law, for example, by reversion on the failure of a condition under which sovereignty was transferred. For example, the independence of Monaco is subject to there being no vacancy in the Crown of Monaco.

The notion of reversionary sovereignty was applicable for example to the mandate system established under the League of Nations whereby the Principal Powers who placed their territories under mandate retained a reversionary interest in the territory until it attained independence.

Other territorial regimes

In addition to territorial sovereignty three other territorial regimes are recognised by international law:

1. Territory not subject to the sovereignty of any State or States and which possesses a status of its own (eg mandate and trust territories).
2. The *res nullius*, being land legally susceptible to acquisition by States but not as yet placed under territorial sovereignty.
3. The *res communis*, consisting of the high seas and also outer space, which is not capable of being placed under the sovereignty of any State.

7.2 The acquisition of territory

Traditional international law distinguishes several modes by which sovereignty can be acquired over territory. They were originally based on Roman law rules regarding acquisition of property. The Roman law analogy was well suited to the system of absolute monarchy prevalent in Europe during the formative years of European expansion in the sixteenth and seventeenth centuries where the Prince was regarded as 'owner' of his State's territory. However, with the decline of private law notions in the eighteenth and nineteenth centuries the analogy with the Roman law rules became less distinct and today, under current international law, it can be argued that such an analogy serves no useful purpose and indeed gives a distorted view of current practice.

The five modes by which territory has traditionally said to have been acquired are: (1) occupation; (2) prescription; (3) accretion; (4) cession; and (5) conquest. These modes are not, however, exclusive or exhaustive. In practice it is unlikely that any single mode would be evident in isolation. The modes are interrelated and in complex cases may be used in conjunction to the extent that no one mode appears dominant. In addition, these modes do not adequately describe the acquisition of territory by newly independent States exercising a right to self-determination. It must also be borne in mind that the traditional modes of acquisition of territory found a place in legal reasoning during the formative stages of international law. In a number of cases it will, therefore, still be evident that these modes are based on a Western perception of the status of the territory prior to acquisition. As is illustrated in more detail below, acquisition of territory by occupation, for example, is based on the fundamental perception that the territory was previously *terra nullius*, ie not under the sovereignty of any State. By *terra nullius* it was, however, implied that the territory was not under the sovereignty of any other *recognised state*, ie one of the small club of State entities to which international law was deemed to have application. It would not defeat a claim for acquisition by occupation to show that the territory in question was inhabited.

The historical origins of the traditional modes of acquisition of territory thus makes it important to examine disputed claims to sovereignty in the light, also, of contemporary principles of international law.

7.3 Occupation

This is an original mode of acquisition whereby a State acquires sovereignty over a *terra nullius* (ie territory not under the sovereignty of any State). The territory may be new land having previously never belonged to any State. It may have been abandoned by the former sovereign or it may have been occupied by a people lacking the social and political organisation necessary to constitute a sovereign State under international law. For example, the existence of the Australian aborigines notwithstanding, Australia was regarded as *terra nullius* at the time of its original settlement by the UK.

What constitutes occupation?

Territory is occupied when it is placed under *effective control* and as *terra nullius* becomes scarcer so the requirements of effective control have become stricter in international law. Today effective control is a relative concept varying according to the nature of the territory concerned. For instance, it will be much easier to establish effective control over territory which is uninhabited than over territory which is inhabited albeit by primitive people.

The intention and will to act as sovereign

In the legal status of *Eastern Greenland Case* (1933) the Permanent Court of Justice said:

'... a claim to sovereignty based not upon some particular act or title such as a treaty of cession but merely upon a continued display of authority, involves two elements each of which must be shown to exist: the intention and will to act as Sovereign; and some actual exercise or display of such authority.'

But is the requirement of the 'will to act as sovereign' a valid requirement?
Brownlie argues that this is a subjective criterion involving the imputation of a state of mind involving a legal assessment and judgment to those ordering various State activities. He says, therefore, that this approach expects too much and is unrealistic in seeking a particular and coherent intention in a mass of activity by numerous individuals.

This requirement of *animus possidendi* also leads to problems where there are competing acts of sovereignty. Today all habitable areas of the earth now fall under the dominion of some State and, therefore, the importance of acquisition by occupation today lies not in the acquisition of new territory but the solving of boundary disputes and competing claims based on past occupation. So in cases where there are competing acts of sovereignty the subjective requirement of the *animus possidendi* of the competing States may be inconclusive. In such cases the tribunal must rely on objective elements of State activity, ie the actual manifestations of sovereignty.

But the intention to act as Sovereign as a requirement of effective occupation is important in three respects:

1. The activity must be that of the State or its authorised agent and not that of a mere individual.
2. The activity must not be exercised by consent of another State.
3. The activity taken as a whole must have no other explanation but the assumption of pre–existing sovereignty.

Effective exercise or continued display of authority

Possession must give the occupying State control over the territory concerned and there must be some display of State activity consistent with sovereignty. The traditional view is one of occupation in terms of settlement and close physical possession. However, under current international law what constitutes the necessary degree of control will vary with the circumstances of the case.

In the *Island of Palmas Case*: *United States* v *Holland* (1928) the USA claimed the Island of Palmas which lies half-way between the Philippines and what was then the Dutch East Indies. The USA founded its title upon the 1898 Treaty of Paris by which Spain ceded the Philippine Islands to the USA. In this Treaty the island of Palmas was described as forming part of the Philippines. However, the island was actually under Dutch control. The issue was therefore whether sovereignty over the island belonged to Spain at the time she purported to cede the island to the USA.

The Arbitrator held that even if Spain did originally have sovereignty over the island the Dutch had administered it since the early eighteenth century, thereby supplanting Spain as the sovereign. He stated that:

'... the continuous and peaceful display of territorial sovereignty (peaceful in relation to other States) is as good as a title ...

Manifestations of territorial sovereignty assume, it is true, different forms, according to conditions of time and place. Although continuous in principle, sovereignty cannot be exercised in fact at every moment on every point of a territory. The intermittence and discontinuity compatible with the maintenance of the right necessarily differ according as inhabited or uninhabited regions are involved, or regions enclosed within territories in which sovereignty is incontestably displayed or again regions accessible from, for instance, the high seas.'

The learned arbitrator found ample expression of the Dutch arguments based upon peaceful and continuous display of State authority over the island. These included the close link existing since 1677 between the people of the island and the Netherlands via the Dutch East India Company. Secondly, the unchallenged peaceful display of Dutch sovereignty from at least 1700 to the outbreak of the present dispute in 1906.

In *Clipperton Island Arbitration: France* v *Mexico* (1931) the Arbitrator stated that: 'the actual and not the nominal, taking of possession is a necessary condition of occupation' and the taking of possession consisted of an exercise of State authority sufficient in the circumstances of the territory concerned, ie the inaccessible and uninhabited nature of the island. So that in the particular case an offshore geographical survey of the uninhabited island, a landing by a small shore party, followed by a declaration of sovereignty published in a Honolulu journal were held to be sufficient to support the French claim.

In the *Eastern Greenland Case* (1933) the dispute arose out of the action of Norway in proclaiming its occupation of parts of East Greenland in 1931. Denmark argued that Danish sovereignty extended to the whole of Greenland. On the evidence submitted the Court was satisfied that Denmark's intention to claim title to the whole of Greenland was established, at least after 1721. It was, therefore, necessary to next discover some actual exercise or display of authority by Denmark over the disputed territory. The following factors were submitted in evidence:

1. The absence, until 1931 of any competing claim by another State.
2. The character of the country – the arctic and inaccessible nature of the uncolonised parts of the territory where it would be unreasonable to demand a continuous exercise of authority.
3. The numerous Danish legislative and administrative acts purporting to apply to the whole of Greenland.
4. Treaties with other States acquiescing to the Danish claim to the territory.
5. The granting of a trade monopoly and the granting of trading, mining and other concessions.

The Court held that this pattern of activity between 1721 and 1931 was sufficient to establish Danish title to the whole of the territory.

An example of this more modern and practical approach to occupation was provided by the Anglo-French dispute involving the *Minquiers and Ecrehos Islands* (1953). In appraising the relative strength of the opposing claims to sovereignty over the Ecrehos the Court stated that it: 'attaches, in particular, probative value to the acts which relate to the exercise of jurisdiction and local administration and to legislation'. The Court referred to the exercise of criminal jurisdiction, the holding of inquests, the collection of taxes and to a British Treasury Warrant of 1875 including the 'Ecrehos Rocks' within the Port of Jersey.

A further example of the development of this approach is provided by the *Rann of Kutch Arbitration: India* v *Pakistan* (1968).

In the case of a traditional agricultural economy the tribunal was able to concede that grazing and other economic activities by private landholders may provide acceptable evidence of title.

The critical date

Bound up with the issue of the continuous display of authority is the question of the date at which sovereignty comes to be assessed. This 'critical date' is the date beyond which further evidence of the exercise of sovereign authority will not be allowed. This judicial technique is important for two reasons: firstly, it establishes a point beyond which the parties will not be called upon to provide evidence of authority. Particularly in cases of uninhabited or sparsely inhabited territories it would make little sense to require that the display of authority be constantly in evidence. Secondly, in the case of disputed territories where the dispute arises in respect of the initial circumstances of acquisition rather than the display of authority thereafter, the critical date will be important in determining which factors are to be taken into account by the Court or Tribunal. In the *Taba Arbitration* (1988), for example, involving a boundary dispute between Egypt and Israel in the area of the Sinai along the Gulf of Aqaba, the Tribunal determined that:

> '29 September 1923, the date of the formal entry into force of the Mandate, is the appropriate date in the circumstances.'

While the critical date will invariably be apparent from the facts of the case, its determination by the Court or Tribunal, particularly in the face of conflicting evidence from the parties, may be of great significance to the merits of dispute. The choice of one or other date may, for example, preclude a party from adducing particular evidence or may alter the case from one of occupation to one of prescription. The choice of the critical date is thus a useful practical tool available to the Court to restrict or broaden the scope of the argument.

Acts of appropriation by private persons and acquisitions by chartered corporations

A State may ratify an act by one of its nationals purporting to appropriate territory on its behalf. The activities of chartered companies and corporations to which powers of acquisition and government may have been delegated by the State will also be regarded as State activity in relation to the acquisition of territory.

7.4 Prescription

Prescription

Like occupation this is based on effective control over territory, but whereas occupation is acquisition of *terra nullius*, prescription is the acquisition of territory which belongs to another State.

Lauterpacht/Oppenheim describes prescription as:

> 'The acquisition of territorial sovereignty through continuous and undisturbed exercise of sovereignty over it during such a period as is necessary to create, under the influence of historical development, the general conviction that the present condition of things is in conformity with international order.'

Generally, however, prescription as to title to territory is ill–defined and indeed some writers deny it recognition altogether. Learned writers have, however, described three categories of situations in which the doctrine of prescription may operate: (1) immemorial possession; (2) competing acts of sovereignty; (3) cases of acquiescence.

Immemorial possession

This is the presumption of a legal title in cases where the original basis of title is uncertain. It has been argued, however, that this cannot be a true case of prescription since the origin of the possession is unknown.

Competing acts of sovereignty

In practice the difference between occupation and prescription in claims based upon the nominal exercise of sovereignty may be impossible to ascertain. The very point at issue may be whether the territory was *terra nullius* or whether it was subject to previous sovereignty. In the *Island of Palmas Case,* for example, the court did not make clear whether the Island was under Spanish sovereignty before the Dutch began to exercise control.

When faced with competing claims, international tribunals often decide in favour of the State which can prove a greater degree of effective control over the disputed territory, without basing their judgment on any specific mode of acquisition. Again, therefore, in such cases references to prescription may be misleading.

Acquiescence

A combination of the passage of time and the implied acquiescence of the dispossessed sovereign are the basis of prescriptive rights.

The requirements for acquisitive prescription

1. Possession must be exercised a *titre de soverain*. There must be a display of State authority and the absence of any recognition of sovereignty in another State.
2. Possession must be peaceful and uninterrupted. What conduct is sufficient to prevent possession from being peaceful and uninterrupted? Any conduct indicating a lack of acquiescence, eg protest.

   Effective protests prevent acquisition of title by prescription.

   In the *Chamizal Arbitration* (1911), the USA laid claim to an area of Mexican territory which had become joined to US territory by the movement of the Rio Grande southwards, *inter alia*, on the ground of uninterrupted possession. The claim failed because Mexico had made a number of protests to the USA, and indeed as a result of the protests a convention had been signed in an attempt to settle 'the rights of the two nations with regard to the changes brought about by the action of the waters of the Rio Grande'. Therefore in the opinion of the Commissioners, diplomatic protests by Mexico prevented title arising.

   However, it is doubtful whether diplomatic protests alone are sufficient to preserve the rights of a dispossessed Sovereign. There must be some serious expression of protest, eg the severing of diplomatic relations or the imposition of sanctions as a retaliation. The matter should be raised before the United Nations and reinforced by a bona fide suggestion that the dispute be submitted to arbitration or judicial settlement.

   In the *Minquiers and Ecrehos Islands Case* (1953) the UK argued that French protests against British legislation applying to the disputed islands were ineffective, *inter alia*, on the ground that they should have been reinforced by pressure to have the matter submitted for determination by an international tribunal.

   This will be particularly relevant where the parties are bound by treaty providing for the settlement of their legal disputes by the Permanent Court of Arbitration.

   However, while some jurists do regard protest as merely effecting a postponement for a reasonable period of the process of prescription while advantage is taken of the available machinery for the settlement of international disputes, this approach can be criticised. Should failure to resort to certain organs be penalised by loss of territorial rights? Is it proper to demand all territorial disputes to be referred to international arbitration? Should procedural requirements be introduced into the concept of acquiescence?
3. The possession must be public. If there is to be acquiescence then there must be publicity.

4. The possession must persist. The effective control necessary to establish title by prescription must last for a longer period of time than the effective control which is necessary in cases of occupation. Unlike the situation under municipal law there is no fixed period in international law. The length of time required, therefore, is a matter of fact depending on the particular case.

Prescription and historical consolidation

Whatever limitation may exist in cases of adverse possession there will come a time when there will be created a belief that however wrongful the original taking, or whatever protests have been made, the present condition of things should not be disturbed.

The doctrine was first expressed in the *Anglo-Norwegian Fisheries Case* (1951) with reference to the Norwegian decrees which had the effect of extending the area of internal waters through the use of straight baselines as the base points for the delimitation of the territorial sea. The exercise of sovereignty claimed by Norway was, therefore, over *res communis* and, therefore, general acquiescence of all foreign States was necessary.

The Court commented:

'Since ... these ... constitute ... the application of a well defined and uniform system, it is indeed this system itself which would reap the benefit of general toleration, the basis of an historic consolidation which would make it enforceable as against all States'.

De Visscher cites the decision as an example of the 'fundamental interest of the stability of territorial situations from the point of view of order and peace'.

According to De Visscher's doctrine, consolidation differs from prescription, occupation and recognition:

'... consolidation differs from acquisitive prescription ... in the fact that it can apply to territories that could not be proved to have belonged to another State. It differs from occupation in that it can be admitted in relation to certain parts of the sea as well as of land. Finally, it is distinguished from international recognition ... by the fact that it can be held to be accomplished ... by a sufficiently prolonged absence of opposition either, in the case of land, on the part of States interested in disputing possession or, in maritime waters, on the part of the generality of States.'

In addition historic consolidation also takes cognisance of other special factors including economic interests and resources.

Criticisms of the doctrine

Jennings points out that, however important consolidating factors might be, it is still the fact of possession which is the foundation of the process of consolidation. The process cannot begin until actual possession is enjoyed and this is a necessary prerequisite in order to prevent evidence of an alleged political right or claim to have title transferred, being adduced as the foundation of a legal title.

7.5 Accretion

A State has the exclusive right of sovereignty over any additions made to its territory as a result of silting or other deposits or resulting from the formation of islands within its territorial waters. Although not of great importance it can be of significance where a State boundary follows the course of a river. Where a boundary river undergoes a sudden change of course (avulsion) this will not change the boundary line which will remain usually the centre line of the former main channel.

In the *Chamizal Arbitration* (1911) the question arose as to which State had title to the tract of land between the old and the new river beds. The boundary commission held that the part of the tract that had occurred by accretion belonged to the USA, ie the USA has acquired title by accretion. That part of the land that had resulted from a flood, in contrast, remained with Mexico.

In *Louisiana* v *Mississippi* (1931) the United States Supreme Court applied international law principles to a boundary dispute between the two federal States. The Court held that the gradual erosion of soil from the Mississippi bank and its deposit on the Louisiana bank between 1823 and 1912 passed title to Louisiana. But when the river suddenly changed course in 1913 across the accretion of the previous 90 years this did not divest Louisiana of the territory already acquired. This change was an avulsion and therefore the pre-1913 boundary remained.

7.6 Cession

This is the transfer of territory, usually by treaty, from one State to another, the treaty forming the legal basis of sovereignty. It may be either gratuitous or for some consideration, eg the sale to the USA by Denmark of the Danish West Indies in 1916.

Cession is an example of a derivative title. If there were defects in the ceding State's title, the purported cession from the previous sovereign cannot cure the defect.

In the *Island of Palmas Case* the USA claimed that by the Treaty of Paris 1898 it acquired title to the island of Palmas from Spain. However, the Arbitrator found that at the time of the purported transfer of the island in 1898 sovereignty over the island lay not with Spain but with the Netherlands. Spain could not transfer more rights than she herself possessed. Therefore since Spain had no title to the island in 1898, the USA could not acquire title from Spain.

In order to effect a valid cession there should normally be both a treaty and an actual transfer of possession: *Iloilo Case* (1925). The Treaty of Paris, signed on 10 December 1898, provided that on exchange of ratifications, Spain should evacuate the Philippines in favour of the USA. However, on 24 December local insurgents forced the Spanish to withdraw and it was not until 10 February that American troops captured Iloilo from the insurgents. On the following day the insurgents set fire to the town damaging property of British subjects. The British-American tribunal hearing claims for damaged property held that as the treaty did not take effect until ratification on 11 April, the transfer of *de jure* sovereignty to the USA, and its resulting obligations, did not commence until that date.

There is, however, no need for a transfer of possession if the State to which the territory is ceded is already in possession. Similarly, in cases such as Lombardy which was ceded by Austria to France in 1860 and then immediately retroceded by France to Italy, there was no requirement for France to actually enter into possession.

7.7 Conquest

Under traditional international law conquest was recognised as a means of acquiring territory even in the absence of a treaty of cession, but the acquisition of territory by conquest was not lawful until hostilities had come to an end. Therefore, in the absence of a peace treaty evidence was necessary that all resistance by the enemy State and by its allies had ceased so that there were no longer forces in the field to free the occupied territory from the control of the conquering power. Thus, the German annexation of Poland during the Second World War was invalid, because Poland's allies continued to struggle against Germany.

But even when a State had been completely subjugated there would be no transfer of sovereignty in the absence of an intention to annex it. Thus, in 1945 the victorious Allies expressly disclaimed the intention of annexing Germany, although they had occupied all German territory and defeated her Axis allies.

While acquisition of territory by conquest may have been acceptable during the period when there was no legal restriction upon the right of a State to wage war, it is now generally accepted that the Covenant of the League of Nations, the Pact of Paris, and, more importantly, Article 2(4) of the United Nations Charter restrict the ability of a State to acquire territory by conquest.

The effect of the change

Once the proposition is accepted that an aggressor State cannot acquire territory by conquering another State through the illegal use of force, it follows that an aggressor cannot now acquire territory by conquest alone and that any treaty of cession imposed by the victor on the vanquished will be invalid.

Can an 'innocent party' to a war still acquire territory by conquest?

Can a State acting in self-defence acquire territory by conquest? The Soviet view has been that States acting in self-defence may impose sanctions on a defeated aggressor: in particular, they are empowered to take away part of the territory of the aggressor in order to prevent a recurrence of the aggression.

However, the Declaration on Principles of International Law Concerning Friendly Relations and Co-operation among States in Accordance with the Charter of the United Nations, passed by the General Assembly in 1970, suggests otherwise.

'The territory of a State shall not be the object of military occupation resulting from the use of force in contravention of the provisions of the Charter. The territory of a State shall not be the object of acquisition by another State resulting from the threat or use of force.'

So any threat or use of force, whether in contravention of the United Nations Charter or not, invalidates the acquisition of territory. For example, both the General Assembly and the Security Council of the United Nations have repeatedly declared that Israel is not entitled to annex any of the territory it captured following the war of June 1967. The Security Council affirmed in 1968 that the 'acquisition of territory by military conquest is inadmissible' and that all measures taken by Israel in the occupied territories were invalid and ineffective to change the status of that territory.

But it must be remembered that as long as the international community of States is not determined to prevent aggressors from enjoying their spoils the principle that an aggressor cannot acquire a good title to territory is liable to produce serious discrepancy between the law and the facts. It will depend upon political rather than legal circumstances.

The invasion of Goa 1961

Portugal retained this colony on the Indian subcontinent until it was invaded by India and incorporated into its own territory. This illegal use of force by India and the subsequent annexation of Goa received the approval of many Members of the United Nations and there was no condemnation of the act by either the Security Council or the General Assembly.

It can be argued that India has obtained a basis of title which, even if there is no express recognition of the fact, will become consolidated over a relatively short period of time, by the acquiescence of the international community into a fully valid title.

Consider the case of Namibia, one of the last instances of conquest. If the ICJ had not declared South Africa's occupation of the territory illegal and if there had been no opposition to this state of affairs, would the international community have eventually acknowledged the reality of South Africa's title?

Similarly with the Falkland Islands. If Britain had not repossessed the islands by force would the illegal Argentinian invasion and occupation have eventually been regarded by the international community as confirming Argentina's claim to sovereignty over the islands?

The invasion of Kuwait 1990

On 2 August 1990, Iraqi armed forces invaded Kuwait and subsequently the Iraqi Government announced its intention to establish a 'comprehensive and eternal merger' between the two states. On 8 August, Iraq again declared its intention to annex Kuwait and that Kuwait was to become the nineteenth province of Iraq and instructed all foreign diplomats to leave Kuwait. Foreign embassies and consulates were closed by the Iraqi authorities.

In response, the UN Security Council adopted Resolution 662 (1990) of 9 August 1990, which declared that the 'annexation of Kuwait by Iraq under any form and whatever pretext has no legal validity and is considered null and void'. The Resolution also called upon all States to refrain from extending recognition to the purported annexation and to abstain from any actions that could be construed as indirect recognition of the annexation.

This Resolution was ignored by Iraq and preparations were made by the Iraqi Government to declare Kuwait as its nineteenth province. The Security Council therefore adopted a second Resolution relating to the Iraqi claim to have acquired the territory of Kuwait by means of conquest and annexation. Specifically referring to the obligations of Iraq under international law, Security Council Resolution 664 (1990) reaffirmed that the annexation of Kuwait by Iraq was null and void and demanded that the Government of Iraq rescind its orders for the closure of the diplomatic and consular missions in Kuwait and the withdrawal of immunity of their personnel.

Both these Resolutions are evidence that the acquisition of territory by means of annexation and conquest is no longer a valid method of obtaining title under international law.

7.8 Other circumstances relevant to the acquisition of territory

Contiguity

Contiguity alone is not a basis of title. However, it is a fact which may influence the decision of an international tribunal in cases, for instance, where sovereignty has not been exercised uniformly in every part of the territory or where only the coast of a barren territory has been occupied or in cases where it is desired to give effect to principles of geographic unity. For example, in the *Eastern Greenland Case* where Danish sovereignty over the whole of Greenland was conferred, the actual areas of the disputed territory settled by Denmark were few.

Contiguity is also the basis of the law concerning territorial waters, the contiguous zone and the continental shelf.

Recognition, acquiescence and estoppel

Although they are not strictly speaking modes of acquisition they do play an important role in the acquisition of territory in the sense that they may provide evidence of control where there are competing acts of possession.

Recognition

Recognition refers to the attitude of third States. This may take the form of a unilateral express declaration or may occur in treaty provisions with third States. In the *Eastern Greenland Case* the Court referred to treaties between Denmark and States other than Norway as constituting evidence of recognition of Danish sovereignty over Greenland in general.

Recognition and acquisition by conquest

Although States are no longer permitted to acquire territory by conquest the invalidity of such territorial acquisitions may be cured by recognition, subject to certain conditions:

1. The recognition must take the form of an express statement and cannot be implied.
2. The recognition must be *de jure* and not merely *de facto*.
3. The recognition must be acknowledged not only by the victim but also by third States.

Acquiescence

This applies to the attitude of the 'losing' State and is inferred from failure to protest against the exercise of control by one's opponent in circumstances where protest might reasonably be expected. Recognition or acquiescence by one State has little or no effect unless it is accompanied by some measure of control over the territory by the other State. So, for instance, failure to protest against a purely verbal assertion of title unsupported by any degree of control does not constitute acquiescence.

Estoppel

Recognition or acquiescence may give rise to an estoppel. In the context of international disputes over territory the rule would mean that a State which had recognised another State's title to particular territory would be estopped from denying the other State's title if the other State had taken some action in reliance on the recognition.

Novation

This is a distinct mode of acquisition defined by Verzijl as follows:

> 'It consists in the gradual transformation of a right in *territorio alieno*, for example a lease, or a pledge, or certain concessions of a territorial nature, into full sovereignty without any formal and unequivocal instrument to that effect intervening.'

For example, British claims to British Honduras (Belize) resulting from the Treaty of Paris 1763 allowing British nationals to cut compeachy wood in the Spanish territories bordering the Bay of Honduras.

Discovery

It was believed in the sixteenth century that discovery alone conferred a complete title to territory and such discovery was usually accompanied by symbolic acts such as the planting of a flag. The modern view, however, is that discovery merely gives an option to the discovering State to consolidate its claim by proceeding to effective occupation within a reasonable time. This was the view stated by the Arbitrator in the *Island of Palmas Case*.

Symbolic annexation

Symbolic annexation has been defined by Brownlie as:

'A declaration or other act of sovereignty or an act of private persons duly authorised or subsequently ratified by a State, intended to provide unequivocal evidence of the acquisition of sovereignty over a parcel of territory or an island.'

In the *Clipperton Island Case*, a declaration of French sovereignty was proclaimed and subsequently published by a duly authorised Lieutenant in the French navy, while cruising near the island in 1858. It was held that in the absence of any effective rival claim and taking into account the inaccessible and uninhabited nature of the island, that France acquired the island when sovereignty was proclaimed on 17 November 1858 and that the purported annexation, though symbolic in form, had legal effect.

Uti possidetis

Uti possidetis, a principle first developed among the Spanish colonies of Latin America, provides that the old administrative boundaries would be recognised as the new borders of the independent States. This principle was adopted by the Organisation of African Unity in a resolution of 1964 which provides that all States should respect the colonial boundaries. The function of this principle is to preserve the territorial integrity of newly independent States. The principle was followed by the Court in its judgment on the boundary dispute in *Burkina Faso* v *Mali* (1986).

The principle was again followed in the *Case Concerning Land, Island and Maritime Frontier Disputes* (1992), which involved a dispute between El Salvador and Honduras concerning the land frontiers between their respective territories. Both parties agreed that the matter should be resolved according to the principle of *uti possidetis* and the Court delimited the disputed boundaries by applying this principle. The original colonial boundaries were, therefore, transformed into international frontiers.

7.9 The acquisition of territory in polar regions

The Arctic

The polar regions create unique problems in the context of territorial acquisition. In the case of the North Pole there is the additional problem in that the region is mostly ice territory over a frozen sea and not over land. In polar regions where the contiguity principle cannot be applied, the 'sector principle' has been used, according to which all land lying within the triangle between the east-west extremities of a State contiguous to the Pole and the Pole itself should be subject to its dominion, unless the territory already belongs to another State.

Whilst the sector principle does not give title which would not arise otherwise, if the necessary State activity occurs it does represent a reasonable application of the principles of effective occupation as applied in the *Eastern Greenland Case*. Both Canada and the USSR have adopted the sector principle.

Antarctica

Sector claims in Antarctica have been made by the UK, New Zealand, Australia, France, Norway, Germany, Argentina and Chile. Some of these claims are based not on contiguity but on discovery and in some cases there are overlapping claims to the same territory. The claimants are not confined to peripheral neighbours as in the Arctic. Neither the USA nor the USSR recognise these territorial claims.

The Antarctic Treaty of 1959, *inter alia*, puts into abeyance all existing claims to territorial sovereignty over Antarctica as long as the Treaty should remain in force and provides for the use of the area for peaceful purposes only.

Notwithstanding that the satisfaction of territorial claims in the Antarctic region has not yet been achieved, the Convention on the Regulation of Antarctic Mineral Resource Activities 1988 creates a legal regime for the exploration and exploitation of the mineral resources of Antarctica. All 39 Antarctic Treaty nations are parties to this agreement. The purpose of the agreement is to facilitate the commercial development of the minerals of Antarctica and to that end, the agreement contains a number of provisions allowing prospecting, exploration and exploitation of the mineral resources of the territory.

The agreement does not alter or compromise the legal rights of the States claiming territory in Antarctica. It expressly preserves the legal positions of those States claiming sovereign rights in the region, and no acts or activities are to be construed as constituting a basis for asserting, supporting or repudiating a claim to territorial sovereignty.

An Antarctic Mineral Resource Commission was established under the Agreement to issue permits for these activities to operators. Operators are strictly liable for any environmental damage to the Antarctic environment caused by their activities. The system of liability is based on the 'polluter pays' principle and operators are required to restore the status quo ante in the event of pollution.

The exploration and exploitation system envisaged by the agreement has not yet come into operation because the convention expressly provides that no mineral resource activities are to take place until it is agreed that the technology and procedures are available to allow safe mining operations, compliance with the terms of the agreement and the capacity to monitor key environmental parameters and ecosystems components. To date, two meetings have taken place among the participating states to decide when these conditions will be satisfied. The first conference was held in Chile in November 1990 and the second in Madrid in April 1991. Both the USA and the UK are seeking a moratorium on development of an unspecified nature which would effectively prohibit mineral resource activities indefinitely. A number of other contracting parties, including Australia, France, Italy and Belgium, oppose this policy.

Unlike the deep sea-bed, the Antarctic area has not been declared the common heritage of mankind. Nevertheless, in the event that the exploration and exploitation regime proposed by the agreement comes into effect, the *res nullius/res communis* debate may be revived. While the agreement does require that payments are made for development permits, commercial viability is the major factor in the exploration and exploitation of minerals in the Antarctic area.

The Antarctic Minerals Act 1989 incorporates the operative provisions of the Convention into the domestic law of the UK.

7.10 Restrictions on the transfer of territory

States may enter into treaty agreements not to alienate certain areas of territory under any circumstances or they may contract not to transfer territory to a particular State or States. An obligation not to acquire territory may also be undertaken. By the State Treaty of 1955, Austria agreed not to enter into political or economic union with Germany.

By the Treaty of Utrecht 1713, Great Britain agreed to offer Gibraltar to Spain before attempting to transfer sovereignty over Gibraltar to any other State.

However, it is doubtful whether a breach of such treaty not to alienate or acquire territory will affect the title of the grantee of such territory.

7.11 Intertemporal law

As a result of changes in the law relating to the acquisition of territory, problems have arisen as to which legal regime should be applied when determining title. For example, should title to territory acquired by conquest in the nineteenth century be assessed according to the rules relating to conquest at the time (title would be lawful) or according to the law on conquest today (title would be unlawful)?

The general rule – known as the principle of intertemporal law – is that title should be assessed according to the rules of law that prevailed at the time of the acquisition of territory. In the *Island of Palmas Case*, however, Arbitrator Huber suggested that title to territory needed to be confirmed against the *changing standards* of international law, ie he appears to suggest that title should be assessed by reference to *current* rules rather than by reference to the rules existing at the time of the acquisition. A number of writers have argued that the modified rule developed by Huber would be highly disruptive, as every State would constantly have to review and confirm its title. Huber's interpretation should, therefore, probably best be seen in terms of the facts of the case in issue, ie as *discovery* only formed an incomplete title, whether or not title had been 'made good' had to be assessed by reference to the law as it applied to subsequent possession.

7.12 The loss of territory

Where the territory falls automatically under the sovereignty of another State

1. By treaty of cession – a transfer of rights by one State to another.
2. By prescription.
3. Where a new State is created: by transfer of sovereignty from the former colonial power; or where the former sovereign is destroyed by revolution.

*Where the territory is abandoned (*derelictio*)*

A State may by its conduct or by express admission acquiesce in the extension of another State's claim to its territory. In such cases absence of a reasonable level of State activity may cause loss of title. It has been argued that dereliction requires both a physical abandonment and an intention to abandon dominion. For reasons of stability, however, abandonment is not to be presumed and certainly in the case of remote and uninhabited areas it would seem that international tribunals require little in the way of maintenance of sovereignty. Such a rule was applied in the *Clipperton Island Case* and was referred to in the *Eastern Greenland Case*. In less inhospitable territories it may well be, however, that dominion will only remain if a physical manifestation of sovereignty subsists.

7.13 The external territorial rights of a State

A State might have powers to regulate the foreign relations of a protectorate, a trusteeship territory or other colonial possession, or even to regard such a non-self-governing community as part of its own territory for legislative and administrative purposes.

Colonial and other possessions

Mandate and trust territories
State authority over mandated or trusteeship territories cannot be described in terms of sovereignty. As was stated in the *South West Africa Case*, the territory of the non-self-governing community is held on trust by the administering power and cannot be considered as part of the territory of that power.

Colonies
These have usually been considered as under the sovereignty of the colonial power even where, as in the case of the British Colonies, they are not incorporated as part of the UK. Thus matters concerning the internal affairs of the territories are regarded by the UK as falling within its domestic jurisdiction.

The rights of a State over the territory of another State

Leases
Examples include the grants made by China in favour of France, Russia, Germany and Great Britain in 1898, the best known being the 'New Territories' attached to Hong Kong. Such leases amount to a transfer of sovereignty by the grantor for the period of the lease. Such a lease is a right in rem. It attaches to the territory and remains enforceable against the territory even if the territory subsequently passes under the dominion of another State.

Use and possession granted in perpetuity
In 1903 Panama granted to the USA 'in perpetuity the use, occupation and control' of the Panama Canal Zone. In such a case residual sovereignty remains with the grantor.

Leases of military bases
The status of such bases is doubtful and would depend upon the terms of the actual treaty which granted the disposition. It is unlikely, however, that they create real rights under international law and are best considered as leases in the municipal sense.

Servitudes
By treaty or otherwise a State may have acquired rights over the territory of a neighbouring State, eg a right to exercise a right of way. Such rights may be divided into two categories:

1. Rights benefitting the international community: international servitudes may exist, not for the benefit of a single State but for the benefit of the international community.

Aaland Islands Dispute (1920): in 1856 Russia entered into a treaty obligation not to fortify the Aaland Islands. Although the islands lay near Stockholm, Sweden was not a party to this treaty. In 1918 the islands became part of Finland which started fortifying them. Sweden complained to the League of Nations. It was decided that Finland had succeeded to Russia's obligations and that Sweden could claim the benefit of the 1858 Treaty, although she was not a party to it. The treaty was designed to preserve the balance of power in Europe and could, therefore, be invoked by all the States which were 'directly interested', including Sweden.

2. Rights benefitting only a single State: these include mining rights, rights to run an oil or gas pipeline across a neighbouring State, rights to take water for irrigation, rights of way, etc.

   In the *Rights of Passage Case* (1960) it was held that Portugal had a right of passage over Indian territory between the coastal district of Daman and the 'enclaves' in respect of private persons, civil officials and goods in general, and this right was binding on India.

   However, international tribunals seem reluctant to find servitudes in favour of a single State where those servitudes are of an economic nature. For example, in the North Atlantic Fisheries Case, it was held that a treaty between the USA and Great Britain of 1818 granting the inhabitants of the USA the liberty to take fish from the sea off Newfoundland did not create a servitude preventing Great Britain from limiting the fishing rights of all persons, including US nationals, in the area concerned.

   But if evidence of the intention to create such a servitude is found to exist on the part of the State granting it then it will be upheld.

   In *Aix-la-Chappelle Maastricht RR Co* v *Thewis* (1914) it was held that the Netherlands was able to exercise control over a coal mine which was owned by the Dutch Government but ran under German territory, in accordance with a binding treaty of 1816 between Prussia and the Netherlands. By the treaty, Prussia was in no way to interfere with or restrict the mining of coal.

7.14 Assessment

At the outset of this discussion relating to acquisition of territory mention was made of the fact that the traditional modes of acquisition of territory are unhelpful in explaining the most significant form of acquisition of territory on the post-war period, ie acquisition by newly independent States.

Although the acquisition of territory by newly independent States can be explained in terms of cession or prescription, such analysis fails to take into account the developments in international law since the late 1950s which have underpinned the independence movement. Most significant among these developments has been the recognition of a right to self-determination which has a specific content going beyond the broad principles outlined in, *inter alia*, Article 1(2) of the United

Nations Charter and common Article 1 of the 1966 Covenants on Civil and Political and Social, Economic and Cultural Rights.

A second important limitation in the traditional approach is that it gives little mention to the fact that title in international law is a *relative* rather than absolute concept. In the *Eastern Greenland Case*, for example, the PCIJ was concerned to assess the strength of the Danish claim relative to that of Norway. This is not to say that a State's control over its own territory will always be open to challenge. Rather, it is a recognition of the fact that disputes over territory arise in the context of competing claims. In these circumstances, the function of the Court is to determine which of the competing claims has greater merit, not which of the claims is good against the world at large.

Given these two substantive limitations regarding the traditional modes of acquisition, any assessment of current entitlement can only take place on the basis of a full analysis of the circumstances of the dispute.

(Note: for a discussion about the right to self-determination see Chapter 12 below.)

8

Jurisdiction

8.1 Introduction

The jurisdiction of a State describes the power of State under international law to exercise its authority over persons and property by the use of its municipal law. It includes both the power to prescribe rules (prescriptive or legislative jurisdiction) and the power to enforce them (enforcement or prerogative jurisdiction). Described in these terms, jurisdiction is fundamental to the concept of sovereignty. It describes both the extent of sovereign powers and the scope or limitation of these powers in the international system.

Jurisdiction is, therefore, that aspect of State sovereignty relating to legislative, executive and judicial competence. There are three groups of powers: (1) the power to legislate in respect of persons, property and events, (2) the power of physical interference exercised by the executive (arrest, seizure of property, etc), (3) the power of the State's courts to hear the cases concerning the persons, property and events.

Distinction between the executive and the judicial competence of States

It is essential to distinguish between these three groups of powers and in particular between the executive and the judicial competence of States. The governing principle – one of the fundamental tenets of the concept of sovereignty – is that a State cannot take measures on the territory of another State by way of enforcement of its national laws without that other State's consent. For example, a person may commit an offence in England and then escape to Brazil. The English courts have jurisdiction to try him, but the English police cannot enter Brazilian territory and arrest him. If they did, this would be contrary to the well-established rule of international law that one State may not commit acts of sovereignty on the territory of another State. So persons may not be arrested, police investigations may not be

97

mounted, summonses may not be served, on the territory of another State except under the terms of a treaty or with other consent.

In *Attorney-General of the Government of Israel v Eichmann* (1962) the accused, a German national, had been head of the Jewish Office of the German Gestapo. He was discovered living in Argentina in 1960 and was abducted to Israel without the knowledge of the Argentine Government. He was there prosecuted under the Israeli Nazi Collaborators (Punishment) Law of 1951, for war crimes and crimes against the Jewish people. He was convicted and sentenced to death.

Argentina lodged a complaint with the Security Council of the United Nations that the transfer of Eichmann to the territory of Israel constituted a violation of the sovereignty of the Argentine Republic. The Security Council resolved as follows:

'The Security Council ...
1) Declares that acts such as that under consideration which affect the sovereignty of a Member State and therefore cause international friction, may, if repeated, endanger international peace and security.
2) Requests the Government of Israel to make appropriate reparations in accordance with the Charter of the United Nations and the rules of international law ...'
Similarly, the same rules of international law will be applied where trickery or fraud induces the prisoner to leave the sanctuary of one State for the territory of another where he is then arrested.
In the *Colunje Claim* (1933) an officer of the Panama Canal Zone had gone to Colunje's offices in Panama and induced him to return to the Canal Zone where he was then arrested. In a claim against the USA, the American-Panamanian Claims Commission stated that it was 'evident that the police agent of the Zone by inducing Colunje by false pretences to come with him to the Zone with the intent of arresting him there unduly exercised authority within the jurisdiction of the Republic of Panama'.

The legislative competence of States in respect of extra territorial acts

The extent to which a State might legislate in respect of events taking place entirely abroad is uncertain. The general principle is that there should exist some link between either the offence or the offender and the State claiming jurisdiction.

Criminal v civil jurisdiction

There has been some debate as to whether the rules of international law on the question of jurisdiction apply only to criminal law or to civil law as well. Akehurst, for example, has taken the view that international law applies to criminal matters only. Bowett, in contrast, has taken a broader view although he accepts that some private matters will not come within the scope of international law. Brownlie has suggested that there is no relevant distinction to be drawn. Civil matters will in the first instance be regulated by reference to conflict of law rules. However, the scope of application of the conflict rules will be determined by principles of public international law.

8.2 The traditional principles of jurisdiction

The discussions surrounding, and the text of, the *Harvard Draft Convention 1935* on jurisdiction with respect to *crime* is commonly cited as identifying five traditional bases under which jurisdiction has been exercised:

1. the territorial principle;
2. the nationality principle;
3. the protective principle;
4. the passive personality principle;
5. the universality principle.

Of these, the principles most widely accepted were territorialty and nationality. The Harvard researchers also found evidence in State practice for the protective and universality principles. Although some evidence of passive personality was apparent, the researchers were of the opinion that this was insufficient to bring it within the ambit of customary law.

Territorial principle

The essence of this principle is that every State has jurisdiction over crimes committed in its own territory. This principle has been widely recognised. Normally, the application of the principle will be straightforward. An individual, present within a State, committing a crime in that State, will be subject to the enforcement jurisdiction of that State. In two circumstances, however, the application of the territorial principle will be more complicated – where an offence, *commenced* within the territory of another State, is *completed* in the territory of the State concerned and where the offence is commenced within the territory of the State concerned but only completed in the territory of another State.

The Harvard Draft approached this problem by providing that a State would have territorial jurisdiction in respect of acts which occur in whole or *in part* within the territory of the State. 'In part' was defined as an essential constituent element of the act in question. Thus, whether the act commenced in the territory (subjective jurisdiction) or was completed in the territory (objective jurisdiction) the State concerned would be able to exercise its authority.

Objective territoriality, ie jurisdiction on the grounds that the act was completed in the State in question, received general support in the *Lotus Case* (1927). The *Lotus* was a French ship that collided on the high seas with a Turkish collier, the *Boz-Kourt*, which sank with loss of life. When the *Lotus* reached Constantinople, the French officer of the watch at the time of the collision was arrested, tried and convicted of involuntary manslaughter, before a Turkish court. France protested about the legality of the Turkish action and the PCIJ was asked to decide whether Turkey had acted in conflict with international law by instituting proceedings and thereby exercising criminal jurisdiction. By the casting vote of the President, the Court decided that Turkey had not acted in conflict with the principles of international law by exercising such jurisdiction.

France had put forward two main contentions:

1. that international law did not allow a State to take proceedings with regard to offences committed by foreigners abroad;
2. that international law recognised the exclusive jurisdiction of the flag state over events occurring on board a ship on the high seas.

The second contention was rejected. The Court reserved its opinion on the first point but went on to hold that:

'... the offence produced its effects on the Turkish vessel and consequently in a place assimilated to Turkish territory in which the application of Turkish criminal law cannot be challenged, even in regard to offences committed there by foreigners'.

The majority of the Court, therefore, by assimilating the Turkish vessel to Turkish territory, brought the case under the principle of the objective territorial jurisdiction.

Nationality principle

The competence of the State to prosecute and punish its nationals on the sole basis of their nationality is based upon the allegiance which the person charged with the crime owes to the State of which he is a national. It is now universally accepted that a State may prosecute its nationals for crimes committed anywhere in the world. The application of the principle may be extended by reliance on residence or other connections as evidence of allegiance owed by aliens.

In *Joyce v DPP* (1946) the accused, William Joyce, was charged with treason under the Treason Act 1351 for having made propaganda broadcasts to the UK from Germany during the Second World War. Joyce was a US citizen born in the USA of Irish parents but he had spent most of his adult life in England. It was contended that because the accused was a US citizen he did not owe allegiance to the Crown and could not, therefore, be guilty of committing treason.

The House of Lords accepted that allegiance was necessary and found that the accused, who also held a British passport, still in force at the time of his broadcasts, was entitled to protection by the Crown and, therefore, owed the Crown allegiance. The fact that the passport had been obtained by fraud was immaterial.

It is, however, recognised that the application of the nationality principle may create parallel jurisdiction, ie jurisdiction by more than one State, and possible double jeopardy in cases of dual nationality or where the territorial and national jurisdiction overlap. Many States, therefore, place limitations on the nationality principle. For instance, English courts may only claim such jurisdiction in the case of serious offences such as treason, murder and bigamy. The UK does not, however, challenge the application of the principle by other States in less serious criminal cases.

Protective principle — *agst. security of State*

Almost all States assume jurisdiction to punish acts prejudicial to their security, even when they are committed by aliens abroad. Such acts, not necessarily confined to political matters, include spying, plots to overthrow the government, forging currency, immigration and economic offences.

For example, Article 7 of the French Criminal Code provides:

'Every foreigner who is outside the territory of the Republic and renders himself guilty, either as perpetrator or accomplice of a felony or misdemeanour against the security of the State or the counterfeiting of the seal of the State or current national monies may be prosecuted and tried according to the provisions of French law if he is arrested in France or if the Government obtains his extradition.'

The protective principle was accepted by the courts as alternative bases for jurisdiction in both the *Joyce* case and the *Eichmann Case*. In the latter case, the court assimilated the State of Israel – which did not exist at the time of the offences – to the Jewish people, holding that the protective principle permitted the Israeli court to exercise jurisdiction in respect of crimes against the Jewish people.

Although most States use this principle to some extent, thereby confirming its legitimacy, there is nevertheless always the danger that some States may abuse the principle by giving a very broad interpretation to the concept of protection. *danger of abuse*

For example, Nazi Germany decreed that it would endanger the racial composition of its nation if a German married a non-Aryan. On that basis a Jew who married a German girl in Czechoslovakia was charged under the relevant German law. *Nazi example of abuse*

The growth in international terrorism and drug smuggling has made the courts of the Western democratic countries less hostile to the reception of the protective principle of jurisdiction. Even the courts of the common law countries, which have traditionally rejected the protective principle, have been compelled to embrace a change of heart. *effect of drug smuggling + terrorism*

This change of policy was most evident in the Privy Council decision in *Liangsiriprasert* v *United States Government* [1990] 3 WLR 606. This case involved the extradition of a Thai national from Hong Kong to the USA on charges of drug smuggling. However, the defendant had been lured into Hong Kong territory by an American agent posing as a fellow smuggler and the defendant had committed no offence under Hong Kong law. The charges made as grounds for extradition related to offences outside the territory and in fact the only connection of the defendant with the territory was his physical presence.

The Privy Council rejected the contention that the courts could not exercise jurisdiction to extradite the defendant to the USA. The court continued to reject the notion that the protective principle could not be relied upon by pointing out that:

'Unfortunately in this century crime has ceased to be largely local in origin and effect. Crime is now established on an international scale and the common law must face this new reality. Their Lordships can find nothing in precedent, comity or good sense that should *international origin + effect of some crimes* inhibit the common law from regarding as justiciable in England inchoate crimes committed abroad which are intended to result in the commission of criminal offences in England...'

The court, however, qualified its decision by deciding that the charge in question could be construed as involving illicit trade in drugs which could be considered to amount to a potential conspiracy to traffic drugs in Hong Kong. But, despite this qualification, the decision signals a definite change of policy on the part of the British courts towards the acceptance of the protective principle.

Passive personality principle

According to this principle a State has jurisdiction to punish aliens for harmful acts committed abroad against its nationals. This has been described as the most difficult principle to justify in theory, and while some States such as Italy and Turkey claim jurisdiction on this ground others, such as the UK and the USA, tend to regard it as contrary to international law.

Although this principle was in evidence in State practice, it was not indicated as one of the accepted bases of jurisdiction in the Harvard Draft because of opposition from the common law countries. In the *Lotus Case*, for example, although the Court ultimately did not have to decide on jurisdiction under the passive personality principle because they had already accepted the principle of territoriality, all of the dissenting judges expressly rejected the application of this principle.

Despite this opposition, however, passive personality has been successfully relied upon as an alternative basis for jurisdiction in a number of cases. In *US v Yunis* (1989), for example, involving the prosecution in the USA of a Lebanese national for his alleged involvement in the hijacking of a Jordanian airliner in the Middle East, the US-based jurisdiction in part on passive personality. The only nexus between the aircraft and the USA was the presence of a number of US nationals on the flight. The court nevertheless accepted that passive personality did provide an appropriate basis for jurisdiction.

Similarly, although this issue did not come before the courts, the USA based its extradition request in the *Achille Lauro* incident on the fact that the victim murdered by the hijackers of the Italian pleasure cruiser off the Egyptian coast was a US national.

Universality principle

According to this principle a State may exercise jurisdiction in respect of all crimes, committed anywhere, solely on the basis of custody of the alleged offender. Usually the principle is limited to allow jurisdiction over acts of non-nationals in cases where the repression of such acts is justified as a matter of international public policy.

Subject to certain exceptions, States have generally rejected this principle. Indeed it is a principle open to misuse and injustice. However, there can be no objection when the acts are recognised as crimes in all countries. For example, for centuries there has been universal jurisdiction to try pirates and today a similar universal jurisdiction probably exists in cases of slave trading, trafficking in narcotics, counterfeiting and hijacking.

Universality has been successfully relied upon in a number of cases. In *Yunis*, for example, the US Government based its arguments on jurisdiction, in part, on universality. The Court accepted that aircraft piracy and hostage taking were the subject of international conventions which demonstrated the international community's commitment to punish this acts wherever they occured. Furthermore, the court accepted that 'international legal scholars unanimously agree that these crimes fit within the category of heinous crimes for the purposes of exerting universal jurisdiction'.

Jurisdiction under the universality principle will, therefore, be dependent on the nature of the crime rather than its place of occurrence or the nationality of the perpetrator or the victim.

Crimes under international law

These would include, for instance, crimes against humanity and breaches of the laws of war, especially breaches of the 1907 Hague Conventions and the Geneva Conventions of 1949. Persons responsible for such breaches may be punished by any State which obtains custody.

There is a distinction between crimes under international law and the principle of universality. In the former case what is being punished is the breach of international law, whereas the latter is concerned with the punishment under national law of certain acts which international law gives the right to all States to punish but does not itself declare to be criminal.

Notwithstanding the possibility that jurisdiction for the prosecution of war crimes in the UK could be founded on the basis that such offences constituted international crimes, British legislation does not rely on this principle as a basis for prosecution of war crimes against individuals present within the UK. The War Crimes Act 1991 instead relies on both the nationality principle and the territorial principle to supply the basis for jurisdiction.

Prosecutions for war crimes in the UK are restricted to offences taking place in Germany between 1939 and 1945, and even then only against individuals who were, or have subsequently become, British nationals or who are resident within the UK. International law allows States to prosecute nationals for crimes regardless of where the crime itself was committed and it is no defence to a charge to claim that at the time the offence was committed the accused was not a national if he subsequently acquires the nationality of the prosecuting State.

Jurisdiction conferred by treaty

As is illustrated in the *Yunis* case, jurisdiction in the case of some crimes may be derived from treaties. The most obvious examples of jurisdiction derived in this way is in the case of piracy, hijacking and hostage-taking. Article 19 of the 1958 Geneva Convention on the High Seas (corresponding to Article 105 of the 1982 Convention) provides, for example, that:

> '... on the high seas, or in any other place outside the jurisdiction of any state, every state may seize a pirate ship or aircraft, or a ship taken by piracy and under the control of pirates, and arrest the persons and seize the property on board. The Courts of the State which carried out the seizure may decide upon the penalties to be imposed, and may also determine the action to be taken with regard to the ships, aircraft or property, subject to the rights of third parties acting in good faith.'

The key elements of most of the treaties dealing specifically with crimes of an international nature – such as the Hague Convention on the Unlawful Seizure of Aircraft or the 1988 Rome Convention for the Suppression of Unlawful Acts against the Safety of Maritime Navigation (concluded in the aftermath of the *Achille Lauro* incident) – are as follows:

1. certain acts are categorised as offences under international law;
2. the treaty establishes an obligation on the States party to make the acts in question offences under their municipal legal systems;
3. the treaty goes on to require that the States concerned be in a position to establish jurisdiction over these offences. Invariably, territorality and nationality are indicated as mandatory sources of jurisdiction. Other principles are permitted as optional sources of jurisdiction;
4. the offences created are deemed to be extraditable offences;
5. the State is placed under a duty to either extradite or prosecute.

Notwithstanding this approach, it remains open to debate as to whether these treaties create a regime of universal jurisdiction in respect of the offences concerned. The better view is probably that jurisdiction is based on the terms of the treaty rather than on any generally accepted principle of customary international law.

The defects in establishing jurisdiction over persons accused of crimes specified in multilateral treaties such as these were recently highlighted in the *Case Concerning Questions of Interpretation and Application of the 1971 Montreal Convention Arising from the Aerial Incident of Lockerbie* (1992). Libya sought from the International Court an order for interim protection to prevent the Security Council from imposing sanctions in response to the refusal of the Libyan authorities to extradite two persons suspected of carrying out the destruction of Pan Am Flight 103.

The application was based on the contention made by Libya that the matter was governed by the Montreal Convention for the Suppression of Unlawful Acts against the Safety of Civil Aircraft and not an issue that constituted a threat to international peace and security justifying the Security Council's decision to adopt sanctions.

The Montreal Convention specifies that if a person suspected of a terrorist act is arrested in the territory of a contracting party, that State is required to prosecute the accused for the offences or, alternatively, it must extradite the accused to any contracting State that is seeking to exercise jurisdiction over the accused. Thus, the

State in which an accused person is found has the option of prosecuting itself or extraditing to a requesting State.

Since the accused were Libyan nationals, Libya opted to conduct the prosecution itself and refused to extradite the suspects to either the UK or the USA. Both the UK and the USA feared that the trial of the accused in Libya would be a sham, and the accused would escape proper trial. Hence, both states sponsored the Security Council Resolution imposing sanctions in an attempt to compel Libya to extradite as opposed to conducting the trial itself.

Libya's application was designed to secure provisional measures to protect its rights under the Montreal Convention.

In fact the Court rejected the application on the ground, *inter alia*, that Libya was required to carry out the decisions of the Security Council in accordance with Article 25 of the UN Charter. To permit Libya to rely on the Montreal Convention as a reason for evading the decisions of the Security Council would be inconsistent with the principle that the UN Charter prevails over the inconsistent terms of any other international agreements.

While in this particular case, Libya was not allowed to avoid its UN Charter obligations, the existence of alternative grounds for exercising jurisdiction clearly will cause problems when one of the States permitted to exercise jurisdiction has a connection with the accused such as nationality. Since the international community is increasingly employing multilateral treaties as a means of establishing jurisdiction over persons accused of perpetrating cross-border offences, this is regrettable.

Concurrent jurisdiction

The existence of these different grounds of jurisdiction inevitably means that several States may have concurrent jurisdiction. Where more than one State has jurisdiction it seems that priority to exercise enforcement jurisdiction depends solely upon custody. Even a State with territorial jurisdiction has no prior claim over another State having custody of a person and relying on some extra-territorial basis for jurisdiction. A conviction or acquittal in a foreign State is treated as a bar to a subsequent prosecution in some countries, but not in all.

8.3 Limitations of the traditional principles and 'new' bases of jurisdiction

As suggested above, the application of the traditional principles establishing jurisdiction has remained relatively uncontroversial in the case of 'normal' transactions. The principles have, however, been the subject of some debate in the context, largely, of business transactions which are deemed to have a national interest dimension. So, for example, if two foreign companies enter into an agreement abroad on the question of a co-ordinated pricing policy for goods marketed in the territory of State X, the question may arise as to whether this agreement infringes the municipal law in that State and, if so, whether State X is in a position to do anything about it.

First analysis may suggest that such situations fall neatly within the scope of the territorial principle. The act in question has been completed within the territory of the State seeking to exert its authority over the parties concerned. Such an interpretation, however, involves a fundamental and controversial extension of the basic relationship at the core of the territorial principle. The PCIJ in the *Lotus Case* accepted the principle of objective territoriality, ie jurisdiction based on the territoriality of the place of completion. However, as is evident from the fact of that case, it was intrinsic to objective territoriality that there existed a *direct and immediate* link between the initiation and completion of the act. A number of commentators have noted that remoteness will defeat a claim to jurisdiction based on objective territoriality.

remoteness

In the example noted above the question of remoteness between the initiating act and the act of completion is clearly in issue. The initiating act would be the anti-competitive agreement on pricing policy. This may well be *prima facie* unlawful. It is, however, not clear that there is a direct and immediate link between that act and any results flowing therefrom within the territory of the State in question.

The problems posed by the limited scope of the objective territorial principle led the US courts to develop what has become known as the 'effects doctrine' of jurisdiction. The question first arose for determination in the *Alcoa Case* (1945) where the question in issue was whether a Canadian company could be liable under US anti-trust legislation. The US court held that it did have jurisdiction as the acts in question were intended to have effect within the USA and did indeed have such an effect.

This doctrine has since undergone a measure of refinement in the case law of US courts. In *Timberlane* (1976) the issue was once again whether foreign companies, acting outside the USA, could be subject to US anti-trust jurisdiction. The Court of Appeals held that it was too simplistic to look only at the effect that the agreements in question would have on trade within the USA. This approach failed to take into account the interests of other States. The court indicated, therefore, that a *balancing of interests* approach should be applied to determine whether the US courts should assume jurisdiction. This *balancing of interests* approach was developed further in the *Mannington Mills Case* (1979) where the court indicated a number of factors that should be taken into consideration before jurisdiction could be assumed. This *weighing of competing interests* required the US court before which the case was heard to consider such matters as the nature of the alleged violation, the nationality of the parties involved, the interests of other States and the effect of an assumption of jurisdiction.

The 'competing interests' or 'reasonableness' approach is now clearly recognised in US jurisprudence as a legitimate basis of jurisdiction. There has been some debate as to whether this should be considered as a legitimate extension of objective territoriality or whether it should rather be considered as an independent basis of jurisdiction. Whatever its origins, it is now certainly the case that the 'effects doctrine' is widely in evidence in US State practice.

The permissive approach of the USA towards the effects doctrine has, however, encountered substantial opposition. The UK in particular has taken the view that jurisdiction based on effects is contrary to international law. A failure to reach agreement between the USA and its major trading partners led the UK to pass the Protection of Trading Interests Act 1980 in an attempt to ameliorate some of the harsher effects of USA legislative and enforcement jurisdiction over foreign companies. The substantive provisions of the Act prohibit, *inter alia*, the production of evidence on compulsion from the US courts and allows a UK company to recover that proportion of an award of damages by the US court that is non-compensatory, ie it provides for the recovery of punitive damages.

UK opposition to the effects doctrine as applied by the US courts has been mirrored by similar opposition to attempts by the European Commission to rely on effects for the purposes of EC Competition policy. While the European Commission has sought to rely on the effects doctrine, in cases such as *Beguelin* and *ICI* v *Commission (Dyestuffs Case)* (1972), the ECJ has been cautious about endorsing resort to these principles. The most recent decision by the ECJ in the *Woodpulp Case* (1988) suggests, however, that the Court is finding it increasingly difficult not to sanction some extraterritorial extension of jurisdiction. In *Woodpulp*, the question arose as to whether pricing and marketing agreements by non-EC woodpulp producers made outside the Community could be subject to the jurisdiction of the Commission for the purposes of competition policy regulation. The Commission argued in favour of jurisdiction based on effects. The Court, however, remained cautious about endorsing effects, preferring to distinguish two elements to the agreements in question, ie the place of agreement and the place of implementation. As the EC was the place of implementation of the agreements the ECJ accepted that the Commission could exercise jurisdiction.

A number of commentators have suggested that the approach by the ECJ steps back from endorsing the effects doctrine as an accepted principle of law. This view has not, however, been universally accepted as others, including the US Justice Department, have suggested that there is no distinction of substance between jurisdiction based on the place of implementation and jurisdiction based on the place of effect.

The debates about the place of the effects doctrine and theories of extraterritorial jurisdiction in international law are likely to continue for some time to come. The existence of the debate and the extent of the exercise of jurisdiction extraterritorially is perhaps illustrative of the difficulty that arises – particularly in the sphere of international business – in applying the traditional principles of jurisdiction to highly complex multinational transactions. A number of commentors have suggested that one way in which to reconcile these competing claims to jurisdiction would be through the development of the notion of economic sovereignty such that the courts of one State will refuse jurisdiction in cases involving the sovereign interests of another State. The difficulty in achieving such a solution is, however, exemplified by the recent US court decision in the *Transnor Case* (1990) in which the court assumed jurisdiction on the basis that the Brent Oil futures market (ie dealing with futures trading in North Sea oil) had even the 'slightest connection' with the USA. The economic consequences in the UK oil markets of the assumption of jurisdiction were substantial. It would seem as well that jurisdiction based on the 'slightest connection' goes some way towards extending the concept of effects yet further. It is evident, however, that at least in the eyes of the US court this issue fell within the sovereign interests of the USA as defined by the relevant piece of US legislation.

But, it is not only in commercial or business relationships that the traditional principles of jurisdiction have become strained. Crimes committed in one State, or planned in one State, may have effects in separate States. Hi-jacking, drug-trafficking, terrorism and international fraud are, unfortunately, part of modern life. Due to the ease of international travel and communication, crime can now be planned and perpetrated on an international basis and co-ordinated in such a manner that at least some of the perpetrators are far from the scene of the crime, while others can escape with relative ease. Often, those involved are of different nationalities and are involved at different levels in the commission of the offence.

The traditional grounds for establishing jurisdiction have struggled to accommodate this development and, more and more frequently, courts in which persons are accused of such offences are unwilling to relinquish jurisdiction to try accused persons simply because the traditional principles of jurisdiction are so rigorous.

The US courts especially have been willing to abandon the rigorous application of these principles in favour of asserting jurisdiction where possible over persons accused of committing offences against the national security of that country or against its nationals.

This propensity was most recently manifested in the Supreme Court in *United States* v *Alvarez-Machain* (1992). In 1985, a US Special Agent in the Drug Enforcement Administration was kidnapped in Mexico and afterwards tortured and murdered. The victim of the crime was American, but the crime took place in Mexico and was allegedly committed by Mexican nationals.

The accused was a medical doctor suspected of participating in the crime. Special agents from the Drug Enforcement Agency seized Alvarez-Machain, a Mexican citizen, in Mexico and flew him against his will to the USA by private aircraft. There he was arrested and charged with having participated in the torture and killing of the special agent.

At his arraignment, the accused argued that the US courts had no jurisdiction over him because his abduction had been carried out without the consent of the Mexican Government contrary to the terms of the US-Mexico extradition treaty. This argument was accepted by the court of first instance and the court of appeal. The matter eventually came before the US Supreme Court.

The US Supreme Court established the principle that the US courts had jurisdiction to try an accused charged with harming an American national as long as the manner in which the accused was brought before the court did not violate the terms of any treaty between the States involved. The court then analysed the extradition treaty to determine whether or not it prohibited abduction.

Ultimately, the court held that there was no express or implied term of the treaty prohibiting such an abduction. Therefore, the prosecution was allowed to continue even though the US courts did not have jurisdiction on the traditional grounds of jurisdiction.

In rendering this decision, the Supreme Court displayed contempt for the traditional grounds for establishing jurisdiction. The accused was a non-US national, the offence was committed in another State and was not an international crime, and the accused had not entered the USA other than against his own free will.

Even if the rationale of the court's decision is accepted, the abduction constituted an infringement of Mexican territorial sovereignty and was therefore a violation of customary law. The US authorities had in fact brought the accused to trial only by themselves engaging in an unlawful act.

This is undoubtedly a dangerous precedent for the US Supreme Court to have set but it is no doubt an expression of the frustration that is felt when the traditional grounds for jurisdiction allow perpetrators of transnational crimes to escape justice. However, if the traditional grounds of jurisdiction are no longer of any relevance, what rules should replace them?

8.4 The relationship of nationality and jurisdiction

Much of the theory of jurisdiction goes towards establishing a link between the State seeking to exercise jurisdiction and the persons in respect of whom that exercise of jurisdiction will lie. Territoriality and nationality are the two clearest examples of such a nexus.

The bond of nationality is, however, particularly important in that it provides a formal link between the State and its citizens, and also between the State and other legal persons such as corporations and other entities over which, without that link of nationality, the task of exercising control would be inordinately complex. Chief amongst the 'other entities' are ships and aircraft which carry the nationality of the State within which they are registered and whose flag they fly. In respect of ships, for example, Article 91 of the 1982 Law of the Sea Convention provides that:

'Every state shall fix the conditions for the grant of its nationality to ships ... Ships have the nationality of the State whose flag they are entitled to fly.'

Article 92 goes on to provide that:

'Ships shall sail under the flag of one state only and, save in exceptional cases ... shall be subject to its exclusive jurisdiction on the high seas.'

9

Nationality and Personal Jurisdiction

9.1 Nationality

9.2 Acquisition of nationality

9.3 Loss of nationality

9.4 The nationality of ships, aircraft and corporations

9.5 Extradition and asylum

9.1 Nationality

Nationality has been defined as the status of belonging to a State for certain purposes of international law. A State may bestow its nationality with complete freedom on whomsoever it chooses, but for the grant of nationality to be recognised by other States it must conform with certain general principles of international law.

In the *Nottebohm Case*: *Liechtenstein* v *Guatemala* (1955) the court said:

> 'It is for Liechtenstein, as it is for every Sovereign State to settle by its own legislation the rules relating to the acquisition of its nationality, and to confer that nationality by naturalisation granted by its own organs in accordance with that legislation ...
>
> The reason for this is that the diversity of demographic conditions has thus far made it impossible for any general agreement to be reached on the rules relating to nationality, although the latter by its very nature affects international relations. It has been considered that the best way of making such rules accord with the varying demographic conditions in different countries is to leave the fixing of such rules to the competence of each State. On the other hand, a State cannot claim that the rules it has thus laid down are entitled to recognition by another State unless it has acted in conformity with this general aim of making the legal bond of nationality accord with the individual's genuine connection with the State which assumes the defence of its citizens by means of protection as against other States.'

9.2 Acquisition of nationality

Nationality acquired by birth

The laws of every State provide for the acquisition of its nationality by birth. Two principles apply: *jus sanguinis* – acquisition of nationality by descent, by being born of parents who are nationals – and *jus soli* – acquisition of nationality by being born in the territory of the State itself.

Jus sanguinis – descent

In practice the nationality laws of most States adopt the nationality of the father in conferring nationality in respect of a legitimate child. In some cases a child may be entitled to the nationality of a particular State even though no member of his family has resided in that State for generations.

For example, the Nationality Law of Belgium confers Belgian nationality on 'the legitimate child, born, even in a foreign country, of a father having the status of a Belgian on the day of the birth'.

Some States do not distinguish between legitimate or illegitimate children, or the sex of a parent. For example, the French Nationality Code provides that 'a child, whether legitimate or natural, is French if at least one of his parents is French'.

The British Nationality Act 1981 provides for the transmission of citizenship by descent for one generation only, subject to exceptions in respect of those working abroad on government service. Citizenship may be transmitted through either parent in respect of a legitimate child, but an illegitimate child takes his mother's citizenship.

Jus soli – born on territory

Jus soli provides the basic principle of many nationality laws. For example, it is provided under the Paraguay Constitution of 1940 that a person is a Paraguayan national if he was born in Paraguayan territory. However, for a person born abroad of Paraguayan parents to be a national, one of the parents must have been in the service of the Republic of Paraguay at the time of the birth.

In some States the *jus soli* principle may supplement the *jus sanguinis* principle. For example, under the French Nationality Code a child born in France will acquire French nationality if his parents are unknown or if his parents are foreign and he does not acquire their nationality.

The British Nationality Act 1981 abolishes the *jus soli* principle so far as British nationality law is concerned. The government was afraid that the principle could be abused by people coming to the UK to give birth here for the express purpose of having their child acquire UK citizenship. It was also felt to be undesirable that children born to parents temporarily resident in the UK should be able to obtain an indefinite right to re-enter.

A British birth certificate is, therefore, no longer evidence of British citizenship.

Births on ships and aircraft registered under the flag

The British Nationality Act 1981 provides that for the purposes of the Act a person born outside the UK aboard a ship or aircraft shall be deemed to have been born in the UK if:

1. at the time of the birth his father or mother was a British citizen; or
2. he would, but for this subsection, have been born Stateless, and (in either case) at the time of the birth the ship or aircraft was registered in the UK or was an unregistered ship or aircraft of the government of the UK.

Nationality subsequently acquired

Marriage

Two rules were commonly applied under the nationality legislation of many States:

1. a foreign woman marrying a national automatically acquired his nationality;
2. a woman who was a national lost her nationality on marrying a foreigner.

These rules were out of step with contemporary thinking regarding the equality of the sexes and this change in attitude has resulted in a re-evaluation of the position of married women under nationality legislation.

The General Assembly Convention on the Nationality of Married Women 1957 provides that each contracting State agrees that the celebration of marriage between one of its nationals and an alien, the dissolution of a marriage between one of its nationals and an alien, or the change of nationality by the husband during marriage, will not automatically affect a wife's nationality.

Naturalisation

Naturalisation is the voluntary admission to citizenship of a foreign national. However, certain requirements must usually be satisfied before naturalisation may be granted. For instance most States require a minimum period of residence, a knowledge of the language and good character of the applicant.

For example, under the British Nationality Act 1981 an applicant for naturalisation must have, *inter alia*:

1. been in the UK for five years without any absence in excess of 450 days;
2. must not have been absent for more than 90 days during the 12 months preceding the application;
3. must not during the 12 months preceding the application have been under any restriction under the immigration laws, on the period for which he might remain in the UK;
4. must not during the five years preceding the application have been in breach of the UK immigration laws;
5. the applicant must be of good character;
6. the applicant must have a sufficient knowledge of the English, Welsh, or Scottish Gaelic language;
7. the applicant must intend to make his main or principal home in the UK, or enter into or continue in Crown service or employment in a company or association established in the UK.

Other means of acquiring nationality

Adoption
Most State legislation recognises that an adopted minor acquires the nationality of the adoptive parent.

For example, the British Nationality Act 1981 Section 1(5) provides:

> 'Where after commencement an order authorising the adoption of a minor who is not a British citizen is made by any Court in the United Kingdom, he shall be a British citizen as from the date on which the order is made if the adopter or, in the case of a joint adoption, one of the adopters is a British Citizen on that date.'

Legitimation
The nationality law of most States provide that legitimated children acquire the nationality of the father.

The British Nationality Act 1981, s47(1) provides:

> 'A person born out of wedlock and legitimated by the subsequent marriage of his parents shall, as from the date of the marriage, be treated for the purpose of this Act as if he had been born legitimate.'

9.3 Loss of nationality

Renunciation of citizenship

The nationality legislation of many States provides for the voluntary renunciation of that State's nationality by its citizens.

The British Nationality Act 1981, s12 provides:

> '1) If any British citizen of full age and capacity makes in the prescribed manner a declaration of renunciation of British citizenship, then subject to subsections (3) and (4), the Secretary of State shall cause the declaration to be registered.
>
> 2) On the registration of a declaration made in pursuance of this section the person who made it shall cease to be a British citizen.
>
> 3) A declaration made by a person in pursuance of this section shall not be registered unless the Secretary of State is satisfied that the person who made it will after the registration have or acquire some citizenship or nationality other than British citizenship; and if that person does not have any such citizenship or nationality on the date of registration and does not acquire some such citizenship or nationality within six months from that date, he shall be, and be deemed to have remained, a British citizen notwithstanding the registration.
>
> 4) The Secretary of State may withhold registration of any declaration made in pursuance of this section if it is made during any war in which Her Majesty may be engaged in right of Her Majesty's Government in the United Kingdom.
>
> 5) For the purposes of this section any person who has been married shall be deemed to be of full age.'

Acquisition of a new nationality

A person acquiring a foreign nationality or taking an oath of allegiance to another State may automatically lose his nationality. However, some States simply give a citizen who acquires a foreign nationality the option of renouncing his old nationality.

Under British nationality legislation the acquisition of another citizenship will not, of itself, affect a person's British citizenship. But some States do not recognise dual nationality and, therefore, a British citizen wishing to become a citizen of such a State will have to renounce his British citizenship.

Deprivation of citizenship

For example, the British Nationality Act 1981, s40 provides:

'1) Subject to the provisions of this section, the Secretary of State may by order deprive any British citizen to whom this subsection applies of his British citizenship if the Secretary of State is satisfied that the registration or certificate of naturalisation by virtue of which he is such a citizen was obtained by means of fraud, false representation or the concealment of any material fact. ....

3) Subject to the provisions of this section, the Secretary of State may by order deprive any British citizen to whom this subsection applies of his British citizenship if the Secretary of State is satisfied that that citizen: (a) has shown himself by act or speech to be disloyal or disaffected towards Her Majesty; or (b) has, during any war in which Her Majesty was engaged, unlawfully traded or communicated with an enemy or been engaged in or associated with any business that was to his knowledge carried on in such a manner as to assist an enemy in that war; or (c) has, within the period of five years from the relevant date, been sentenced in any country to imprisonment for a term of not less than twelve months. ...'

The deprivation of citizenship may result in a person becoming Stateless. Thus a large number of Jews in Central Europe became Stateless during the Nazi era and more recently many people in Communist Eastern Europe have been deprived of their citizenship.

9.4 The nationality of ships, aircraft and corporations

Ships

International law recognises that ships have nationality. Article 91 of the 1982 Law of the Sea Convention, corresponding to Article 5 of the Geneva Convention on the High Seas 1958, provides:

'1. Each State shall fix the conditions for the grant of its nationality to ships, for the registration of ships in its territory, and for the right to fly its flag. Ships have the nationality of the State whose flag they are entitled to fly. There must exist a genuine link between the State and the ship.

2. Each State shall issue to ships to which it has granted the right to fly its flag documents to that effect.'

The requirement of a genuine link is a direct application of the *Nottebohm* principle. It was introduced partly in an attempt to limit the use of flags of convenience. For instance, the majority of ships registered in Panama, Liberia and Honduras are owned by foreigners who register their ships in these States for fiscal and economic reasons.

Article 92 of the 1982 Convention, corresponding to Article 6 of the High Seas Convention 1958, provides:

'1. Ships shall sail under the flag of one State only and, save in exceptional cases expressly provided for in international treaties or in this Convention, shall be subject to its exclusive jurisdiction on the high seas. A ship may not change its flag during a voyage or while in a port of call, save in the case of a real transfer of ownership or change in registry.

2. A ship which sails under the flags of two or more States, using them according to convenience, may not claim any of the nationalities in question with respect to any other State, and may be assimilated to a ship without nationality.'

Problems of dual nationality in respect of ships, therefore, do not arise.

Aircraft

The Chicago Convention on International Civil Aviation 1944 provides:

Article 17: aircraft have the nationality of the State in which they are registered.

Article 18: an aircraft cannot be validly registered in more than one State, but its registration may be changed from one State to another.

The question of jurisdiction over aircraft is dealt with under the Tokyo Convention on Offences and Certain Other Acts Committed on Board Aircraft 1963.

Article 3 of the Convention provides:

'1. The State of registration of the aircraft is competent to exercise jurisdiction over offences and acts committed on board.

2. Each contracting State shall take such measures as may be necessary to establish its jurisdiction as the State of registration over offences committed on board aircraft registered in such State.

3. This Convention does not exclude any criminal jurisdiction exercised in accordance with national law.'

Article 4 provides:

'A Contracting State which is not the State of registration may not interfere with an aircraft in flight in order to exercise its criminal jurisdiction over a offence committed on board except in the following cases: (a) the offence has effect on the territory of such State; (b) the offence has been committed by or against a national or permanent resident of such State; (c) the offence is against the security of such State; (d) the offence consists of a breach of any rules or regulations relating to the flight or manoeuvre of aircraft in force in such State; (e) the exercise of jurisdiction is necessary to ensure the observance of any obligation of such State under a multilateral international agreement.'

The UK Government ratified the Convention by the Tokyo Convention Act 1967.

Corporations

The general rule is that a corporation has the nationality of the State under the laws of which it is incorporated and in whose territory it has its registered office.

In *Barcelona Traction, Light and Power Co Case: Belgium* v *Spain* (1970) the ICJ observed in its judgment:

> 'In allocating corporate entities to States for purposes of diplomatic protection, international law is based, but only to a limited extent, on an analogy with the rules governing the nationality of individuals. The traditional rule attributes the right of diplomatic protection to a corporate entity to the State under the laws of which it is incorporated and in whose territory it has its registered office. These two criteria have been confirmed by long practice and by numerous international instruments.'

9.5 Extradition and asylum

Extradition

A criminal may seek refuge in a State which has no jurisdictional competence to try him, or is unwilling to try him, in respect of offences committed by him within the territory of another State.

International law, therefore, allows the State in which a suspected or convicted criminal has sought refuge to extradite him by surrendering him to the State exercising jurisdictional competence to try him.

In the absence of a treaty of extradition between the States concerned there is no duty under customary international law to extradite. Treaties of extradition may be multilateral or bilateral and usually confer reciprocal rights and duties upon the States parties. The following matters are usually included:

1. the principle of double criminality. The crime in respect of which extradition is sought must usually be a crime under the laws of both the States concerned. Such crimes will usually be restricted to the most serious offences under their respective criminal laws;
2. the crime in respect of which extradition is sought must usually have been committed within the territory of the State seeking extradition;
3. a State will usually be under no obligation to extradite its own nationals;
4. a State is usually under no obligation to extradite in respect of offences of a political character;
5. the principle of speciality. A fugitive who is surrendered may only be tried in respect of the particular crime for which he was extradited.

In the UK, the Extradition Act 1989 contains the relevant principles and procedures for extradition to and from the UK. This statute governs the procedure for extraditing a person accused of the commission of an extradition crime in the requesting State, or who is allegedly at large after conviction of an extradition crime by a court in such a State. An extradition crime is defined as conduct which, if it occurred in the UK, would constitute an offence punishable by a term of imprisonment of 12 months or longer and which is also punishable in the law of the foreign State.

A number of exceptions are made to this general rule. A person cannot be extradited under the 1989 Act, if it can be shown that:

1. the offence of which a person is accused, or was convicted, is an offence of a political character;
2. the offence is a crime under military law and not an offence under the general criminal law;
3. the request for extradition was made for the purpose of prosecuting or punishing an individual on account of race, religion, nationality or political views; and
4. upon return to the requesting State, the accused would be denied a fair trial by reason of race, religion, nationality or political opinions.

Nor can a person who is alleged to be unlawfully at large after conviction by a foreign State be extradited if the conviction was obtained in their absence, or if it would not be in the interests of justice to return the individual on the ground of the conviction.

The procedures of the Extradition Act 1989 apply not only when the UK has entered into a bilateral extradition agreement with another State, but also when the UK is a party to a multilateral agreement which creates offences of an international character. Offences which are established by international convention, and therefore constitute extradition crimes under the statute, include:

1. hijacking, under the Tokyo Convention 1963, the Hague Convention 1970 and the Montreal Convention 1971;
2. offences against diplomats and protected persons, under the Internationally Protected Persons Convention 1973;
3. hostage-taking, under the Hostages Convention 1979;
4. the unlawful transfer of nuclear materials, under the Nuclear Material Convention 1980; and
5. torture, under the Torture Convention 1984.

Special provisions have been drafted into the statute to deal with the problem of terrorism. In particular, under this legislation, no offence similar to that created by s1 of the Suppression of Terrorism Act 1978 applies shall be deemed a political offence.

The courts have recently had cause to interpret the Extradition Act 1989 in *R v Governor of Brixton, ex parte Osman (No 3)* [1992] 1 WLR 36. The applicant in this case was arrested on charges of conspiracy to defraud and conspiracy to steal and an application was made by the Governor of Hong Kong for his extradition to stand trial for these charges in the territory. The Governor of Hong Kong gave undertakings in terms of the 1989 Act that, if extradited, the applicant would not be tried for offences other than those for which the extradition application had been made.

In his defence, the applicant claimed that the Governor was not in a position to provide such undertakings because the British lease to the territory expired after 1997. After this period the Chinese authorities would resume sovereignty over the colony and, if convicted, the applicant would, from that time on, be subject to detention at the instance of the Chinese authorities. The question was, therefore, whether the Governor of Hong Kong could make the necessary undertakings required by the statute.

In rejecting the appeal, the Divisional Court held that in the construction of the statute it was merely necessary that a State existed at the time the request was made. It was unnecessary for the court to consider the future sovereignty and destiny of the colony. Therefore, the undertaking of the Governor amounted to an arrangement in terms of s6(4) of the 1989 Act and extradition was granted.

Asylum

In the exercise of its territorial sovereignty a State may permit an alien to take refuge within its territory, subject to any treaty obligations the State may be under to extradite the individual concerned. Asylum is most frequently granted in respect of political offenders – where there is usually no duty to extradite.

Article 14 of the Universal Declaration of Human Rights 1948 provides:

'1) Everyone has the right to seek and enjoy in other countries asylum from persecution.

2) This right may not be invoked in the case of prosecutions genuinely arising from non-political crimes or from acts contrary to the purposes and principles of the United Nations.'

Diplomatic asylum and asylum on warships

It is doubtful that any general legally recognised right to seek asylum on diplomatic premises exists. However, there may be a regional custom in Latin American States permitting such asylum to be granted in certain circumstances in accordance with local conventions and the principles enunciated in the *Asylum Case*: *Colombia* v *Peru* (1950).

It is also doubtful that any right exists to seek asylum on board foreign warships or other public vessels. However, the practice of some States permits such refuge to be granted during 'political disturbances or popular tumults to persons fleeing from imminent personal danger'.

10

Immunity from Jurisdiction

10.1 Introduction

10.2 State immunity

10.3 English judicial practice regarding State immunity

10.4 The State Immunity Act 1978

10.5 Waiver of immunity

10.6 Diplomatic immunity

10.1 Introduction

There are certain categories of persons and bodies to whom international law accords immunity from the jurisdiction of municipal courts. The two principal categories are: foreign States (State immunity) and diplomatic agents (diplomatic immunity).

The principle underlying the doctrine of immunity from jurisdiction developed as a natural extension of the immunity of the individual sovereign. The principle was authoritatively expressed by Marshall CJ in the US Supreme Court in the case of *The Schooner Exchange* v *McFadden* (1812):

'This full and absolute territorial jurisdiction being alike the attribute of every Sovereign, and being incapable of conferring extra-territorial power, would not seem to contemplate foreign Sovereigns nor their sovereign rights as its objects. One Sovereign being in no respect amenable to another, and being bound by obligations of the highest character not to degrade the dignity of his nation, by placing himself or its sovereign rights within the jurisdiction of another, can be supposed to enter a foreign territory only under an express licence, or in the confidence that the immunities belonging to his independent Sovereign station, though not expressly stipulated, are reserved by implication and will be extended to him.

   This perfect equality and absolute independence of Sovereigns, and this common interest compelling them to mutual intercourse, and an interchange of good offices with each other, have given rise to a class of cases in which every Sovereign is understood to waive the exercise of a part of that complete exclusive territorial jurisdiction which has been stated to be the attribute of every nation.'

10.2 State immunity

The basic principle behind the doctrine of State immunity is that since States are independent and equal they should not be subjected to the jurisdiction of other States without their consent.

In *De Haber* v *Queen of Portugal* (1851) the plaintiff had issued writs against the defendant and a number of agents of the Portuguese Government, claiming that the Portuguese Government had wrongfully received money which was in fact due to him. The defendant succeeded in having all further proceedings stayed.

Lord Campbell LJ stated the law as follows: 'to cite a foreign potentate in a municipal court ... is contrary to the law of nations and an insult which he is entitled to resent'.

Basis of State immunity – immunity and non-justiciability

State immunity may be said to rest upon two principles:

The principle of *par in parem non habet jurisdiction em*:
legal persons of equal standing cannot have their disputes
settled in the courts of one of them

This is founded upon the principle of sovereign equality and independence of States and rests upon the historical proposition that as a sovereign could not himself be sued before his own municipal courts, so the sovereign of another State was similarly exempt from the jurisdiction of the local law.

This principle is based upon the immunity of the sovereign. It is possible, therefore, for a sovereign in the exercise of his equality to waive this immunity in which case the municipal courts of the other State may exercise jurisdiction.

The principle of non-intervention in the internal affairs of other States

The exercise of this principle produces an area of issues which are essentially non-justiciable and, therefore, the municipal court has no competence to assert jurisdiction.

In *Buck* v *Attorney-General* (1965) the Court of Appeal refused to make declarations on the validity or otherwise of the constitution of Sierra Leone as created by Order in Council at Independence. The court held that it had no jurisdiction to make a declaration of the kind claimed.

Diplock LJ said:

'... the application of the doctrine of sovereign immunity does not depend upon the persons between whom the issue is joined, but upon the subject matter of the issue. For the English Court to pronounce upon the validity of a law of a foreign Sovereign State within its own territory, so that the validity of that law becomes the *res* of the *res judicata* in the suit, would be to assert jurisdiction over the internal affairs of that State. That would be a breach of the rules of comity. In my view, this Court has no jurisdiction so to do.'

The theory of State immunity – absolute restrictive immunity

So long as State activity was restricted to governmental matters the principle of State immunity and the application of absolute immunity in relation to such matters was universally accepted. However, the dramatic expansion of State activity and the increasing involvment of States in commercial activities and enterprises have meant that many economies have a State controlled public sector. The problem is, therefore, whether States should enjoy the same absolute immunity in respect of their commercial activities as they do in respect of their governmental activities.

Faced with this growing involvement of the State in commercial activities, courts began to distinguish between acts *jure imperii* – acts of a sovereign nature – and acts *jure gestionis* – acts of a commercial nature. While absolute immunity would still be granted in respect of acts *jure imperii*, acts of a commercial nature would not attract immunity. This approach has become known as the doctrine of restrictive immunity.

Various arguments have been put forward against granting full immunity in the case of State acts *jure gestionis*.

1. If a sovereign engages in commerce then he should be assumed to have waived his immunity.
2. The tendency of municipal law is to place the State and State corporations on an equal footing with other legal persons, eg the Crown Proceedings Act 1947.
3. The fact that in practice many States waive their immunity in such cases anyway, by treaty or otherwise.

Distinction between acts **jure imperii** *and* **jure gestionis**

The major problem is one of identifying a distinction between the governmental and commercial activities of a State, that is sufficient to justify denying the latter full immunity. Attempts have been made to make the necessary distinction on the basis of the following criteria:

The nature of the act
This is the traditional test. If the act undertaken by the State is one which can be performed by an individual, then it is *jure gestionis.* However, the strict application of such a test may give rise to odd results. For example, an individual can enter into a contract. Therefore, if a State enters into a contract to purchase, for example, clothing for its army or goods and supplies necessary for the maintenance of the national economy, does it lose its immunity from jurisdiction because they are contracts and an individual can make a contract?

The purpose of the act
This suffers from the practical difficulty that it simply restates the problem and involves the exercise of a value judgment as to the role of the State.

General State practice with regard to immunity
The distinction may be deduced by the exercise of or by drawing analogy with existing State practice.

Is such a distinction justified?

It has been argued that there is no justification for such a distinction if account is taken of the modern role of the State. Under current international conditions the commercial activities of the State are just as important as the more traditional State activities. The maintenance of a strong economic and industrial base may be just as important to the survival of a State as its military capability.

10.3 English judicial practice regarding State immunity

Whereas absolute immunity always attached itself to a sovereign in relation to his public acts, it remained for most of the nineteenth century unsettled whether this immunity attached to him in an absolute sense. In *The Charkich* (1873) Sir Robert Phillimore held that a vessel owned by the Khedive of Egypt forfeited its immunity because it was chartered to a private individual and engaged in commercial activity. This approach, founded on a division between *jure imperii* and *jure gestionis* did not survive the century.

In *The Parlement Belge* (1879) the defendant ship was owned by the King of the Belgians. It was a mail boat engaged in channel crossings. Phillimore remained consistent to his reasoning in *The Charkich*: the mail boat was not to be accorded immunity because it was involved in a commercial enterprise. His decision was reversed by the Court of Appeal, but the rule subsequently adopted may have been far wider than was necessary. The Court of Appeal had the option of deciding that the vessel was primarily operating for the public benefit, the carrying of cargo and passengers being secondary to the carrying of mail. However, the principle applied by the Court of Appeal was that of absolute immunity resting on the theory of the independence of States.

This principle was re-affirmed in *The Porto Alexandre* (1920). This ship had gone aground in the Mersey and had been refloated with the assistance of three tugs. The tug owners could not obtain payment and so issued a writ in rem against the ship itself. The facts were that the ship had been requisitioned by the Portuguese Government, but was being employed entirely for carrying cargoes for private individuals. In upholding a claim to immunity, the Court of Appeal had no doubt that this case was covered by the previous Court of Appeal decision in *The Parlement Belge*. The judges in the Court of Appeal were aware of the blatant injustice of the decision, but demurred that they had no alternative in the light of the strong dicta in *The Parlement Belge*.

Stronger dicta, particularly in the judgment of Lord MacMillan, is evident in the case of *The Christina* (1938). But these cases are of interest in that they illustrate the stranglehold the doctrine of precedent had over thinking. The virtue of flexibility is that it can take account of changes in public policy; and in this area the change in public policy was the increase of State activity in commerce. The doctrine of absolute immunity was justifiable when it applied to a sovereign in person, but when great corporations receive immunity on account of the fact that they are State controlled the whole doctrine must be called into question.

Foreign governmental agencies like the United States Shipping Board and the Tass News Agency were accorded immunity, but in 1957 in *Baccus SRL* v *Servicio Nacional del Trigo* the Court of Appeal went further. The defendant was a department of the Spanish Ministry of Agriculture, but, according to expert advice was an independent legal personality. Nevertheless, the majority of the Court of Appeal upheld the plea of immunity, even though it was in Spanish law a separate company and the subject matter of the dispute was a commercial transaction.

The stranglehold of precedent was, however, broken in 1975 with *The Philippine Admiral.* The ship in question was owned by the Philippine Reparation Commission, an agency of the Philippines Government, but it was being operated at the time current to the dispute by the Liberation Steamship Company under a conditional sale agreement with the Commission. The company had employed the ship for normal commercial purposes. The Privy Council refused to uphold the plea for immunity. It did not follow from *The Parlement Belge* that any vessel owned by the sovereign or government was automatically immune from jurisdiction, and that the Court of Appeal was drawing such a conclusion.

This was followed in *Trendtex Trading Corp* v *Central Bank of Nigeria* (1977). The Central Bank of Nigeria claimed sovereign immunity. Lord Denning MR concluded that international law now recognised the doctrine of restrictive immunity and that a distinction must be drawn between acts *jure imperii* and acts *jure gestionis*. The only satisfactory test was to look to the functions and control of the organisation. It was necessary to look at all the evidence to see whether the organisation was under government control and exercised governmental functions.

At common law, therefore, the British courts abandoned the doctrine of absolute immunity in respect of both actions *in rem* and actions *in personam*, thereby anticipating the enactment of the State Immunity Act 1978.

10.4 The State Immunity Act 1978

The position of English law on the question of State immunity is now regulated by the State Immunity Act 1978. This Act, broadly implementing the provisions of the 1972 European Convention on State Immunity, embodies the restrictive theory of immunity accepted by the Court of Appeal the previous year in *Trendtex*. The approach of the Act is, however, to affirm the *general principle* of *absolute immunity* in s1(1) and then go on to indicate a number of exceptions to this rule. In this approach the UK legislation accords with the Foreign Sovereign Immunities Act 1976 adopted by the USA.

Section 2 of the SIA 1978 lays down the general provisions regarding waiver of immunity. 'A State is not immune as respects proceedings in respect of which it has submitted to the jurisdiction of the courts of the United Kingdom.' Further, 'a State may submit after the dispute giving rise to the proceedings has arisen or by a prior written agreement'. Section 2(3) provides that a State will be deemed to have waived immunity in cases where it has instituted proceedings. Under s13, however, a State must give a *separate* waiver of immunity before execution and enforcement of a judgment can take place against any State property not in use for commercial purposes.

The substantive provisions of the Act following Article 2 go on to establish exceptions from the basic rule of absolute immunity set out under s1(1). Perhaps the most important of these provisions is s3 which provides that a State will not be immune in respect of proceedings relating to commercial transactions or obligations which under contract stand to be performed in whole or in part in the UK. 'Commercial transactions' is defined in s3(3) as meaning:

'(a) any contract for the supply of goods or services;
(b) any loan or other transaction for the provisions of finance and any guarantee or indemnity in respect of any such transaction or of any other financial obligation; and
(c) any other transaction or activity ... into which a State enters or in which it engages otherwise than in the exercise of sovereign authority.'

A transaction that falls within any one of these definitions will be a commercial transaction for the purposes of the Act with the exception that a contract of employment is not to be regarded as a commercial transaction within the meaning of the section. There are specifically covered by s4 which provides, *inter alia*, that a State will not be able to claim immunity in respect of a contract of employment made in the UK or in respect of work to be performed in whole or in part in the UK.

Other substantive provisions of the Act establish exceptions to absolute immunity in the case of:

1. proceedings for personal injury, death or loss or damage to tangible property in the UK (s5);
2. proceedings relating to any interest in or possession or use of immovable property in the UK (s6);
3. proceedings relating to patents or trademarks registered or protected in the UK (s7);
4. proceedings relating to a State's membership of a body corporate, unincorporated association or partnership which has members other than States and in which is incorporated or constituted under UK law or controlled from or has its principal place of business in the UK (s8);
5. proceedings in the UK courts with respect to arbitration to which the State has agreed to submit (s9);
6. actions in *rem* against a ship belonging to that State or actions in *personam* for enforcing a claim in connection with such a ship (s10); and
7. proceedings in respect of liability for VAT, customs and excise duties, agricultural levies or rates in respect of premises occupied for commercial

purposes (s11). Immunity from indirect taxes does not however extend to liability for income tax payable by foreign governments on earnings from investments in the UK: see *R* v *IRC, ex parte Camacq Corp* (1990).

The leading case dealing with the application of the 1978 Act to commercial transactions is *A Company Limited* v *Republic of X* [1990] 2 Lloyd's Rep 250. This case involved an attempt to obtain an injunction to prevent the disposal of assets held by the government of State X in the UK in both bank accounts and property in order to enforce any decree obtained from an action for payment for the price of a consignment of rice ordered by the government of State X.

The defendants argued that such an action was incompetent because of the immunity conferred by s1(1) of the 1978 Act, despite the exception in s2(1) of the statute which allows jurisdiction when the government of the foreign State has submitted to adjudication or arbitration in England. The contract of sale provided for the exercise of such jurisdiction and the plaintiffs claimed that this was sufficient to found jurisdiction in the English courts.

The court agreed with the submissions of the plaintiffs and held that the intention and purpose of the clause in the contract was to place State X in the same position as a private individual for the purposes of legal proceedings. However, the action was dismissed because, even if the plaintiffs were successful, no decree could be enforced against the assets of the State X in the UK without the consent of the government of that State.

Remedies

Section 13 establishes the general rule that relief may not be given against a State by way of injunction, specific performance or order for the recovery of land or other property and that the property of a State shall not be subject to enforcement save where the State concerned has consented to such measures being taken. This principle of absolute immunity in respect of enforcement is, however, subject to an important limitation in the case of 'property which is for the time being in use or intended for use for commercial purposes' (s13(4)). Section 13(5) then goes on to provide that the head of the State's diplomatic missions shall be deemed to have the authority to certify whether or not the property in question is in use or intended for use for commercial purposes. Such a certificate shall constitute sufficient evidence of the fact unless the contrary is proved.

The issue of execution and enforcement was considered in *Alcom* v *Republic of Colombia* (1984) where the question arose as to whether the plaintiffs could enforce an order for execution against monies in a bank account in the name of the Colombian mission in the UK. The House of Lords, refusing enforcement, accepted a certificate from the head of the mission under s13(5) that the funds were not used for the day-to-day running of the mission and were thus not property used for commercial purposes under the meaning of the section.

Entities entitled to claim immunity

Given the uncertainty that can arise in deciding whether an entity is to be considered part of the State for the purposes of a claim of immunity, entities entitled to claim immunity under the Act are specified in s14. Section 14(1) provides that the immunities and privileges of the Act will apply to any foreign State. For these purposes a State will include the head of State acting in his public capacity, the government of that State and any department of that government. By s21, a certificate from the Secretary of State shall be conclusive on the question of whether an entity is a State for the purposes of the Act.

In addition to States, entities distinct from the executive organs of the government (known as 'separate entities') will be entitled to claim immunity if the proceedings relate to something done by it in the exercise of its sovereign authority *and* the circumstances are such that a State would have been immune. Constituent territories or federal entities are to be regarded as separate entities unless an Order in Council provides differently. Whether or not an entity is a 'separate entity' or a department of government will probably fall to be determined in accordance with the municipal law of the State concerned.

As well as these two entities, s14 also provides that the property of a State's central bank or other monetary authority are not to be regarded as intended for use for commercial purposes in respect of execution and enforcement proceedings.

10.5 Waiver of immunity

As noted above, waiver of immunity is covered by ss2 and 13 of the SIA 1978. The position regarding the waiver may be usefully summarised as follows:

1. a State may waive its immunity from jurisdiction either expressly or by conduct. Such waiver may occur by treaty, diplomatic communication or by actual submission to the jurisdiction in respect of those proceedings and all matters incidental to them;
2. if a foreign sovereign comes to the court as plaintiff or appears without protest as defendant in an action he has submitted to the jurisdiction in respect of these proceedings and all matters incidental to them;
3. even if the sovereign waives his immunity and a decision is given against him, it is not possible for the successful plaintiff to execute the judgment against the sovereign. A separate act of waiver of immunity from execution will be necessary before execution can be levied;
4. whether the foreign sovereign appears as plaintiff or defendant, he submits not only to the jurisdiction of the court of first instance, but also to all necessary stages of appeal;
5. the submission must be a genuine act of submission in the face of the court. Thus a prior agreement by a foreign sovereign to submit to the jurisdiction of the municipal courts will not constitute a waiver of immunity.

10.6 Diplomatic immunity

'Diplomacy comprises any means by which States establish or maintain mutual relations, communicate with each other, or carry out political or legal transactions, in each case through their authorised agents.'

Throughout history diplomats and other envoys have needed privileges and immunities for the effective performance of their functions. The preamble to the Vienna Convention on Diplomatic Relations of 1961 recites that: 'the purpose of such privileges and immunities is not to benefit individuals but to ensure the efficient performance of the functions of diplomatic missions as representing States'.

The international law on diplomatic and consular immunity is to be found principally in two conventions, the Vienna Convention on Diplomatic Relations of 1961 and the Vienna Convention on Consular Relations of 1963. As regards the Convention on Diplomatic Relations, this came into force on 24 April 1964 and was incorporated into English law by the Diplomatic Privileges Act of 1964. The Convention does not itself provide that it was intended to be declaratory of customary international law and it is probably best to regard its provisions as a mixture of codification and development of the law. However, given that upwards of 150 States are party to the Convention, most members of the international community will be bound by the provisions by virtue of their treaty obligation if not by virtue of any obligation under customary law.

The essence of the Convention is to provide for the inviolability of the diplomatic mission from the executive jurisdiction of the receiving State and for the immunity from the executive and enforcement jurisdiction of the State for diplomatic agents. It is up to the sending State to decide whether or not immunity should be waived.

Article 2 of the Vienna Convention on Diplomatic Relations 1961 provides that 'the establishment of diplomatic relations between States, and of permanent diplomatic missions takes place by mutual consent'.

Function of missions

Article 3 of the Vienna Convention provides:

'The functions of a diplomatic mission consist, *inter alia*, in:
a) representing the sending State in the receiving State;
b) protecting in the receiving State the interests of the sending State and of its nationals, within the limits permitted by international law;
c) negotiating with the Government of the receiving State;
d) ascertaining by all lawful means conditions and developments in the receiving State and reporting thereon to the Government of the sending State;
e) promoting friendly relations between the sending State and the receiving State, and developing their economic, cultural and scientific relations.'

Staff

Classification: Article 1 of the Vienna Convention divides the staff of the mission into the following categories:

1. diplomatic staff, namely, members of the mission having diplomatic rank, eg counsellors, diplomatic secretaries or attachés;
2. administrative and technical staff, such as clerical assistants;
3. service staff, being staff 'in the domestic service of the mission'.

A 'diplomatic agent' is the head of the mission or a member of the diplomatic staff of the mission.

Heads of missions

The head of the mission is the person charged by the sending State with the duty of acting in that capacity. The receiving State's consent is necessary for the selection of the head of the mission (Article 4(1) Vienna Convention).

Appointment of the other members of the mission

Article 7 of the Vienna Convention provides as follows:

> 'Subject to the provisions of Articles 5, 8, 9 and 11, the sending State may freely appoint the members of the staff of the mission. In the case of military, naval or air attachés, the receiving State may require their names to be submitted beforehand, for its approval.'

Size of the mission

Article 11 of the Vienna Convention provides:

> '1. In the absence of specific agreement as to the size of the mission, the receiving State may require that the size of a mission be kept within limits considered by it to be reasonable and normal, having regard to circumstances and conditions in the receiving State and to the needs of the particular mission.'

Expulsion of individual diplomatic staff

Article 9 of the Vienna Convention provides:

> '1. The receiving State may at any time and without having to explain its decision, notify the sending State that the head of the mission or any member of the diplomatic staff of the mission is *persona non grata* or that any other member of the staff of the mission is not acceptable. In any such case, the sending State shall, as appropriate, either recall the person concerned or terminate his functions with the mission. A person may be declared *non grata* or not acceptable before arriving in the territory of the receiving State.
>
> 2. If the sending State refuses or fails within a reasonable period to carry out its obligations under paragraph 1 of this Article, the receiving State may refuse to recognise the person concerned as a member of the mission.'

Scope of the immunity

Personal immunities from local jurisdiction

Diplomats enjoy an immunity from the jurisdiction of the local courts and not an exemption from the substantive law. Immunity can be waived in which case the local law will then apply.

Immunity from criminal jurisdiction

Article 31(1) also provides that a diplomatic agent:

'... shall also enjoy immunity from its civil and administrative jurisdiction (except) in the case of:

a) a real action relating to private immovable property situated in the territory of the receiving State, unless he holds in on behalf of the sending State for the purposes of the mission:

b) an action relating to succession in which the diplomatic agent is involved as executor, administrator, heir or legatee as a private person and not on behalf of the sending State;

c) an action relating to any professional or commercial activity exercised by the diplomatic agent in the receiving State outside his official functions.'

Immunity from jurisdiction for official acts

A diplomatic agent has permanent immunity in respect of official acts and this continues to subsist even after he leaves his post. There is no authoritative definition of an official act but it presumably encompasses all matters in the course of official duties.

Other immunities

A diplomatic agent is not obliged to give evidence as a witness. He has immunity from measure of execution and he is exempt from most taxes. He has certain exemption from social security legislation, customs duties, personal and public duties and military service.

Categories of persons entitled to privileges and immunities

The persons entitled to the various degrees of immunity are divided into the following categories:

Diplomatic agents and their families

Diplomatic agents who are not nationals of or permanently resident in the receiving State are entitled to the privileges and immunities under the Vienna Convention. Members of the family of a diplomatic agent forming part of his household shall, if they are not nationals of the receiving State, also enjoy the privileges and immunities specified.

Administrative and technical staff and their families

For example, clerks, archivists, wireless operators etc. These are non-diplomatic members of staff and they have complete immunity from criminal jurisdiction but civil and administrative immunities are limited to their official acts.

Article 37(2) of the Vienna Convention provides:

'Members of the administrative and technical staff of the mission, together with members of their families forming part of their respective households, shall, if they are not nationals of or permanently resident in the receiving State, enjoy the privileges and immunities specified in Article 29 to 35, except that the immunity from civil and administrative jurisdiction of the receiving State specified in paragraph 1 of Article 31 shall not extend to acts performed outside the course of their duties. They shall also enjoy the privileges specified in Article 36, paragraph 1, in respect of articles imported at the time of first installation.'

Service staff

These are 'members of the staff of the mission in the domestic service of the mission'. Article 37(3) of the Vienna Convention provides:

'Members of the service staff of the mission who are not nationals of or permanently resident in the receiving State shall enjoy immunity in respect of acts performed in the course of their duties, exemption from dues and taxes on the emoluments they receive by reason of their employment and the exemption contained in Article 33 (social security legislation).'

Private servants

Article 37(4) of the Vienna Convention provides that private servants of members of the mission shall, if they are not nationals of or permanently resident in the receiving State, be exempt from tax on emoluments received by reason of their employment, but in other respects they may enjoy privileges and immunities entirely at the discretion of the receiving State. The receiving State should, however, exercise jurisdiction in such a manner as not to interfere unduly with the performance of the functions of the mission.

Existence of diplomatic status

Section 4 of the Diplomatic Privileges Act 1964, provides as follows:

'If in any proceedings any question arises whether or not any person is entitled to any privilege or immunity under this Act a certificate issued by or under the authority of the Secretary of State stating any fact relating to that question shall be conclusive evidence of that fact.'

Inviolability of diplomatic agents

Article 29 of the Vienna Convention provides:

'The person of a diplomatic agent shall be inviolable. He shall not be liable to any form of arrest or detention. The receiving State shall treat him with due respect and shall take all appropriate steps to prevent any attack on his person, freedom or dignity.'

Article 30 of the Vienna Convention provides:

'1. The private residence of a diplomatic agent shall enjoy the same inviolability and protection as the premises of the mission.
  2. His papers, correspondence, and, except as provided in paragraph 3 of Article 31, his property, shall likewise enjoy inviolability.'

Inviolability of the mission, its records and communications

Premises
Article 1(i) of the Vienna Convention defines the 'premises of the mission' as:

'... the buildings or parts of buildings and the land ancilliary thereto, irrespective of ownership, used for the purposes of the mission including the residence of the head of the mission'.

Article 22 of the Vienna Convention states the position as follows:

'1. The premises of the mission shall be inviolable. The agents of the receiving State may not enter them, except with the consent of the head of mission.

2. The receiving State is under a special duty to take all appropriate steps to protect the premises of the mission against any intrusion or damage and to prevent any disturbance of the peace of the mission or impairment of its dignity.

In the *Hostages Case*: *US* v *Iran* (1980) the ICJ accepted that Iran was under a 'categorical obligation' to take appropriate steps to protect the US mission.

'3. The premises of the mission, their furnishings and other property thereon and the means of transport of the mission shall be immune from search, requisition, attachment or execution.'

Article 30 provides explicitly that the private residence and correspondence of the diplomatic agent shall also be inviolable.

Diplomatic premises are not extra-territorial; acts occurring there are regarded as taking place on the territory of the receiving State, not on that of the sending State.

Diplomatic premises are also protected against the enforcement of a judgment, decree or arbitral award made against the government of the State maintaining the premises: *A Company Limited* v *Republic of X* [1990] 2 Lloyd's Rep 520.

Archives, documents and official correspondence
Article 24 of the Vienna Convention lays down the inviolability of the archives and documents of the mission 'at any time and wherever they may be'.

Under Article 27(1) of the Convention, the receiving State must permit and protect free communication on the part of the mission for all official purposes.

Article 27(2) declares official correspondence of the mission inviolable.

Article 27(3) states that the diplomatic bag shall not be opened or detained.

Article 27(5) provides that the diplomatic courier shall be 'protected by the receiving State in the performance of his functions' and 'shall enjoy personal inviolability and shall not be liable to any form of arrest or detention'.

Application to third States
Article 40(3) of the Vienna Convention provides that official correspondence and other official communications in transit shall be allowed the same freedom and protection by third States as must be provided by the receiving State. They shall accord to diplomatic couriers and diplomatic bags in transit the same inviolability and protections as the receiving State is bound to accord.

Duration of immunity

Article 39 of the Vienna Convention provides:

'1. Every person entitled to privileges and immunities shall enjoy them from the moment he enters the territory of the receiving State on proceeding to take up his post or, if he already is in its territory, from the moment when his appointment is notified to the Ministry of Foreign Affairs or such other ministry as may be agreed.

2. When the functions of a person enjoying privileges and immunities have come to an end, such privileges and immunities shall normally cease at the moment when he leaves the country, or on expiry of a reasonable period in which to do so, but shall subsist until that time even in case of armed conflict. However, with respect to acts performed by such a person in the exercise of his functions as a member of the mission, immunity shall continue to subsist.'

Foreign diplomats and their families are not entitled to diplomatic immunity, or the right to residence or to expedited immigration procedure, after the expiry of their secondment to their mission. Once a person's appointment at a mission has ceased he or she is no longer a member of the mission and if the official or his or her family remain in the UK after the termination of an appointment, it is without the leave of the immigration authorities: *R* v *Secretary of State for the Home Department, ex parte Bagga* [1990] 3 WLR 1013.

Waiver of immunity

Article 32(1) of the Vienna Convention provides that it is for the sending State to waive immunity at its discretion and by Article 32(2) 'waiver must always be express'.

However, Section 2(3) of the British Diplomatic Privileges Act 1964 provides that the waiver by the head of a mission shall be deemed to be a waiver by the State he represents. But there is nothing in the Act to suggest that a subordinate official requires approval from his State or the head of his mission before waiving his immunity by taking proceedings in the English courts. But a subordinate member of the staff of a mission cannot, by appearing as defendant in an action, waive an immunity which is primarily that of his State and not his own.

Article 32(3) of the Vienna Convention provides that if he commences proceedings, a diplomatic agent is precluded from invoking immunity from jurisdiction in respect of any counterclaim directly connected with the principal claim. While Article 32(4) provides that waiver of immunity from civil or administrative jurisdiction shall not be held to imply waiver in respect of the execution of the judgment, for which a separate waiver shall be necessary.

Hostages Case *(1980)*

The *Hostages Case* between the USA and Iran before the ICJ arose out of the events following the overthrow of the Shah during which the US embassy in Iran was occupied, its contents seized and its personnel held captive, with similar violations taking place in the case of consular missions. There were two phases to the events giving rise to the proceedings: first, the attack on the embassy by militant students and others and, second, the adoption of these acts by the Iranian State. In respect of the first phase, the ICJ found Iran to be responsible under Article 22(2) of the Vienna Convention for its *failure to take steps to protect the embassy*. In respect of the second phase, the Court held Iran *directly responsible* for the breaches of the inviolability of the mission, its premises and correspondence.

Quasi-diplomatic privileges and immunities

Consuls, although representatives of their States in another State are not accorded the degree of immunity within the receiving State enjoyed by diplomatic agents. Their functions are varied and include the protection of the interests of the sending State and its nationals, the development of economic and cultural relations, the issuing of passports and visas, the registration of births, marriages and deaths and the supervision of vessels and aircraft attributed to the sending State.

However, while as a general rule a consul is not immune from local jurisdiction, under the provisions of the Consular Relations Act 1968, which gives effect to the 1963 Vienna Convention on Consular Relations, a consul does enjoy a limited degree of immunity in respect of his official functions.

The Convention provides that Career Consuls (as opposed to Honorary Consuls) are exempted from taxation and customs duties in the same way as diplomats. Consular premises are made inviolable and are given exemption from taxation. Immunity and protection afforded by customary law are maintained. For example:

Article 40: protection of consular offices.

Article 33: inviolability of consular archives and documents.

Article 43: immunity from jurisdiction in respect of acts performed in the exercise of consular functions.

Article 53: exemptions from personal services and contributions.

Article 41 of the Convention provides:

'1. Consular officers shall not be liable to arrest or detention pending trial, except in the case of grave crime and pursuant to a decision by the competent judicial authority.

2. Except in the case specified in paragraph 1 of this article, consular officers shall not be committed to prison or liable to any other form of restriction on their personal freedom save in execution of a judicial decision of final effect.

3. If criminal proceedings are instituted against a consular officer, he must appear before the competent authorities. Nevertheless, the proceedings shall be conducted with the respect due to him by reason of his official position and, except in the case specified in paragraph 1 of this article, in a manner which will hamper the exercise of consular functions as little as possible. When, in the circumstances mentioned in paragraph 1 of this article, it has become necessary to detain a consular officer, the proceedings against him shall be instituted with the minimum delay.'

11

State Responsibility

11.1 Introduction

11.2 The theory of responsibility

11.3 The question of attribution or imputability

11.4 Direct international wrongs

11.5 The treatment of aliens

11.6 Expropriation of foreign property

11.7 Breaches and annulment of State contracts

11.8 The admissibility of State claims

11.9 Remedies

11.1 Introduction

In any legal system there is responsibility for failure to observe obligations imposed by its rules. In international law responsibility arises from the breach of any obligation owed under international law. A State may be responsible, for example:

1. if it fails to honour a treaty;
2. if it damages the territory or property of another State;
3. if it violates the territorial sovereignty of another State;
4. if it uses armed force against another State;
5. if it injures the diplomatic representative of another State;
6. if it injures the nationals of another State.

As a State cannot itself commit breaches of the law, responsibility will be engaged by the acts or omissions of individuals – whether officials (ministers, judges, soldiers, police etc) or private persons. However, it is not all acts, nor the acts of all individuals that will give rise to responsibility. The essence of the law on responsibility is therefore to determine:

1. what *type of actions* will give rise to responsibility, and
2. *by whom* must they be committed if they are to give rise to responsibility?

134

11.2 The theory of responsibility

a) *Existence of responsibility*

All States are responsible in law for their illegal acts. Internationally illegal acts of a State entail the international responsibility of that State.

In the *Spanish Zones of Morocco Claims: Great Britain v Spain* (1925), Judge Huber said:

> 'Responsibility is the necessary corollary of a right. All rights of an international character involve international responsibility. If the obligation in question is not met, responsibility entails the duty to make reparations.'

b) *Civil and criminal responsibility*

International law makes no distinction between tortious and contractual liability. The breach of a treaty or customary obligation will in general give rise to the same remedy, usually a declaration or an award of damages. There is, however, some controversy as to whether States may be criminally liable. The ILC, in Article 19 of its Draft Articles on State Responsibility, suggests that a State may be criminally liable if it breaches an obligation 'so essential for the protection of fundamental interests of the international community'. Such obligations can be identified from the consensus amongst States that the breach of these norms would be particularly serious and would be of concern to all States, not just those immediately effected (ie obligations *erga omnes*). The breach of these obligations would attract penalties more severe than would be the case in an ordinary delictual/civil breach. The ILC identifies four such categories of international crime:

1. the breach of an obligation essential to the maintenance of peace and security, eg the use of force;
2. the breach of an obligation safeguarding the right to self-determination;
3. the breach of an obligation essential for the safeguarding of the human being;
4. the breach of an obligation essential for the safeguarding of the human environment.

Commenting on State practice the ILC in 1976 put the argument thus:

> 'It seems undesirable that today's unanimous and prompt condemnation of any direct attack on international peace and security is paralleled by almost universal disapproval on the part of States towards certain other activities. Contemporary international law has reached the point of condemning outright the practice of certain States in forcibly keeping other peoples under colonial domination or forcibly imposing internal regimes based on discrimination and the most absolute racial segregation in imperilling human life and dignity in other ways, or in so acting as gravely to endanger the preservation and conservation of the human environment. The international community as a whole, and not merely one or other of its members, now considers that such acts violate principles formally embodied in the Charter and, even outside the scope of the Charter, principles which are now so deeply rooted in

the conscience of mankind that they have become particularly essential rules of general international law. There are enough manifestations of the views of States to warrant the conclusion that in the general opinion, some of these acts genuinely constitute "international crimes", that is to say, international wrongs which are more serious than others and which, as such, should entail more severe legal consequences.'

The Commission went on to stress that it was concerned with State and not individual criminal responsibility:

'... in adopting the designation "international crime" the Commission intends only to refer to "crimes" of the State, to acts attributable to the State as such. Once again it wishes to sound a warning against confusion between the expression "international crime" as used in this article and similar expressions, such as "crime under international law", "war crime", "crime against peace", "crime against humanity", etc, which are used in a number of conventions and international instruments to designate certain heinous individual crimes for which those instruments require States to punish the guilty persons adequately, in accordance with the rules of their internal law. Once again, the Commission takes this opportunity of stressing that the attribution to the State of an internationally wrongful act characterised as an "international crime" is quite different from the incrimination of certain individuals – organs for actions connected with the commission of an "international crime" of the State, and that the obligation to punish such individual actions does not constitute the form of international responsibility specially applicable to a State committing an "international crime" or, in any case, the sole form of this responsibility.'

In contrast to the ILC, Brownlie argues that there is no consensus in support of the existence of a separate category of international crimes. Furthermore, he doubts whether such a category would serve any useful purpose as a result of the difficulty that international law would face in trying to impose criminal sanctions.

'The sources of international law indicate that the State is only liable for delicts, ie to give compensation; the individual directly responsible for a crime against peace is liable to trial and punishment. The Charter of the Nuremberg Tribunal, the Draft Code of Offences, the Nuremberg Principles, recent peace treaties and State practice ignore the concept of State criminality. ... The imposition of collective sanctions would in any case violate general principles of justice and there is a strong presumption against vicarious responsibility in criminal law. ... The International Military Tribunal at Nuremberg expressed the matter clearly: "crimes against international law are committed by men, not by abstract entities, and only by punishing individuals who commit such crimes can the provisions of international law be enforced".'

The basis of responsibility

Does the responsibility of the State arise from the commission of the prohibited act alone or does it arise only when it is accompanied by some degree of intention or negligence on the part of the delinquent State?

There are two theories:
(1) the 'risk' or 'objective' theory of responsibility; and (2) the 'fault', 'culpa', or 'subjective' theory of responsibility.

Objective responsibility. The principle of strict liability on the part of States has been followed both in State practice and in the jurisprudence of the International Court and arbitral tribunals. This objective responsibility rests on the doctrine of the voluntary act: provided that agency and causal connection are established, there is a breach of duty by result alone.

In the *Caire Claim: France* v *Mexico* (1929) Caire, a French national, was killed in Mexico by Mexican soldiers after they had demanded money from him. The President of the *Franco-Mexican Claims Commission*, applied:

'... the doctrine of the "objective responsibility" of the State, that is the responsibility for the acts of the officials or organs of a State which may devolve upon it even in the absence of any "fault" of its own ... The State also bears an international responsibility for all acts committed by its officials or its organs which are delictual according to international law, regardless of whether the official organ has acted within the limits of its competency or has exceeded those limits. ... However, in order to justify the admission of this objective responsibility of the State for acts committed by its officials or organs outside their competence, it is necessary that they should have acted, at least apparently, as authorised officials or organs, or that, in acting, they should have used powers or measures appropriate to their official character'.

Subjective responsibility – the culpa doctrine. Some jurists support the Grotian view that culpa or *dolus malus* provide the proper basis of State responsibility in all cases.

The term culpa is used to describe types of blameworthiness based upon fault arising from negligent conduct or recklessness. The view that culpa or fault is a necessary basis for State responsibility has been supported in some arbitral awards.

In *Home Missionary Society Claim: United States* v *Great Britain* (1920) the collection of a new tax imposed by Britain in 1898 on the natives of the Protectorate of Sierra Leone led to a serious and widespread revolt during which missions were attacked and either destroyed or damaged and some missionaries were murdered.

The tribunal dismissed the USA claim, saying:

'It is a well established principle of international law that no Government can be held responsible for the act of rebellious bodies of men committed in violation of its authority, where it is itself guilty of no breach of good faith, or of no negligence in suppressing insurrection.'

Evidence of negligence or fault on the part of State organs may be difficult to find. In many cases, therefore, the issue involved becomes one of causation.

In the *Lighthouses Arbitration: France* v *Greece* (1956) a claim arose from the eviction of a French firm from their offices in Salonika and the subsequent loss of their stores when a fire destroyed their temporary premises. The Permanent Court of Arbitration said:

'Even if one were inclined ... to hold that Greece is in principle responsible for the consequences of that evacuation, one could not ... admit a causal relationship between the damage caused by the fire, on the one part, and that following on the evacuation, on the other, so as to justify holding Greece liable for the disastrous effects of the fire ... The damage was neither a foreseeable nor a normal consequence of the evacuation, nor attributable to any want of care on the part of Greece. All causal connection is lacking, and in these circumstances (the claim) must be rejected.'

Even when a State engages in lawful activities, responsibility will attach in respect of culpa in the execution of those lawful activities.

In *Re Rizzo* (1955) concerning the sequestration of Italian property in Tunisia by the French Government after the defeat of Italy, the Conciliation Commission said:

> '... the act contrary to international law is not the measure of sequestration, but an alleged lack of diligence on the part of the French State – or, more precisely, of him who was acting on its behalf – in the execution of the said measure'.

Assessment

Of these two approaches, the objective school appears to have wider support. However, a number of writers have argued that to see state responsibility exclusively in the light of either of these two approaches is misleading. The better view, according to Brownlie, is that:

> '... the content of a particular duty ... will depend not upon a general principle but upon the precise formulation of each obligation of international law. The relevance of fault, the relative "strictness" of the obligation, will be determined by the content of each rule.'

The ILC have avoided involvement in the debate by noting that responsibility arises on the breach of an international obligation but by not defining those obligations specifically.

One area where fault, intention or knowledge will be important, however, is in determining the responsibility of States for acts of private individuals or other entities over which they should be exercising control, ie in cases where there is a positive *obligation* on the State. In these cases negligence may be important in establishing responsibility for failure to act. The *Home Missionary Case*, for example, was based, arguably, on the tribunals finding that the UK authorities had done everything reasonably possible to maintain order.

Furthermore, motive and intention may be specific elements in the definition of permitted conduct. For example:

1. expropriation of foreign property is unlawful if done as a political reprisal or in retaliation;
2. an act of lawful self-defence against an aggressor may cease to be lawful if the State is found to be using the application of self-defence for purposes of annexation.

Abuse of rights

In some cases an act is not unlawful but nevertheless a State may be responsible for the consequences if the act is committed.

For example: the Convention on the High Seas 1958 – Article 22 provides that a warship which encounters a foreign merchant ship on the high seas may board her if there is reasonable ground for suspecting piracy, slave trading etc.

Paragraph 3 of the Article provides however:

'If the suspicions prove to be unfounded, and provided that the ship boarded has not committed any act justifying them, it shall be compensated for any loss or damage that may have been sustained.'

11.3 The question of attribution or imputability

State responsibility is engaged by the acts or omissions of individuals. It is fundamental to the question of responsibility, therefore, to be able to distinguish those acts that are to be attributable to the State from those that are not. Attribution thus has the effect of indicating that the act in question is an act of the State concerned.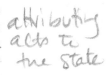

As a general rule, if a State, through the activities of its organs or representatives, has committed a wrongful act against the person or property of a foreign national within its territory, then that act will *prima facie* constitute a breach of international law.

The question of attribution arises in the context of three different groups:

1. the acts of *the State and its officials*;
2. the acts of *private persons*;
3. the acts of *insurrectionaries*.

Acts of the State and its officials

A State can only act through its organs and representatives. The organs and representatives of a State include the following: (1) the executive and administration, (2) the judicature, (3) the legislature, (4) the armed forces, and (5) federal States and provinces.

The general rule regarding State organs and officials is found in Article 5 of the ILC Draft Articles:

'... conduct of any State organ having that status under the internal law of that State shall be considered as an act of the State concerned under international law, provided that organ was acting in that capacity in the case in question'.

Article 6 goes on to provide that the status of the organ or official is of no importance. Thus, an act, whether carried out by the legislature (eg *Fisheries Jurisdiction Cases* in which Iceland had unlawfully extended its jurisdiction), the executive (eg *Naulilaa Case* in which German forces damaged Portuguese property), the judiciary, an official in a superior position or one in a subordinate position, will involve the same measure of responsibility.

In the *Massey Case: United States v Mexico (1927)* a US national was murdered in Mexico by a Mexican named Saenz. Saenz was later arrested, but escaped from gaol when the assistant gaoler allowed him to leave. The Mexican Government argued that it was not liable for this denial of justice because it stemmed from the misconduct of a *minor official* who was acting in violation of Mexican law and of his duty.

Commissioner Nielson stated:

'To attempt by some broad classification to make a distinction between some "minor" or "petty" officials and other kinds of officials must obviously at times involve practical difficulties. Irrespective of the propriety of attempting to make any such distinction at all, it would seem that in reaching conclusions in any given case with respect to responsibility for acts of public servants, the most important considerations of which account must be taken are the character of the acts alleged to have resulted in injury to persons or to property, or the nature of functions performed whenever a question is raised as to their proper discharge.'

Liability of the State where an official acts outside his authority

If the act falls within the apparent scope of the official's authority then *prima facie* the State will be liable notwithstanding the fact that the official has exceeded his actual authority.

In two cases, *The Jessie* and *The Wonderer,* the USA was held responsible for the acts of its revenue officers in the exercise of their right of visit and search over British ships on the high seas. The officers had acted in good faith but had exceeded their powers under the relevant Anglo-American agreement. Although acting outside their actual authority, the tribunal confirmed that so long as the officers were acting within the scope of their duties then the State would be responsible.

Article 8(a) of the ILC Draft Articles provides that the conduct of a person or group shall also engage the responsibility of the State if it is established that they were in fact acting on behalf of the State. This may occur if acts committed by private parties are subsequently adopted by the State such as took place in the *Hostages Case* (ICJ, 1980).

The liability of the State in such cases is not limited to mere errors of judgment on the part of its officials.

In the *Maal Case,* officers of the Venezuelan police in the exercise of their powers to refuse aliens admission to the country, arrested Maal, a Netherlands subject whom they suspected of being a revolutionary. The officers then proceeded, in excess of their authority, to strip Maal in public. The Umpire acquitted the Venezuelan Government:

'... from any other purpose or thought than the mere exclusion of one regarded as dangerous to the welfare of the Government, but the acts of their subordinates in the line of their authority, however odious their acts may be, the Government must stand sponsor for'.

Similarly in the *Quintanilla Claim: Mexico v United States* (1926) the USA was held responsible for the death of a young Mexican national who was found murdered soon after being taken into custody by a deputy sheriff. The Commission found it clear that Quintanilla was taken into custody by a State official, and while it would go too far to hold that the Government is liable for everything which may befall him, it does have to account for him. Whether the deputy sheriff or some other person had deliberately killed him, the State could not absolve itself of responsibility by ignoring what happened.

Liability for *ultra vires* acts of organs and officials

The traditional view was that the activities of an official which fell outside the scope of his authority could not be imputed to the State.

Thus in the *Cibich Claim: United States* v *Mexico* the USA presented a claim on behalf of one of its nationals who had been arrested for drunkenness. Money in his possession was taken by the local chief of police for safe keeping. During the night a gang of liberated prisoners and defecting policemen stole the money. However, as the defecting policemen were no longer purporting to act in their official capacity, their presence in the gang could not impute responsibility to the State and in the absence of evidence showing a lack of reasonable care on the part of the local police authorities, the Mexican Government was not responsible.

The jurisprudence of international tribunals and the writings of jurists today supports the rule that States may be responsible for *ultra vires* acts of their officials if committed within the scope of their apparent authority. The test has therefore become objective.

In the *Union Bridge Company Claim: United States* v *Great Britain* (1924) in 1899, shortly after the outbreak of war between Great Britain and the Orange Free State, a British official of the Cape Government Railway appropriated neutral property under the mistaken belief that it was not neutral. The tribunal found that

'... liability is not affected either by the fact that (the official appropriated the property) under a mistake as to the character and ownership of the material or that it was a time of pressure and confusion caused by war, or by the fact, which, on the evidence, must be admitted, that there was no intention on the part of the British authorities to appropriate the material in question'.

The official acted within the scope of his general duty and liability was, therefore, fixed on the British Government.

Similarly, where the persons employed have abused the governmental powers entrusted to them their State may be liable.

In the *Caire Claim: France* v *Mexico* (1929) Caire, a French national, was killed in Mexico by Mexican soldiers after they had demanded money from him. The Presiding Commissioner considered the responsibility of Mexico for actions of individual military personnel, acting without orders or against the wishes of their commanding officers and independently of the needs and aims of the revolution ...

In holding Mexico responsible for the murder, the Presiding Commissioner continued:

'The State also bears international responsibility for all acts committed by its officials or its organs ... regardless of whether the official or organ has acted within the limits of his competency or has exceeded those limits ... However, in order to justify the ... responsibility of the State for acts committed by its officials or organs outside their competence, it is necessary

used powers in that capacity

that they should have acted, *at least apparently*, as authorised officials or organs, or that, in acting, they should have used powers or measures appropriate to their official character'.

Where the persons employed make use of the powers and means put at their disposal in their official capacity, to commit the wrongful act, then the State may be liable in respect of those acts.

soldiers killed 3 americans

In the *Youmans Case: United States* v *Mexico* (1926) a group of three US nationals was being attacked by a Mexican mob. Troops sent to protect them joined in the attack, which resulted in the death of the Americans. The Mexican Government argued that as the soldiers had acted in complete disregard of their instructions, Mexico could not be responsible for the deaths.

soldiers (even if rejected their orders) acted for state ≠ private capacity

The Commission rejected the Mexican argument that the soldiers having disregarded their orders were then acting in a private capacity.

'We do not consider that the participation of the soldiers in the murder ... can be regarded as acts of soldiers committed in their private capacity when it is clear that at the time of the commission of these acts the men were on duty under the immediate supervision and in the presence of a commanding officer. Soldiers inflicting personal injuries or committing wanton destruction or looting always act in disobedience of some rules laid down by superior authority. There could be no liability whatever for such misdeeds if the view were taken that any acts committed by soldiers in contravention of instructions must always be considered as personal acts.'

This approach now finds support in Article 10 of the ILC Draft Articles which provides that the conduct of an entity with government authority will be attributable to the State even if the organ was acting *ultra vires*.

distinct bt. case law + ILC draft

An apparent distinction between the case law and the ILC Articles, however, is that the cases stress the requirement of *apparent authority*. The ILC, in contrast, does not. This notwithstanding, it is probably the case that some notion of apparent authority or use of official powers will be necessary for a claim to be founded. In *Yeager* v *Iran* (I-USCT, 1987), the Iran-US Claims Tribunal disallowed a claim by a US national to recover money extorted from him by an Iranair official at the time of his expulsion from the country as the act in question was beyond the scope of the apparent authority of the official in question.

not acting in apparent authority

The responsibility of the State may also arise from the negligent acts of its officers. In the *Zafiro Claim: Great Britain* v *United States* (1925) the USA was held responsible for looting committed by the Chinese civilian crew of a merchant vessel employed as a supply vessel by the US navy, under the command of a merchant captain, under the orders of an American naval officer. The tribunal found that in the particular circumstances of the case there had been an absence of proper diligence on the part of the ship's officers who allowed the crew to go ashore uncontrolled.

Ⓑ
The acts of private persons

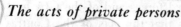

The general rule is stated in Article 11, ILC Draft Articles:

'The conduct of a person or a group of persons *not* acting on behalf of the State shall not be considered as an act of the State under international law.'

The principal exception to this rule is that found in Article 8(a) to the effect that if it is subsequently established that the person(s) were *in fact* acting on behalf of the State, eg because the State adopts the acts in question, then responsibility will arise. Thus, the ICJ in the *Hostages Case* (1980) held that Iran, by adopting the acts of the revolutionary guards, became responsible for the acts in question. Note, however, that in the first phase (where the acts had been carried out by the revolutionary guards but before the State had adopted them as its own) the Court was quite clear that even congratulatory and approving statements made by the Iranian leadership did not have the effect of attributing the acts to the State. It was only when the acts in question were *adopted* by the State that responsibility arose. (The whole question of responsibility for incitement is unclear. There is, no doubt a very fine line betweeen approving statements – that do not give rise to responsibility – and adoption of the acts (or possibly, incitement) which does give rise to responsibility.)

In the *Nicaragua Case* (1986), the question arose as to whether the acts of the Contras could be attributed to the USA. In considering this question the Court noted that it had to determine

'... whether or not the relationship of the Contras to the US Government was so much one of *dependence* on the one side and *control* on the other that it would be right to equate the Contras, for legal purposes, with an organ of the US Government or as acting on behalf of that Government'.

In deciding the issue the Court noted that there was no clear evidence that the USA '*actually exercised such a degree of control* in all fields as to justify treating the Contras acting on its behalf'. The Court continued to note that:

'US participation, even if preponderant or decisive, in the financing, organising, training, supplying and equipping of the Contras, the selection of its military or paramilitary targets, and the planning of the whole of its operation, is still insufficient in itself ... for the purpose of attributing to the US the acts committed by the Contras in the course of their military or paramilitary operations in Nicaragua. All the forms of US participation mentioned above, and even the general control by the respondent State (the US) over a force with a high degree of dependency on it, would not in themselves mean, without further evidence, that the US directed or enforced *the perpetration of the acts contrary to human rights and humanitarian law alleged* by the applicant State. Such acts could well be committed by the Contras without the control of the US. *For this conduct to give rise to legal responsibility of the US, it would in principle have to be proved that that State had effective control of the military or paramilitary operations in the course of which the alleged violations were committed.* The Court does not consider that the assistance given by the US to the Contras warrants the conclusion that these forces are subject to the US to such an extent that any acts they have committed are imputable to that State.'

Judge Ago, in his Separate Opinion in the *Nicaragua Case*, agreed with the Court in their finding that acts of the members of the US armed forces and of the CIA *were* attributable to the USA. He also supported the view that the acts of the Contras were *not* attributable to the USA. While he agreed with the view that attribution rested on the issue of whether the USA *directed or enforced* the acts in question, he questioned whether the requirement of *control* was appropriate.

Taken together, the *Hostages* and *Nicaragua* cases indicate a strict test of attribution. Dependence or 'moral' support will not be sufficient. What is required will be evidence of *actual control* such that the activities could be said to have been directed or enforced by the State concerned.

Liability for the acts of insurrectionaries

The development of the law in this area has been complicated by the fine line between insurrection and mob violence. In the latter, the contention has long been that a State would be liable for failure to take the necessary measures. In the former, such a view was less certain as a number of writers took the view that a State engaged in repressing insurgents was not responsible for harm caused to foreigners.

Lord McNair states five principles regarding the responsibility of lawful governments for the consequences of insurrection and rebellion:

1. a State on whose territory an insurrection occurs is not responsible for loss or damage sustained by a foreigner unless it can be shown that the government of that State was negligent in the use of, or in the failure to use, the forces at its disposal for the prevention or suppression of the insurrection.

   In the *Sambaggio Case: Italy v Venezuela* (1903) the Umpire rejected a claim by an Italian national for compensation in respect of damage caused by unsuccessful revolutionaries in Venezuela. The following general principles were stated as the basis for that decision: (a) revolutionaries are not the agents of Government, and a natural responsibility does not exist; (b) their acts are committed to destroy the Government, and no one should be held responsible for the acts of an enemy attempting his life; (c) the revolutionaries were beyond governmental control, and the Government cannot be held responsible for injuries committed by those who have escaped its restraint;

2. this is a variable test, dependent on the circumstances of the insurrection;

3. such a State is not responsible for the damage resulting from military operations directed by its lawful government unless the damage was wanton or unnecessary, which appears to be substantially the same as the position of belligerent States in an international war;

4. such a State is not responsible for loss or damage caused by the insurgents to a foreigner after that foreigner's State has recognised the belligerency of the insurgents;

5. such a State can usually defeat a claim in respect of loss or damage sustained by resident foreigners by showing that they have received the same treatment in the matter of protection or compensation, if any, as its own nationals.

Article 14 of the ILC Draft Articles now states the general proposition that a State will *not* be responsible for acts of an insurrectionary movement. The position changes if the movement subsequently becomes the government of the State or establishes a new State. In such cases, Article 15 provides that the new government – ie that composed of the insurgents – *will* be responsible for the acts of the movement during the insurgency. It will also bear responsibility for any acts committed by the previous government.

A number of cases on the responsibility of the State in cases of insurrection were put to the Iran-US Claims Tribunal. In *Short* v *Iran* (1987) a US national was forced to leave after threats from private persons during the revolution. He claimed against Iran for wrongful expulsion. The Tribunal, while accepting that the revolutionary Government was liable for acts committed during the revolution, held that Iran was not responsible for acts of private parties who had no status within the revolutionary movement. He would have been able to recover had he been compelled to leave by revolutionary officials. In a dissenting opinion, the US member of the Tribunal queried how to distinguish between mere enthusiastic supporters and members of the revolutionary movement. In *Yeager* v *Iran* (1987), the applicant was expelled by revolutionary guards. The Tribunal held in his favour as these acts were clearly attributable to the new Government.

11.4 Direct international wrongs

An *indirect* wrong arises when a State is in breach of an obligation owed to the national of another State, eg an unlawful expropriation of private property. In contrast, a *direct* wrong arises when one State is in direct breach of an obligation owed to another State.

The following are examples of direct wrongful acts by one State against another:

Breach of treaty

A breach of a treaty by a State is a breach of an obligation owed by that State to the other party to the treaty and that other party thereby suffers a direct wrong.

In the *Chorzow Factory (Indemnity) Case: Germany* v *Poland* (1927) the Permanent Court of Justice stated that it was 'a principle of international law that the breach of an engagement involves an obligation to make reparation' and that reparation was therefore 'the indispensable complement of a failure to apply a convention'.

Damage to State property

If a State through its acts or omissions is the direct cause of damage to the property of a foreign State, then it is liable to pay reparation for the damage so caused.

Corfu Channel Case: United Kingdom v Albania (1949)

On 22 October 1946 a squadron of British warships, the cruisers *Mauritius* and *Leander* and the destroyers *Saumarez* and *Volage*, left the port of Corfu and proceeded northwards through a channel previously swept for mines in the North Corfu Strait. Outside the Bay of Saranda, *Saumarez* struck a mine and was heavily damaged. Whilst towing the damaged ship, *Volage* struck a mine and was much damaged.

The Court held the People's Republic of Albania:

'... responsible under international law for the explosions which occurred on 22 October 1946, in Albanian waters, and for the damage and loss of human life which resulted therefrom ... the laying of the minefield which caused the explosion ... could not have been accomplished without the knowledge of the Albanian Government ... The obligation incumbent upon the Albanian authorities consisted in notifying, for the benefit of shipping in general, the existence of a minefield in Albanian territorial waters and in warning the approaching warships of the imminent danger to which the minefield exposed them. Such obligations are based ... on certain general and well recognised principles namely: elementary considerations of humanity ...; the principle of the freedom of maritime communication; and every States obligation not to allow knowingly its territory to be used for acts contrary to the rights of other States.'

Failure to respect the territorial rights of other States

A failure to respect the territorial rights of another State may occur in a number of ways:

By the invasion or other use of force against a State

Article 2(4) of the Charter of the United Nations provides:

'All Members shall refrain in their international relations from the threat or use of force against the territorial integrity or political independence of any State, or in any other manner inconsistent with the Purposes of the United Nations.'

The unlawful arrest of a wanted criminal on the territory of another State

In the *Eichmann Case* (1962) Eichmann, the former Head of the Jewish Office of the German Gestapo, was found in Argentina in 1960 by Israeli Government agents and abducted to Israel without the knowledge of the Argentinian Government. Argentina complained to the Security Council of the United Nations which adopted a resolution stating that: 'acts such as that under consideration, which affect the sovereignty of a Member State ... endanger international peace and security' and 'requests the Government of Israel to make appropriate reparations in accordance with the Charter of the United Nations and the rules of international law'.

rep. to Argentina

Illegal flights in the airspace of another State

In the U-2 incident of May 1960 a US aircraft engaged in espionage activities over the Soviet Union was forced down by the Russian authorities.

The carrying out of activities in the territorial waters of a State

In the *Corfu Channel Case (Merits): United Kingdom* v *Albania* (1949) the ICJ held that the Royal Navy, in carrying out minesweeping operations in Albanian territorial waters, violated the sovereignty of the Albanian Peoples Republic.

By allowing toxic fumes to escape into the territory of another State

The *Trail Smelter Arbitration: United States* v *Canada* (1938 and 1941) a Canadian company began smelting lead and zinc at Trail, on the Columbia River about 10 miles from the US-Canadian border, on the Canadian side. By 1930 over 300 tons of sulphur, containing considerable quantities of sulphur dioxide, were being emitted daily. Some of the fumes were being carried down the Columbia River valley and across into the USA where they were allegedly causing considerable damage to land and other interests in the State of Washington. The USA claimed compensation, and the matter was referred to the International Joint Commission.

The tribunal found that: 'under the principles of international law ... no State has the right to use or permit the use of its territory in such a manner as to cause injury by fumes in or to the territory of another or the properties of persons therein'.

Insult to the State

These acts are generally termed 'insults to the flag' and constitute international wrongs for which the State responsible should make suitable reparations: the *I'm Alone: Canada v United States (1935)*.

In this case, the *I'm Alone*, a British schooner, registered in Canada, was ordered to heave to by a US coastguard vessel, on suspicion of smuggling liquor at the time of prohibition in the USA. She fled, and when more than 200 miles from the US coast was fired upon and sunk, with the loss of the boatswain and the cargo.

The Commission found the sinking of the vessel to be unjustified. However, although the *I'm Alone* was a British ship of Canadian registry the Commission found the vessel to be *de facto* owned by citizens of the USA and that therefore no compensation ought to be paid in respect of the ship or cargo. But the Commission continued:

> 'The act of sinking the ship, however, by officers of the United States Coast Guard, was, as we have already indicated, an unlawful act; and the Commissioners consider that the United States ought formally to acknowledge its illegality, and to apologise to His Majesty's Canadian Government therefor; and, further, that as a material amend in respect of the wrong the United States should pay the sum of $25,000 to His Majesty's Canadian Government; and they recommend accordingly.'

In the majority of such cases a public apology and an undertaking to punish those responsible for the act will usually comprise adequate amends.

11.5 The treatment of aliens

State and individual

Vattal stated that an injury to a citizen is an injury to the State. This relationship between the individual and his State gives rise to two principles:

Responsibility
The State is responsible for the acts of its citizens of which its agents know or ought to know and which cause harm to the legal interests of another State.

Protection

The State has a legal interest in its citizens and in protecting this interest the State may call to account those harming its citizens.

In the *Mavrommatis Palestine Concessions Case (Jurisdiction): Greece v United Kingdom* (1924) the Court said:

'... it is an elementary principle of international law that a State is entitled to protect its subjects, when injured by acts contrary to international law committed by another State, from whom they have been unable to obtain satisfaction through the ordinary channels. By taking up the case of one of its subjects and by resorting to diplomatic action or international judicial proceedings on his behalf, a State is in reality asserting its own right – its right to ensure, in the person of its subjects, respect for the rules of international law.'

Failure to protect these principles, therefore, may lead the injured State to exercise its right of diplomatic protection. The injured State may make a claim through diplomatic channels against the offending State or, failing satisfaction, may present a claim on the international plane.

The defendant States duties are owed not to the injured alien, but to the alien's national State. Thus: (1) the claimant State may refrain from making a claim; (2) the claimant State may abandon its claim; (3) the claimant State is under no obligation to pay any compensation obtained to its injured national.

In *Rustomjee* v *The Queen* (1876) money had been paid to Great Britain by China as compensation for damage suffered by British nationals in China.

Lush J stated:

'No doubt a duty arose as soon as the money was received to distribute that money amongst the persons towards whose losses it was paid by the Emperor of China; but then the distribution when made would be, not the act of an agent accounting to a principal, but the act of the Sovereign in dispensing justice to her subjects. For any omission of that duty the Sovereign cannot be held responsible.'

International minimum standard or national treatment?

Much of the controversy regarding the treatment of aliens stems from the difference in approach between those States that consider that there is an 'international minimum standard' of treatment which must be accorded to aliens by all States irrespective of how they treat their own nationals and those that argue that aliens may only insist upon 'national treatment', ie treatment equal to that given by the State concerned to its own nationals.

The standard of national treatment

The principle of national treatment has been favoured by the newer and developing States. For example, it has received support in Latin America and today many of the post-colonial Afro-Asian States support the principle. The main justifications for granting aliens equality of treatment under the local law have been stated as follows: (1) To give the alien a special status would be contrary to the principles of territorial jurisdiction and equality of States. (2) By residing in the particular State the alien is deemed to have submitted to both the benefits and the burdens incidental to residence in that State, ie he takes conditions as he finds them.

The standard does not apply to every area of activity.

Certain sources of inequality are admissible. Customary international law recognises that in certain areas of activity States may treat aliens less favourably than their own nationals.

For example, aliens may be restricted in: (1) the ownership of property; (2) participation in public life and politics; (3) the taking of employment; (4) receiving legal aid and welfare benefits.

In the UK for instance, an alien may not own a British ship, may not vote in parliamentary elections and may face restrictions in joining the civil service.

The international minimum standard

The older and more economically developed States of Western Europe and North America have generally supported the international minimum standard of treatment of aliens. This principle is also supported by the great majority of international tribunals.

In the *Neer Claim: United States v Mexico* (1926) the USA claimed that Mexico had failed to exercise due diligence in finding and prosecuting the murderer of a US national. In rejecting the claim the Commission expressed the applicable standard as follows:

> '... the propriety of governmental acts should be put to the test of international standards ... the treatment of an alien, in order to constitute an international delinquency, should amount to an outrage, to bad faith, to wilful neglect of duty, or to an insufficiency of governmental action so far short of international standards that every reasonable and impartial man would readily recognise its insufficiency. Whether the insufficiency proceeds from deficient execution of an intelligent law or from the fact that the laws of the country do not empower the authorities to measure up to international standards is immaterial.'

The two standards – the treatment of aliens and fundamental human rights

The national standard of treatment and the international minimum standard of treatment reflect conflicting economic and political interests. Critics of the international minimum standard cite the past effects of maintaining a privileged status for aliens: foreign armed intervention to enforce these privileges and large sections of the national economy under alien control.

The International Law Commission in its Debate on the Second Report on State Responsibility in 1957 attempted to move away from the conflict between national treatment and minimum international standards by linking the question of the protection of aliens to the rapidly developing law regarding the protection of human rights in general.

The Rapporteur – the Cuban jurist Garcia Amador – proposed in Article 1 of his second report of 1956 that:

> '1. The State is under a duty to ensure to aliens the enjoyment of the same civil rights, and to make available to them the same individual guarantees as are enjoyed by nationals [national standard]. These rights and guarantees shall not, however, in any case be less

than the "fundamental human rights" recognised and defined in contemporary international instruments [international minimum standard].

2. In consequence, in case of violation of civil rights, or disregard of individual guarantees, with respect to aliens, international responsibility will be involved only if internationally recognised "fundamental human rights" are affected.'

This proposal would have made substantial inroads upon the domestic jurisdiction of States and was felt to be quite unacceptable in the light of current State practice. Furthermore, it was felt by non-European States that the 'fundamental human rights' protected were reflective of Western European standards and ideals, and were not necessarily suitable for the Third World States, with their particular economic, social and political problems. However, with the rapid growth of international instruments dealing with human rights since 1956, there is a growing body of opinion that this approach is now correct. Thus, the standard of treatment to be accorded to non-nationals should be the standard established by the international law of human rights.

Admission and expulsion of aliens

These are matters essentially within the domestic jurisdiction of States.

Admission of aliens

A State may refuse to admit aliens or may impose conditions or restriction upon their admission.

In *Attorney-General for Canada* v *Cain* (1906) the Judicial Committee of the Privy Council stated:

'One of the rights possessed by the supreme power in every State is the right to refuse to permit an alien to enter that State, to annex what conditions it pleases to the permission to enter it, and to expel or deport from the State, at pleasure, even a friendly alien, especially if it considers his presence in the State opposed to its peace, order and good Government, or to its social or material interests.'

Expulsion

Providing the State acts in good faith it may exercise the power of expulsion at its discretion. However certain exceptions do exist which limit this discretion:

1. expulsion may constitute the crime of genocide or may infringe the rule of non-discrimination under customary international law;
2. there may be no right of expulsion where persons by long residence have acquired effective nationality of the foreign host State.

Denial of justice

The term 'denial of justice' has been given widely differing interpretations by international tribunals and its precise meaning is, therefore, uncertain and controversial. In its widest sense it has been equated with any wrongful treatment of aliens for which the respondent State would be accountable. In its narrow sense it has been used to cover only those situations in which foreigners have either been refused access to the local courts, or where such access has been hindered.

A definition somewhere between these two views is that contained in the 1929 Harvard Draft Convention on the Responsibility of States for Damage Done in Their Territory to the Person or Property of Foreigners.

Article 9 states:

> 'Denial of justice exists when there is a denial, unwarranted delay or obstruction of access to courts, gross deficiency in the administration of judicial or remedial process, failure to provide those guarantees which are generally considered indispensable to the proper administration of justice, or a manifestly unjust judgment. An error of a national court which does not produce manifest injustice is not a denial of justice.'

[handwritten margin note: denial of justice]

This draft has been criticised as being too general. It is this generality which has resulted in the wide interpretation given to the phrase and has led to its erratic application and uncertainty of meaning.

The international standard of denial of justice

It is generally agreed that if 'denial of justice' is to achieve a degree of certainty and be used as a basis of international responsibility then it must be defined in terms of an international law standard.

The international standard is founded upon two principles:

1. it is no defence to show that an alien has been treated no worse than nationals of the respondent State if the standard of treatment is lower than the minimum standard required by international law; *[handwritten margin note: at least min.]*
2. if the local standards of the administration of justice are higher than those of the minimum standard required by international law, the alien must receive the benefit of that higher standard and not the international minimum, ie there must be no discrimination. *[handwritten margin note: no discriminate]*

However, when the special circumstances of many States are taken into account it is obvious that any international standard will be a variable concept. Allowance must be made for derogation from the international standard in special circumstances. Special measures may have to be introduced by a State to meet an emergency, eg war, rebellion or other civil disorder. Some account may also have to be taken of the special difficulties involved in administering justice in the underdeveloped, less stable parts of the world. For example, inadequate communications may make the local police and judicial authorities virtually autonomous from the central authorities of the State.

The international standard and local conditions

If the international standard is not to impose unreasonably high standards on the less developed States, the standard must take into account local conditions and not be a reflection of those standards applied in the more advanced Western States. *[handwritten margin note: less developed States]*

The problem is illustrated by the cases involving injury to American nationals heard by the Mexican-United States Claims Commission.

In many cases before the Commission, Mexico argued that if foreigners came to work in Mexico they must accept life as they found it and should not be entitled to more favourable treatment than that enjoyed by Mexican nationals. This defence was usually rejected. For example, in *Roberts Claim: United States v Mexico* (1926) the Commission found:

> '... the jail in which he was kept was a room thirty five feet long and twenty feet wide with stone walls, earthen floor, straw roof, a single window, a single door and no sanitary accommodation, all the prisoners depositing their excrement in a barrel kept in a corner of the room ... thirty or forty men were at times thrown together in this single room ... the prisoners were given no facilities to clean themselves ... the room contained no furniture ... they were afforded no opportunity to take physical exercise ... the food given them was scarce, unclean, and of the coarsest kind. The Mexican Agent ... stated that Roberts was accorded the same treatment as that given to all other persons, and with respect to the food Roberts ... was given "the food that was believed necessary, and within the means of the municipality".
>
> Facts with respect to equality of treatment of aliens and nationals may be important in determining the merits of a complaint of mistreatment of an alien. But such equality is not the ultimate test of the propriety of the acts of authorities in the light of international law. That test is broadly speaking whether aliens are treated in accordance with ordinary standards of civilisation. We do not hesitate to say that the treatment of Roberts was such as to warrant an indemnity on the ground of cruel and inhuman imprisonment.'

The failure of international law to establish a compromise between the international standard and local conditions led the South American States to reject the international minimum standard and adopt instead the standard of national treatment when dealing with aliens.

The 1947 Panamanian Draft on the Rights and Duties of States provided that foreigners were not entitled to claim rights 'different from, or more extensive than, those enjoyed by nationals'.

However, this approach has had to be adapted to meet the developments in international human rights generally, and today even the advocates of the national standard of treatment accept the need for some limitation on the application of their municipal laws so as not to contravene fundamental human rights.

The International Law Commission Revised Draft on International Responsibility of the State for Injuries Caused on its Territory to the Person or Property of Aliens 1961 reflects this changing attitude.

Article 1 provides:

> '... aliens enjoy the same rights and the same legal guarantees as nationals, but these rights and guarantees shall in no case be less than the "human rights and fundamental freedoms" recognised and defined in contemporary international instruments'.

The requirement of 'bad faith'

There may be no denial of justice where the failure arises through deficiencies in the administration of justice, unless those deficiencies are such as to raise a presumption of bad faith.

In the *Neer Claim: United States v Mexico* (1926) the USA claimed that Mexico had failed to exercise due diligence in finding and prosecuting the murderer of a US national. In rejecting the claim the Commission said there was:

> '... a long way between holding that a more active and efficient course of procedure might have been pursued on the one hand, and holding that this record presents such a lack of diligence and of intelligent investigation as constitutes an international delinquency on the other hand'.

[handwritten margin note: not very efficient]

However, this may be contrasted with: *Janes Claim: United States v Mexico* (1926) where the Commission stated that in its opinion:

> 'Carbajal, the person who killed Janes, was well known in the community where the killing took place. Numerous persons witnessed the deed. The slayer, after killing his victim, left on foot. There is evidence that a Mexican police magistrate was informed of the shooting within five minutes after it took place ... Eight years have elapsed since the murder and it does not appear from the records that Carbajal has been apprehended at this time ... there was clearly such a failure on the part of the Mexican authorities to take prompt and efficient action to apprehend the slayer as to warrant an award of indemnity.'

[handwritten margin note: bad faith]

11.6 Expropriation of foreign property

Introduction

A State may restrict or place conditions upon the acquisition of certain kinds of property by aliens. In the absence of such restrictions an alien is free to acquire and enjoy title to property in accordance with the provisions of the local law.

Expropriation, or the compulsory taking of private property by the State has always been considered as a ground for diplomatic intervention as constituting a breach of international law. Whereas in the nineteenth century the problem was usually one of the destruction or expropriation of the property of one individual, today it is likely to be one of general expropriation of all foreign property, or the expropriation of all property in certain key areas of the State's economy, eg railways, banks, oil companies and mines.

Nature of the problem

The acquisition and control of property by aliens is of considerable political importance to States. The economies of many States, both underdeveloped and developed, are dominated by foreign companies and foreign investors. Many States resent this foreign dominance and see it as a threat to their independence and as inhibiting their freedom to implement their chosen economic and social policies.

The problem has become particularly acute following the spread of socialism and the emergence of the post-colonial States in Asia and Africa who resent the interests retained by their former colonial powers and seek ways to sever their former colonial ties completely.

The rules of expropriation

Although it is generally agreed that expropriation may occur, the wide divergence of political and economic beliefs among States has resulted in little agreement as to the rules to be applied in cases of expropriation.

The Communist countries believe that States may expropriate the means of production, distribution and exchange without paying any compensation, ie confiscation.

The developing States believe the matter should be left to the expropriating State to regulate at its discretion and in accordance with its national law.

Western capital exporting States have, however, advocated *an international minimum standard* based on three principles: the principle of *non-discrimination*, the principle that the expropriation most be for a *public purpose;* and the principle that expropriation must be followed by *adequate compensation.*

Non-discrimination

While the requirement of non-discrimination is not expressly stated in either of the principal international instruments dealing with this question (see below), it is a general principle of good faith and has been widely upheld in arbitral awards such as *BP* v *Libya* and *LIAMCO* v *Libya*. In *Aminoil* v *Kuwait* (1982) Kuwait was pursuing a general policy of nationalisation but was doing so in stages. At the time of the nationalisation of Aminoil, a Japanese company operating in the same region was left unaffected. Aminoil alleged discrimination. This was, however, rejected by the Tribunal on the grounds that there were legitimate reasons for the nationalisation not having included the Japanese company. To establish discrimination a company would, therefore, have to show that it had been singled out on the basis of its nationality. The most striking example of this arose in the *BP Case* in which Libya expressly stated that it was expropriating BP's assets in response to what was regarded as improper action by the British Government in the Gulf. The expropriation thus arose directly as a result of the British nationality of BP.

Public purpose

In the *Certain German Interests in Polish Upper Silesia Case* (1926) the Court acknowledged that 'expropriation for reasons of public utility, judicial liquidation and similar measures' was permissible in international law.

This is stated as a requirement in GAR 1803 (1962) but not in GAR 3281 (1974) (see below). There has thus been some debate as to whether this forms part of the international law test of lawfulness. Arbitrator Lagergren in *BP* accepted that this was a requirement of international law. In that case, the Libyan nationalisation of BP took place in the context of a specific anti-British policy. The nationalisation was, therefore, unlawful because it 'was made for purely extraneous political reasons' rather than as part of a policy of public utility. In the *LIAMCO* award, however, arbitrator Mahmassani expressly rejected the notion that international law included a public policy test.

As in the *BP Case* (1974), there will frequently be an overlap between the non-discrimination requirement and the public purpose principle. In *BP*, for example, the Libyan nationalisation decree was contrary to both principles: 'the taking ... violates public international law as it was made for purely extraneous political reasons and was arbitrary and discriminatory in character'. This does not clarify, however, whether Lagergren saw non-discrimination as part of the public policy test or a separate test in its own right. In *LIAMCO*, Mahmassani accepted the non-discrimination principle but rejected the public policy requirement. These decisions can be reconciled only if it is accepted either that the two principles form part of the same test or that, while they are separate tests, the public policy principle will be easily satisfied on evidence that the act in question was motivated other than by purely political considerations.

Compensation

While there is general acceptance that there is a requirement to compensate in the case of expropriation the *standard* of the compensation required has been much in issue. The debate has focused on the divide between those seeking an international standard of compensation and those in favour of a standard of compensation determined in accordance with the municipal law of the state concerned.

Those in favour of an international standard of compensation have pointed to numerous examples of State practice in support of the proposition. US Secretary of State Hull, in 1940, argued that the right to expropriate was 'coupled with and conditioned on the obligation to make adequate, effective and prompt compensation'.

In the *Anglo-Iranian Oil Company Case* the UK pleaded the following before the ICJ:

'... it is clear that the nationalisation of the property of foreigners, even if not unlawful on any other ground, becomes an unlawful confiscation unless provision is made for compensation which is adequate, prompt and effective ... By "adequate" compensation is meant "the value of the undertaking at the moment of dispossession, plus interest to the day of judgment" ... There have, in fact, been pronouncements that prompt compensation means immediate payment in cash. Thus in the arbitration between the United States and Norway relating to the requisitioning of contracts for the building of ships in the United States, it was held: The Tribunal is of opinion that full compensation should have been paid ... at the latest on the day of the effective taking ... The Government of the United Kingdom is, however, prepared to admit that deferred payments may be interpreted as satisfying the requirement of payment in accordance with the rules of international law if: (a) the total amount to be paid is fixed promptly; (b) allowance for interest for late payment is made; (c) the guarantees that the future payments will in fact be made are satisfactory, so that the person to be compensated may, if he so desires, raise the full sum at once on the security of the future payments ... The third requirement is summed up in the word "effective" and means that the recipient of the compensation must be able to make use of it. He must, for instance, be able, if he wishes, to use it to set up a new enterprise to replace the one that has been expropriated or to use it for such other purposes as he wishes .. The compensation ... must be freely transferrable from the country paying it and, so far as that country's restrictions are concerned, convertible into other currencies.'

Similarly, GAR 1803 (1962) on the Permanent Sovereignty over Natural Resources, indicates a requirement to pay 'appropriate compensation ... in accordance with international law'. While the definition of what was meant by 'appropriate' was left unstated, it was generally accepted that the resolution firmly established an international standard of compensation. The international standard argument has been put in numerous cases since that resolution (eg *Texaco, BP, Aminoil*).

There are nevertheless exceptions to the compensation rule in the case of:

1. treaty provisions;
2. confiscation as a penalty for crimes;
3. legitimate exercise of police power;
4. measures of defence;
5. seizure by way of taxation;
6. destruction of property of neutrals arising from military operations;
7. taking of enemy property as reparations.

In opposition, developing States have argued in favour of a standard of compensation set by the municipal law of the State concerned. They point in particular to GAR 3281 (1974) – The Charter of Economic Rights and Duties of States – which provides, in para 2(c), that 'where the question of compensation gives rise to a controversy, it shall be settled under the *domestic* law of the nationalising State'.

In terms of this debate, the weight of opinion would appear to rest with an international standard of compensation. The arbitrator in the *Texaco* case, following an assessment of the two GA resolutions, came to the conclusion that GAR 1803 reflected customary law while GAR 3281 did not. This conclusion notwithstanding, the debate on the international v domestic standard of compensation, has lost much of its vigour for two main reasons:

1. in an attempt to encourage foreign investment in order to stimulate economic growth, a large number of developing States have been willing to conclude bi-lateral investment agreements, clauses that subject the agreement to international law and that provide for the submission of any dispute to international settlement;
2. the growth in the number of cases involving questions of compensation before international tribunals is leading to the development of specialised rules on the payment of compensation.

Much in the same way as international human rights instruments are establishing a common body of rules and standards applicable to the treatment of aliens, so it is likely that the jurisprudence of international tribunals will give rise to specialised rules and agreed standards of compensation.

The General Assembly Resolution on Permanent Sovereignty Over Natural Resources 1962 (GAR 1803)

Widespread nationalisation following the Second World War and the emergence of the new post-colonial States in Africa and Asia has led to a dramatic shift in international opinion regarding the expropriation of foreign property. This Resolution of the General Assembly illustrates the emerging attitudes of the developing States by emphasising that foreign ownership of the means of production should not deprive a State of its sovereignty or its ability to control and plan its economy.

The General Assembly declares that:

'1. The right of peoples and nations to permanent sovereignty over their natural wealth and resources must be exercised in the interest of their national development and of the well-being of the people of the State concerned;

2. The exploration, development and disposition of such resources, as well as the import of the foreign capital required for these purposes, should be in conformity with the rules and conditions which the peoples and nations freely consider to be necessary or desirable with regard to the authorisation, restriction or prohibition of such activities;

3. In cases where authorisation is granted, the capital imported and the earnings on that capital shall be governed by the terms thereof, by the national legislation in force, and by international law. The profits derived must be shared in the proportions freely agreed upon, in each case, between the investors and the recipient State, due care being taken to ensure that there is no impairment, for any reason, of that States sovereignty over its natural wealth and resources;

4. *Nationalisation, expropriation or requisitioning shall be based on grounds or reasons of public utility, security or the national interest which are recognised as overriding purely individual or private interests, both domestic and foreign. In such cases the owner shall be paid appropriate compensation in accordance with the rules in force in the State taking such measures in the exercise of its sovereignty and in accordance with international law. In any case where the question of compensation gives rise to a controversy, the national jurisdiction of the State taking such measures shall be exhausted. However, upon agreement by Sovereign States and other parties concerned, settlement of the dispute should be made through arbitration or international adjudication;*

5. The free and beneficial exercise of the sovereignty of peoples and nations over their natural resources must be furthered by the mutual respect of States based on their Sovereign equality;

6. International co-operation for the economic development of developing countries, whether in the form of public or private capital investments, exchange of goods and services, technical assistance, or exchange of scientific information shall be such as to further their independent national development and shall be based upon respect for their sovereignty over their natural wealth and resources;

7. Violation of the rights of peoples and nations to sovereignty over their natural wealth and resources is contrary to the spirit and principles of the Charter of the United Nations and hinders the development of international co-operation and the maintenance of peace;

8. Foreign investment agreements freely entered into by, or between Sovereign States shall be observed in good faith; States and international organisations shall strictly and conscientiously respect the sovereignty of peoples and nations over their natural wealth and resources in accordance with the Charter and the principles set forth in the present resolution.'

As suggested above, paragraph 4 of the Resolution would seem to reflect the Western States' position regarding expropriation.

The Charter of Economic Rights and Duties of States 1974 (GAR 3281)

This Charter, adopted by a Resolution of the General Assembly of the United Nations, reflects the viewpoint of the developing States on the matter of expropriation of foreign property. The Charter illustrates the great strength of support for the developing States' viewpoint now present within the United Nations. Article 2 of the Charter provides:

> '1. Every State has and shall freely exercise full permanent sovereignty, including possession, use and disposal, over all its wealth, natural resources and economic activities.
> 2. Each State has the right:
> (a) To regulate and exercise authority over foreign investment within its national jurisdiction in accordance with its laws and regulations and in conformity with its national objectives and priorities. No State shall be compelled to grant preferential treatment to foreign investment;
> (b) To regulate and supervise the activities of transnational corporations within its national jurisdiction and take measures to ensure that such activities comply with its laws, rules and regulations and conform with its economic and social policies. Transnational corporations shall not intervene in the internal affairs of a host State. Every State should, with full regard for its Sovereign rights, co-operate with other States in the exercise of the right set forth in this sub-paragraph;
> (c) *To nationalise, expropriate or transfer ownership of foreign property in which case appropriate compensation should be paid by the State adopting such measures, taking into account its relevant laws and regulations and all circumstances that the State considers pertinent. In any case where the question of compensation gives rise to a controversy, it shall be settled under the domestic law of the nationalising State and by its tribunals, unless it is freely and mutually agreed by all States concerned that other peaceful means be sought on the basis of the Sovereign equality of States and in accordance with the principle of free choice of means.'*

The resolutions and customary international law

As will be evident, the two resolutions differ in a number of important respects. While both accept that there is a right to nationalise, GAR 1803 specifies the requirement of *public utility* whereas GAR 3281 does not. Both acknowledge the requirement for compensation to be paid. GAR 1803, however, specifies that this should accord with international law while GAR 3281 establishes a domestic standard of compensation.

The status of these resolutions was reviewed by arbitrator Dupuy in *Texaco* (1977). In contrast to GAR 1803, which had the support of both developed and developing states, GAR 3281 had little or no support from industrialised nations (ie the investors).

The Charter was adopted by 120 votes to six, with ten abstentions. The States voting against were Belgium, Denmark, the Federal Republic of Germany, the UK and the USA. The abstaining States were Austria, Canada, France, Ireland, Israel, Italy, Japan, the Netherlands, Norway and Spain. The nature of this opposition to the Charter was regarded by Dupuy as being of sufficient size and significance to deny it the status of customary international law.

Disguised expropriation

This may involve placing a company under 'temporary' government control which is then maintained indefinitely, or by more subtle processes of discrimination against foreign companies. These may take the form of controls on prices or profits, promoting nationally owned competition or creating delays in the granting of licenses, supplying equipment, manpower etc. This question was considered by the Iran-US Claims Tribunal in *Starrett Housing* (1984). The Tribunal concluded that any significant interference with property rights, such that these rights were rendered useless, would amount to an expropriation even though there was no actual change in ownership or legal title. Thus, the appointment by Iran of a temporary manager, with a right to control and use the assets of the housing project, amounted to a taking. The question was raised again in the *ELSI Case* (ICJ, 1989). The USA argued that the taking of property would include not only an outright expropriation but also any unreasonable interference with the use, enjoyment or disposal of that property. While the court did not rule directly on this point, it implied that any act that amounted to a significant deprivation of interest would satisfy the requirement of a taking.

[handwritten margin notes: such interference which rendered rights useless = expropriation; sig. deprivat of interest = taking]

National monopolies *— are legal*

Legislation may be enacted by the State establishing a national monopoly in certain areas of the economy by restricting or excluding foreign competition.

For instance, in 1973 Mexico introduced legislation under which certain areas – petroleum and hydrocarbons, exploitation of radioactive minerals and nuclear energy, certain mining activities, electricity, railways, telegraphic and wireless communications – were 'reserved exclusively for the State'.

Other activities – radio and television, gas distribution, forestry, transport – were reserved exclusively to Mexican nationals and companies.

Limited foreign participation was to be allowed in certain other areas – secondary petrochemicals, exploitation and use of minerals.

Investment protection

Many developing countries in order to attract new investment have passed laws, or in some cases inserted provisions into their Constitutions, guaranteeing foreign investments against expropriation or providing for payment of compensation in the event of expropriation.

Some developing States have also entered into treaties with developed countries with respect to foreign investment guarantees and payment of compensation in the event of expropriation.

Other Western States, including the USA and the UK, encourage their nationals to invest in developing countries by insuring their nationals against the risk involved in such investment, in return for a small premium.

The available methods of settling investment disputes have been supplemented by the Convention on the Settlement of Investment Disputes Between States and Nationals of Other States 1965. This established an International Centre for the Settlement of Investment Disputes, under the auspices of the International Bank for Reconstruction and Development.

The Centre was established to settle investment disputes by conciliation and arbitration and has jurisdiction over:

> '... any legal dispute arising directly out of an investment, between a Contracting State ... and a national of another Contracting State, which the parties to the dispute consent in writing to submit to the Centre'.

Around 100 States are now party to the Convention, including the USA, the UK, the majority of Western States and most Afro-Asian States.

The Calvo clause

It has long been the practice of many Latin American governments to insert a 'Calvo clause' when making concession contracts with aliens, under which the alien agrees not to seek the diplomatic protection of his own State and submits any matters arising from the contract to the local jurisdiction.

Many governments deny the validity of such clauses on the principle that a clause in a private law contract cannot deprive a State of the right of diplomatic protection, or deny an international tribunal jurisdiction.

For example, in the *North American Dredging Company Case* (1926), one of the terms of the contract between the American company and the Mexican Authorities provided:

> 'The contractor and all persons who, as employees or in any other capacity, may be engaged in the execution of the work under this contract either directly or indirectly, shall be considered as Mexicans in all matters, within the Republic of Mexico, concerning the execution of such work and the fulfilment of this contract. They shall not claim, nor shall they have, with regard to the interests and the business connected with this contract, any other rights or means to enforce the same than those granted by the laws of the Republic to Mexicans, nor shall they enjoy any other rights than those established in favour of Mexicans. They are consequently deprived of any rights as aliens, and under no conditions shall the intervention of foreign diplomatic agents be permitted, in any matter related to this contract.'

The Mexican/US General Claims Commission held that by agreeing to such a clause, an individual could not:

> '... deprive the Government of his nation of its undoubted right of applying international remedies to violations of international law committed to his damage. Such Government frequently has a larger interest in maintaining the principles of international law than in recovering damage for one of its citizens in a particular case, and manifestly such citizens cannot by contract tie in this respect the hands of his Government.'

Generally, a breach of a private law contract will not be an international wrong unless there is a denial of justice in the course of exhausting local remedies. In practice, therefore, the effect of the Calvo clause in arbitration has, in the absence of a denial of justice, been to prevent contractual disputes becoming inter-State proceedings.

11.7 Breaches and annulment of State contracts

The general view is that in the absence of a denial of justice, a breach of contract does not create State responsibility on the international plane. Most contracts between States and aliens are governed by municipal law (usually the municipal law of the contracting State). However, in some circumstances it is possible for contractual obligations to create State responsibility over and above that arising from a denial of justice.

Breaches of contractual obligations having an international character

The following factors may give a contract an international character thereby creating State responsibility on the international plane:

Legislative interference
The contracting government may legislate in such a way as to make the contract worthless. For example, it may impose export or currency restrictions, or it may legislate to annul the contract or otherwise alter its existing contractual obligations. By so acting it can be argued that the State is taking the matter out of the field of private law and is creating an issue of international character.

In the *Norwegian Loans Case: France v Norway* (1957) French nationals had purchased bonds issued by two Norwegian banks on behalf of the Norwegian State. The bonds were redeemable by the payment of their gold value. The Norwegian Government introduced legislation prohibiting the convertibility of Norwegian currency into gold and suspending all payments in gold.

Although the Court, after upholding a preliminary objection raised by Norway, did not decide upon the merits of the dispute, individual judges did comment upon Norway's international responsibility under the bond agreements.

Judge Read was of the opinion that when the bondholders purchased the Norwegian bonds the transaction was solely within the jurisdiction of the municipal law. However, the passing of the Norwegian legislation and the suspension of payments in gold raised the question 'whether Norway could, in conformity with the principles of international law by legislative action unilaterally modify the substance of the contracts'. In the opinion of Judge Read the action of the Norwegian Government, which breached the contracts, automatically 'internationalised' the dispute and became *prima facie* a breach of international law.

Where the contract is internationalised

Most contracts between States and aliens are governed by the municipal law of the debtor State. However, it is possible for a State to enter into a contract which is either expressly or by implication subject to some foreign system of law.

In *R* v *International Trustee for Protection of Bondholders Aktiengesellschaft* (1937) the House of Lords held that while the fact that a State is a party to a contract is a factor of general significance in determining the applicable law, nevertheless it is not of itself conclusive. It may still be possible to infer from the circumstances as a whole that the contract is governed by some other legal system.

In *Texaco* (1977) arbitrator Dupuy set out three ways in which a contract could be internationalised:

1. if there was an express choice of law clause subjecting the contract to general principles of law (or international law);
2. if there was a clause providing that in the event of a dispute the matter was to be submitted to international arbitration;
3. if the agreement was in the nature of an 'international development agreement', that is, agreements which continue over long period of time and involve investment in the developing country in question.

A contract may also become internationalised if it contains a 'stabilisation' clause, ie a clause purporting to restrict the right of the state to unilaterally vary the terms of the contract. This will invariably also include a clause subjecting the contract to international or general principles of law.

Contracts of a quasi-public nature

It has been argued that contracts of a quasi-public nature entered into between a State and a foreign individual are governed not by municipal law but by general principles of international law. In this respect the contract is internationalised. This internationalisation may be by express choice of the parties or may be inferred by the Court from the circumstances of the case.

This proposition that contracts between States and non-international persons can, either expressly or by implication, be subject to international law has been supported in several commercial arbitrations involving concessions granted to oil companies, eg the *Abu Dhabi Arbitration* (1951)

This case concerned a dispute over the interpretation of the terms of an oil concession contract granted by the Sheikh of Abu Dhabi in 1939. The sole arbitrator had to decide firstly upon the law governing the contract.

The contract was made in Abu Dhabi and was wholly to be performed in that country. If any municipal system of law were applicable therefore it would *prima facie* be that of Abu Dhabi. But as the Arbitrator pointed out:

> '... no such law can reasonably be said to exist. The Sheikh administers a purely discretionary justice with the assistance of the Koran; and it would be fanciful to suggest that in this very primitive region there is any settled body of legal principles applicable to the construction of modern commercial instruments.'

Nor could the Arbitrator see any basis on which the municipal law of England could apply:

> 'On the contrary (the substance) of the agreement ... repels the notion that the municipal law of any country, as such, could be appropriate. The terms ... invite, indeed prescribe, the principles rooted in the good sense and common practice of the generality of civilised nations – a sort of "modern law of nations".'

The 'modern law of nations'

Two theories have been advanced in order to identify this 'modern law of nations'.

This is a new system of international commercial law based upon general principles of law derived from municipal systems
The system provides a choice of law that can be used to reconcile the interests of the State on the one hand and the foreign individual on the other. Breach of the contract by the State concerned is not a breach of international law giving rise to a claim on the international plane but simply a breach according to the law of the contract. Therefore, because the system of law is not international law in its true sense there is no conflict with the principle that international law only governs relations between entities having international personality.

If one of the parties to the contract is endowed with international personality then it is possible for that contract to be governed by public international law
In theory, therefore, a breach of such a contract governed by 'international law' would amount to a breach of an international obligation.

In the *Lena Goldfields Arbitration* (1929–30) the tribunal had to consider the law governing a concession granted by the Soviet Union to a British company. Under the concession agreement, it was provided that the parties should base their relations:

> '... on the principle of good will and good faith as well as on reasonable interpretation of the terms of the Agreement'.

The majority of the tribunal accepted the argument of the complainant company that in regard to performance of the contract inside the Soviet Union, Russian law was applicable but that for other purposes:

> '... the general principles of law such as those recognised by Article 38 of the Statute of the Permanent Court of International Justice ... should be regarded as "the proper law of the contract".'

Does a reference to 'general principles of law' in such a contract mean 'international law'? With regard to these contracts, McNair stated:

> 'If then, as is submitted, one can reasonably infer that the parties do not regard the national law of either of them as affording an adequate or appropriate legal system within which these contracts can operate, and if we may also assume that they contain an international

element, what legal system can be regarded as appropriate to govern them? What is the legal system which best satisfies the intention of the parties? One can truly infer from these contracts – both from what they do say and from what they do not say – the parties are groping after some legal system which is not the territorial law of either party.

The answer to these questions is not that these contracts are governed by public international law *stricto sensu*, for this system is an inter-State system – *jus inter gentes*. It is true that a corporation operating in a foreign country can be said to be under the protection of public international law because it can invoke the diplomatic protection of its own Government if it should meet with wrongful treatment at the hands of the Government of the country in which it is operating; but that is not the same thing as saying that the contract is governed by public international law. My submission is that in contracts of this type the parties, if they specify no particular legal system, intend that their contracts should be governed by the general principles of law recognised by civilised nations.'

In the *Aramco Arbitration (1958)*, under the arbitration agreement between Saudi-Arabia and the Arabian American Oil Company (Aramco), the Tribunal was required to decide disputes over the concession agreement in accordance with Saudi Arabian law in so far as matters within the jurisdiction of Saudi Arabia were concerned, and in accordance with the law deemed by the tribunal to be applicable in so far as matters beyond the jurisdiction of Saudi Arabia were concerned.

The Tribunal stated that as the concession was not an agreement between two States but between a State and a private American Corporation, it could not be governed by public international law. The tribunal found that the concession agreement itself constituted 'the fundamental law' of the parties and in so far as doubts might remain as to the content or meaning of the agreement, it was:

'... necessary to resort to the general principles of law and to apply them in order to interpret, and even to supplement, the respective rights and obligations of the parties'.

The *Aramco Arbitration*, therefore, strongly supports the view that contracts of a concessionary type not governed by the municipal law of the grantor State are subject to general principles of law and not international law.

Breach of a commercial contract is not *ipso facto* a breach of international law

If the principle is accepted that the proper law in such cases is not public international law, a breach of a commercial contract subject to general principles of law is not *ipso facto* a breach of international law. Such a case would only assume an international character if: (1) a State that is a party to an 'international contract' refuses to go to arbitration as required by the contract; or (2) refuses to abide by the Tribunal's ruling.

Internationalisation of a contract by a collateral understanding or treaty arrangement between States

In some cases a treaty specifically lays down that a particular contract between one of the States party to the treaty and nationals of the other State which is a party to the treaty shall be performed, or that rights under the contract shall be recognised. In such cases a breach of the contract by the State concerned is, therefore, a breach of an international obligation owed to the other State.

Many of the capital-exporting States have entered into such bilateral agreements to promote and protect investments by their nationals in a number of the developing States.

Breach of contract and expropriation

Some writers contend that if a State exercises its executive or legislative authority to destroy contractual rights then the act comes within the ambit of expropriation and will lead to State responsibility on that basis.

11.8 The admissibility of State claims

treatm^t of aliens

A case involving the treatment of aliens brought before an international tribunal may be lost on a preliminary objection by the defendant State, which, if successful, will stop all proceedings in the case.

The principal factors giving rise to a preliminary objection are:

1. Non-compliance with the rules regarding nationality of claims.
2. Failure to exhaust local remedies.
3. Unreasonable delay in bringing the claim.
4. Waiver of the claim.
5. Improper behaviour by the injured alien.

Nationality of claims

The general rule on the nationality of claims is that a State may only assert an international claim on behalf of one of its nationals. Rule I of the UK Rules Applying to International Claims provides that 'HMG will not take up the claim unless the claimant is a UK national and was so at the date of the injury.'

The rule was stated by Oppenheim as follows:

'... from the time of the occurrence of the injury until the making of the award the claim must continuously and without interruption have belonged to a person or to a series of persons: (a) having the nationality of the State by whom it is put forward, and (b) not having the nationality of the State against whom it is put forward.'

The requirement of continuity, evident in the rule, has been criticised on two *Continuity* main grounds: (1) it allows incidental matters, eg a change of nationality by operation of law, to defeat a valid claim. (2) If an injury to the individual is an injury to the State of origin, then the wrong matures at the time of the injury and should not be affected by any subsequent change in the status of the individual.

In many cases, the question of the nationality of the injured party will be complicated by additional factors. Two situations are of particular importance:

1. where the injured persons is a national of more than one State;
2. where the injured person has a stronger link with the respondent State than with the national State seeking to exercise diplomatic protection.

Protection in cases of dual nationality

Position where the individual is also a national of the respondent State – the test applicable in such cases is that of 'dominant nationality'.

In the *Canevaro Case: Italy v Peru* (1912) the Arbitral Tribunal was asked to decide whether Italy could claim on behalf of Raphael Canevaro who had both Italian and Peruvian nationality.

The Tribunal held that:

'Whereas, as a matter of fact, Raphael Canevaro has on several occasions acted as a Peruvian citizen, both by running as a candidate for the Senate where none are admitted except Peruvian citizens and where he went to defend his election, and also especially by accepting the office of Consul General of the Netherlands, after soliciting the authorisation of the Peruvian Government and then of the Peruvian Congress ... under these circumstances, whatever Raphael Canevaro's status may be in Italy with respect to his nationality, the Government of Peru has a right to consider him as a Peruvian citizen and to deny his status as an Italian claimant.'

This principle denying admissibility in the case of dual nationals found support in Article 4 of the Hague Convention on the Conflict of Nationality Laws of 1930. Rule III of the UK Rules on International Claims further provides that 'HMG will not normally take up [the] claim [of] a UK national if the respondent State is the State of his second nationality'.

These examples of State practice notwithstanding, a number of cases have sought to modify the rule against dual nationality. In the *Merge Claim* (1955), for example, the USA brought a claim under the 1947 Italian Peace Treaty. The claimant was, however, of both US and Italian nationality and the Treaty which permitted claims on behalf of 'United Nations nationals' contained no provisions governing the case of dual nationality. The Commission decided that the question whether the USA could bring the claim against Italy must be decided according to 'the general principles of international law' and agreed that these included the principle of the *dominant and effective* nationality. The Commission gave the following examples of dominant US nationality:

'i) Children born in the United States of an Italian father when the children have habitually lived there;

ii) Italians who, having acquired United States nationality by naturalisation and having thus lost their Italian nationality, later re-acquire it by Italian law by staying in Italy for more than two years though without the intention of residing there permanently;

iii) American women married to Italian nationals where the family has had habitual residence in the United States and the interests and the permanent professional life of the head of the family were established in the United States;

iv) A widow who at the termination of her marriage transfers her residence from Italy to the United States when her conduct, especially with regard to the raising of her children shows her new residence to be of a habitual nature.'

The principle of dominant and effective nationality has since been upheld in two important cases before the Iran-US claims Tribunal, namely, *Esphahanian* v *Bank Tejarat* (1983) and *Case A/18* (1984). Despite these recent decisions, however, it is by no means clear that the principle of dominant and effective nationality has become part of customary law.

Position where the individual is the national of a third State as well as of the claimant State – the practice of international tribunals seems to treat an individual's connection with a third State as immaterial.

In the *Salem Case: Egypt* v *United States* (1932) the Tribunal stated that it is the practice of several governments, where two powers are both entitled by international law to treat a person as their national, that neither of these powers can raise a claim against the other in the name of such person. Accordingly Egypt may oppose the American claim if they can bring evidence that Salem was an Egyptian subject and that he acquired American nationality without the express consent of the Egyptian Government.

> 'In the opinion of the Arbitral Court the Egyptian Government is unable to bring such evidence. Indeed from the circumstances it must be assumed that Salem was not an Egyptian subject but a Persian subject when he acquired American nationality ...
>
> It is beside the point to ask whether Salem lost his Persian nationality or not by the acquisition of American nationality. ... Whatever may be the true interpretation, the Egyptian Government cannot set forth against the United States the eventual continuation of the Persian nationality of George Salem; the rule of international law being that in a case of dual nationality a third power is not entitled to contest the claim of one of the two powers whose national is interested in the case by referring to the nationality of the other power.'

In the *Merge Claim* (1955) the Italian-US Conciliation Commission accepted the principle that the respondent State could not raise the second dominant nationality of a third State.

> 'United States nationals who do not possess Italian nationality, but the nationality of a third State can be considered "United Nations nationals" under the Treaty, even if their prevalent nationality was the nationality of the third State.'

Position where an individual has close ties with, but not the nationality of, the respondent State

In the *Nottebohm Case: Liechtenstein* v *Guatemala* (1955) Nottebohm was born in Hamburg and held German nationality by birth. In 1905 he went to Guatemala, took up residence there and made that country the headquarters of his business activities. He had business connections in Germany and sometimes went there on business. He also paid a few visits to a brother who had lived in Liechtenstein since 1931. In 1939 Nottebohm applied for admission as a national of Liechtenstein. His request was granted and his passport was issued, the three years residence requirement being waived. Nottebohm returned to Guatemala and when Guatemala later declared war on Germany he was interned and his property confiscated.

In 1951 the Government of Liechtenstein instituted proceedings before the ICJ in which it claimed restitution and compensation on the ground that the

Government of Guatemala had 'acted towards the person and property of Mr Friedrich Nottebohm, a citizen of Liechtenstein, in a manner contrary to international law'.

The Court held that Liechtenstein was not entitled to exercise diplomatic protection and present a claim to the Court on behalf of Nottebohm against Guatemala because there was no genuine link between Nottebohm and Liechtenstein:

> 'At the time of his naturalisation does Nottebohm appear to have been more closely attached by his tradition, his establishment, his interests, his activities, his family ties, his intentions for the near future to Liechtenstein than to any other State? ...
>
> He had been settled in Guatemala for 34 years. He had carried on his activities there. It was the main seat of his interests. He returned there shortly after his naturalisation, and it remained the centre of his interests and of his business activities. He stayed there until his removal as a result of war measures in 1943. He subsequently attempted to return there, and he now complains of Guatemala's refusal to admit him. There, too, were several members of his family who sought to safeguard his interests.
>
> In contrast, his actual connections with Liechtenstein were extremely tenuous. No settled abode, no prolonged residence in that country at the time of his application for naturalisation: the application indicates that he was paying a visit there and confirms the transient character of this visit by its request that the naturalisation proceedings should be initiated and concluded without delay. No intention of settling there was shown at that time or realised in the ensuing weeks, months or years – on the contrary, he returned to Guatemala very shortly after his naturalisation and showed every intention of remaining there ... There is no allegation of any economic interests or of any activities exercised or to be exercised in Liechtenstein and no manifestation of any intention whatsoever to transfer all or some of his interests and business activities to Liechtenstein ...
>
> These facts clearly establish, on the one hand, the absence of any bond of attachment between Nottebohm and Liechtenstein and, on the other hand, the existence of a long-standing and close connection between him and Guatemala, a link which his naturalisation in no way weakened ...'

It is, however, important to bear in mind that the ICJ decided that Liechtenstein could not bring a claim *against Guatemala*. It did *not* decide that Liechtenstein could not bring a claim against a third state with which Nottebohm had no connection. Thus, for example, a claim by Liechtenstein against, say, Japan may well have been admissible, the link of nationality serving to establish Liechtenstein's interest in exerting diplomatic protection.

Position where the individual while not being a national of a third State nevertheless has a close connection with a third State – if the 'genuine link' theory of the *Nottebohm Case* is now the paramount aspect of diplomatic protection, then a 'genuine link' with a third State might be of greater significance than actual nationality of a third State.

However, it must be remembered that the Nottebohm decision is of limited application. This fact was recognised by the Italian-US Conciliation Commission in the *Flegenheimer Claim* (1958).

In the opinion of the Commission:

> '... it is doubtful that the International Court of Justice intended to establish a rule of general international law in requiring, in the Nottebohm case, that there must exist an

effective link between the person and the State in order that the latter may exercise its right of diplomatic protection on behalf of the former. The Court itself restricted the scope of its Decision by affirming that the acquisition of nationality in a State must be recognised by all other States, ... subject to the twofold reservation that, in the first place, what is involved is not recognition for all purposes but merely for the purposes of the admissibility of the Application, and, secondly, that what is involved is not recognition by all States but only by Guatemala. ... But when a person is vested with only one nationality ... the theory of effective nationality cannot be applied without the risk of causing confusion. It lacks a sufficiently positive basis to be applied to a nationality which finds support in a State law. There does not in fact exist any criterion of proven effectiveness for disclosing the effectiveness of a bond with a political collectively, and the persons by the thousands who, because of the facility of travel in the modern world, possess the positive legal nationality of a State, but live in foreign States where they are domiciled and where their family and business centre is located, would be exposed to non-recognition, at the international level, of the nationality with which they are undeniably vested by virtue of the laws of their national State, if this doctrine were to be generalised.'

So where there exists a 'genuine' single nationality, the connection by residence or otherwise of the individual with another State is irrelevant.

Position where the individual is Stateless – the position of Stateless persons was indicated in the *Dickson Car Wheel Company Case: United States v Mexico* (1931).

'A State ... does not commit an international delinquency in inflicting a injury upon an individual lacking nationality and consequently, no State is empowered to intervene or complain on his behalf either before or after the injury.'

Corporations and their shareholders

Protection of corporations created under the domestic laws of the claimant State

Prima facie a corporation has the nationality of the State under the laws of which it is incorporated and in whose territory it has its registered office. Therefore, incorporation may be relied upon by States when pursuing claims against respondent States who have seized corporation property. However, State practice requires something more than mere registration. If a State is to pursue a claim on behalf of a corporation there must be some degree of national control or beneficial ownership of shares in the company concerned.

British State practice is illustrated by the case of *Enrique Cortes and Company* in 1896. This company was incorporated in England, but its principal members and all its shareholders were Colombian citizens. The company inquired whether, in case of disorder in Colombia, the company could seek the protection of the British Government. The Law Officers after considering the matter reported that in their opinion:

'... the principle ought not to be recognised that foreigners, by registering themselves here as a limited company, are entitled to claim from Her Majesty's Government the protection accorded to British subjects in foreign countries'.

Application of the *Nottebohm* 'genuine connection' principle to corporations – practice suggests that the principle of a real or genuine link advanced by the court in the *Nottebohm Case* does apply to corporations. However, this has not been accepted by the ICJ.

In *Barcelona Traction, Light and Power Co Case: Belgium v Spain* (1970) the claim was presented by Belgium on behalf of its nationals who were shareholders in the company incorporated and having its registered office in Canada. The ICJ treated the question whether the company was entitled to Canadian diplomatic protection as being of only indirect relevance. Nevertheless, the Court explained its view that Canada was the national State in the following terms:

'In allocating corporate entities to States for purposes of diplomatic protection; international law is based, but only to a limited extent, on an analogy with the rules governing the nationality of individuals. The traditional rule attributes the right of diplomatic protection of a corporate entity to the State under the laws of which it is incorporated and in whose territory it has its registered office. These two criteria have been confirmed by long practice and by numerous international instruments. This notwithstanding, further or different links are at times said to be required in order that a right of diplomatic protection should exist. Indeed it has been the practice of some States to give a company incorporated under their law diplomatic protection solely when it has its seat or management or centre of control in their territory, or when a majority or a substantial proportion of the shares has been owned by nationals of the State concerned. Only then, it has been held, does there exist between the corporation and the State in question a genuine connection of the kind familiar from other branches of international law. However, in the particular field of the diplomatic protection of corporate entities, no absolute test of the "genuine connection" has found general acceptance. Such tests as have been applied are of a relative nature, and sometimes links with one State have had to be weighed against those with another. In this connection reference has been made to the Nottebohm Case. In fact the Parties made frequent reference to it in the course of the proceedings. However, given both the legal and factual aspects of protection in the present case the Court is of the opinion that there can be no analogy with the issues raised or the decision given in that case.

In the present case, it is not disputed that the company was incorporated in Canada and has its registered office in that country. The incorporation of the company under the law of Canada was an act of free choice. Not only did the founders of the company seek its incorporation under Canadian law but it has remained under that law for a period of over 50 years. It has maintained in Canada its registered office, its accounts and its share registers. Board meetings were held there for many years; it has been listed in the records of the Canadian tax authorities. Thus a close and permanent connection has been established, fortified by the passage of over half a century. This connection is in no way weakened by the fact that the company engaged from the very outset in commercial activities outside Canada, for that was its declared object. Barcelona Tractions links with Canada are thus manifold.'

Thus, the Court rejects the analogy of the *Nottebohm Case* and the 'genuine connection' principle. However, the Court's conclusion on this point may not be regarded as authoritative.

1. Neither Belgium nor Spain contested the Canadian character of the Barcelona Traction Company so the reference to 'genuine connection' was not at issue.

2. The Court does in fact set out the 'manifold' links of the company with Canada.

3. Many jurists do favour the application of the Nottebohm principle to the diplomatic protection of limited companies.

The decision in the *Barcelona Traction Case* does, however, preserve the principle that a claim can only have one 'nationality', and thus helps to limit the number of international claims and helps restrict the powers of the large multinational corporations.

The protection of shareholders – generally, a State cannot intervene on behalf of a foreign corporation solely on the basis that some of its nationals are shareholders in the company. The shareholders must rely upon the diplomatic protection available to the corporation itself.

The principles governing the admissibility of claims on behalf of shareholders were clarified by the ICJ in the *Barcelona Traction Case (1970).*

The company was established under Canadian law in 1911 in connection with the development of electricity supplies in Spain. In 1948 it was declared bankrupt by a Spanish court. Canada intervened on behalf of the company but later withdrew. At the time 88 per cent of the shares in the company were allegedly owned by Belgian nationals and Belgium brought this claim in respect of the injury to its nationals who were shareholders, resulting from the injury to the company.

Spain objected that since the injury was to the company, not the shareholders, Belgium lacked *locus standi* to bring the claim.

The Court ruled in favour of the respondent State, Spain, upon the ground that Belgium had no *locus standi* to espouse before the Court claims of alleged Belgian nationals who were shareholders in the company, inasmuch as the company was incorporated in Canada and was, in an international legal sense, of Canadian nationality. The reasoning relied upon by the Court may be expressed as follows:

1. International law must recognise the general principle of municipal legal systems which provides that an infringement of the rights of a company by outsiders did not involve liability towards the shareholders, even if their interests were detrimentally affected by the infringement. The Court will not look behind the corporate veil.

2. It is a general rule of international law that it is the national State of the company concerned which is entitled to exercise diplomatic protection and seek redress for an international wrong done to the company.

3. *A different principle might apply if the wrong were aimed at the direct rights of the shareholders as such*, eg their right to attend and vote at general meetings. However, the present case was not concerned with the infringement of the shareholders' direct rights but with the alleged illegal measures taken by Spain against the company.

4. The exclusive entitlement of the national State of the company to exercise diplomatic protection might conceivably, in certain cases, give way to the right of the national State of the shareholders, eg *where (1) the company itself had ceased to exist; or (2) the protecting national State of the company lacked capacity to exercise diplomatic protection.*

But in the present case, the company had not ceased to exist as a corporate entity in Canada, nor was the Canadian Government incapable of exercising diplomatic protection – it merely chose not to do so.

The Court rejected the argument that for reasons of equity a State should be entitled in certain cases to take up the protection of its nationals who were shareholders in a company, the victim of a breach of international law. The court was afraid that any such alleged equitable justification would open the door to competing claims on the part of different States thereby creating an atmosphere of confusion and insecurity in international economic relations.

The ICJ therefore is reluctant to 'pierce the corporate veil' in order to allow a State, other than the national State of the company, to seek redress for an international wrong done to the company.

In summary, therefore, the Court provided that, as a general rule, the genuine link principle does not apply to companies. However, in three cases the national State of the shareholders will be entitled to assert a claim for diplomatic protection. These three exceptions have been incorporated into the UK Rules on International Claims. Thus, a State may claim on behalf of its nationals as shareholders if:

1. the wrong alleged was directed against the shareholders by reason of their nationality (Rule III, UK Rules);
2. the company has ceased to exist (Rule V, UK Rules);
3. the national State of the company lacked the capacity to bring an international claim (Rule VI, UK Rules).

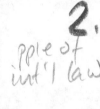

Nottebohm ≠ apply to Co's.

Exhaustion of local remedies

pple of int'l law

It is an established principle of international law that a claim brought by a State on behalf of its national will not be admissible before an international tribunal unless the foreign national has exhausted all the legal remedies available to him under the local courts of the defendant State.

For example, Rule VII of the UK Rules on International Claims provides that:

'Her Majesty's Government will not normally take over and formally espouse a claim of a United Kingdom national against another State until all the legal remedies, if any, available to him in the State concerned have been exhausted.'

Comment: failure to exhaust any local remedies will not constitute a bar to a claim if it is clearly established that in the circumstances of the case an appeal to a higher municipal tribunal would have had no effect. Nor is a claimant against another State required to exhaust justice in that State if there is no justice to exhaust.

Justification for the rule

1. National courts are a more suitable and convenient forum for hearing the claims of individuals and corporations.
2. By residing and operating within the foreign State the individual or corporation has associated himself with the local jurisdiction.

3. It avoids the multiplication of small claims on the level of diplomatic protection.
4. The local courts are in a better position to adduce the facts of the case and assess the damage caused.
5. The foreign State should be given the opportunity of righting any wrong it has committed and to force its immediate submission to international adjudication would be an interference with its sovereignty.

Situations where the rule does not apply

Where there is direct injury to the complainant State itself. The rule applies with regard to claims by a State on behalf of its national. It does not apply to claims by a State in respect of direct injuries to itself. For example, if the State's embassy is damaged there is no obligation upon that State to seek redress in the municipal courts of the foreign State concerned.

In the *Aerial Incident Case (1955)* an Israeli airliner which had strayed into Bulgarian airspace was shot down by Bulgarian fighter aircraft. Bulgaria argued *inter alia* that the ICJ had no power to hear the action because Israel had failed to exhaust local remedies. Israel contended that as the incident had been a direct inter-State wrong, the local remedies rule was inapplicable. The Israeli agent before the ICJ said he could:

'... recall no precedent in which a Government complaining of actions performed by another Government *jure imperii* has been referred to the Courts of the respondent State as a preliminary condition to the obtaining of international satisfaction'.

Where there is no connection between the injured alien and the respondent State. The general principle is that by entering the territory of a foreign State, an individual is presumed to subject himself to the jurisdiction of the local courts. However, it can be argued that where the connection between the injured national and the respondent State is involuntary or purely fortuitous then the local remedies rule should not be applied.

In the *Aerial Incident Case*, for example, Israel argued *inter alia* that there was no link between the victims and the Bulgarian State. Therefore, even assuming the claim could be regarded as being made on behalf of Israeli nationals, there was no need to exhaust local remedies because the connection with Bulgaria was only caused by the illegal act of the Bulgarian Authorities in bringing down the plane.

Where the State concerned has already committed a breach of international law. If there has been no breach of international law, but only a breach of local law, then no responsibility arises on the international plane in respect of the breach, unless the individual concerned is denied justice in the local courts.

If the individual is denied justice in the local courts it would seem absurd to require him to seek redress in those same courts. In such a case there may be no justice to exhaust and therefore the rule should not apply.

d) Where there is no breach of local law. Where there is a breach of international law which does not involve any breach of local law then the rule is inapplicable.

3. Function of the rule

The function of the rule is to give the respondent State the opportunity, before being subjected to international adjudication, of doing justice in its own way and of having an investigation and adjudication of the issues of law and fact. International relations thus stand to benefit since it prevents a vast number of trivial disputes souring relations between States and the international tribunals from being inundated with cases.

4. The scope of 'local remedies'

There would seem to be no requirement for the 'local remedies' to be restricted to those remedies of a judicial nature available only through the local courts. The International Law Commission in its 1961 draft Convention proposed a definition which would include all administrative or judicial remedies or proceedings available under the local law. Thus if a State has an established procedure for remedying the particular injury, the individual suffering such injury must avail himself of that procedure even if it is of a non-judicial form.

In the *Barcelona Traction Case (1970)* Judge Bustamente, President of the Court, made reference to Barcelona Traction's failure to appeal against the Spanish Institute of Foreign Exchange's refusal to sanction proposals to deal with the company's overseas bonds payments. He pointed out that in accordance with well established principles, a complaint should have been made to the Minister of Commerce, for:

> '... only a higher authority is able to discern whether a subordinate official has exceeded the limits of a reasonable discretion and ventured into the unlawful domain of arbitrariness or unjust discrimination'.

Thus, it would appear that provided the administrative remedy is based upon some established procedure, then it will constitute a local remedy for the purposes of the exhaustion rule.

The rule does not apply to extra-legal remedies or remedies as of grace. For example, the right to petition the Queen under the Royal Prerogative is an act of grace and not a local remedy which must be exhausted under the rule.

5. Only effective remedies need be exhausted

Although the local remedies rule is generally strictly applied, it does not mean that it is necessary for the individual to exhaust remedies which, though available in theory, would nevertheless be ineffective or insufficient to redress the injury of which he complains.

For example, there are no local remedies to exhaust where:

1. the local courts are bound by statute or precedent which compels them to reject the claim;
2. the local courts are notoriously corrupt or known to discriminate against foreigners;

3. the wrong has been committed by the legislative itself or by some high official and the local courts refuse to challenge their authority;

4. having lost his claim in the lower court, appeal would be futile because the point at issue is one of fact and the court of appeal may deal only with points of law.

If the conditions within the State are such that the processes available for pursuing local remedies are corrupt or insufficient and unreliable, a foreign national may be excused recourse to such processes.

If corrupt etc may be excused.

In the *Robert E Brown Case: United States v Great Britain* (1923) Brown, an American citizen, had applied for licences to prospect for gold in South Africa. Under the law of South Africa he was entitled to have the licences granted, but the law was suspended by the Executive Council. He commenced proceedings before the South African courts alleging that this suspension of the law was *ultra vires*, and obtained judgment that the act of the Executive Council was unconstitutional. The court held that his licence had been wrongfully refused and granted him leave to claim damages.

Before this claim could be heard the Chief Justice was dismissed and a law was introduced directing that the judiciary were to apply resolutions to the Volksraad (lower chamber of Parliament) without referring to their validity under the Constitution). The new court refused Brown leave to claim damages by way of motion and held that any claim for such damages must involve a retrial of the case.

← Commons changed the law before his case was dismissed

The Great Britain/US Arbitral Tribunal rejected a claim of non-exhaustion of local remedies on the ground that under the prevailing circumstances a retrial of the case would be futile. The Tribunal referred to 'the frequently quoted language of an American Secretary of State: "A claimant in a foreign State is not required to exhaust justice in such State when there is no justice to exhaust".' The Tribunal commented that in *Brown's Case*:

> 'All three branches of the Government (of the South African Republic) conspired to ruin his (Brown's) enterprise ... The judiciary, at first recalcitrant, was at length reduced to submission and brought into line with a determined policy of the Executive ...'

Where the laws of the respondent State are the basis of the breach of duty – in some cases the injured national may be deprived of any remedy before the local courts as a result of legislation enacted by the offending State. In such cases, if the local courts are bound by that legislation, there can be no local remedies to exhaust.

In the *Norwegian Loans Case: France v Norway* (1957) the French Government claimed that a number of international loans issued by Norwegian banks on behalf of the Norwegian State were redeemable by the payment of their gold value and not their original face value. The Norwegian Government objected to the Court's jurisdiction *inter alia* on the ground that the bondholders had failed to exhaust local remedies. However, by Norwegian legislation convertibility of Norwegian currency into gold was prohibited. France, therefore, argued that recourse to the Norwegian courts by the bondholders would have been pointless.

Although in the event the Court was not called upon to consider the matter of non-exhaustion of local remedies, Judge Lauterpacht and Judge Read did deal with the issue in their separate opinions.

Lauterpacht's view was that there may have been a remedy under Norwegian law notwithstanding the legislation: *(ie may regard PIL as part of national law)*

'There has been a tendency in the practice of courts of many States to regard international law, in some way, as forming part of national law or as entering legitimately into the national conception of ordre public. Although the Norwegian Government has admitted that in no case can a Norwegian Court overrule Norwegian legislation on the ground that it is contrary to international law, it has asserted that it is possible that a Norwegian Court may consider international law to form part of the law of the Kingdom to the extent that it ought, if possible, to interpret the Norwegian legislation in question so as not to impute to it the intention or the effect of violating international law.'

Judge Read on the other hand believed that recourse to the local courts under the particular circumstances would be 'obviously futile'. He accepted the French excuse for the failure to institute proceedings before the Norwegian courts. In effect Norway was arguing that the bondholders must exhaust local remedies while at the same time contending that the matter was unquestionably governed by their legislation. In Read's view the local remedies rule had no application where the right of the foreign national had been impaired by the direct intervention of the respondent government or Parliament. Unless Norway could show that it was possible for the bondholders to challenge governmental activities authorised by the legislature, in the Norwegian courts the defence of non-exhaustion of local remedies must fail.

If it is possible for the injured alien to seek redress in the local courts against executive or legislative action on the part of the respondent State, then the exhaustion of local remedies rule will apply.

In the *Interhandel Case: Switzerland* v *United States of America* (1959) the Swiss Government had instituted proceedings before the ICJ against the USA. The US Government had in 1942 under the provisions of the Trading with the Enemy Act, seized the assets of the General Aniline and Film Company (GAF), which was incorporated in the USA. The majority of GAF shares were owned by Interhandel, a Swiss firm, which, in the opinion of the US Government was under the control of IG Farben, a German company. The Swiss Government contended that Interhandel had severed its ties with IG Farben in 1940 ie before the USA entered the war. Therefore, the foreign interest in GAF was Swiss and not German.

In 1946 the Washington Accord was signed between the Allies (Great Britain, France, and the USA) and Switzerland under which it was agreed to unblock all Swiss assets. However, the USA continued to hold the assets of GAF as being beneficially German they were not covered by the agreement. Between 1948 and 1957 the Swiss Government and Interhandel brought proceedings in the US courts, but when these proved abortive Switzerland made application to the ICJ. However, while the application was being made the Supreme Court of the United States had granted a writ of *certiorari* and remanded Interhandel's case to the District Court. It was therefore open to Interhandel to avail itself again of the remedies available to it under the Trading with the Enemy Act, and to seek the restitution of its shares by proceedings in the US courts.

The USA thereupon objected to the admissibility of the claim on the ground that local remedies had not been exhausted. Switzerland argued that the local remedies rule did not apply, since the failure of the USA to comply with the terms of the Washington Accord, constituted a direct breach of international law, causing immediate injury to the rights of the applicant State.

The Court rejected this argument, it:

> '... must attach decisive importance to the fact that the laws of the United States make available to interested persons who consider that they have been deprived of their rights by measures taken in pursuance of the Trading with the Enemy Act, adequate remedies for the defence of their rights against the Executive.'

Thus the presumption that where the injury is caused by the activities of the foreign executive or legislature, there may be no remedy available, is rebuttable by the respondent State if, as in the *Interhandel Case*, it can show that its actions may be subject to judicial review in its municipal courts.

The decision of the ICJ in the *Interhandel Case* has, however, come in for a good deal of criticism in that it arguably establishes an unrealistic test be satisfied before local remedies will be exhausted. In that case nine years of otherwise futile litigation in the US courts were held to be insufficient to satisfy the local remedies rule.

The ICJ, in a judgment of a chamber of the court in the *ELSI Case* (1989), reconsidered the application of the rule. In this case, domestic remedies had been pursued by the allegedly injured US companies for a long period of time. Prior to the USA adopting the claims of the international level expert advice was obtained from two Italian lawyers, both of whom confirmed that every domestic remedy avenue had been pursued. In addition, the Italian Government had failed to draw attention to the fact that an additional remedy was available under Italian law during protracted pre-litigation negotiations with the USA. Against this background the chamber of the Court held that, even though there was a remedy in Italian law that had not been pursued, the claim would be admissible, ie the local remedies rule had been satisfied. The following points emerge from the judgment of the chamber:

1. the onus will be on the State raising the objection of non-exhaustion to adduce the evidence;
2. the local remedies rule will be satisfied if the party has *in substance* exhausted all available local remedies and has behaved reasonably;
3. whether or not local remedies have been exhausted must be considered in the light of all the circumstances of the case and the principle of good faith.

The process of appeals

Generally local remedies will not be exhausted until the injured party has pursued his claim through the various channels of appeal available to him under the municipal law. Until the highest appellate tribunal determines the issue, the local remedies are not exhausted. However, there is no need to pursue a fruitless course of appeals.

In the *Panevezys-Saldutiskis Railway Case*: *Estonia* v *Lithuania* (1939) the Permanent Court of International Justice said: 'There can be no need to resort to the municipal courts if ... the result must be a repetition of a decision already given.'

Freeman in his *The International Responsibility of States for Denial of Justice*, states:

> 'Just as the concept of "exhaustion" in the ensemble is not absolute, neither is this particular aspect of the rule. It is not a mechanical device requiring the claimant to pursue aimless appeals against adverse decisions. The rule requiring local remedies to be invoked and exhausted would be a meaningless thing were it interpreted as applying to every means of recourse whether it promised hope of redress or not ... A "remedy" which offers no hope of effective redress is not worthy of the name and does not fall within the ambit of the rule.'

In the *Finnish Ships Arbitration*: *Finland* v *Great Britain* (1934) the Arbitrator was asked to decide whether the local remedies rule had been exhausted by Finland in seeking compensation from Great Britain for the hire of Finnish ships requisitioned during the Great War. Finland had sought compensation before the Admiralty Transport Arbitration Board but had been unsuccessful because the Board had found as a fact that, although used during the war by Great Britain, the ships had been requisitioned by or on behalf of Russia and not Great Britain.

The Arbitrator ruled that Finland's failure to appeal to the Court of Appeal did not mean that it had not exhausted local remedies. Such an appeal would have been futile because the Court of Appeal could not have reversed the Board's finding of fact: it could only have considered questions of law.

Where the alien fails to present his claim effectively or pursue it fully there will be no exhaustion of local remedies.

In the *Ambatielos Arbitration*: *Greece* v *United Kingdom* (1956) Ambatielos, a Greek national, agreed in 1919 to purchase a number of ships from the British Government. The British Government had given credit on the sale but had retained a mortgage over the vessels and in due course proceedings were taken to enforce the mortgage. Ambatielos claimed in his defence that the British Government had given an undertaking that the vessels would be delivered by specific dates and that he had suffered loss as a result of the late delivery of some of the vessels and sought to cancel the contract of purchase in respect of two of the ships. However, the British Government refused to allow the discovery of certain documents relating to the negotiations, under the plea of Crown privilege, and Ambatielos was therefore unable to prove that such an undertaking as to delivery dates had been given.

On appeal to the Court of Appeal Ambatielos asked for leave to call as a witness Major Laing, the British civil servant who had negotiated the contract for the purchase of the ships. The Court held that it could not allow Ambatielos to produce a new witness who could have been called in the Court of first instance and leave was therefore refused. Ambatielos did not appeal to the House of Lords. The claim was submitted to a Commission of Arbitration in accordance with the provisions of the

Anglo-Greek Treaty of Commerce and Navigation of 1886. Before the Tribunal Great Britain invoked the local remedies rule and submitted that the procedural remedies available to Ambatielos in the English courts had not been exhausted. The Greek Government contended that in the present case the remedies which English law offered Ambatielos were ineffective and that, accordingly, the rule is not applicable.

The Commission found that the local remedies had not been exhausted:

> 'These ... "local remedies" include not only reference to the courts and tribunals, but also the use of the procedural facilities which municipal law makes available to litigants before such courts and tribunals. It is the whole system of legal protection, as provided by municipal law, which must have been put to the test before a State, as the protector of its nationals, can prosecute the claim on the international plane.
>
> It is clear, however, that (this view) ... cannot be strained too far. Taken literally, it would imply that the fact of having neglected to make use of some means of procedure – even one which is not important to the defence of the action – would suffice to allow a defendant State to claim that local remedies have not been exhausted, and that, therefore, an international action cannot be brought. This would confer on the rule of the prior exhaustion of local remedies a scope which is unacceptable.
>
> In view of the Commission the non-utilisation of certain means of procedure can be accepted as constituting a gap in the exhaustion of local remedies only if the use of these means of procedure were essential to establish the claimant's case before the municipal courts'.

Furthermore, it was not possible for the Greek Government to argue that the remedies had been exhausted because a further appeal would have been pointless.

> 'It would be wrong to hold that a party who, by failing to exhaust his opportunities in the court of first instance, has caused an appeal to become futile should be allowed to rely on this fact in order to rid himself of the rule of exhaustion of local remedies.'

3. *Unreasonable delay: extinctive prescription*

There is no rule of international law which lays down a time limit within which claims must be presented. Nevertheless, a claim will fail if it is presented after an unreasonable delay by the claimant State. What is reasonable is a question for the tribunal to decide at its discretion.

A claim which is delayed may be denied:

1. where the delay creates difficulty for the defendant State in establishing the facts alleged by the claimant State;
2. where the delay is evidence of acquiescence or waiver on the part of the claimant State.

4. *Waiver of the claim*

A claim, once waived by the claimant State, cannot be resurrected. But as the claim belongs to the State and not the injured national, any waiver of the claim by the national in his private capacity does not bind his government.

5 *Improper behaviour by the injured alien*

The doctrine of 'clean hands' provides that where the claimant is involved in activities which are illegal, either under municipal or international law, this may bar the claim.

However, the injury caused to such an alien must be proportionate and reasonable in relation to the illegality committed by him.

11.9 Remedies

Remedies potentially available under international law include the following:

1. satisfaction
2. declarations
3. injunction
4. restrictions
5. damages.

Which remedy is available will invariably depend on the powers of the tribunal in each given case. These powers may be limited either by the constitution of the court of tribunal itself or by the agreement – the compromise – between the parties submitting the case to the court of tribunal.

Satisfaction — what the other state v. PIL demands.

Satisfaction has been defined as 'any measure which the author of a breach of duty is bound to take under customary law or under an agreement by the parties to a dispute, apart from restitution or compensation'.

Satisfaction usually involves three objects:

1. an apology or other acknowledgement of wrongdoing by means of a salute to the flag or payment of an indemnity;
2. the punishment of the individuals concerned; and
3. the taking of measures to prevent a recurrence of the harm.

The forms that satisfaction may take are illustrated by the *Borchgrave Case: Belgium v Spain (1937)*.

A Belgian national working at the Belgian Embassy in Madrid was found dead on the roadside in Spain in 1936. Belgium sought the following reparation in diplomatic proceedings with Spain:

'In consequence, proceeding on the principles of international law relating to the responsibility of States, the Belgian Government demands as reparation:
  1) an expression of the Spanish Government's excuses and regrets;
  2) transfer of the corpse to the port of embarkation with military honours;
  3) the payment of an indemnity of one million Belgian francs;
  4) just punishment of the guilty.'

A declaration by a court or tribunal that a State has acted illegally may itself be sufficient satisfaction in some cases.

In the *Corfu Channel Case* (1949) the Court declared that the mine sweeping operation by the Royal Navy in Albanian territorial waters was a violation of her sovereignty. Albania did not seek damages and the Court held that 'This declaration is in accordance with the request made by Albania through her counsel, and is in itself appropriate satisfaction.'

Declaration — stating the point,

In some cases, eg those concerning title to territory, a declaration by an international tribunal as to the true legal position will be sufficient.

For example, by a Special Agreement between the United Kingdom and France, ratified by the two States in 1951, the ICJ was:

'... requested to determine whether the sovereignty over the islets and rocks ... of the Minquiers and Ecrehos groups respectively belongs to the United Kingdom or the French Republic'.

Injunction — an order not to

The ICJ has power under its statute to grant interim measure of protection. For instance, it may enjoin a party from taking any steps which may prejudice the position of the other party to the dispute before the case can be heard on its merits.

For example, in the *Nuclear Test Cases* (1974), Australia asked the ICJ to adjudge and declare that the 'carrying out of further atmospheric nuclear weapons tests in the South Pacific Ocean is not consistent with applicable rules of international law' and also 'order' that 'the French Republic shall not carry out any further such tests'.

Restitution — rtn to status quo ante,

In the *Chorzow Factory Case* (1927), involving a claim by Germany against Poland arising out of the expropriation of a factory, the PCIJ held that:

'... reparation must, as far as possible, wipe out all the consequences of the illegal act and re-establish the situation which would, in all probability, have existed if that act had not been committed'.

This dicta of the Court has since been relied upon frequently in aid of arguments that restitution is the primary remedy at international law. While there is a great deal of controversy about the correctness of this ascertion, there have nevertheless been circumstances in which courts and tribunals have awarded restitution. In the *Free Zones Case* (1932), the PCIJ ordered France to withdraw its customs line and to return to the *status quo ante* regarding the border and customs arrangements between France and Switzerland. Similarly, in the *Temple Case* (1962), the ICJ ordered

Thailand to return to Cambodia religious objects removed unlawfully from the Temple of Preah Vihear.

More controversial has been the question of the power of the court or tribunal to award restitution or specific performance in expropriation cases. The question was discussed in the Libyan oil nationalisation cases. In *Texaco* (1977) Arbitrator Dupuy, relying on the judgment of the court in the *Chorzow Factory Case*, accepted that restitution was the primary remedy under international law. This aspect of his judgment has, however, come in for severe criticism on the grounds that an order requiring a State to perform its obligations under a concession agreement does not sit easily with the principle of permanent sovereignty over natural resources. It is also unrealistic to assume that an order for restitution will be effective given the circumstances. Certainly, in the *BP Case* (1974) Arbitrator Lagergren accepted that restitution would be an inappropriate remedy.

The criticisms levelled at the Dupuy approach are reflected in Article 7 of Part II of the ILC Draft Articles on State responsibility. This provides that restitution will not be available if it is not possible, or if it would be in breach of *jus cogens* or if such an order would be *extremely onerous* for the State committing the wrong (eg if it would seriously jeopardise the political, economic or social system of the State concerned). This provision constitutes a clear rejection of Dupuy's approach in *Texaco*.

The question of restitution as a remedy under international law was considered in the recent case of the *Rainbow Warrior* (1990). This case between New Zealand and France arose out of the facts subsequent to the sinking of the Greenpeace Ship in the New Zealand harbour in July 1985 by agents from the French secret service. Two of the agents involved were caught and tried in New Zealand for the sabotage and the killing of a Dutch photographer on board. Following the sentencing a dispute arose between New Zealand and France – France demanding the release of the agents and New Zealand claiming compensation. An agreement was reached between the two countries, following mediation by the UN Secretary-General, which involved the payment by France of a sum of $7 million to New Zealand and an agreement between New Zealand and France that the two agents would serve a three-year term on a French military base on the remote Pacific Island of Hao. Under the terms of the agreement the agents were to be 'prohibited from leaving the island for any reason, except with the mutual consent of the two governments'.

At various stages *before* the three-year sentence was up the agents were *unilaterally* removed from the island and returned to France. New Zealand brought an action against France requiring, *inter alia*, that the two agents be returned to Hao to serve out the remainder of their sentence. In its award, the Tribunal accepted that France had been in breach of its obligation under the agreement in removing the agents and failing to return them to the island. The Tribunal continued to hold, however, by a majority of two votes to one, that, as the three-year period of isolation had expired in the interim, France was *no longer* in breach. The New Zealand application – which was in reality a request for an order for the cessation of the unlawful conduct of the French – was not available as the conduct had ceased to be unlawful. There was little discussion by the Tribunal on the content of the law applicable to claims for restitution.

5 Damages

In the *Chorzow Factory Case (1927)* the PCIJ expressed the principle as follows:

'The essential principle contained in the actual notion of an illegal act – a principle which seems to be established by international practice and in particular by the decisions of arbitral tribunals – is that reparation must, as far as possible, wipe out all the consequences of the illegal act and re-establish the situation which would, in all probability, have existed if that act had not been committed. Restitution in kind, or, if this is not possible, payment of a sum corresponding to the value which a restitution in kind would bear; the award, if need be, of damages for loss sustained which would not be covered by restitution in kind or payment in place of it – such are the principles which should serve to determine the amount of compensation due for an act contrary to international law.'

Reparation in the case of direct State wrongs

Damages in such cases are awarded to compensate for the actual loss resulting from the damage or injury suffered.

In the *Corfu Channel Case: United Kingdom v Albania* (1949) the Court approved the UK's claim for damages in respect of:

1. the actual material damage sustained by the two British naval vessels which had struck the mines while proceeding through the Corfu Channel;
2. the cost of pensions and awards and of medical treatment in respect of ships' company who had been killed or injured in the explosions.

Damages may be awarded in respect of the insult to the national honour of the claimant State.

In the *I'm Alone Case (1933–35)*, for example, the Commissioners recommended the payment by the USA of $25,000 'as a material amend in respect of the wrong' committed by the USA in sinking the *I'm Alone*. The compensation was related to the indignity suffered by His Majesty's Canadian Government by the unlawful sinking of a ship registered in Montreal; it was not related to the value of the ship or its cargo.

Such measures demanded by way of an apology should not take forms which are humiliating and excessive.

Claims on behalf of nationals

The principle was expressed by the PCIJ in the *Mavrommatis Palestine Concessions Case: Greece v United Kingdom* (1924):

'By taking up the case of one of its subjects and by resorting to diplomatic action or international judicial proceedings on his behalf, a State is in reality asserting its own right, its right to ensure, in the person of its subjects, respect for the rules of international law.'

The measure of damages in cases of diplomatic protection was considered by the PCIJ in the *Chorzow Factory Case*, who stated the position as follows:

'The reparation due by one State to another does not ... change its character by reason of the fact that it takes the form of an indemnity for the calculation of which the damage suffered by a private person is taken as the measure. The rules of law governing the reparation are the rules of international law in force between the two States concerned, and not the law governing relations between the State which has committed the wrongful act and the individual who has suffered damage. Rights or interests of an individual the violation of which rights causes damage are always on a different plane to rights belonging to a State, which rights may also be infringed by the same act. The damage suffered by an individual is never therefore identical with that which will be suffered by a State; it can only afford a convenient scale for the calculation of the reparation due to the State.'

Factors taken into account by international tribunals in calculating the amount of compensation to be awarded in respect of injury to an individual national:

Wrongful acts against property

Where a claim arises out of interference with property, the amount of the award depends not only upon the value of the property but also upon the degree of interference.

In the *Union Bridge Company Claim: United States v Great Britain* (1924) the claimant company in 1899, after the outbreak of war between Great Britain and the Orange Free State, delivered material to Port Elizabeth under contract with the Government of the Orange Free State. It claimed damages arising out of the removal of the material from Port Elizabeth to Bloemfontein without its consent by an agent of the British Government and its subsequent sale.

The tribunal observed that the conduct of the British agent fell to be considered:

'... not by reference to nice distinctions between trover, trespass and action on the case, but by reference to that broad and well recognised principle of international law which gives what, in all the circumstances, is fair compensation for the wrong suffered'.

The extent of the award depends on what happens to the property concerned – whether it is returned or whether it is destroyed or expropriated. In the *Chorzow Factory Case* the Court said that if the respondent State cannot or will not make restitution, it has the alternative option of paying the value of the property 'at the time of indemnification, which value is designed to take the place of restitution'.

Wrongful acts against the person

Cases involving a denial of justice: *Janes Claim: United States v Mexico* (1926).

The USA presented a claim based on a failure by Mexico to take adequate steps to apprehend the murderer of an American citizen.

In the Opinion of the Commission:

'The international delinquency in this case is one of its own specific type, separate from the private delinquency of the culprit. The culprit is liable for having killed or murdered an American national; the Government is liable for not having measured up to its duty of diligently prosecuting and properly punishing the offender ... The damage caused by the culprit is the damage caused to Janes' relatives by Janes' death; the damage caused by the Government's negligence is the damage resulting from the non-punishment of the murderer. If the murderer had not committed his delinquency – if he had not slain Janes – Janes (but for other occurrences) would still be alive and earning the livelihood for his family; if the Government had not committed its delinquency – if it had apprehended and punished Carbajal – Janes's family would have been spared indignant neglect and would have had an opportunity of subjecting the murderer to a civil suit.'

Where there has been a denial of justice the value of the award may depend upon the degree of misconduct by the respondent State – the degree of 'shock, outrage, and suffering inflicted upon the claimants by the wrongful acts'.

In the *Maal Case: Netherlands* v *Venezuela* Maal, a Dutch subject, was stripped in public by the Venezuelan police. The Tribunal awarded him $500 in respect of the indignity suffered by him as a result.

Cases not involving a denial of justice – in such cases, where the injury suffered arises directly from the activities of officials of the respondent State, the measure of damages is that of the actual injuries caused.

Compensation may therefore be awarded in respect of medical expenses, loss of earnings, degree of disablement etc, or, in the case of fatal injuries, the extent of the financial loss of the dependents and the suffering caused to them.

Punitive damages

Although, in some cases, the award of damages exceeds the actual loss suffered it is clear that international law does not recognise the award of punitive, vindictive or exemplary damages.

In the *Lusitania Claims* the Commission stated:

'That one injured is, under the rules of international law, entitled to be compensated for an injury inflicted resulting in mental suffering, injury to his feelings, humiliation, shame, degradation, loss of social position or injury to his credit or to his reputation, there can be no doubt, and such compensation should be commensurate to the injury. Such damages are real, and the mere fact that they are difficult to measure or estimate by money standards makes them none the less real and affords no reason why the injured person should not be compensated therefor as compensatory damages, but not as a penalty. ... The industry of counsel has failed to point us to any money award by an international arbitral tribunal where exemplary, punitive or vindictive damages have been assessed against one sovereign nation in favour of another presenting a claim on behalf of its nationals.'

12

Human Rights and Self-Determination

12.1 Introduction

12.2 The United Nations Charter

12.3 The Universal Declaration of Human Rights 1948

12.4 The Covenants on Human Rights 1966

12.5 The United Nations Commission on Human Rights

12.6 Regional protection of human rights

12.7 The European Convention for the Protection of Human Rights and Fundamental Freedoms

12.8 Self-determination

12.1 Introduction

Under international law some restrictions were recognised as being imposed on a State's treatment of aliens residing within its territory, but so far as the treatment of its own nationals was concerned this was a matter solely within the domestic jurisdiction of the State.

Following the First World War some treaty provisions for the protection of the inhabitants of mandated territories and the national minorities in Eastern and Central Europe were concluded, either as special minorities treaties or under the peace treaties themselves. But no attempt was made to protect individual human rights generally. However, the Second World War and the suffering inflicted under the Nazi regime gave new impetus to those demanding international recognition and enforcement of fundamental human rights and freedoms. These aspirations were met by the draftsmen of the Charter of the United Nations who included among its provisions the foundations for the international protection of human rights.

12.2 The United Nations Charter

The Charter of the United Nations contains a variety of provisions on human rights and is generally regarded as setting the standard for their international protection. In the preamble to the Charter the Peoples of the United Nations reaffirm their:

'... faith in fundamental human rights, in the dignity and worth of the human person, in the equal rights of men and women and of nations large and small, and to establish conditions under which justice and respect for the obligations arising from treaties and other sources of international law can be maintained, and to promote social progress and better standards of life in larger freedom.'

Article 1(3) of the Charter lists among the Purposes and Principles of the United Nations:

'To achieve international co-operation in solving international problems of an economic, social, cultural, or humanitarian character, and in promoting and encouraging respect for human rights and for fundamental freedoms for all without distinction as to race, sex, language or religion.'

Article 55 of the Charter provides that: — Human rights

'With a view to the creation of conditions of stability and well-being which are necessary for peaceful and friendly relations among nations based on respect for the principle of equal rights and self-determination of peoples, the United Nations shall promote ... (c) universal respect for, and observance of human rights and fundamental freedoms for all without distinction as to race, sex, language or religion.'

Under Article 56:

'All Members pledge themselves to take joint and separate action in co-operation with the Organisation for the achievement of the purposes set forth in Article 55.'

Under the Charter human rights functions are also conferred on various organs of the United Nations.

Under Article 13(1):

'The General Assembly shall initiate studies and make recommendations for the purpose of ... (b) ... assisting in the realisation of human rights and fundamental freedoms for all without distinction as to race, sex, language, or religion.'

Under Article 60 responsibility for discharging the functions contained in Articles 55 and 56:

'... shall be vested in the General Assembly and, under the authority of the General Assembly, in the Economic and Social Council'.

The Economic and Social Council, under Article 62(2), may, when discharging this responsibility 'make recommendations for the purpose of promoting respect for, and observance of, human rights and fundamental freedoms for all'.

Under Article 68:

'The Economic and Social Council shall set up commissions in economic and social fields and for the promotion of human rights'.

Article 76 lists as one of the basic objectives of the United Nations International Trusteeship System:

'... to encourage respect for human rights and for fundamental freedoms for all without distinction as to race, sex, language, or religion, and to encourage recognition of the inter-dependence of the peoples of the world'.

Article 87 provides that the General Assembly and Trusteeship Council in carrying out their functions under the International Trusteeship System may consider reports, accept petitions and provide for periodic visits to the trust territories.

Under Article 73 regarding Non-Self Governing Territories, the Administering States:

'... recognise the principle that the interests of the inhabitants of these territories are paramount, and accept as a sacred trust the obligation to promote to the utmost ... the well-being of the inhabitants of these territories, and to this end: ... to ensure, with due respect for the culture of the peoples concerned, their political, economic, social and educational advancement, their just treatment, and their protection against abuses.'

These provisions of the Charter clearly express the obligation upon every Member not to violate human rights. However, most of these human rights clauses of the Charter are very vague and are stated in general terms. Nevertheless, they do create basic duties which all Members must fulfil in good faith. Failure to promote and observe human rights principles constitutes a violation of the Charter.

For example, in the Advisory Opinion on Namibia (1971) the ICJ declared that:

'... to establish ... and to enforce distinctions, exclusions, restrictions and limitations exclusively based on grounds of race, colour, descent or national or ethnic origin which constitute a denial of fundamental human rights is a flagrant violation of the purposes and principles of the Charter'.

12.3 The Universal Declaration of Human Rights 1948

The Universal Declaration of Human Rights was adopted by the General Assembly of the United Nations in 1948 as a first step towards defining more clearly what was meant by the provisions of the Charter. The *resolution* (not a treaty) was adopted by 48 votes to zero with eight abstentions (Saudi Arabia, South Africa, Byelorussia, Czechoslovakia, Poland, Ukraine, USSR and Yugoslavia).

The Declaration lists a wide range of human rights and freedoms to be protected ranging from the traditional civil and political rights to the more recent economic, cultural and social rights.

The civil and political rights clauses prohibit slavery, servitude, torture, cruel inhuman and degrading treatment or punishment, arbitrary arrest, detention and exile, and discrimination on grounds of race, colour, sex, language, religion, political opinion, national or social origin, property or birth. They also proclaim the right to life and liberty, equality before the law, a fair hearing, privacy and family life, freedom of movement and residence, asylum, nationality, to marry, to own property, religion, opinions, assembly and association and to take part in government.

The economic, social and cultural rights include the rights to work, equal pay, social security, join trade unions, rest and leisure, adequate standard of living, education, and to participate in the cultural life of the community.

The Declaration did not impose an immediate duty upon Members to implement its provisions. This would have been unacceptable to many States: 'It is not and does not purport to be a statement of law or of legal obligation.' The Declaration simply states therefore that:

> '... every individual and every organ of society, keeping this Declaration constantly in mind, shall strive by teaching and education to promote respect for these rights and freedoms and by progressive measures, national and international, to secure their universal and effective recognition and observance ... It is a common standard of achievement for all peoples of all nations.'

At first there was disagreement on the legal effect of the Declaration. But the practice of the United Nations now shows that even those states which originally questioned the legality of the Declaration have not hesitated to invoke its provisions against other States.

The International Conference of Human Rights, held at Teheran in 1968 unanimously proclaimed that the Declaration:

> '... states a common understanding of the peoples of the world concerning the inalienable and inviolable rights of all members of the human family and constitutes an obligation for all members of the international community'.

The Declaration therefore constitutes an authoritative interpretation of the Charter obligations and provides a comprehensive list of human rights and freedoms to be protected. It represents a consensus of the international community regarding human rights which each of its members must respect, promote and observe. It has had considerable influence in shaping subsequent treaties on human rights and some of its provisions undoubtedly reflect general principles of law.

12.4 The Covenants on Human Rights 1966

On 16 December 1966 the General Assembly adopted two Covenants on Human Rights, dealing respectively with civil and political rights, and with economic, social and cultural rights. These Covenants, which entered into force in 1976, differ in several respects from the Declaration.

First, they are more precise and provide detailed guidelines for the conduct of governments, specific legal protection for individuals, and detail instances in which public order, safety, health, morals etc, can be invoked to limit individual freedom.

Second, the Covenants contain various measures of implementation, in some cases recognising the right of individuals to seek redress of their grievances on the international plane.

Third, the Covenants were not proclaimed by the General Assembly as immediately applicable instruments, but were made subject to ratification and would only enter into force when ratified or acceded to by 35 States.

Although the Covenants are treaties binding only those who ratify them they also constitute a detailed codification of human rights and, like the Declaration, serve as an authoritative interpretation of the human rights provisions embodied in the Charter of the United Nations. In particular, they will serve to interpret the obligations under the Charter of the non-ratifying States.

The International Covenant on Civil and Political Rights

The Covenant is generally based upon the European Convention on Human Rights. The implementation machinery includes the obligation to submit reports to the Human Rights Committee consisting of 18 members elected by the contracting parties, on measures adopted to give effect to the rights recognised by the Covenant.

A contracting party may accept, on condition of reciprocity, the right of other contracting parties to bring a claim alleging violation of the Covenant by it.

An optional protocol provides that individuals who claim to be victims of violations of the Covenant and who have exhausted all available domestic remedies may submit applications to the Human Rights Committee. However, unlike the European system there is no judicial determination of the issue. The Committee merely forwards its views to the State party and to the individual. The machinery for enforcement is thus much weaker than under the European Convention.

The provisions of the Covenant include, *inter alia*:

Article 1:   the right to self-determination
Article 2:   no distinction as to race, colour, sex, religion etc
Article 6:   the right to life
Article 7:   prohibition of torture
Article 8:   prohibition of slavery
Article 9:   right to liberty
Article 18:   freedom of thought and religion
Article 22:   freedom of association.

The Covenant on Economic, Social and Cultural Rights

This protects the corresponding economic and social rights listed in the Universal Declaration. The Covenant is supervised by means of reports on measures adopted to implement the Covenant, which are submitted for examination to the Economic and Social Council of the United Nations.

The provisions of the Covenant include, *inter alia*:

Article 1:   the right to self-determination
Article 6:   the right to work
Article 8:   the right to joing a trade union
Article 9:   the right to social security
Article 13:   the right to education.

Part IV of the Covenant on Civil and Political Rights establishes a Human Rights Committee to be comprised of 18 members. By Article 40, States party to the Covenent undertake to submit reports to the committee detailing measures they have adopted to give effect to the rights recognised in the Covenant. By Article 41, States may declare that they accept the right of other parties to bring allegations of abuses against it within the Committee. By Article 42, the Committee may attempt to achieve a settlement in the case of any such complaints.

12.5 The United Nations Commission on Human Rights

The Commission was established by the Economic and Social Council in 1946. Its principal duties have been the preparation of the Universal Declaration and the 1966 Covenants. Since 1971 the Commission has also been able to debate complaints submitted to it by the Sub-Commission on the Prevention of Discrimination and Protection of Minorities, which was authorised in 1970 by Resolution 1503 to form a group to examine the many individual petitions relating to violations of human rights received by the Secretary General of the United Nations, and then report to the Sub-Commission those which 'appear to reveal a consistent pattern of gross and reliably attested violations of human rights'.

However, the Sub-Commission is especially vulnerable to political pressures and its effectiveness has thus been limited.

12.6 Regional protection of human rights

Perhaps the best-known example of attempts at the regional protection of human rights has been the *European Convention on Human Rights*, drawn up by the Council of Europe, which entered into force in September 1953. Other examples include the *American Convention on Human Rights* of 1978 and the *Inter-American Commission on Human Rights* established in 1959 under the auspices of the Organisation of American States and the *Banjul Charter* adopted by the Organisation of African Unity in 1981 dealing with individual and peoples' rights.

12.7 The European Convention for the Protection of Human Rights and Fundamental Freedoms

The Convention, prepared under the auspices of the Council of Europe, entered into force on 3 September 1953. It currently has 22 States party to it, with Finland, a signatory, still to ratify it. Of the 22 parties, all have made declarations accepting the right of individual petition under Article 25. All but Turkey have accepted the compulsory jurisdiction of the European Court of Human Rights.

Machinery for enforcement

Article 1 of the Convention lays down that:

'The High Contracting Parties shall secure to everyone within their jurisdiction the rights and freedoms defined in Section 1 of this Convention.'

To achieve compliance with this objective the Convention establishes an effective system for enforcement comprising three principal institutions – the Committee of Ministers, the Commission of Human Rights and the Court of Human Rights.

The Committee of Ministers is an executive body. Under Article 31, the *Commission* must submit a report on any unsettled matter to the Committee. Under Article 32 the Committee decides whether a violation has occurred in the case of any matter that remains unresolved and that has not been submitted to the Court within 3 months.

Article 19 provides that:

'To ensure the observance of the engagements undertaken by the High Contracting Parties in the present Convention, there shall be set up:
   (1) A European Commission of Human Rights ...
   (2) A European Court of Human Rights ...'

The European Commission of Human Rights

Article 20 provides:

'The Commission shall consist of a number of members equal to that of the High Contracting Parties. No two members of the Commission may be nationals of the same State.'

Members are elected by the Committee of Ministers of the Council of Europe (Article 21); for a period of six years (Article 22).

Article 24 provides for inter-State applications:

'Any High Contracting Party may refer to the Commission, through the Secretary-General of the Council of Europe, any alleged breach of the provisions of the Convention of another High Contracting Party.'

Several applications have been made by States under Article 24. For example, in 1956 and 1957 two cases were brought against the UK by Greece, alleging breach of the Convention by the British authorities in Cyprus. In 1967 Denmark, Norway, Sweden and the Netherlands brought an application against Greece in respect of alleged violations of the Convention by the military government. In 1971 and 1972 Ireland brought two actions against the UK in respect of breaches of the Convention by the security forces in Northern Ireland.

Article 25 provides for the right of individual petition:

'(1) The Commission may receive petitions addressed to the Secretary-General of the Council of Europe from any person, non-governmental organisation or group of individuals claiming to be the victim of a violation by one of the High Contracting Parties of the rights set forth in this convention, provided that the High Contracting Party against which the complaint has been lodged has declared that it recognises the competence of the Commission to receive such petitions. Those of the High Contracting Parties who have made such a declaration undertake not to hinder in any way the effective exercise of this right.

(2) Such declaration may be made for a specific period ...'

The practice of most States has been to make their declaration under Article 25 valid for a specific period – usually three to five years.

All domestic remedies must have been exhausted and the matter must be referred to the Commission within six months from the date on which the final decision was taken (Article 26).

Article 27 provides:

'(1) The Commission shall not deal with any petition submitted under Article 25 which:
(a) is anonymous, or
(b) is substantially the same as a matter which has already been examined by the Commission or has already been submitted to another procedure of international investigation or settlement and if it contains no relevant new information.
(2) The Commission shall consider inadmissible any petition submitted under Article 25 which it considers incompatible with the provisions of the present Convention, manifestly ill-founded, or an abuse of the right of petition ...'

About 90 per cent of the petitions submitted by individuals under Article 25 are declared inadmissible by the Commission at this stage.

In the event of the Commission accepting a petition referred to it, then under Article 28:

'(a) it shall, with a view to ascertaining the facts, undertake, together with the representatives of the parties, an examination of the petition and, if need be, an investigation, for the effective conduct of which the States concerned shall furnish all necessary facilities, after an exchange of views with the Commission.

(b) it shall place itself at the disposal of the parties concerned with a view to securing a friendly settlement of the matter on the basis of respect for Human Rights as defined in this Convention.'

The examination and investigation under Article 28 are conducted on the basis of written and oral pleadings by the parties.

If the Commission succeeds in effecting a friendly settlement in accordance with Article 28:

'... it shall draw up a Report which shall be sent to the States concerned, to the Committee of Ministers and to the Secretary General of the Council of Europe for publication' (Article 30).

If a solution is not reached then under Article 31:

'(a) the Commission shall draw up a Report on the facts and state its opinion as to whether the facts found disclose a breach by the State concerned of its obligations under the convention...

(b) the Report shall be transmitted to the Committee of Ministers ... together with such proposals as the Commission thinks fit.'

Article 32(1) provides that if the question is not referred to the Court of Human Rights within three months of the transmission of the report to the Committee of Ministers the Committee of Ministers shall decide by a two-thirds majority whether there has been a violation of the Convention.

If it decides that there has been a violation the Committee shall prescribe a period during which the High Contracting Party concerned must take the measures required by the decision of the Committee of Ministers. If the party concerned does not comply with this decision the Committee shall decide by a two-thirds majority what effect shall be given to its original decision and shall publish the report.

Under Article 32(4):

'The High Contracting Parties undertake to regard as binding on them any decision which the Committee of Ministers may take in application of the preceding paragraph.'

The European Court of Human Rights

Article 38 provides that:

'The European Court of Human Rights shall consist of a number of judges equal to that of the Members of the Council of Europe. No two judges may be nationals of the same State.'

'The members of the Court shall be elected by the Consultative Assembly by a majority of the votes cast from a list of persons nominated by the Members of the Council of Europe' (Article 39(1)).

'The candidates shall be of high moral character and must either possess the qualifications required for appointment to high judicial office or be jurisconsults of recognised competence' (Article 39(3)).

Members of the Court are elected for nine years (Article 40).
Article 43 provides:

'For the consideration of each case brought before it the court shall consist of a chamber composed of seven judges. There shall sit as an ex-officio member of the Chamber, the judge who is a national of any State party concerned, or, if there is none, a person of its choice who shall sit in the capacity of judge'.

Only the High Contracting Parties and the Commission have the right to bring a case before the Court (Article 44). An individual applicant cannot initiate proceedings or plead his case before the Court.

Under Article 45, 'The jurisdiction of the Court shall extend to all cases concerning the interpretation and application of the present convention which the High Contracting Parties or the commission shall refer to it', providing that: the High Contracting Parties have declared that they recognise as compulsory the jurisdiction of the Court in all matters concerning the interpretation and application of the present convention (Article 46(1)) and: that if the case is brought before the Court by a High Contracting Party that party must be:

1. a party whose national is alleged to be a victim; or
2. the party which referred the case to the Commission; or
3. the party against which the case has been lodged (Article 48).

Under Article 50 the Court has the power to 'afford just satisfaction to an injured party'.

The judgment of the Court shall be final (Article 52) and execution of the Court's judgment shall be supervised by the Committee of Ministers (Article 54).

The parties undertake to abide by the decision of the Court in any case to which they are parties (Article 53).

The rights protected under the Convention

Article 2:	protects the right to life. No one shall be deprived of life intentionally, save in the execution of a sentence of death by a court. Although the death penalty is permitted when imposed by a court of law, and after due legal process, extradition to a State which permits capital punishment may contravene the prohibition on torture and inhuman and degrading treatment contained in Article 3 if the accused would be subject to the so-called 'death row phenomenon' which involves unreasonable delay between the passing of sentence and the execution of that sentence: see *Soering* v *United Kingdom* (1989).
Article 3:	no one shall be subjected to torture or inhuman or degrading treatment.
Article 4:	no one shall be held in slavery or servitude, or be required to perform forced labour.
Article 5:	right to liberty and security of person. In the event of arrest, a detained person is entitled to be brought promptly before a judicial authority and shall be entitled to release within a reasonable period, or to release pending trial: see *Brogan and Ors* v *United Kingdom* (1989).
Article 6:	right to a fair and public hearing within a reasonable time before an independent and impartial tribunal established by law.
Article 7:	prohibition on retrospective legislation creating any criminal offence or increasing the penalty for an existing offence.
Article 8:	right to respect for private and family life, home and correspondence.
Article 9:	right to freedom of thought, conscience and religion.
Article 10:	right to freedom of expression.

Article 11:   right to freedom of peaceful assembly and freedom of association, including the right to form and join trade unions.

Article 12:   right of men and women of marriageable age to marry and found a family.

Article 13:   right to an effective remedy before a national authority where the rights and freedoms set forth in the Convention are violated.

Non-discrimination

Article 14 provides that:

'The enjoyment of the rights and freedoms set forth in this Convention shall be secured without discrimination on any ground such as sex, race, colour, language, religion, political or other opinion, national or social origin, association with a national minority, property, birth or other status.'

Limitation on protection

A number of Articles contain express exemption provisions. For example, Article 11(2) provides:

'No restrictions shall be placed on the exercise of these rights other than such as are prescribed by law and are necessary in a democratic society in the interests of national security or public safety. For the prevention of disorder or crime, for the protection of health or morals or for the protection of the rights and freedoms of others.'

Similar provisions are contained in Articles 8(2) 9(2) and 10(2).

Derogation in time of war or public emergency

Article 15 provides that:

'(1) In time of war or other public emergency threatening the life of the nation any High Contracting Party may take measures derogating from its obligations under this Convention to the extent strictly required by the exigencies of the situation, provided that such measures are not inconsistent with its other obligations under international law.'

But:

'(2) No derogation from Article 2, except in respect of deaths resulting from lawful acts of war, or from Articles 3, 4(1) and 7 shall be made under this provision.'

Restrictions on political activities of aliens

Article 16 provides:

'Nothing in Article 10 (freedom of expression), Article 11 (freedom of assembly) and Article 14 (non-discrimination) shall be regarded as preventing the High Contracting Parties from imposing restrictions on the political activity of aliens.'

The protocols to the Convention

The First Protocol to the Convention 1952 provides: Article 1: right to peaceful enjoyment of possessions; Article 2: right to education; Article 3: right to free elections by secret ballot.

The Fourth Protocol to the Convention 1963 provides, Article 1: no one shall be deprived of his liberty for failure to fulfil a contractual obligation; Article 2: right to liberty of movement and freedom of residence; Article 3: freedom from expulsion and right to enter state of which a national; Article 4: prohibition on collective expulsion.

12.8 Self-determination

The right of self-determination is the clearest example of a collective right, ie it is a right open to exercise by peoples, not individuals.

Recognition by the international commnity

In recent history self-determination has been recognised by the international community in two situations:

1. Following the First World War, Woodrow Wilson proclaimed the right of self-determination in respect of those people in Eastern Europe, the Balkans and the Middle East who were formerly a part of the Austro-Hungarian, German, Russian and Turkish empires. This right of self-determination was given effect through the Mandate System of the League of Nations.
2. Following the Second World War, the disintegration of the overseas empires of the colonial powers has given impetus to those demanding self-determination for all peoples of colonial territories.

Recognition by writers

Today self-determination is recognised by many writers as being a legal right – at least in the colonial context. This right to self-determination finds expression in Articles 1(2) and 55 of the UN Charter, the common Article 1 of the two 1966 Covenants of Human Rights and a host of General Assembly resolutions. Chief amongst the last of these is *General Assembly Resolution 1514 of 1960 – The Declaration on the Granting of Independence to Colonial Territories and Peoples*. This resolution declares:

1. the subjection of peoples to alien subjugation and exploitation constitutes a denial of fundamental human rights, is contrary to the Charter of the United Nations and is an impediment to the promotion of world peace and co-operation;
2. *all peoples have the right to self-determination; by virtue of that right they freely determine their political status and freely pursue their economic, social and cultural development;*

3. inadequacy of political, economic, social or educational preparedness should never serve as a pretext for delaying independence;
4. all armed action or repressive measures of all kinds directed against dependent peoples shall cease in order to enable them to exercise peacefully and freely their right to complete independence, and the integrity of their national territory shall be respected;
5. immediate steps shall be taken, in the trust and non–self-governing territories or all other territories which have not yet attained independence, to transfer all power to the peoples of those territories, without any conditions or reservations, in accordance with their freely expressed will and desire, without any distinction as to race, creed or colour, in order to enable them to enjoy complete independence and freedom;
6. *any attempt aimed at the partial or total disruption of the national unity and the territorial integrity of a country is incompatible with the purposes and principles of the Charter of the United Nations;*
7. all States shall observe faithfully and strictly the provisions of the Charter of the United Nations, the Universal Declaration of Human Rights and the present Declaration on the basis of equality, non-interference in the internal affairs of all States, and respect for the sovereign rights of all peoples and their territorial integrity.

As well as GAR 1514 (1960), the right to self-determination is reaffirmed in GAR 2625 (1970) on the Principles of International Law. Both of these resolutions are widely regarded as reflecting customary international law.

The content of the principle of self-determination came up for discussion before the ICJ in the *Western Sahara* Advisory Opinion in 1975. The Court, reiterating GAR 2625 (1970) voted that self-determination could be exercised in a variety of ways, namely:

'(a) emergence as a sovereign independent State;
(b) free association with an independent State; or
(c) integration with an independent State.'

It is clear, therefore, that the exercise of self-determination does not require the entity concerned to become an independent State. Whatever route is chosen, however, the opinion of the Court emphasises that the essential component of the exercise of this right is that it must conform to the 'freely expressed will of peoples'.

In his separate opinion in the same case Judge Dollard considered whether the right of self-determination could qualify as a norm of contemporary international law. Reviewing GAR 1514 (1960) and the opinion of the ICJ in the *Namibia Case* (1971), he concluded thus:

'The pronouncements of the court thus indicate, in my view, that a norm of international law has emerged applicable to the decolonization of these non-self-governing territories which are under the aegis of the United Nations.
    It seemed hardly necessary to make more explicit the cardinal restraint which the legal right of self-determination imposes. That restraint may be captured in a single sentence.

It is for the people to determine the destiny of the territory and not the territory the destiny of the people.'

The scope of the right of self-determination

Self-determination has gained general recognition as a right where colonial peoples are involved and its implementation cannot be delayed by a plea of Article 2(7) on the part of the colonial powers. Beyond colonial situations, however, the content of the right to self-determination is less clear. Was there, for example, a right of self-determination in the case of the Biafran attempt to secede from Nigeria? What about self-determination on the part of the Soviet republics such as the Ukraine or Byelorussia? Does the 'people' to whom the right applies include minorities within a State? Can it include the *majority* within a State attempting to throw off the shackles of a dictatorship? In other words, does the principle of self-determination imply a commitment to political self-expression such that it can be equated – however loosely – with the concept of democracy?

These questions do not admit of clear answers. Until very recently the collective wisdom would have limited self-determination to colonial situations with the maintenance of the territorial integrity of States taking priority over the claims of 'peoples' to establish their own separate political identity. This point was made by Secretary-General U Thant in 1970 in relation to the attempt by Biafra to gain independence from Nigeria:

'So far as the question of secession of a particular section of a Member State is concerned, the United Nations' attitude is unequivocable. As an international organisation, the United Nations has never accepted and does not accept and I do not believe it will ever accept the principle of secession of a part of a Member State.'

The circumstances of late 1989 and the start of the 1990s, plus the growing emphasis being placed on a broad vision of human rights, perhaps requires these views to be reassessed. This is not to say that the principle of self-determination may now be successfully invoked by any and every dissident group seeking to assert their own brand of nationalism. It may mean, however, that greater merit will be placed on assessing the right of self-determination within a broader context of the protection of human rights.

13

The Law of Treaties

13.1   Introduction

13.2   The formalities of a treaty

13.3   Unilateral acts

13.4   The making of treaties

13.5   Validity of treaties

13.6   Application of treaties

13.7   Amendment and modification of treaties

13.8   Interpretation of treaties

13.9   Termination of treaties

13.10   Settlement of disputes

13.11   Treaties by international organisations

13.1 Introduction

The expression 'treaty' is used as a generic term to cover a multitude of international agreements and contractual engagements between States. These international agreements are called by various names including treaties, conventions, pacts, declarations, charters, concordats, protocols and covenants. They may be quasi-legislative or purely contractual. They may lay down rules binding upon States concerning new areas into which international law is expanding, or they may codify, clarify and supplement the already existing customary international law on a particular matter.

The Vienna Convention on the Law of Treaties 1969

The law of treaties has now been codified in the Vienna Convention on the Law of Treaties which came into force on 27 January 1980. By 1990 around 60 States

[handwritten: to Law of treaties Convention]

(including the UK), were parties. Although the Convention only applies to treaties made after its entry into force, it is nevertheless important in that most of its provisions attempt to codify the customary law.

13.2 The formalities of a treaty

Article 2(1)(a) of the Vienna Convention on the Law of Treaties defines a treaty for the purposes of the Convention, as:

[handwritten margin: Definition Art. 2 (1) (a) Viena Conv.]

> '... an international agreement concluded between States in written form and governed by international law, whether embodied in a single instrument or in two or more related instruments, and whatever its particular designation'.

[handwritten margin: includes an intention to create legal relations]

To qualify as a 'treaty' therefore, the agreement must satisfy the following criteria: (1) it should be a written instrument or instruments between two or more parties; (2) those parties must be endowed with international personality; (3) it must be governed by international law; (4) it should be intended to create legal obligations.

A written instrument between two or more parties

Although the Vienna Convention does not apply to international agreements which are not made in writing, Article 3 of the Convention expressly states that the legal force of such non-written agreements shall not be affected by that fact.

Article 3 of the Vienna Convention provides:

[handwritten margin: Article 3 must be written]

> 'The fact that the present Convention does not apply to international agreements concluded between States and other subjects of international law or between such other subjects of international law, or to international agreements not in written form, shall not affect:
> a) the legal force of such agreements;
> b) the application to them of any of the rules set forth in the present Convention to which they would be subject under international law independently of the Convention;
> c) the application of the Convention to the relations of States as between themselves under international agreements to which other subjects of international law are also parties.'

[handwritten margin: Still subj. to int'l law outside the convention]

Note, however, that Article 102 of the Charter of the United Nations provides:

> '1. Every treaty and every international agreement entered into by any Member of the United Nations after the present Charter comes into force shall as soon as possible be registered with the Secretariat and published by it.
> 2. *No party to any such treaty or international agreement which has not been registered in accordance with the provisions of paragraph 1 of this Article may invoke that treaty or agreement before any organ of the United Nations.*'

[handwritten margin: requirement of registrat? + publicat?]

This requirement of registration and publication would seem to exclude verbal agreements from the status of 'treaty' as the term is understood and applied by the Charter of the United Nations with particular reference to the ICJ, the principal judicial organ of the UN.

A treaty must be between parties endowed with international personality

The Vienna Convention applies only to those international agreements concluded between States. Other subjects of international law such as international organisations are therefore excluded. The reason for limiting the Convention to treaties entered into between States was the fear that if other agreements were included, the differing rules of international law applicable to such agreements would make the Convention too complicated and delay its drafting.

But again Article 3 of the Vienna Convention provides that notwithstanding the exclusion of such 'international agreements concluded between States and other subjects of international law or between such other subjects of international law' from the Convention, this does not affect 'the legal force of such agreements'.

Article 3 of the Vienna Convention therefore recognises that under customary international law entities other than States may have the requisite international personality allowing them to make treaties.

States

Article 6 of the Vienna Convention provides: 'Every State possesses capacity to conclude treaties.'

In this respect the Convention reflects customary international law. According to the International Law Commission commentary, the term 'State' is used in Article 6:

'... with the same meaning as in the Charter of the United Nations, the Statute of the Court, the Geneva Convention on Diplomatic Relations; ie it means a State for the purpose of international law'.

Federal States and colonial and similar territories are not within the Convention, but nevertheless they may have treaty-making powers.

Federal States

The Draft Articles of the International Law Commission include the following paragraph, omitted from the Vienna Convention, regarding federal States: 'States members of a federal union may possess a capacity to conclude treaties if such capacity is admitted by the federal constitution and within the limits there laid down.'

Some examples of federal States in which States of the federation have the power to make treaties are the USSR and the Federal Republic of Germany.

Article 32(3) of the Bonn Constitution provides: 'In so far as the Lander have power to legislate, they may, with the consent of the Federal Government, conclude treaties with foreign States.'

In accordance with this Article the Lander of Baden-Wurtemberg and Bavaria are parties with Austria and Switzerland to a 'Convention for the Protection of Lake Constance against Pollution' of 1960.

Colonial and other non-self-governing territories

Some colonial and non-self-governing territories have been recognised as having capacity to conclude treaties. For example, Canada, Australia, New Zealand, South

Africa and India were invited to take part in the 1919 Paris Peace Conference and became parties to the Treaty of Versailles.

International organisations

The power of an international organisation to enter into a treaty can arise in two ways:

By express grant contained in the constitution of the organisation. For example, Articles 57 and 63 of the Charter of the United Nations gives the United Nations power to enter into relationship agreements with the various specialised agencies.

Article 43 of the Charter empowers the United Nations to enter into agreements with Member States on the provision of military contingents.

By implication, in order to carry out the duties imposed by the constitution upon the organisation. For example, in the Advisory Opinion on *Reparations for Injuries Suffered in the Service of the United Nations Case (1949)*, it was stated:

> 'Under international law the organisation must be deemed to have those powers which, though not expressly provided for in the Charter, are conferred by necessary implication as being essential to the performance of their duty.'

Limitations on the implied powers

The existence of an implied treaty making power does not mean that an organisation can conclude any sort of agreement. An organisation cannot act in total disregard of the limitations placed upon it in its constitution. As Brierly states:

> '... the inherent treaty-making capacity of an international organisation ... is confined to capacity to make treaties compatible with the letter and spirit of its constitutions'.

If the organisation did exceed its implied powers the act would be ineffective and the treaty void.

Individuals or corporations created under municipal law

Individuals and corporations have never been recognised as having the capacity to make treaties, whether with States, other individuals or with other international persons with treaty-making capacity. It is possible for a State to enter into a contract with an individual or a corporation, but such an agreement will not have the status of a treaty under international law.

In the *Anglo-Iranian Oil Company Case (1952)* the UK alleged that a concessionary agreement between the Iranian Government and the Oil Company of 1933 was in the nature of an international agreement. The UK argument was founded upon the fact that the concession had been negotiated in order to settle a dispute between the UK and Iran which had been before the Council of the League of Nations and therefore the UK had played a part in its negotiation although it was not itself a party to the actual final agreement.

The Court held that the background against which the agreement was negotiated could not give the concession the international character suggested by the UK. The UK was not a party. It was therefore nothing more than a concessionary contract between a government and a foreign corporation.

The agreement must be governed by international law

These rules represent a significant innovation compared to the position under customary international law. Under customary international law, international courts and commissions do not have jurisdiction over all cases concerning claims that a treaty is invalid, but only over those cases where the parties agree to submit the matter to such a court or commission.

Simply because two entities endowed with international personality and possessing treaty making capacity enter into an agreement, it does not follow that the agreement is necessarily a treaty. Certain inter-State agreements can be subject to municipal law, either expressly or by implication.

For example, during the period 1966 to 1968 Denmark entered into a series of loan agreements with other States (eg Malawi) which stipulated that, except as otherwise provided therein; 'the Agreement and all rights and obligations deriving from it shall be governed by Danish law'.

There would seem to be no reason why an agreement must be governed exclusively by either international law or by municipal law. Many agreements between States are of a hybrid nature and as such are binding on the international plane as well as being directly governed by municipal law.

The International Law Commission Fourth Special Rapporteur stated in his First Report (1962):

> '... the Commission felt in 1959 that the element of subjection to international law is so essential a part of an international agreement that it should be expressly mentioned in the definition. There may be agreements between States, such as agreements for the acquisition of premises for diplomatic missions or for some purely commercial transaction, the incidents of which are regulated by the local law of one of the parties or by a private law system determined by reference to conflict of law principles. Whether in such cases the two States are internationally accountable to each other at all may be a nice question; but even if that were held to be so, it would not follow that the basis of their international accountability was a treaty obligation. At any rate, the Commission was clear that it ought to confine the notion of an 'international agreement' for the purposes of the law of treaties to one, the whole formation and execution of which (as well as the obligation to execute) is governed by international law.'

The agreement should create a legal obligation

The intention to create legal relations is not mentioned in the Vienna Convention.

The International Law Commission's Rapporteur stated that: '... in so far as this [requirement] may be relevant in any case, the element of intention is embraced in the phrase "governed by international law".'

There are, however, practical reasons for excluding any specific reference to intention. States may wish to reach an agreement as to political intent without going to the extent of making it legally enforceable. Therefore what may appear to be a treaty may in fact be devoid of any legal content. This is particularly true of the so-called 'joint declaration' by States, examples being the Atlantic Charter of 1941 and the Cairo Declaration of 1943. Such declarations are statements of 'common principles' or 'common purpose' imposing no legal obligation upon the parties to pursue those policies.

Similarly, The Final Act of the Helsinki Conference on Security and Co-operation in Europe, 1975, was stated to be: 'not eligible for registration under Article 102 of the Charter of the United Nations' and the general understanding expressed at the conference was that the Act would not be binding in law.

However, such agreements, even if not creating rights and obligations directly, may provide the basis for new rights and obligations in the future. So that today, for instance, it is of little practical significance that the United Nations Declaration of Human Rights adopted by the General Assembly in 1948 was agreed to by Member States only on the understanding that it did not create binding obligations upon them.

13.3 Unilateral acts

Acts and conduct by governments, although not intended to formulate agreements may nevertheless result in legal effect.

Unilateral declarations

A State may accept obligations *vis-à-vis* other States by the making of a public declaration expressing a clear intention on its behalf.

In the *Legal Status of Eastern Greenland Case: Denmark v Norway* (1933) the Danish Government notified the Norwegian Government through the Danish Minister in Norway that Denmark would not raise objections to Norway's claim to Spitzbergen. The intention was to obtain a reciprocal undertaking from the Norwegian Government with respect to Denmark's claim to Greenland. The Danish Government stated that it was 'confident' that the Norwegian Government 'would not make any difficulties in the settlement of this question'. The Norwegian Foreign Minister, Ihlen replied to the effect that his Government would make no such difficulties. The Court held that even if this declaration by Ihlen could not be considered as recognition of Denmark's claim to Greenland, it nevertheless created an obligation binding upon Norway to refrain from contesting Danish sovereignty over Greenland.

The Court stated:

'The Court considers it beyond all dispute that a reply of this nature given by the Minister of Foreign Affairs on behalf of his Government in response to a request by the diplomatic representative of a foreign Power, in regard to a question falling within his province, is binding upon the country to which the Minister belongs.'

Juridical nature of the declaration

The juridical nature of unilateral declarations was considered by the ICJ in the *Nuclear Test Case: Australia v France; New Zealand v France* (1974).

Australia and New Zealand had sought a decision of the Court that the French testing of nuclear weapons in the atmosphere was contrary to international law. The French Government refused to comply with the Court's interim order requiring it to refrain from commencing the tests until the Court reached a decision in the case.

However, in a series of public pronouncements, members of the French Government had stated that France was going to commence underground testing in the following year and at a press conference the President of the Republic stated that he had 'made it clear that this round of atmospheric tests would be the last'.

The Court concluded that as these pronouncements were binding upon France the applicants had achieved their objective and therefore the dispute between the parties no longer existed. The Court said it had 'no doubt' that declarations made by way of unilateral acts, concerning legal or factual situations, may have the effect of creating legal obligations.

The criteria for such an obligation are:

1. the intention of the State making the declaration that it should be bound according to its terms; and
2. that the undertaking be given publicly. 'No subsequent acceptance of the declaration, nor even any reply or reaction from other States, is required for the declaration to take effect.'

When, as in the *Nuclear Test Case*, the declaration is not directed to a specific State or States but is merely expressed generally the question as to whether there is an intention to be legally bound will require very careful consideration.

In the *North Sea Continental Shelf Cases* (1969) the ICJ stated that the unilateral assumption of the obligations of a convention by conduct was 'not lightly to be presumed' and that 'a very consistent course of conduct' was required in such cases.

13.4 The making of treaties

Negotiation

This is carried out by the accredited representatives of the State in question. Article 7 provides that the representative of the state will be someone equipped with an instrument of 'full powers' or if it appears from the normal practice of the State that the person concerned has such powers. Article 7(2) of the Vienna Convention then indicates three categories of person who are deemed to have 'full powers':

1. heads of State, heads of government and ministers of foreign affairs;
2. heads of diplomatic missions, ie ambassadors to the State concerned;
3. representatives accredited to international conferences or organisations.

Following negotiation, Article 9 provides that the text of the treaty may be *adopted* by consent between the parties. In the case of an international conference, adoption will take place by a two-thirds majority vote of States present at the conference. Note: adoption will not of itself create legal obligations.

Adoption of the text of a treaty

The adoption of the text is the first stage of the conclusion of a treaty.

Article 9 of the Vienna Convention provides:

'1. The adoption of the text of a treaty takes place by the consent of all the States participating in its drawing up except as provided in paragraph 2.

2. The adoption of the text of a treaty at an international conference takes place by the vote of two-thirds of the States present and voting, unless by the same majority they shall decide to apply a different rule.'

Therefore, unanimity remains the general rule for bilateral treaties and for those treaties drawn up between few States. But Article 9(2) recognises that it would be unrealistic to demand unanimity as the general rule for the adoption of treaties drawn up at conferences or within organisations, where the widest possible measure of agreement between the participants is desirable.

The adoption of the text does not by itself create any obligations. A treaty is of no effect until two or more States consent to be bound by it. This consent to be bound usually follows the adoption of the text and is an entirely separate process.

Authentication of the treaty

The authentication of the text of the treaty in the form which the parties may later ratify may be done in a number of ways. The method of authentication to be adopted is a matter for the parties themselves to agree, but the two usual methods are: signing and initialling. The text may, however, be authenticated in other ways, eg by incorporating the text in the final act of the conference.

Consent to be bound

Article 11 of the Vienna Convention provides: 'The consent of a State to be bound by a treaty may be expressed by signature, exchange of instruments constituting a treaty, ratification, acceptance, approval or accession; or by any other means if so agreed.'

The traditional methods of expressing consent to a treaty are signature, ratification and accession.

Signature

The legal effects of signature are as follows:

1. the signing of a treaty may represent simply an authentication of its text;

2. where such a signature is subject to ratification, acceptance or approval, signature does not establish consent to be bound.

In the case of a treaty which is only to become binding upon ratification, acceptance or approval there is some uncertainty as to the relationship of the parties to the instrument before that step is taken. Such a treaty, unless declaratory of customary law, will not be enforceable against a party until the treaty is formally ratified.

In the context of the *North Sea Continental Shelf Cases* (1969) the Federal Republic of Germany had been a signatory to the 1958 Geneva Convention on the Continental Shelf, but had not ratified it. The Court held that Article 6 of that Convention was not binding on the Federal Republic because its signature had only been 'a preliminary step: it did not ratify the Convention, is not a party to it and therefore cannot be contractually bound by its provisions'.

However, under Article 18 of the Convention, the act of signing the treaty creates an obligation of good faith on the part of the signatory: to refrain from acts calculated to frustrate the objects of the treaty; and to submit the treaty to the appropriate constitutional machinery for approval.

Signature does not, however, create an obligation to ratify.

3. Where a treaty is not subject to ratification, acceptance or approval, signature will signify consent to be bound.

In such cases guidance is provided by Article 12(1) of the Vienna Convention which provides:

'The consent of a State to be bound by a treaty is expressed by the signature of its representative when: (a) the treaty provides that signature shall have that effect; (b) it is otherwise established that the negotiating States were agreed that signature should have that effect; or (c) the intention of the State to give that effect to the signature appears from the full powers of its representative or was expressed during the negotiations.'

Ratification

Meaning of ratification. Ratification is the formal act whereby one State declares its acceptance of the terms of the treaty and undertakes to observe them. Ratification is used to describe two distinct procedural acts, one municipal and one international.

1. *Ratification in municipal law.* In the municipal law sense ratification may be the formal act of the appropriate organ of the State and may be called ratification in the constitutional sense. For example, according to English law, ratification is effected in the name of the Crown.

2. *Ratification in international law.* In the international law sense ratification is the procedure which brings a treaty into force, ie formal exchange or deposit of the instrument of ratification. It is not concerned with the question as to whether a State has complied with the requirements of its constitutional law.

Reasons why ratification may be required. Despite the fact that a treaty may be made effective by signature alone in many cases States still insist upon formal ratification. There are several reasons for this.

1. Historically the subsequent ratification by the Sovereign prevented diplomats from exceeding their instructions and confirmed the power of the representative to negotiate the treaty.
2. The delay between signature and ratification allows the Sovereign time to reconsider the matter and allows time for expression of public opinion on the matter.
3. Consent of the legislature may be required for ratification in accordance with the State municipal law.

national acceptance

Ratification under the Vienna Convention. Article 14(1) of the Vienna Convention provides:

> 'The consent of a State to be bound by a treaty is expressed by ratification when: (a) the treaty provides for such consent to be expressed by ratification; (b) it is otherwise established that the negotiating States were agreed that ratification should be required; (c) the representatives of the State has signed the treaty subject to ratification; or (d) the intention of the State to sign the treaty subject to ratification appears from the full powers of its representative or was expressed during the negotiations.'

Art. 14(1) ratificato = binding when?...

Thus, if a treaty should contain no express provision on the subject of ratification Article 14 will regulate the matter by reference to the intention of the parties.

Ratification by performance. Performance of a treaty may constitute tacit ratification. If a State successfully claims rights under an unratified treaty it will be estopped from alleging that it is not bound by the treaty.

estoppel

Accession

Accession or adherence or adhesion occurs when a State which did not sign a treaty formally accepts its provisions. Accession may occur before or after the treaty has entered into force. It is only possible if it is provided for in the treaty, or if all the parties in the treaty agree that the acceding State should be allowed to accede. Accession, therefore, has the same effect as signature and ratification combined.

Reservations

A State may be willing to accept most provisions of a treaty, but it may, for various reasons, wish to object to other provisions of the treaty.

Definition of a reservation

A reservation is defined in Article 2(1)(d) of the Vienna Convention as:

reservations 2(1)(d)

> '... a unilateral statement, however phrased or named, made by a State, when signing, ratifying, accepting, approving or acceding to a treaty, whereby it purports to exclude or to modify the legal effect of certain provisions of the treaty in their application to that State'.

The effect of such a reservation depends upon whether it is accepted or rejected by the other States concerned.

Traditional view

The traditional view was that reservations were valid only if the treaty concerned permitted reservations and if all the other parties to the treaty accepted the reservation. In 1927 for instance, the League of Nations adopted the following approach to reservations with regard to multilateral treaties:

> 'In order that any reservation whatever may be validly made in regard to a clause of the treaty, it is essential that this reservation should be accepted by all the other contracting parties, as would have been the case if it had been put forward in the course of the negotiations. If not, the reservation, like the signature to which it is attached, is null and void.'

Limitation of the traditional approach

In the case of a bilateral treaty or a treaty involving few parties no real difficulty arose in deciding whether a reservation had been accepted by the other party. However, the increasing numbers of multilateral treaties made the situation more complicated, and particularly with regard to those conventions drafted through the auspices of the United Nations it was soon apparent that this traditional approach would have to change.

Reservations to the Convention on the *Genocide Case* (1951)

Following the adoption of the Convention on the Prevention and Punishment of the Crime of Genocide by the General Assembly of the United Nations in 1948 a conflict of opinion arose on the admissibility of reservations to the Convention. The Convention contains no reservations clause and so the questions as to the effects of the reservations were submitted to the ICJ for an advisory opinion.

The Court held:

> '... in so far as concerns the Convention on the Prevention and Punishment of the Crime of Genocide, in the event of a State ratifying or acceding to the Convention subject to a reservation made either on ratification or on accession, or on signature followed by ratification,
>
> On Question I:
>
> that a State which has made and maintained a reservation which has been objected to by one or more of the parties to the Convention but not by others, can be regarded as being a party to the Convention if the reservation is compatible with the *object and purpose* of the Convention; otherwise, that State cannot be regarded as being a party to the Convention.
>
> On Question II:
>
> a) that if a party to the Convention objects to a reservation which it considers to be incompatible with the *object and purpose* of the Convention, it can in fact consider that the reserving State is not a party to the Convention;
>
> b) that if, on the other hand, a party accepts the reservation as being compatible with the *object and purpose* of the Convention, it can in fact consider that the reserving State is a party to the Convention.

object & purpose.

On Question III:

a) that an objection to a reservation made by a signatory State which has not yet ratified the Convention can have the legal effect indicated in the reply to Question 1 only upon ratification. Until that moment it merely serves as a notice to the other State of the eventual attitude of the signatory State;

   b) that an objection to a reservation made by a State which is entitled to sign or accede but which has not yet done so, is without legal effect.'

The Advisory Opinion therefore laid the foundations for a more flexible approach to the problem of reservations to multilateral treaties. However, the classification of reservations into those that are 'compatible' and those that are 'incompatible' with the 'object and purpose' of a Convention was rejected by the International Law Commission who considered the test too subjective and preferred the traditional rule of unanimous consent.

Present approach of the United Nations

Faced with this conflict of opinion between the traditional view and the view of the Court as expressed in the *Genocide Case*, the General Assembly of the United Nations in 1952 requested the Secretary General to follow the Court's Opinion as depositary for the Genocide Convention and, as depositary of future multilateral conventions, to continue to act as depositary in connection with the deposit of documents containing reservations or objections, without passing upon the legal effect of such documents; and to communicate the text of such documents relating to reservations or objectives to all States concerned, leaving it to each State to draw legal consequences from such communications.

In 1959 this directive was extended to cover all conventions concluded under the auspices of the United Nations, unless they contain provisions to the contrary.

Position under the Vienna Convention

Articles 19 to 21 of the Vienna Convention follow the principles laid down by the Court in the *Genocide Case* but do, however, make some concessions to the traditional rule by recognising that every reservation is incompatible with certain types of treaty unless accepted unanimously.

Permissible and impermissible reservations

The Vienna Convention distinguishes between 'permissible' and 'impermissible' reservations. This distinction derives from the will of the parties in that they may either prohibit certain reservations or expressly authorise certain reservations.

Freedom to formulate the reservation

Article 19 of the Vienna Convention provides as follows:

'A State may, when signing, ratifying, accepting approving or acceding to a treaty, formulate a reservation unless:

a) the reservation is prohibited by the treaty;

b) the treaty provides that only specified reservations, which do not include the reservation in question, may be made; or

c) in cases not falling under sub-paragraphs (a) and (b), the reservation is incompatible with the object and purpose of the treaty.'

Acceptance of and objection to reservations other than those expressly authorised by a treaty

Article 20 of the Vienna Convention provides as follows:

'1. A reservation expressly authorised by a treaty does not require any subsequent acceptance by the other contracting States unless the treaty so provides.

2. When it appears from the limited number of the negotiating States and the object and purpose of a treaty that the application of the treaty in its entirety between all the parties is an essential condition of the consent of each one to be bound by the treaty, a reservation requires acceptance by all the parties.

3. When a treaty is a constituent instrument of an international organisation and unless it otherwise provides, a reservation requires the acceptance of the competent organ of that organisation.

4. In cases not falling under the preceding paragraphs and unless the treaty otherwise provides:

a) acceptance by another contracting State of a reservation constitutes the reserving State a party to the treaty in relation to that other State if or when the treaty is in force for those States;

b) an objection by another contracting State to a reservation does not preclude the entry into force of the treaty as between the objecting and reserving States unless a contrary intention is definitely expressed by the objecting State;

c) an act expressing a State's consent to be bound by the treaty and containing a reservation is effective as soon as at least one other contracting State has accepted the reservation.

5. For the purpose of paragraphs 2 and 4 and unless the treaty otherwise provides, a reservation is considered to have been accepted by a State if it shall have raised no objection to the reservation by the end of a period of twelve months after it was notified of the reservation or by the date on which it expressed its consent to be bound by the treaty, whichever is later.'

The beneficial results of this more flexible approach are obvious. In its Commentary the International Law Commission stated:

'The majority of reservations relate to a particular point which a particular State for one reason or another finds difficult to accept, and the effect of the reservation on the general integrity of the treaty is often minimal; and the same is true even if the reservation in question relates to a comparatively important provision of the treaty, so long as the reservation is not made by more than a few States. In short, the integrity of the treaty would only be materially affected if a reservation of a somewhat substantial kind were to be formulated by a number of States. This might no doubt, happen; but even then the treaty itself would remain the master agreement between the other participating States. What is essential to ensure both the effectiveness and the integrity of the treaty is that a sufficient number of States should become parties to it, accepting the great bulk of its provisions ... But when today the number of the negotiating States may be upwards of one hundred States with very diverse cultural, economic and political conditions, it seems necessary to assume that the power to make reservations without the risk of being totally excluded by the objection of one or even a few States may be a factor in promoting a more general acceptance of multilateral treaties.'

Interpretative declarations

Some States have adopted the practice of classifying as reservations declarations which are no more than statements as to their understanding or interpretation of a particular treaty provision.

The International Law Commission has commented:

'States ... not infrequently make declarations as to their understanding of some matter or as to their interpretation of a particular provision. Such a declaration may be a mere clarification of the State's position or it may amount to a reservation, according as to whether it does or does not vary or exclude the application of the terms of the treaty as adopted.'

The test is the effect the statement purports to have, and it turns upon whether the statement seeks to exclude or modify the legal effect of the provisions of the treaty.

The point is illustrated by the USSR's reservation to Article 11(1) of the Vienna Convention on Diplomatic Relations: 'any difference of opinion regarding the size of a diplomatic mission should be settled by agreement between the sending State and the receiving State'.

Given that Article 11 allowed the receiving State the sole power to limit the size of a mission in the absence of agreement, a number of States objected to this reservation on the ground that it did not 'modify any rights or obligations'. In other words, it was not a true reservation.

Effect of such a declaration

It has become increasingly common for a State to couch a unilateral statement in the language of an interpretative declaration and announce that it is only prepared to enter into the treaty on the basis of its interpretation being accepted. Such an approach causes a dilemma for the other parties to the treaty. If the other States accept the statement as a reservation and therefore as being impermissible this may lead to one of two courses: disregarding the 'reservation' as a nullity; or rejecting the treaty relations entirely.

The better view would be to accept the declaring State's characterisation, but refuse to accept the interpretation thus forcing the issue to some form of independent adjudication as a matter of treaty interpretation.

If a statement is determined to be an interpretative declaration although some parties may accept it and others not, there is no question of non-acceptance as if it were an objection for purposes of Articles 20 and 21, so as to exclude the affected provision or even exclude the treaty from entering into force between the reserving State and the objecting State.

A dispute over interpretative declaration goes to interpretation of the treaty and no more. The only problem arises when there is a dispute as to whether the expression is a true reservation or an interpretative declaration. This problem can be disposed of by recourse to a recognised judicial tribunal.

The issue arose for consideration in the *UK/France Continental Shelf Arbitration (1977)* where France argued that a statement it had made at the time of the 1958 Geneva Convention on the Continental Shelf was in fact a reservation. The UK argued, in contrast, that it was an interpretative declaration and that it, therefore, had no binding force. The tribunal, however, held that it was a reservation as it expressed a condition to the French acceptance of the treaty obligations. Similarly, in the recent decision in the *Belilos Case* (1988) before the European Court of Human Rights, the question arose as to whether a Swiss statement was an interpretative declaration or a reservation. The Court held that the character of the statement would not depend on how it was described. If the statement purported to exclude or vary the legal effect of the treaty it would be a reservation. In the case in issue the Court held that the statement did constitute a reservation but that it was an unpermissible reservation and that, as a result, it had no legal effect.

Entry into force

Where the treaty does not specify a date, there is a presumption that the treaty is intended to enter into force as soon as all the negotiating States have expressed their consent to be bound by it.

In the case of multilateral treaties negotiated by many States it is very unlikely that they will all proceed to ratify it. In such cases the treaty usually provides that it shall enter into force when it has been ratified by a specified number of States. When the minimum number of ratifications is reached the treaty enters into force between those States which have ratified it.

Registration

Article 102 of the Charter of the United Nations provides as follows:

'1. Every treaty and every international agreement entered into by any Member of the United Nations after the present Charter comes into force shall as soon as possible be registered with the Secretariat and published by it.
   2. No party to any such treaty or international agreement which has not been registered in accordance with the provision of paragraph 1 of this Article may invoke that treaty or engagement before any organ of the United Nations.'

Article 102 was intended to prevent States from entering into secret agreements without the knowledge of their nationals, and without the knowledge of other States, whose interests might be affected by such agreements.

13.5 Validity of treaties

Article 42(1) of the Vienna Convention provides: 'The validity of a treaty or of the consent of a State to be bound by a treaty may be impeached only through the application of the present Convention.'

This is to prevent a State from attempting to evade an inconvenient treaty obligation by alleging spurious grounds of invalidity.

Non-compliance with provisions of municipal law

Many States have provisions in their constitutions which prevent their government from entering into treaties, or into certain types of treaty, without the consent of the legislature or some organ of the legislature.

Effect of non-compliance with municipal law

What is the position if a competent representative, ie head of State, foreign secretary, etc disregards the requirements of his State's constitutional law when entering into a treaty? Is the treaty valid or not?

The extent to which such constitutional limitations on the treaty-making power can be invoked on the international plane is a matter of controversy and the following views have been put forward:

1. the treaty is void if there is a failure to comply with the requirements of the State's constitutional law;
2. the treaty is only void if the constitutional rule in question is 'notorious', ie a well-known constitutional limitation;
3. the treaty is valid irrespective of non-compliance with the constitutional law of the State;
4. the treaty is valid except where one party to the treaty knew that the other party was acting in breach of a constitutional requirement.

This latter view, which involves a presumption of competence and excepts manifest irregularity is the one favoured by most States and is reflected in the Vienna Convention.

Article 46 of the Vienna Convention provides:

'1. A State may not invoke the fact that its consent to be bound by a treaty has been expressed in violation of a provision of its internal law regarding competence to conclude treaties as invalidating its consent unless that violation was manifest and concerned a rule of its internal law of fundamental importance.

2. A violation is manifest if it would be objectively evident to any State conducting itself in the matter in accordance with normal practice and in good faith.'

Treaties entered into by a representative who lacks authority

Who is a representative?
Article 7(1) of the Vienna Convention provides:

'A person is considered as representing a State for the purpose of ... expressing the consent of the State to be bound by a treaty if: he produces appropriate full powers; or it appears from the practice of the States concerned or from other circumstances that their intention was to consider that person as representing the State for such purposes and to dispense with full powers.'

Article 7(2) of the Vienna Convention provides:

'In virtue of their functions and without having to produce full powers, the following are considered as representing their State: Heads of State, Heads of Government and Ministers for Foreign Affairs ... heads of diplomatic missions ... representatives accredited by States '.

Article 8 of the Vienna Convention provides:

'An act relating to the conclusion of a treaty performed by a person who cannot be considered under Article 7 as authorised to represent a State for that purpose is without legal effect unless afterwards confirmed by that State.'

Specific restrictions on authority:

If the authority of a representative to express the consent of his State to be bound by a particular treaty has been made subject to a specific restriction, then if he fails to observe the restriction what is the position?

Article 47 of the Vienna Convention provides:

'If the authority of a representative to express the consent of a State to be bound by a particular treaty has been made subject to a specific restriction, his omission to observe that restriction may not be invoked as invalidating the consent expressed by him unless the restriction was notified to the other negotiating States prior to his expressing such consent.'

Corruption of a State representative

Article 50 of the Vienna Convention provides:

'If the expression of a State's consent to be bound by a treaty has been procured through the corruption of its representative directly or indirectly by another negotiating State, the State may invoke such corruption as invalidating its consent to be bound by the treaty.'

The 'corruption' must be a 'substantial influence'. A small courtesy or favour shown to a representative will be insufficient.

Error

Article 48 of the Vienna Convention provides:

'1. A State may invoke an error in a treaty as invalidating its consent to be bound by the treaty if the error relates to a fact or situation which was assumed by that State to exist at the time when the treaty was concluded and formed an essential basis of its consent to be bound by the treaty.

2. Paragraph 1 shall not apply if the State in question contributed by its own conduct to the error or if the PUBLIC circumstances were such as to put that State on notice of a possible error.

3. An error relating only to the wording of the text or a treaty does not affect its validity'.

Thus, only if the error is essential or fundamental to the obligations that a State believed it had undertaken will it be a reason for invalidating the treaty.

Article 48 is reflective of current law. As the International Law Commission pointed out, in practice most alleged errors 'concern geographical errors, mostly errors on maps'.

In the *Temple Case* (1962) the ICJ was asked to rule that Cambodia and not Thailand had sovereignty over the Temple of Preah Vihear. In 1904, the boundary between Cambodia (a French protectorate) and Thailand (then Siam) was determined by treaty between France and Siam. The treaty stated that it was to follow the watershed line and surveys were conducted by experts on the basis of which a map was prepared. The map placed the Temple in Cambodia and it was this map upon which Cambodia relied for its claim. Thailand argued, *inter alia*, that the map embodied a material error in that it did not follow the watershed line as required by the treaty. This was argued despite the fact that the map had been received and accepted by the Siamese. The Court rejected Thailand's arguments as follows:

> 'It is an established rule of law that the plea of error cannot be allowed as an element vitiating consent if the party advancing it contributed by its own conduct to the error, or could have avoided it, or if the circumstances were such as to put that party on notice of a possible error. The Court considers that the character and qualifications of the persons who saw the ... map on the Siamese side would alone make it difficult for Thailand to plead error in law'.

Fraud

Article 49 of the Vienna Convention provides:

> 'If a State has been induced to conclude a treaty by the fraudulent conduct of another negotiating State, the State may invoke the fraud as invalidating its consent to be bound by the treaty.'

Coercion of a State's representatives

Article 51 of the Vienna Convention provides:

> 'The expression of a State's consent to be bound by a treaty which has been procured by the coercion of its representative through acts or threats directed against him shall be without any legal effect.'

Such coercion may include, for example, blackmailing threats or threats against the representative's family. Such coercion must be directed at the representative personally and not at coercion of him through a threat of action against his State.

Coercion of a State

The traditional doctrine prior to the Covenant of the League of Nations was that the validity of a treaty was not affected by the fact that it had been brought about by the threat or use of force. However, Article 2(4) of the Charter of the United Nations which prohibits the threat or use of force, together with other developments, now justifies the conclusion that a treaty procured by such coercion shall be void.

Article 52 of the Vienna Convention provides:

> 'A treaty is void if its conclusion has been procured by the threat or use of force in violation of the principles of international law embodied in the Charter of the United Nations.'

This modern rule against the use of force does not operate retroactively. If a treaty was procured by force before the use of force was made illegal the validity of the treaty is not affected by this subsequent change in the law.

Force, in the context of Article 52, does not include 'economic and political' pressure. An amendment defining force to include these matters was withdrawn.

Unequal treaties

Soviet writers have for some years propounded the doctrine of 'equal treaties':

> 'The principle that international treaties must be observed does not extend to treaties which are imposed by force, and which are unequal in character ...
>
> Equal treaties are treaties concluded on the basis of the equality of the parties; unequal treaties are those which do not fulfil this elementary requirement. Unequal treaties are not legally binding'.

Treaties must be based upon the sovereign equality of the contracting parties; examples cited include the Munich Agreement of 1938 and the Anglo-Egyptian Treaty of Alliance of 1936.

Western jurists oppose the doctrine on the ground of its vagueness but it is attracting considerable support especially from the newly independent States.

Conflict with a peremptory norm of general international law – jus cogens

It has been argued that there exist principles of customary law which are in some sense fundamental to the international legal order, forming a body of *jus cogens*. These rules of customary law cannot be set aside by treaty or acquiescence, but only by the formation of a subsequent customary rule of contrary effect. Examples include prohibitions on the trade in slaves, piracy and of wars of aggression. The law of genocide, crimes against humanity and the principle of non-discrimination on grounds of race.

The concept was included in the Vienna Convention, Article 53 of which provides:

> 'A treaty is void if, at the time of its conclusion, it conflicts with a peremptory norm of general international law. For the purposes of the present Convention, a peremptory norm of general international law is a norm accepted and recognised by the international community of States as a whole as a norm from which no derogation is permitted and which can be modified only by a subsequent norm of general international law having the same character.'

Article 64 of the Vienna Convention further provides:

'If a new peremptory norm of general international law emerges, any existing treaty which is in conflict with that norm becomes void and terminates.'

13.6 Application of treaties

Territorial application

Article 29 of the Vienna Convention provides:

'Unless a different intention appears from the treaty or is otherwise established, a treaty is binding upon each party in respect of its entire territory.'

Colonial territories: in the absence of any territorial cause or other indication of a contrary intention, a treaty is presumed to apply to all the territories for which the contracting States are internationally responsible. So treaties made by the UK automatically extend to its overseas territories unless the treaty indicates otherwise. The use of the 'territorial' or 'colonial' clause enables the wishes of the inhabitants of the colony to be considered before the treaty is extended to the colony.

Inconsistent treaties

Where a party to a treaty subsequently enters into another treaty with overlapping provisions then the position is regulated by Article 30 of the Vienna Convention which provides as follows:

'1. Subject to Article 103 of the Charter of the United Nations, the rights and obligations of States parties to successive treaties relating to the same subject matter shall be determined in accordance with the following paragraphs.

2. When a treaty specifies that it is subject to, or that it is not to be considered as incompatible with, an earlier or later treaty, the provisions of that other treaty prevail.

3. When all the parties to the earlier treaty are parties also to the later treaty but the earlier treaty is not terminated or suspended in operation under Article 59, the earlier treaty applies only to the extent that its provisions are compatible with those of the later treaty.

4. When the parties to the later treaty do not include all the parties to the earlier one:

   a) as between States parties to both treaties the same rule applies as in paragraph 3.

   b) as between a State party to both treaties and a State party to only one of the treaties, the treaty to which both States are parties governs their mutual rights and obligations.

5. Paragraph 4 is without prejudice to Article 41, or to any question of the termination or suspension of the operation of a treaty under Article 60 or to any question of responsibility which may arise for a State from the conclusion or application of a treaty the provisions of which are incompatible with its obligations towards another State under another treaty.'

Third States

The general rule

The general rule is that a treaty applies only between the parties to it, and this principle is a corollary of the principle of consent and the sovereignty and independence of States.

Article 34 of the Vienna Convention provides: 'A treaty does not create either obligations or rights for a third State without its consent.'

This general rule is known by the maxim *pacta tertiis nec nocent nec prosunt* and Article 34 undoubtedly reflects customary international law in this respect.

Exceptions to the general rule

Whether such exceptions exist is a matter of controversy. The International Law Commission was of firm opinion that a treaty cannot of itself create obligations for non-parties.

Article 35 of the Vienna Convention provides:

'An obligation arises for a third State from a provision of a treaty if the parties to the treaty intend the provision to be the means of establishing the obligation and the third State expressly accepts that obligation in writing.'

The International Law Commission commenting upon this provision acknowledged that the requirements in it are so strict that when they are met

'... there is, in effect, a second collateral agreement between the parties to the treaty, on the one hand and the third State on the other; and that the juridical basis of the latters obligation is not the treaty itself but the collateral agreement.'

However, two exceptions to the general rule have been recognised:

1. a treaty may become binding on non-parties if it becomes a part of international customary law. An example is the 1907 Hague Convention on the rules of land warfare which now reflect customary international law and therefore have application to States generally;
2. a treaty may provide for sanctions to be imposed on aggressor States which violate the law.

In this respect the effect of Article 2(6) of the Charter of the United Nations must be noted.

Article 2(6) provides: 'The Organisation shall ensure that States which are not Members of the United Nations act in accordance with these Principles so far as may be necessary for the maintenance of international peace and security.'

One view is that this provision creates duties and liabilities for non-members of the Organisation to impose sanctions under the enforcement provisions of the Charter.

However, it can be argued that the only justification for such an interpretation would be that the principles set out in Article 2 of the Charter of the United Nations reflect customary international law.

Can a treaty confer rights on a third party?

Some treaties contain provisions in favour of specified third States or in respect of States generally. Examples of such third party rights are contained for instance in the treaty provisions guaranteeing freedom of passage for ships through the Suez and Kiel Canals. For example, Convention Respecting Free Navigation of the Suez Canal 1888:

Article 1 provides: 'The Suez Maritime Canal shall always be free and open, in time of war as in time of peace, to every vessel of commerce or of war, without distinction of flag'.

When, if at all, does such a right conferred upon a third State become established and enforceable by it?

Two opposing views have been expressed on this point:

1. the accepted view is that the third State may only claim the benefit if it assents, either expressly or impliedly, to the creation of the right;
2. the right created in favour of the third party is not conditional upon any express act of acceptance by the third party.

The International Law Commission adopted the view that in practice the effects of the two opposing views would be substantially the same. The matter was given effect in Article 36 of the Vienna Convention which provides:

'1. A right arises for a third State from a provision of a treaty if the parties to the treaty intend the provision to accord that right either to the third State, or to a group of States to which it belongs, or to all States, and the third State assents thereto. Its assent shall be presumed so long as the contrary is not indicated, unless the treaty otherwise provides.

2. A State exercising a right in accordance with paragraph 1 shall comply with the conditions for its exercise provided for in the treaty or established in conformity with the treaty.'

So this Article creates a presumption of assent on the part of the third State.

Revocation and modification of third party rights

Article 37 of the Vienna Convention provides:

'1. When an obligation has arisen for a third State in conformity with Article 35, the obligation may be revoked or modified only with the consent of the parties to the treaty and of the third State, unless it is established that they had otherwise agreed.

2. When a right has arisen for a third State in conformity with Article 36, the right may not be revoked or modified by the parties if it is established that the right was intended not to be revocable or subject to modification without the consent of the third State.'

13.7 Amendment and modification of treaties

Amendment

The normal method of amending a treaty is by the unanimous agreement of the parties and Article 39 of the Vienna Convention provides that: 'A treaty may be amended by agreement between the parties'.

If all the parties agree to the amendment no difficulty arises. But in a large multilateral convention it may not be possible to obtain unanimous agreement to a proposed amendment.

Many treaties contain provisions for an amendment procedure.

For example, Article 109 of the Charter of the United Nations provides for the holding of a General Conference of Member States 'for the purpose of reviewing the present Charter'.

Other multilateral treaties provide for possible revision at the end of specified periods. For example, the Geneva Conventions on the Law of the Sea provide that any party, after the expiry of five years from the entry into force of the Convention, may request the revision of the Convention by a notification in writing to the United Nations Secretary General.

Cases where the treaty contains no reference to amendment

In these cases Article 40 of the Vienna Convention provides as follows:

'1. Unless the treaty otherwise provides, the amendment of multilateral treaties shall be governed by the following paragraphs.

2. Any proposal to amend a multilateral treaty as between all the parties must be notified to all the contracting States, each one of which shall have the right to take part in:

   a) the decision as to the action to be taken in regard to such proposals;

   b) the negotiation and conclusion of any agreement for the amendment of the treaty.

3. Every State entitled to become a party to the treaty shall also be entitled to become a party to the treaty as amended.

4. The amending agreement does not bind any State already a party to the treaty which does not become a party to the amending agreement; Article 30, paragraph 4(b) applies in relation to such State.

5. Any State which becomes a party to the treaty after the entry into force of the amending agreement shall, failing an expression of a different intention by that State:

   a) be considered as a party to the treaty as amended; and

   b) be considered as a party to the unamended treaty in relation to any party to the treaty not bound by the amending agreement.'

Effects of amendment

In general, therefore, an amendment will only bind parties that have agreed to it and if one State has agreed to the amendment and another State has not, then the terms of the original treaty will remain operative between them.

'Legislative' amendment

In some cases a State may consent in advance to accept amendments agreed upon by a majority of the parties to the treaty.

For example, Article 108 of the Charter of the United Nations provides:

'Amendments to the present Charter shall come into force for all Members of the United Nations when they have been adopted by a vote of two-thirds of the Members of the General Assembly and ratified in accordance with their respective constitutional processes by two thirds of the Members of the United Nations, including all the permanent Members of the Security Council.'

Modification

This occurs where a number of parties to the treaty formally agree to modify the effects of the treaty amongst themselves, while continuing to be bound by the treaty in their relations with the other parties.

This matter is covered by Article 41 of the Vienna Convention:

'1. Two or more of the parties to a multilateral treaty may conclude an agreement to modify the treaty as between themselves alone if:
    a) the possibility of such a modification is provided for by the treaty; or
    b) the modification in question is not prohibited by the treaty and
        i) does not affect the enjoyment by the other parties of their rights under the treaty or the performance of their obligations;
        ii) does not relate to a provision, derogation from which is incompatible with the effective execution of the object and purpose of the treaty as a whole.
2. Unless in a case falling under paragraph 1(a) the treaty otherwise provides, the parties in question shall notify the other parties of their intention to conclude the agreement and of the modification to the treaty for which it provides.'

Modification by subsequent practice

A consistent practice, if it establishes common consent of the parties to be bound by a different rule from that laid down in the treaty, will have the effect of modifying the treaty. The following is an illustration of the process in operation:

The Italian Peace Treaty of 1947 was signed and ratified by nearly 20 States. It provided for the setting up of a Free Territory of Trieste, but this proved impracticable owing to disagreements between the Great Powers. It was subsequently agreed by four of the signatories that Italy and Yugoslavia should each administer half the territory. This agreement was acted upon by Yugoslavia and Italy and was not objected to by the other States. Thus, the terms of the original Peace Treaty were modified by subsequent practice.

13.8 Interpretation of treaties

The Vienna Convention states the general rules as follows in Article 31:

'1. A treaty shall be interpreted in good faith in accordance with the ordinary meaning to be given to the terms of the treaty in their context and in the light of its object and purpose.

2. The context for the purpose of the interpretation of a treaty shall comprise, in addition to the text, including its preamble and annexes:

　a) any agreement relating to the treaty which was made between all the parties in connection with the conclusion of the treaty;

　b) any instrument which was made by one or more parties in connection with the conclusion of the treaty and accepted by the other parties as an instrument related to the treaty.

3. There shall be taken into account, together with the context:

　a) any subsequent agreement between the parties regarding the interpretation of the treaty or the application of its provisions;

　b) any subsequent practice in the application of the treaty which establishes the agreement of the parties regarding its interpretation;

　c) any relevant rules of international law applicable in the relations between the parties.

4. A special meaning shall be given to a term if it is established that the parties so intended.'

Article 32 of the Vienna Convention further provides:

'Recourse may be had to supplementary means of interpretation, including the preparatory work of the treaty and the circumstances of its conclusion, in order to confirm the meaning resulting from the application of Article 31, or to determine the meaning when the interpretation according to Article 31:

　a) leaves the meaning ambiguous or obscure; or

　b) leads to a result which is manifestly absurd or unreasonable.'

In the *Fisheries Jurisdiction Case* (1972) the UK introduced the entire record of the negotiations leading to the exchange of notes into the case. In the case of the EC treaties, however, the travaux preparatoires are generally *un*available to the Court as an aid to interpretation. This may explain the emphasis on the 'aims and objects' approach.

The Vienna Convention lays emphasis on a textual approach to interpretation. The words used should be given their natural and ordinary meaning. If the words used are clear and unambiguous then an international tribunal must give effect to the treaty in the sense required by the clear and unambiguous wording, unless some valid ground can be shown for interpreting the provision otherwise.

In the *Competence of the General Assembly Case* (1950) the ICJ stated the position as follows:

'The Court considers it necessary to say that the first duty of a tribunal which is called upon to interpret and apply the provisions of a treaty, is to endeavour to give effect to them in their natural and ordinary meaning in the context in which they occur. If the relevant words in their natural and ordinary meaning make sense in their context, that is an end of the matter. ... When the Court can give effect to a provision of a treaty by giving to the words used in it their natural and ordinary meaning, it may not interpret the words seeking to give them some other meaning'.

The textural approach includes the following principles:

1. the words used should be given their ordinary and natural meaning;
2. the words must be interpreted in the context of the treaty as a whole;
3. the natural and ordinary meaning must be unambiguous;
4. the ordinary and natural meaning must not lead to an absurd or unreasonable result.

In addition to the textual approach, attention must also be drawn to the 'objects and purposes' test, otherwise known as the *principle of effectiveness*. In the *Peace Treaties Case* (ICJ, AO, 1949), the Court interpreted the effectiveness principle narrowly, holding that the duty of the Court was to interpret treaties, not to revise them. In the *SWA* Advisory Opinion (1950), however, the Court's opinion that the UN trusteeship system had succeeded the Mandate System under the League was, arguably, based on the notion of effectiveness as there was no clear indication of this in the Charter. Of interest, also, is the strong emphasis in favour of effectiveness adopted by the European Court of Justice in its interpretation and application of the Treaty of Rome (see, for example, *van Gend en Loos* (1963)).

13.9 Termination of treaties

The rule, *pacta sunt servanda*, is the fundamental principle of the law of treaties and is expressed in Article 26 of the Vienna Convention: 'Every treaty in force is binding upon the parties to it and must be performed by them in good faith.'

A State cannot release itself from its treaty obligations whenever it feels like it. If it could, treaties would become worthless. However, few treaties last for ever, and in order to prevent the law from becoming too rigid some provision is made for the termination of treaties. But in so doing, the law regarding the termination of treaties tries to steer a middle course between the two extremes of rigidity and insecurity.

Article 42(2) of the Vienna Convention in seeking to protect the security of legal relations provides:

'The termination of a treaty, its denunciation or the withdrawal of a party, may take place only as a result of the application of the provisions of the treaty or of the present Convention. The same rule applies to suspension of the operation of a treaty.'

Termination in accordance with the terms of the treaty

Article 54 of the Vienna Convention provides: 'The termination of a treaty or the withdrawal of a party may take place: a) in conformity with the provisions of the treaty'.

The following are examples of the most frequently used provisions for the termination of or the withdrawal from treaty obligations.

1. The treaty may be for a specified period.
2. The treaty may be for a minimum period with a right to withdraw at the expiry of that period.

3. The treaty may be for a specific purpose and terminate on completion of that purpose.
4. The treaty may allow withdrawal at any time.
5. The treaty may allow withdrawal in special circumstances.

Termination by agreement

Article 54(b) of the Vienna Convention provides: 'The termination of a treaty or the withdrawal of a party may take place: ... b) at any time by consent of all the parties after consultation with the other contracting States.'

Implied right of denunciation or withdrawal

The agreement of the parties to terminate the treaty may be implied. In this respect Article 56 of the Vienna Convention provides:

'1. A treaty which contains no provision regarding its termination and which does not provide for denunciation or withdrawal is not subject to denunciation or withdrawal unless:
    a) it is established that the parties intended to admit the possibility of denunciation or withdrawal; or
    b) a right of denunciation or withdrawal may be implied by the nature of the treaty.
2. A party shall give not less than twelve months notice of its intention to denounce or withdraw from a treaty under paragraph 1.'

A right of denunciation or withdrawal may therefore be implied in certain types of treaties because of their very nature, for example, treaties of alliance and commercial treaties.

But under Article 56 a right to denunciation or withdrawal can never be implied if the treaty contains an express provision regarding denunciation, withdrawal or termination.

Implied termination where the parties enter into a similar
treaty on the same subject matter

Article 59 of the Vienna Convention provides:

'1. A treaty shall be considered as terminated if all the parties to it conclude a later treaty relating to the same subject matter and:
    a) it appears from the later treaty or is otherwise established that the parties intended that the matter should be governed by that treaty; or
    b) the provisions of the later treaty are so far incompatible with those of the earlier one that the two treaties are not capable of being applied at the same time.
2. The earlier treaty shall be considered as only suspended in operation if it appears from the later treaty or is otherwise established that such was the intention of the parties.'

Therefore, it is apparent from Article 59 that in the case of multilateral treaties implied termination is less readily established.

Reduction of the parties to a multilateral treaty below the number necessary for its entry into force

If the parties to a multilateral treaty state that it should only enter into force once a certain number of States have ratified it, there is no reason, in the absence of a specific provision to the contrary, why the treaty should terminate if, subsequently, the number of parties falls below the number necessary to bring the treaty into force.

This general rule is laid down in Article 55 of the Vienna Convention:

> 'Unless the treaty otherwise provides, a multilateral treaty does not terminate by reason only of the fact that the number of the parties falls below the number necessary for its entry into force.'

Material breach of the treaty

It is recognised that the material breach of a treaty by one party entitles the other party or parties to the treaty to invoke the breach as a ground of termination or suspension.

Article 60(1) of the Vienna Convention provides:

> 'A material breach of a bilateral treaty by one of the parties entitles the other to invoke the breach as a ground for terminating the treaty or suspending its operation in whole or in part.'

This right of termination or suspension has become accepted as being the main sanction for securing the observance of treaties.

However, the problem has become more complex in the case of breach of a multilateral treaty. There are two aspects to such treaties: the rights of the parties to the treaty as a group, and the rights of the individual States towards the breach.

In this respect Article 60(2) of the Vienna Convention provides:

> 'A material breach of a multilateral treaty by one of the parties entitles:
> a) the other parties by unanimous agreement to suspend the operation of the treaty in whole or in part or to terminate it either;
> i) in the relations between themselves and the defaulting State, or
> ii) as between all parties;
> b) a party specially affected by the breach to invoke it as a ground for suspending the operation of the treaty in whole or in part in the relations between itself and the defaulting State;
> c) any party other than the defaulting State to invoke the breach as a ground for suspending the operation of the treaty in whole or in part with respect to itself if the treaty is of such a character that a material breach of its provisions by one party radically changes the position of every party with respect to the further performance of its obligations under the treaty.'

Paragraph 2(c) applies in respect of those treaties where, 'a breach by one party tends to undermine the whole regime of the treaty as between all the parties' the best example being disarmament treaties. In obligations under the treaty *vis-à-vis* the defaulting State without at the same time violating its obligations to the other parties. Yet, unless it does so, it may be unable to protect itself against the threat resulting from the arming of the defaulting State'.

The breach must be 'material'
Article 60(3) of the Vienna Convention provides:

> 'A material breach of a treaty, for the purposes of this article, consists in: a repudiation of the treaty not sanctioned by the present Convention; or the violation of a provision essential to the accomplishment of the object or purpose of the treaty.'

Such a breach does not automatically terminate the treaty; it merely gives the injured party or parties an option to terminate or suspend the treaty.

Article 45 of the Vienna Convention provides that an injured party will lose this right to exercise the option:

> '... if after becoming aware of the facts: it shall have expressly agreed that the treaty ... remains in force or continues in operation, as the case may be; or it must by reason of its conduct be considered as having acquiesced ... in its (the treaty) maintenance in force or in operation, as the case may be'.

Breaches giving no right of termination or suspension
Article 60(5) of the Vienna Convention provides:

> 'Paragraphs 1 to 3 do not apply to provisions relating to the protection of the human person contained in treaties of a humanitarian character, in particular to provisions prohibiting any form of reprisals against persons protected by such treaties.'

The provisions contained in the 1949 Geneva Convention prohibiting reprisals against the persons protected by those Conventions would come within this Article.

Supervening impossibility of performance

There may be circumstances in which a treaty is literally impossible to perform by one of the contracting parties. The International Law Commission gave examples of the submergence of an island, the drying up of a river or the destruction of a dam, indispensable for the execution of a treaty.

Article 61 of the Vienna Convention therefore provides:

> '1. A party may invoke the impossibility of performing a treaty as a ground for terminating or withdrawing from it if the impossibility results from the permanent disappearance or destruction of an object indispensable for the execution of the treaty. If the impossibility is temporary, it may be invoked only as a ground for *suspending* the operation of the treaty.
>
> 2. Impossibility of performance may not be invoked by a party as a ground for terminating, withdrawing from or suspending the operation of a treaty if the impossibility is the result of a breach by that party either of an obligation under the treaty or of any other international obligation owed to any other party to the treaty.'

Such impossibility of performance does not automatically terminate the treaty, but merely gives a party an option to terminate.

Fundamental change of circumstances

A party is not bound to perform a treaty if there has been a fundamental change of circumstances since the treaty was concluded.

The Vienna Convention in Article 62 confines this rule within very narrow limits:

'1. A fundamental change of circumstances which has occurred with regard to those existing at the time of the conclusion of a treaty, and which was not foreseen by the parties, may not be invoked as a ground for terminating or withdrawing from the treaty unless:
  a) the existence of those circumstances constituted an essential basis of the consent of the parties to be bound by the treaty; and
  b) the effect of the change is radically to transform the extent of obligations still to be performed under the treaty.
2. A fundamental change of circumstances may not be invoked as a ground for terminating or withdrawing from the treaty:
  a) if the treaty established a boundary; or
  b) if the fundamental change is the result of a breach by the party invoking it either of an obligation under the treaty or of any other international obligation owed to any other party to the treaty.
3. If, under the foregoing paragraphs, a party may invoke a fundamental change of circumstances as a ground for terminating or withdrawing from a treaty, it may also invoke the change as a ground for suspending the operation of the treaty.'

This Article reflects the doctrine of *rebus sic stantibus* (things remaining as they are). Some writers base this principle on the fictional rule that every treaty contains an implied term that it shall only remain in force so long as circumstances remain the same. Although State practice supports the principle many jurists dislike the doctrine and prefer to confine its scope within very narrow limits. They see the doctrine as a considerable threat to the security of treaties and the International Law Commission considered the fiction to be undesirable in that it increased the risk of subjective interpretation and abuse.

Article 62(2)(a) excludes treaties fixing boundaries from the operation of the principle in order to avoid threats to the peace.

In the *Fisheries Jurisdiction Case: United Kingdom* v *Iceland* (1973) the ICJ said that Article 62 'may in many respects be considered as a codification of existing customary law on the subject' but held that the dangers to Icelandic interests resulting from new fishing techniques 'cannot constitute a fundamental change with respect to the lapse or subsistence' of the jurisdictional clause in a bilateral agreement.

New peremptory norm of general international law (jus cogens)

Article 64 of the Vienna Convention provides:

'If a new peremptory norm of general internation law emerges, any existing treaty which is in conflict with that norm becomes void and terminates.'

But this does not have retroactive effects on the validity of the treaty.

War and armed conflict

In the past war was regarded as ending all treaties between belligerent States. However, today few belligerent States will admit to being in a state of war and hostilities short of war do not automatically terminate a treaty. Therefore some treaties may be suspended, others may terminate on the grounds of impossibility or fundamental change of circumstances but others will remain binding, eg the Charter of the United Nations and the 1949 Geneva Conventions. Also many multilateral treaties will today include neutral States as well as belligerents among their parties.

The Vienna Convention does not specifically deal with the effects of war on treaties.

13.10 Settlement of disputes

Articles 65 to 68 of the Vienna Convention provide for the situation where a State:

'...invokes either a defect in its consent to be bound by a treaty or a ground for impeaching the validity of a treaty, terminating it, withdrawing from it or suspending its operation'.

Article 65(1) provides that the State must notify the other parties of the 'measures proposed to be taken with respect to the treaty and the reasons therefor'.

Article 65(2) provides that the notification should specify a period within which the other parties should raise objections and this period 'except in the case of special urgency, shall not be less than three months after the receipt of the notification'.

Article 65(3) provides that if an objection is raised the State making the notification and the other party or parties objecting 'shall seek a solution' in accordance with Article 33 of the Charter of the United Nations: viz 'negotiation, equity, mediation, conciliation, arbitration, judicial settlement, resort to regional agencies or arrangements, or other peaceful means of their own choice'.

If no solution has been reached by the means specified in Article 65(3) 'within a period of 12 months following the date on which the objection was raised' Article 66 confers jurisdiction on the ICJ over disputes arising from Article 53 (*jus cogens*) and confers jurisdiction over other disputes on a special conciliation commission set up under an annex to the Convention.

These rules represent a significant innovation compared to the position under customary international law. Under customary international law, international courts and commissions do not have jurisdiction over all cases concerning claims that a treaty is invalid, but only over those cases where the parties agree to submit the matter to such a court or commission.

13.11 Treaties by international organisations

The Vienna Convention on Treaties for International Organisations 1986 regulates the procedures for negotiating treaties between states and international organisations and among international organisations themselves. For the most part, the 1986 Convention repeats the rights and duties contained in the Vienna Convention on the Law of Treaties 1969, relating to matters such as the formalities and negotiating procedures for making treaties, validity, the application of treaties, the amendment and modification of treaties, interpretation and termination.

The capacity of international organisations to enter treaties is governed by Article 6 which provides that 'the capacity of an international organisation to conclude a treaty is governed by the rules of that organisation'.

An international organisation that is a party to a treaty is prohibited from invoking the terms of its constitution or internal rules as a justification for failing to perform its obligations under an international agreement. Nor can an agreement entered into by an international organisation establish rights for third states in the absence of the consent of that state. International organisations express their consent to be bound by the terms of a treaty through agents who have been delegated authority to enter into such commitments by the internal rules and procedures of the organisation.

14

Good Faith

14.1   Estoppel

14.2   Abuse of rights

The principle of good faith has long been accepted as being a part of internatonal law. Bin Cheng, for example, quotes the sole arbitrator in the *Metzger & Co Case* (1900) saying that 'it cannot be that good faith is less obligatory upon nations than upon individuals in carrying out agreements'. The content of the principle is, however, less easy to define. There is no doubt that the principle of good faith is closely bound up with the law of treaties. More generally, however, the concept of good faith probably also includes general considerations of *equity*. In this guise, good faith has found applications in the jurisprudence of the ICJ and has become intrinsic to the methodology of international law. The current discusson of good faith is limited to a discusson of two principles, *estoppel* and *abuse of rights*.

14.1 Estoppel

Bowett states the operation of the principle of estoppel as follows:

> 'The rule of estoppel, whether treated as a rule of substantive law or not, operates so as to preclude a party from denying before a tribunal the truth of a statement of fact made previously by that party to another whereby that other has acted to his detriment or the party making that statement has secured some benefit.'

The basis of this rule, Bowett argues, is in the principle of good faith and as such finds a place in many systems of law.

The essential of an estoppel

A statement of fact which is clear and unambiguous
In the *Serbian Loans Case: France* v *Serbia* (1929) the question arose whether by their conduct in accepting payment of interest upon the loans in French francs as opposed to gold francs, the French bondholders had represented that they were prepared to accept payment in French francs. If they had, then it was arguable that they were henceforth estopped from claiming payment according to the strict terms of the loan. The Permanent Court of International Justice on this point determined

that there had been no clear and unequivocal representation of the bondholders upon which the debtor State was entitled to rely and had relied.

The statement or representation must be voluntary, unconditional and authorised

Leaving aside the question of treaties imposed upon the defeated after a war, a representation that creates an estoppel must be made voluntarily by the party against whom the estoppel is pleaded. Thus, any form of duress or fraud will automatically negate a plea of estoppel.

Reliance in good faith upon the representation of one party by the other party to his detriment (or to the advantage of the party making the representation)

This third essential of the estoppel defined by Bowett:

> '... illustrates how the principle of good faith lies at the very root of the doctrine of estoppel, for that doctrine has binding effect only where the party making the representation has secured some advantage thereby, or the other party relying on the representation has as a result suffered some detriment: the consequent change in the position of the parties means that in order to maintain good faith the party must stand by his representation.'

The most forceful assertion of this requirement was made by Taft CJ in the *Tinoco Arbitration: Great Britain* v *Costa Rica* (1923). Costa Rica argued that the non-recognition by Great Britain of the Tinoco Government during its period of control estopped the British Government from claiming that the Tinoco Government could confer binding agreements. Taft CJ determined that an equitable estoppel 'must rest on previous conduct of the person to be estopped, which has led the person claiming the estoppel into a position where the truth will injure him'.

Professor Bowett, a leading advocate of the doctrine of estoppel in international law, claims that estoppels are of different types. This argument is employed to meet the common criticism that estoppel operates in an incoherent and specialised way, its incidents and effects not being uniform.

Estoppel by treaty, compromise, exchange of notes, etc

This type of estoppel is analogous to the municipal law estoppel by deed. The fact that the obligation is evidenced in writing is significant, for the court will have primary recourse to the deed to ascertain the meaning of the undertaking. The doctrine of estoppel in this case supplements the maxim *pacta sunt servanda*.

In the *Eastern Greenland Case: Denmark* v *Norway* (1933) the Danish contention was that vaious bi-lateral and mutual treaties to which Norway was a party and which described Greenland as a Danish colony or as part of Denmark or by which Denmark was allowed to exclude Greenland from the operation of the agreement, precluded Norway from contesting Danish sovereignty over Greenland. This contention was upheld by the Permanent Court of International Justice.

Estoppel by conduct

Bowett defines this type of estoppel as 'a representation of a state of fact made expressly or impliedly where, upon a reasonable construction of a party's conduct, the conduct presupposes a certain state of facts to exist'. Since there is no instrument, such as a deed as in the former case, it is a stricter test. It is analogous to an equitable estoppel and is more exclusively founded on the principle of good faith.

The representation of fact must be unequivocal in that it must support the meaning attributed to it by the party raising the plea of estoppel, and the party must satisfy the court that it objectively understood the statement to have that meaning. In the *Eastern Greenland Case* the Danish Government tried to adduce the Ihlen declaration as an equitable estoppel precluding Norway from contesting Danish sovereignty over Greenland. But the Court felt that not only was the declaration unambiguous, the Danes could not have inferred the meaning they attributed to the statement.

This form of estoppel plays an important role in claims of nationality. This is because in cases where the basic facts are ambiguous the conduct of governments will provide answers. Thus, in the *Hendry Claim*, the Mexican-US General Claims Commission held that Mexico the respondent State, was estopped from denying the American nationality of the deceased, Hendry, by reason of it having discharged him from employment because he was an American. Similarly in *Kunkel et al v Polish State*, the Tribunal took the view that Poland having liquidated the estates of certain persons on the ground that they were Germans, were estopped from denying their German nationality so as to deprive those persons of legal remedies afforded to German nationals under the Peace Treaties. But in both these examples it acts as a procedural rule.

Although Bowett has argued his case forcefully and drawn on a wealth of examples from international jurisprudence, questions still remain as to its consistency as a concept. In the *Temple Case*: *Cambodia* v *Thailand* (1962), for example, Fitzmaurice thought that the English requirements of reliance and detriment are necessary; but in the *Eastern Greenland Case* such a requirement was not postulated. Sometimes, as in the *Temple Case* it has the effect of making it impossible for a party to contradict his previous statement; at other times it merely makes it difficult. These inconsistencies point to its deficiencies as a concept. Any legal concept requires certain qualities to differentiate it from similar concepts.

It is suggested that the only area where it can have substantial effect is in territorial acquisition. In those situations acquiescence and express admissions are part of the evidence of sovereignty. Estoppel differs merely in that it is a clear assertion of a point of view, possibly where the bulk of the evidence is equivocal. Acquiescence of the kind that is conclusive of the issue – an effect not dissimilar to estoppel – must rest on very cogent evidence.

14.2 Abuse of rights

Lauterpacht defines the doctrine as follows:

> 'The essence of the doctrine is that, as legal rights are conferred by the community, the latter cannot countenance their anti-social use by the individual: that the exercise of a hitherto legal rights becomes unlawful when it degenerates into an abuse of rights; and that there is such an abuse of rights each time the general interest of the community is affected as the result of the sacrifice of an important social or individual interest to a less important though hitherto legally recognised individual right.'

Lauterpacht argued that the use of a right can degenerate as a consequence of social change if that change is not accompanied by a reciprocal change in the law. On the municipal plane there is no real problem; legislators pass new laws and the legal change is effected. But on the international plane there is no mechanism for achieving such ends unless the government responsible for the abuse voluntarily agrees to either control or forfeit the right by treaty. Moreover, customary change is both slow and dependent on the crucial element of acquiescence. Lauterpacht saw the doctrine of abuse of rights as supplying a missing but vital part of the laws of nations; a mechanism for change by the judicial creation of new torts.

Other writers have also acknowledged the doctrine. Hyde states:

> '...the society of nations may at any time conclude the acts which an individual state was previously deemed to possess the right to commit without external interference are so injurious to the world at large as to justify the imposition of restrictions'.

The content of the doctrine

The most thorough investigation into the doctrine of abuse of rights has been carried out by Dr Kiss. He suggests three elements:

1. the use of a State power which interferes with another States use of a power;
2. the use of a power for a reason which was not one for which the power was conferred;
3. the use of power in an unjustifiable or arbitrary manner.

The use of a State power which interferes with another State's use of a power

This probably represents the ultimate basis of abuse of rights. *In practice it appears as bad faith.* A State acts in bad faith where it abuses its rights and does so knowing it has abused its rights. There can be no abuse of rights where a party is acting in good faith: *Lake Lanoux Arbitration: France* v *Spain* (1957).

Lake Lanoux on the French side of the Pyrenees is fed by streams rising in France and flowing only through French territory. Its waters ultimately feed the Spanish river Segre. The Treaty of Bayonne 1856 provided for the joint use of the waters. It was alleged by Spain that certain plans proposed by France would adversely affect Spain's rights and interests contrary to the Treaty and could only be undertaken with the prior agreement of both parties. The text of the Treaty stated that whenever interpretation is necessary, it should be in accordance with the rules of international law. Since the rules of international law were not material the rules of customary international law were examined. The Spanish contention on the need for prior consultation was rejected by the Court on the ground that France had acted in good faith.

The arbitration was governed by the maxim that the Treaty must be interpreted in good faith. The fact of the possible prejudice to Spanish interests was taken into consideration but was discounted because both parties had shown good faith.

International jurisprudence does not disclose many examples of cases where the international tribunal sought specifically to find bad faith. In the *Tacna-Arica Arbitration* (1922) between Chile and Peru such finding was made. By the Treaty of Ancon 1883 the provinces of Tacna and Arica which constituted a part of Peru were to remain in the possession of Chile for ten years from the date of ratification of the Treaty. On the expiry of the ten-year period a plebiscite was to have been held to decide whether the provinces were to remain permanently under Chilean control, or to continue to constitute part of Peru. Peru sought to terminate the Treaty, alleging that Chile was forcing Peruvians out of the disputed provinces and therefore frustrating the impending plebiscite. The Arbitrator rejected these allegations:

> 'The Arbitrator is far from approving the course of Chilean administration and condoning the acts committed against Peruvians to which reference has been made, but finds no reason to conclude that a fair plebiscite in the present circumstances cannot be held under proper conditions or that a plebiscite should not be had ... It is manifest that if abuses of administration could have the effect of terminating such an agreement, it would be necessary to establish such serious conditions as the consequence of administrative wrongs as would operate to frustrate the purpose of the agreement, and, in the opinion of the Arbitrator, a situation of such gravity has not been shown.'

The requirement of bad faith limits the effectiveness of the doctrine since it creates evidential difficulties. In the case concerning *Certain German Interests in Polish Upper Silesia* (1926) it was held that, after the peace treaty came into force and until transfer of sovereignty over Upper Silesia, the right to dispose of State property in the territory remained with Germany. The Court admitted that alienation would constitute a breach of her obligations if there was a misuse of the right. But, as the Court said 'such misuse cannot be presumed, and it rests with the party who states that there has been such a misuse to provide his statement'. And to prove misuse, bad faith would have to be shown. Similarly, in the *Free Zones of Upper Savoy and The District of Gex Case* (1932) the Court held that French fiscal legislation applied to the Free Zones (which were in French territory), but that 'a reservation must be made as regards the abuse of right, an abuse which, however, cannot be presumed by the Court'.

The use of a power for a reason which was not one for which the power was conferred

This heading possesses the greatest scope for growth, but it has no general field of operation in State action. For it to operate there must be a conferred power set out with some measure of precision. State powers are not, in general, conferred. And powers of international organisations are cloaked in such general language for a review of proper purposes to be ineffective. However, there are cases at the lower level in the jurisprudence of the United Nations and the International Labour Organisation which may point to a future way. Lauterpacht saw the doctrine as part of the development of law through the ICJ; and it is clear that in the judicial context the doctrine is analogous to the grounds of review inherent in English administrative law. A corollary of the doctrine, it is contended, is that where an admitted right is exercised in an abusive way the act must be regarded as void or invalid or alternatively that it becomes legitimate to have recourse to means for nullifying its effects.

In the *Admissions Case* (1948) the question arose in relation to the use of the veto for preventing the admission of new members to the United Nations. Article 4(1) of the Charter of the United Nations provides that:

> 'Membership in the United Nations is open to all other peace-loving States which accept the obligations contained in the present Charter and, in the judgment of the Organisation, are able and willing to carry out these obligations.'

A number of legal or entirely political reasons were given by members of the Security Council when voting on applications for admission. At one stage the Soviet Union let it be known that it would not vote against the applications of Finland and Italy only if Bulgaria, Hungary and Roumania were admitted to membership at the same time. This 'package deal' led the General Assembly to seek an opinion of the ICJ on two specific questions.

1. Was a Member State voting on an application for membership entitled to take into account conditions other than those laid down in Article 4(1) of the Charter?
2. Was a Member State entitled to subject its affirmative vote to the additional condition that other applicants be admitted to membership at the same time?

The majority held that the list was exhaustive. It then proceeded to discuss whether the matter came within those to be enumerated, and the Court felt that the voting States were possessed of a considerable margin of appreciation. However, the irrelevant matter was considered and held to be bad since it clearly constitutes a new condition; since it is entirely unconnected with those prescribed in Article 4. But all this objection amounts to is to state that the matter was an irrelevant consideration; this in turn, implies that it was alien to the tenor of the rule, ie it was an improper purpose.

The dissenters held that there was a residual discretion on States to consider matters other than those listed. They looked for an improper purpose. They also looked at the aims and objects of the Article but could only find a reference to the aims and objects of the Organisation.

> 'In the exercise of this power the Member is legally bound to have regard to the principle of good faith, to give effects to the Purposes and Principles of the United Nations and to act in such a manner as not to involve a breach of the Charter.'

It has been contended that this is the correct conclusion, given the postulate that the aim and object of the Article could only be found in the aim and object of the Organisation. It must be recognised that with that postulate as the basis for control, no control can in effect be exercised since the Organisation's aims and objects are so vague and imprecise that an accurate evaluation of any matter is impossible.

One major international judicial review of discretionary action is to be found in the *South West Africa Case*. It was alleged that South Africa had violated its Mandate to govern South-West Africa by misusing its government competence, ie an abuse of rights.

> 'South Africa had violated its obligations under the Mandate, *inter alia*, by unilaterally modifying its terms, by failing to promote to the utmost the material and moral well being and social progress of the inhabitants, by practising apartheid in the territory, by failing to report annually to the United Nations and by failing to transmit petitions to it.'

Two issues were at the heart of the case.

Does the ICJ have the power to review?

South Africa contested this and the question only arose as an alternative submission. It is suggested that the power of judicial review is an inherent power of the ICJ.

The scope of Article 2(2) of the mandate

Article 2(2) requires South Africa to promote to the utmost the material and moral well being and social progress of the inhabitants of the mandated territory.

South Africa's arguments were as follows:

1. The proposition that State actions are only limited by positive provisions of international law.

    In order to base the Court's review on positive provisions, positive restrictions had to be found in the mandate. The only restriction Article 2(2) of the mandate places upon South Africa is that it must act for the material and moral well being and social progress of the inhabitants. Since there was nothing further, South Africa concluded that there could be no control over the power to administer the mandate. All the Court could do was to examine errors of procedure, competence and bad faith.

2. South Africa's alternative contention was that even if the Court could review for improper purposes, the argument necessarily failed.

The applicants had to make their case out in terms of bad faith. Moreover, it is unlikely that a State would pursue improper purposes in relation to Article 2(2) without bad faith. All possible grounds for misuse were the same – bad faith. To show bad faith one has to refer to the decision makers' subjective intention.

Only four judges discussed abuse of discretion – Judges Forster, Tanaka, Jessup and Judge *ad hoc* Van Wyk. Judge Forster saw the issue as excess of power, but did not expand on it. Judge Tanaka spoke of 'general rules which prohibit the Mandatory from abusing his power and being made fides in performing its obligations'. Judge ad hoc Van Wyk took the correct analogy – that of administrative law – but gave no clear indication that he saw them on separate grounds. The right approach is to be found in Judge Jessup's judgment.

Judge Jessup developed the analogy of municipal administrative law. The Permanent Court of International Justice in the *Lotus Case* described the greatest area of State competence – domestic jurisdiction as a discretion. This discretion is clearly analogous to that which exists in municipal law – the discretionary action by government. Municipal courts leave to the person possessing the discretion a margin of appreciation and examine only such questions of law as may be denoted from the legislation conferring the discretion. In this case the power is conferred and as a consequence an international tribunal is in an identical position to the municipal court.

The conclusion which can be deduced from the above observation is one Judge Jessup reached: that if the review is analogous to one conducted by a municipal law court then it is wider than a finding of bad faith. Few systems of administrative law rely on bad faith as the sole ground for judicial review. In England, for example, improper purposes, relevant and irrelevant factors and unreasonableness also figure in the control exercised by the courts over administrative action.

Use of power in an unjustifiable or arbitrary manner

This heading emerges from general international law. Broadly speaking it refers to discrimination and, possibly, unjust enrichment. Its use in international adjudication is infrequent. Something exceptional has to be proved before an action will be held wrongfully discriminatory. An action cannot be deemed discriminatory merely because it helps some to the detriment of others. In fact, legislation of positive discrimination is enacted on the basis that it is necessary to discriminate in favour of backward groups merely to ensure equality of opportunity. And there exists a residual discretion with government bodies to assess whether this action serves the community despite the inequality. Thus in the *El Triunfo Case*, the tribunal was willing to find that the expropriation involved was discriminatory because:

1. the only property taken was that of a US national;
2. relations with the USA at the time indicated that the property had been taken because it belonged to a person of that nationality.

This is a high standard of proof. It is doubtful if the action would have been considered discriminatory if another nationality had had property expropriated.

In the jurisprudence of the European Commission and Court of Human Rights there is no discrimination where the benefitting of some and the harming of others is referrable to a proper reason. Thus, in *Church of Scientology* v *United Kingdom* the Commission noted that:

> '... in deciding whether to recognise an institution as an educational establishment the State is entitled to have regard to certain minimum educational standards ... therefore any governmental measures which are taken to differentiate institutions on such a basis do not constitute discrimination'.

The point was made again with greater force in the Court's decision in *Certain Aspects of the Laws on the Use of Language in Education in Belgium*.

> 'The competent national authorities are frequently confronted with situations and problems which, on account of differences inherent therein, call for different legal solutions; moreover, certain legal inequalities tend only to correct factual inequalities.'

The main criterion was stated to be the existence of an 'objective and reasonable justification for the distinction'.

Another problem where the discriminatory thesis has been applied is the abuse of rights in the expulsion of aliens. The competence to exclude people entering and the competence to remove people from the jurisdiction falls within the ambit of State jurisdiction. It is a unique attribute of sovereignty. The abuse of that power lies not in the expulsion, but in the discriminatory expulsion of a particular linguistic or ethnic group. Oppenheim considers that such expulsion is a classic instance of abuse of rights. This view is not without authority. In the *Boffolo Claim: Italy* v *Venezuela* (1903) the Umpire said:

> 'The country exercising the power (of expulsion) must, when occasion demands, state the reason of such expulsion before an international tribunal, and an inefficient reason or none being advanced, accept the consequences.'

15

The Law of the Sea

15.1 Sources of law

15.2 Internal waters

15.3 The territorial sea

15.4 The contiguous zone

15.5 Exclusive economic zone

15.6 The high seas

15.7 The continental shelf

15.8 The deep sea-bed

15.1 Sources of law

The legal regime of the law of the sea is to be found in a host of general and specific conventions and in customary international law.

The United Nations Conference at Geneva in 1958 codified the law of the sea in four conventions:

1. The Convention on the Territorial Sea and the Contiguous Zone (TSC).
2. The Convention on the High Seas (HSC).
3. The Convention on Fishing and Conservation of the Living Resources of the High Seas (FCC).
4. The Convention on the Continental Shelf (CSC).

The majority of the provisions contained in these conventions codify customary international law.

The 1958 Conventions failed, however, to deal adequately with several questions. Many of their provisions have in addition now been overtaken by advances in technology. The United Nations Conference on the Law of the Sea therefore began meeting in 1973 in order to draft a new convention on the Law of the Sea. The result has been the United Nations Convention on the Law of the Sea which opened for signature in Jamaica on 10 December 1982.

241

The Convention was closed for signature in December 1984 at which time 159 States had signed. Under Article 308, the Convention will enter into force 12 months after the date of deposit of the 60th instrument of ratification. As of the start of 1990 42 States had ratified the Convention.

The 1982 Convention is the result of a nine-year negotiating process. The text itself is a 'package deal' resulting from the compromises agreed during the conference between States with different priorities. While many of the provisions of the 1958 Geneva Convention are reiterated in the 1982 Convention, the Convention goes beyond the earlier texts in a number of important respects. Firstly, a number of issues not spelt out in 1958 were clarified in the 1982. Chief amongst these was the width of the territorial sea. No agreement was reached by the parties in 1958 although it was commonly thought that customary law prescribed a limit of 3 miles. Article 3 of the 1982 Convention now puts the width of the territorial sea at 12 miles. Secondly, with advances in technology and other developments since 1958 a number of the provisions in the earlier treaties had proven to be inadequate to deal with the practical realities of the circumstances. One such example was the definition of the continental shelf in 1958 which provided, *inter alia*, that the continental shelf would include all that part of the sea-bed adjacent to the coast 'where the depth of the waters admit of exploration and exploitation'. Deep sea mining techniques have robbed this definition of any limiting quality whatsoever. Article 76 of the 1982 Convention has therefore now amended the old test and substituted for it a more complex definition.

Thirdly, the 1982 Convention includes within its scope a whole range of developments that had not been considered in 1958. The 1958 Convention, for example, did not include a regime in respect of the exclusive economic zone or the deep sea-bed. Also, the years following the conclusion of the 1958 Convention saw a range of developments in the laws relating to fouling and pollution. Many of these developments are now reflected in the 1982 Convention.

While the Convention was intended as a package deal which would not admit of reservations by individual States, it became apparent that the USA and a number of other industrialised States – including the UK – had some disquiet over the deep sea-bed regime set out in the treaty. As a result, the USA and three other States voted against the adoption of the text. Seventeen other States, including the UK, abstained in the vote. At the present time there is, therefore, some doubt about the application and impact of the treaty *qua* treaty. This notwithstanding, it is evident that many of the provisions of the 1982 Convention do reflect customary international law. In addition, all those States that have signed the treaty have a general obligation – under Article 18 of the Vienna Convention on the Law of Treaties – not to defeat the object and purposes of the treaty. Also, while industrialised States continue to express concern about the deep sea-bed provisions' of the Convention, there are fewer indications of hostility towards the treaty in general. In September 1989, for example, the USA and USSR voted that their 'Governments are guided by the provisions of the 1982 Convention ... which, *with respect to traditional uses of the oceans*, generally constitute international law and practice and balance fairly the interests of all States.' The Convention, while not yet in force, exerts a dominant influence on the maritime practices of States.

15.2 Internal waters

Internal waters consist of ports, harbours, lakes, rivers, canals and waters on the landward side of the baselines from which the breadth of the territorial sea is measured.

The regime of internal waters is found mainly in customary international law. Internal waters are subject to State sovereignty. In the absence of treaty or other agreement, no right of passage, innocent or otherwise exists for foreign vessels in internal waters. But, whereas such a prohibition may be justified in respect of foreign warships, most coastal States have an interest in the preservation and promotion of free maritime navigation and trade between ports and therefore restrictions on passage are unlikely to be placed on foreign merchant ships.

Jurisdiction over foreign ships in internal waters

Warships
The coastal State has limited jurisdiction over foreign warships in its internal waters. Coastal State authorities cannot board a foreign warship or carry out any act on board such a vessel without the consent of its captain or other authority of the flag State. The crew of the vessel are immune from prosecution by the coastal State for crimes committed on board the vessel and for crimes committed ashore, provided that they were in uniform and on official business at the time of committing the crime.

Merchant ships
The coastal State may enforce its national laws against foreign merchant ships in its internal waters. The rule was expressed by Wait CJ in *Wildenhus's Case*, United States Supreme Court 1887 as follows:

> 'It is part of the law of civilised nations that when a merchant vessel of one country enters the ports of another for the purposes of trade, it subjects itself to the law of the place to which it goes, unless by treaty or otherwise the two countries have come to some different understanding or agreement ... As the owner has voluntarily taken his vessels for his own private purposes to a place within the dominion of a Government other than his own, and from which he seeks protection during his stay, he owes that Government such allegiance for the time being as is due for the protection to which he becomes entitled.'

There are, however, a number of exceptions to this rule. The coastal State courts' jurisdiction is not exclusive. The courts of the flag State may also try persons for crimes committed on board the vessel. Ships in distress are accorded a degree of immunity from coastal State jurisdiction. The coastal State cannot seek to take advantage of their distress by imposing harbour duties and taxes in excess of any services rendered. All matters of discipline and all things done on board a foreign ship which affect only the vessel or those belonging to her, and do not involve the peace or dignity of the coastal State, or the tranquillity of the port should be left by the local government to be dealt with by the authorities of the nation to which the vessel belongs.

15.3 The territorial sea

All coastal States have sovereign rights over their territorial sea, its sea-bed and subsoil and the airspace above it.

The Geneva Convention on the Territorial Sea and the Contiguous Zone 1958, provides that subject to the provisions of these articles and to other rules of international law:

Article 1:

'(1) The sovereignty of a State extends beyond its land territory and its internal waters, to a belt of sea adjacent to its coast, described as the territorial sea.'

Article 2:

'The sovereignty of a coastal State extends to the airspace over the territorial sea as well as to its bed and subsoil.'

This rule, which is repeated in Article 2 of the United Nations Convention on the Law of the Sea, 1982 (UNCLOS III), represents customary international law.

The width of the territorial sea

There was no uniform State practice regarding the width of the territorial sea. Some States, in particular Great Britain and the USA supported the 3-mile territorial sea which had developed from the 'cannon-shot rule' in the late eighteenth century. But while most States originally accepted the 3-mile rule other States claimed territorial seas ranging from four to 12 miles and some States, particularly those in South America, claimed a 200 mile territorial sea.

Gradually the 3-mile rule began to be abandoned, but because of the conflicting interests of States it proved impossible to reach agreement as to what the new rule should be. States with large maritime fleets such as Great Britain and the USA argued in favour of a narrow territorial sea which would have minimal effect on the freedom of the high seas. In particular they were afraid that any extension of the territorial sea beyond 3 miles would:

1. restrict the freedom of movement of their naval fleets, particularly submarines which in exercising the right of innocent passage through the territorial sea must navigate on the surface and show their flag;

2. restrict the operations of their distant water fishing fleets which would be excluded from fishing in rich coastal waters;
3. restrict the operations of aircraft, which have no right of innocent passage over the territorial sea;
4. restrict the right of passage through many of the most important international straits which would become the territorial seas of the coastal States.

They also argued that:

1. the safety of shipping would be affected as most landmarks and lighthouses are not visible at a range of 12 miles;
2. ships could not anchor in the deep water outside a 12 mile limit;
3. the cost of patrolling the territorial sea would be increased and would prove impossible for many Third World States;
4. defence of the territorial sea would be difficult; in particular neutral States would have difficulty enforcing their neutrality against incursion of their territorial sea by belligerent ships. Belligerent submarines could also use the extended territorial sea to hide and take sanctuary.

Against this those States in favour of extending the width of the territorial sea argued that the retention of the 3-mile limit would:

1. permit the distant water fishing fleets of the advanced Western nations with their new trawling techniques and refrigeration to exploit the fishery resources of those coastal States which lack the capital and technology to harvest the fish for themselves;
2. permit the maritime powers to exert psychological pressure on weaker coastal States by the display of naval force just outside the 3-mile limit.

Under customary international law therefore the position regarding the width of the territorial sea was far from clear. However, one point was reasonably certain. It was generally accepted by States that any claim to a territorial sea in excess of 12 miles was invalid. This rule was implicit from Article 24 of the Territorial Sea Convention which provides that the contiguous zone (which is an area of high seas stretching beyond the territorial sea) cannot extend more than 12 miles from the baselines from which the breadth of the territorial sea is measured.

Article 3 of the 1982 Convention now provides:

'Every State has the right to establish the breadth of its territorial sea up to a limit not exceeding 12 nautical miles, measured from base lines determined in accordance with this Convention.'

State practice now shows that 12 miles is the width most commonly claimed by States and Article 3 probably reflects the present customary international law position.

Delimitation of the territorial sea

The normal baseline from which the breadth of the territorial sea is measured is the low-water line along the coast. This rule is affirmed in Article 5 of the 1982 Convention (Article 3 TSC):

> 'Except where otherwise provided in these articles, the normal baseline for measuring the breadth of the territorial sea is the low water line along the coast as marked on large scale charts officially recognised by the coastal State.'

The use of straight baselines

In some situations geographical circumstances permit the drawing of straight baselines. This method consists of selecting appropriate points on the low-water mark and drawing straight lines between them. It was the method approved by the ICJ in the *Anglo Norwegian Fisheries Case* (1951) in the particular circumstances of the Norwegian coast and it has also been used by the UK for drawing baselines on the west coast of Scotland.

Article 7 of the 1982 Convention (Article 4 TSC) provides:

> '1. In localities where the coastline is deeply indented and cut into, or if there is a fringe of islands along the coast in its immediate vicinity, the method of straight baselines joining appropriate points may be employed in drawing the baseline from which the breadth of the territorial sea is measured.
>
> 2. Where, because of the presence of a delta and other natural conditions, the coastline is highly unstable, the appropriate points may be selected along the furthest seaward extent of the low-water line and, notwithstanding subsequent regression of the low-water line, the straight baselines shall remain effective until changed by the coastal State in accordance with this Convention.
>
> 3. The drawing of such baselines must not depart to any appreciable extent from the general direction of the coast, and the sea areas lying within the lines must be sufficiently closely linked to the land domain to be subject to the regime of internal waters.
>
> 4. Straight baselines shall not be drawn to and from low-tide elevations, unless lighthouses or similar installations which are permanently above sea level have been built on them, or except in instances where the drawing of baselines to and from such elevations has received general international recognition.
>
> 5. Where the method of straight baselines is applicable under paragraph 1, account may be taken, in determining particular baselines, of economic interests particular to the region concerned, the reality and the importance of which are clearly evidenced by a long usage.
>
> 6. The system of straight baselines may not be applied by a State in such a manner as to cut off the territorial sea of another State from the high seas or an exclusive economic zone.'

This Article confirms the principle laid down by the ICJ in the *Anglo-Norwegian Fisheries Case* (1951).

Article 8 (1982) provides:

> '1. ... waters on the landward side of the baseline of the territorial sea form part of the internal waters of the state.
>
> 2. Where the establishment of a straight baseline in accordance with the method set forth in Article 7 has the effect of enclosing as internal waters areas which previously had been considered as such, a right of innocent passage ... shall exist in those waters.'

Bays

Customary law allowed straight baselines to be drawn across the mouth of a bay from which the width of the territorial sea could then be measured. However, there was no uniform rule as to the maximum permissible length of such lines.

This uncertainty was removed by Article 7 of the TSC which provides that where the coast of the bay belongs to a single State the maximum length of the closing line is 24 miles.

The Convention does not apply to historic bays which are treated under customary international law as the internal waters of the coastal State. For example, Canada claims historic rights over Hudson Bay, the mouth of which is approximately 50 miles wide.

The legal regime applicable inside bays which are not considered historic bays is less certain, particularly where there is more than one coastal state. For example, in *Case Concerning Land, Island and Maritime Frontier Dispute* (1992), the ICJ held that a bay with three adjacent coastal states was subject to the joint authority of all three states except for a 3-mile maritime belt along the coast.

Also Article 7 does not apply in those cases where the straight baseline system provided for in Article 4 is applied. In such cases a coastal State may derive title to a bay as internal waters if enclosed in the exercise of delimitation in accordance with Article 4.

Article 10 of the Law of the Sea Convention reiterates the existing principles governing bays.

Islands

Article 10 of the TSC provides:

> '1. An island is a naturally formed area of land surrounded by water, which is above water at high tide.
>   2. The territorial sea of an island is measured in accordance with the provisions of these articles.'

Thus, permanently submerged banks and reefs do not produce any right to a territorial sea.

Recently small islands have become very important because of the possibility of discovering offshore deposits of oil and gas and also because the State exercising sovereignty over the island may claim an exclusive economic zone of 200 miles from the baselines from which the territorial sea of the island is measured.

For example, the UK claims sovereignty over Rockall, a tiny islet 265 miles north west of Ireland, 298 miles west of Scotland and 350 miles south west of the Faroes. Since 1 January 1977 the UK has claimed an exclusive 200 mile fishing limit around Rockall giving her an additional 100,000 square miles of fishing grounds in the North Atlantic.

Article 121 of the Law of the Sea Convention restates in paragraph 1 the definition of an island contained in Article 10(1) of the Geneva Convention. However, Article 121(3) of the Convention provides:

'Rocks which cannot sustain habitation or economic life of their own shall have no exclusive economic zone or continental shelf.'

Thus, under the Convention the UK would lose the right to an exclusive fishery zone around Rockall – one reason why the UK refuses to ratify the Convention.

Archipelagos

An archipelago is a group of islands. Examples of mid-ocean archipelagos include Indonesia, Philippines, Fiji, Galapagos and the Hawaiian Islands.

The Geneva Convention on the Territorial Sea makes no specific mention of groups of islands and does not provide any special system for delimiting the territorial sea of such groups on any group basis. Under Article 10(2) each island in the group would have its own territorial sea measured around it in the normal way. If the islands are close together so that their individual territorial seas overlap a block of territorial sea may be created. But if there is no overlap, then the waters between the various areas of territorial seas will be high seas.

Several mid-ocean archipelagos, in particular Indonesia, the Philippines and Fiji, have now claimed to delimit their territorial waters by joining the outermost points of their outermost islands through straight baselines. Vast expanses of water, otherwise regarded as high seas have thus been enclosed. These States have sought to justify their action on economic, political and security grounds, placing strong reliance on the judgment of the ICJ in the *Anglo-Norwegian Fisheries Case*:

'A State must be allowed the latitude necessary in order to be able to adapt its delimitation to practical needs and local requirements.'

The Law of the Sea Convention provides for the use of straight baselines by archipelagic States. These are defined in Article 46(a) as States constituted wholly by one or more archipelagos and may include other islands.

'Archipelago' is defined as a group of islands, including parts of islands, interconnecting waters and other natural features which are so closely interrelated that such islands, waters and other natural features, form an intrinsic geographical, economic and political entity, or which historically have been regarded as such.

Article 47 of the Convention provides for the drawing of archipelagic baselines:

'1. An archipelagic State may draw straight archipelagic baselines joining the outermost points of the outermost islands and drying reefs of the archipelago provided that within such baselines are included the main islands and an area in which the ratio of the area of the water to the area of the land, including atolls, is between one to one and nine to one.

2. The length of such baselines shall not exceed 100 nautical miles, except that up to three per cent of the total number of baselines enclosing any archipelago may exceed that length, up to a maximum length of 125 nautical miles.

3. The drawing of such baselines shall not depart to any appreciable extent from the general configuration of the archipelago.'

Article 49 of the Convention provides that the sovereignty of the archipelagic State extends to the waters enclosed by the baselines, the airspace above and the sea-bed and subsoil below, and the resources contained therein.

Article 52 of the Convention provides that ships of all States enjoy the right of innocent passage through archipelagic waters. But, under Article 53 an archipelagic State may designate sea lanes and air routes which must be used by foreign ships and aircraft passing through or over the archipelagic waters and the adjoining territorial sea.

If an archipelagic State does not designate sea lanes or air routes, the right of archipelagic sea lanes passage may be exercised through the routes normally used for international navigation.

Rights of the coastal State over its territorial sea

Article 1 of the TSC, reiterated in Article 2 of UNCLOS III, provides that the coastal State exercises sovereignty over its territorial sea. The following rights and duties are inherent in that sovereignty:

1. The exclusive right over fisheries and the exploitation of the living and non-living resources of the sea-bed and subsoil.
2. The right to exclude foreign vessels from trading along its coast (cabotage).
3. The right to impose regulations concerning navigation, customs, fiscal, sanitary health and immigration.
4. The exclusive enjoyment of the airspace above the territorial sea.
5. The duty of belligerents in time of war to respect the neutral States' territorial sea and refrain from belligerent activities therein.

The right of innocent passage

The sovereignty of the coastal State over its territorial sea is subject to one important limitation. Customary law recognises that foreign vessels have the right of innocent passage through the territorial sea. This right, based upon practical considerations, is necessary to facilitate communications by sea.

The customary rule is restated in Article 14(1) of the TSC and has been developed in Articles 17–19 of the 1982 Convention.

Article 17 sets out the basic right as follows:

'Subject to this Convention, ships of all States, whether coastal or land-locked, enjoy the right of innocent passage through the territorial sea.'

Article 18 goes on to define what is meant by passage:

'1. Passage means navigation through the territorial sea for the purpose of:
   a) traversing that sea without entering internal waters or calling at a roadstead or port facility outside internal waters; or
   b) proceeding to or from internal waters or a call at such roadstead or port facility.
2. Passage shall be continuous and expeditious. However, passage includes stopping and anchoring, but only in so far as the same are incidental to ordinary navigation or are rendered necessary by force majeure or distress or for the purposes of rendering assistance to persons, shops or aircraft in danger or distress.'

Article 19 of the Convention then goes on to enumerate what is meant by 'innocent passage':

'1. Passage is innocent so long as it is not prejudicial to the peace, good order or security of the coastal State. Such passage shall take place in conformity with this convention and with other rules of international law.

2. Passage of a foreign ship shall be considered to be prejudicial to the peace, good order or security of the coastal State, if in the territorial sea it engages in any of the following activities:

a) Any threat or use of force against the sovereignty, territorial integrity or political independence of the coastal State, or in any other manner in violation of the principles of international law embodied in the Charter of the United Nations;

b) Any exercise or practice with weapons of any kind;

c) Any act aimed at collecting information to the prejudice of the defence or security of the coastal State;

d) Any act of propaganda aimed at affecting the defence or security of the coastal State;

e) The launching, landing or taking on board of any aircraft;

f) The launching, landing or taking on board of any military device;

g) The loading or unloading of any commodity, currency or person contrary to the customs, fiscal, immigration or sanitary regulations of the coastal State;

h) Any act of wilful and serious pollution; contrary to this Convention;

i) Any fishing activities;

j) The carrying out of research or survey activities;

k) Any act aimed at interfering with any systems of communication or any other facilities or installations of the coastal State;

l) Any other activities not having a direct bearing on passage.'

Hampering innocent passage

Article 24 of the Law of the Sea Convention, extending Article 15 of the TSC, provides that:

'1. The coastal State shall not hamper the innocent passage of foreign ships through the territorial sea except in accordance with this Convention. In particular ... the coastal State shall not:

a) Impose requirements on foreign ships which have the practical effect of denying or impairing the right of innocent passage, or

b) Discriminate in form or in fact against the ships of any State or against ships carrying cargoes to, from or on behalf of any State.

2. The coastal State is required to give appropriate publicity to any dangers to navigation, of which it has knowledge, within its territorial sea.'

Rights of the coastal State

The coastal State may in accordance with Article 25 of the 1982 Convention:

1. prevent passage which is not innocent;
2. enact laws and regulations in respect of ships proceeding to internal waters;
3. temporarily suspend innocent passage through its territorial sea.

Such suspension:

1. must not discriminate as between foreign vessels;
2. it must be temporary;

3. the area concerned must be specified;
4. it must be for the protection of the coastal State's security;
5. it must be essential;
6. due notification must be published;
7. it can take place only after such publication;
8. there is no right of suspension in respect of passage through international straits.

Article 25 essentially restates the provisions of Article 16 of the TSC except that the right to suspend innocent passage temporarily is extended to cover weapons exercises.

Article 26 of the 1982 Convention provides that no charges may be levied upon foreign ships in respect of mere passage through the territorial sea except for specific services rendered.

Coastal states right to regulate passage

Article 21(4) of the 1982 Convention provides that:

'Foreign ships exercising the right of innocent passage through the territorial sea shall comply with the laws and regulations and all generally accepted international regulations relating to the prevention of collisions at sea.'

Article 21(1) of the Convention provides:

'The coastal State may adopt laws and regulations in conformity with the provisions of this Convention and other rules of international law, relating to innocent passage through the territorial sea, in respect of all or any of the following:
  a) The safety of navigation and the regulation of marine traffic;
  b) The protection of navigational aids and facilities and other facilities or installations;
  c) The protection of cables and pipelines;
  d) The conservation of the living resources of the sea;
  e) The prevention of infringement of the fisheries regulations of the coastal State;
  f) The preservation of the environment of the coastal State and the prevention, reduction and control of pollution thereof;
  g) Marine scientific research and hydrographic surveys;
  h) The prevention of infringement of the customs, fiscal, immigration or sanitary regulations of the coastal State.'

Article 22 of the Convention permits the coastal State to introduce sea lanes and traffic schemes regulating the passage of ships through its territorial sea.

International straits

Problems may arise if the navigable channel of an international strait runs through the coastal State's territorial waters. In order to safeguard the right of passage through such straits at all times, Article 16(4) of the Geneva Convention provides:

'There shall be no suspension of the innocent passage of foreign ships through straits which are used for international navigation between one part of the high seas and another part of the high seas or the territorial sea of a foreign State.'

This reaffirms the customary international law position expressed by the ICJ in the *Corfu Channel Case* (1949). The Court stated:

> 'It is the opinion of the Court, generally recognised and in accordance with international custom that States in time of peace have a right to send their warships through straits used for international navigation between two parts of the high seas without the previous authorisation of a coastal State, provided that the passage is innocent. Unless otherwise prescribed in an international convention, there is no right for a coastal State to prohibit such passage through straits in time of peace.'

In practice the right of innocent passage through many international straits is guaranteed by treaty.

As more States extend their territorial seas the question of innocent passage through straits becomes more important. The Law of the Sea Convention now contains detailed provisions regarding passage through straits used for international navigation.

Article 38 of the Convention introduces the right of transit passage which under Article 37 applies to straits which are used for international navigation between one area of the high seas or an exclusive economic zone and another area of the high seas or an exclusive economic zone.

Article 38(1) provides:

> '1. In straits referred to in Article 37, all ships and aircraft enjoy the right of transit passage, which shall not be impeded, except that, if the strait is formed by an island of a State bordering the strait and, its mainland, transit passage shall not apply if there exists seaward of the island a route through the high seas or through an exclusive economic zone of similar convenience with respect to navigational and hydrographical characteristics.'

Transit passage is a much wider right than that of innocent passage and the limitations which a coastal State may impose upon innocent passage are not applicable to it.

Passage of warships through the territorial sea

Some States deny that warships have any right of passage through territorial waters in peacetime and some States require prior authorisation for the passage of warships through their territorial waters.

In the *Corfu Channel Case* the ICJ held that warships have right of passage through international straits but did not decide whether that right extends to the territorial sea in general. The 1958 Geneva Convention provisions regarding innocent passage do not specifically mention warships but some writers argue that their inclusion is implied. For instance Articles 14 to 17 of the Convention are headed 'Rules applicable to All Ships', and Article 14(6) relating to submarines implies that 'all ships' includes men of war.

Also Article 23, under the heading 'Rules applicable to warships' provides:

> 'If any warship does not comply with the regulations of the coastal State concerning passage through the territorial sea and disregards any request for compliance which is made to it, the coastal State may require the warship to leave the territorial sea.'

It has been argued that this Article also implies that warships do have a right of innocent passage through the territorial sea.

The Law of the Sea Convention does not serve to clarify the position regarding warships in the territorial sea.

Article 29 of the Convention defines warships as ships 'belonging to the armed forces of a State bearing the external marks distinguishing such ships of its nationality, under the command of an officer duly commissioned by the Government of the State and whose name appears in the appropriate service list or its equivalent, and manned by a crew which is under regular armed forces discipline'.

Article 30 deals with the non–observance by warships of the laws and regulations of the coastal State – 'the coastal State may require it to leave the territorial sea immediately'.

Article 31 imposes international responsibility upon the flag State for damage caused by warships to the coastal State.

Criminal jurisdiction in respect of ships in passage

Warships and non–commercial government ships enjoy absolute immunity from local jurisdiction. In the case of merchant ships, Article 27(1) of the 1982 Convention (reiterating Article 19(1) of the TSC) provides:

> 'The criminal jurisdiction of the coastal State should not be exercised on board a foreign ship passing through the territorial sea to arrest any person or to conduct any investigation in connection with any crime committed on board the ship during its passage, save only in the following cases:
> a) if the consequences of the crime extend to the coastal State; or
> b) if the crime is of a kind to disturb the peace of the country or the good order of the territorial sea; or
> c) if the assistance of the local authorities has been requested by the master of the ship or by a diplomatic agent or consular officer of the flag State; or
> d) if such measures are necessary for the suppression of illicit traffic in narcotic drugs or psychotropic substances.'

Article 27(5) prohibits the exercise of jurisdiction by the coastal State where the crime was committed before the ship entered the territorial sea if the ship is only passing through the territorial sea without entering internal waters.

Civil jurisdiction in respect of ships in passage

There are two matters to be considered: civil jurisdiction in respect of a person on board; and civil jurisdiction in respect of the vessel herself.

Persons on board

Article 28(1) of the 1982 Convention – reiterating Article 20(1) of the TSC – provides that the coastal State should not stop or divert a foreign ship passing through the territorial sea for the purpose of exercising civil jurisdiction in relation to a person on board the ship.

The vessel herself

Articles 28(2) and (3) of the Convention provide that except in the case of a vessel lying at anchor in the territorial sea or passing through the territorial sea after leaving internal waters, a vessel in passage may not be arrested, nor may execution be levied against her, on civil account, except in respect of obligations assumed, or liabilities incurred, expressly in the course or for the purpose of its voyage through the waters of the coastal State.

15.4 The contiguous zone

Under the regime established by the 1958 TSC, the contiguous zone was a zone which was part of the high seas over which the coastal state could exercise a degree of control. This approach has now changed. With the acceptance of an exclusive economic zone (EEZ), the contiguous zone can no longer form part of the high seas. Article 33 of the 1982 convention provides:

> '1. In a zone contiguous to its territorial sea, described as the contiguous zone, the coastal state may exercise the control necessary to:
>> a) prevent infringement of the customs, fiscal, immigration or sanitary laws and regulations within its territory or territorial sea;
>> b) punish infringement of the above laws and regulations committed within its territory or territorial sea.
>
> 2. The contiguous zone may not extend beyond 24 nautical miles from the baselines from which the breadth of the territorial sea is measured.'

The coastal State exercises control and not jurisdiction. The rights of the coastal State in the zone do not amount to sovereignty.

The contiguous zone must be claimed by the coastal State.

Security zones

Proposals to include security zones in the Convention were not adopted and it is doubtful that such zones have gained general acceptance by States. The International Law Commission Commentary on the Draft Articles reads:

> 'The Commission did not recognise special security rights in the contiguous zone. It considered that the extreme vagueness of the term 'security' would open the way for abuses and that the granting of such rights was not necessary. The enforcement of customs and sanitary regulations will be sufficient in most cases to safeguard the security of the State. In so far as measures of self-defence against an imminent and direct threat to the security of the State are concerned, the Commission refers to the general principles of international law and the Charter of the United Nations.'

15.5 Exclusive economic zone

The concept of the EEZ extending beyond the territorial sea was first developed by certain Latin American States to ensure their exclusive jurisdiction over fishing resources in a belt adjacent to their territorial seas.

The Truman Proclamation of 1945 had made governments aware that by making such a claim themselves they might acquire control over offshore resources, so limiting the operations of the distant water fishing fleets, and thereby conserving fishing stocks off their coasts and reserving them for their own fishermen.

Some States sought to achieve this aim by extending their territorial sea. For instance several South American countries – Brazil, Argentina, Uruguay, Peru, Ecuador, Panama and El Salvador – all claim a territorial sea of 200 miles. Other States, not wishing to attract international protest by claiming a 200 mile territorial sea, sought to claim a 'patrimonial sea', ie a territorial sea of up to 12 miles, plus an economic zone to a maximum distance of 200 miles (including the breadth of the territorial sea). Apart from the freedom of fishing, the freedom of the high seas apply.

This formula was adopted by a group of South American States bordering the Caribbean Sea in the Declaration of Santo Domingo in 1972. This Declaration states that all States exercise 'sovereign rights' over the renewable and non-renewable natural resources found in the waters, in the sea-bed and in the subsoil of an area adjacent to their territorial sea called the patrimonial sea. In this area, ships and aircraft of all States, whether coastal or not, have a right of freedom of navigation and overflight with no restrictions other than those resulting from the exercise by the coastal State of its rights within the area of the patrimonial sea. The freedom of laying submarine cables and pipelines is also recognised.

The EEZ under the law of the sea treaty

The idea of including the EEZ in the Law of the Sea Convention was raised early on in the negotiations. The principles governing this zone are now embodied in Part V of the 1982 Convention. Article 57 provides, for example, that 'the exclusive economic zone shall not extend beyond 200 nautical miles from the baselines from which the breadths of the territorial sea is measured'. This practice has received further support from dicta of the ICJ in the *Tunisia/Libya Continental Shelf Case* (1982) which accepted that the EEZ was part of customary law. There are now around 75 States which claim an EEZ, with a further 20 or so laying claim to an exclusive fishing zone.

Article 55 of the Convention defines the EEZ as 'an area beyond and adjacent to the territorial sea, subject to the specific legal regime established in this Part'.

Article 57 provides that the EEZ shall not extend beyond 200 nautical miles from the baselines from which the breadth of the territorial sea is measured.

Article 56(1) sets out the rights and duties of the coastal State in its EEZ:

'1. In the exclusive economic zone, the coastal State has:

a) sovereign rights for the purpose of exploring and exploiting, conserving and managing the natural resources, whether living or non living, of the waters superjacent to the sea-bed and of the sea-bed and its subsoil and with regard to other activities for the economic exploitation and exploration of the zone, such as the production of energy from the water currents and winds;

b) jurisdiction as provided for in the relevant provisions of this convention with regard to:

   i) the establishment and use of artificial islands, installations and structures;

   ii) marine scientific research;

   iii) the protection and preservation of the marine environment;

c) other rights and duties provided for in this Convention.'

Article 56(2) provides that:

'In exercising its rights and performing its duties under this convention in the exclusive economic zone, the coastal State shall have due regard to the rights and duties of other States and shall act in a manner compatible with the provisions of this Treaty.'

Article 58 of the Convention describes the rights and duties of other States in the EEZ. These include the freedom of navigation and overflight, the laying of submarine cables and pipelines, and other internationally lawful uses of the sea related to these freedoms. Such States shall have due regard to the rights and duties of the coastal State and shall comply with the law and regulations adopted by the coastal State.

The EEZ is not, therefore, in any sense regarded as territorial sea, and the right of navigation through the EEZ is not limited to the restrictive right of innocent passage.

Article 60 of the convention concerns artificial islands, installations, and structures in the zone. The coastal State has exclusive rights regarding their construction operation and use, and exclusive jurisdiction over them, with the obligation to give due notice that such structures exist. The coastal State may establish reasonable safety zones, generally not to exceed 500 metres, around such structures. No artificial islands, structures, or safety zones may be established where they would interfere with the use of recognised sea lanes essential to international navigation.

The Convention contains detailed provisions regarding the allocation of fishing resources within the zone and gives substantial control over them to the coastal State.

Articles 61 and 62 provide for the conservation and utilisation of the living resources of the EEZ.

Article 61(1) of the Convention permits the coastal State to determine the allowable catch of the living resources in its EEZ.

Article 61(2) places the obligation upon the coastal State to establish proper conservation and management measures to prevent overexploitation.

Article 62(1) provides that the coastal State shall promote the objective of optimum utilisation of the living resources of the EEZ without prejudice to Article 61.

One criticism of the EEZ concept was that conferring exclusive rights upon the coastal States over the living resources of the zone might lead to the inadequate utilisation of these resources owing to the fact that a number of coastal States do not have the capability to exploit these resources efficiently.

Article 62(2) of the Convention therefore provides:

'The coastal State shall determine its capacity to harvest the living resources of the exclusive economic zone. Where the coastal State does not have the capacity to harvest the entire allowable catch, it shall, though agreements or other arrangements ... give other States access to the surplus of the allowable catch ...'

Article 62(4) permits the coastal State to establish detailed regulations, with which foreign fishermen must comply, for conservation and utilisation purposes.

These provisions appear to allow the coastal State to subjectively determine the allowable catch and its capacity to harvest it. Wide latitude is also given to the coastal State in determining who shall have access to the surplus resources of the zone.

Article 62(3) merely provides that:

'In giving access to other States to its exclusive economic zone under this article the coastal State shall take into account all relevant factors including, *inter alia*, the significance of the living resources of the area to the economy of the coastal State concerned and its other national interests (the rights of land locked States and States with special geographical characteristics in the same sub-region or region), the requirements of developing States in the sub-region or region in harvesting part of the surplus and the need to minimise economic dislocation in States whose nationals have habitually fished in the zone or which have made substantial efforts in research and identification of stocks.'

Article 63 directs the coastal State to seek agreement on the conservation and utilisation of stocks which are found within the EEZs of two or more coastal States or which are both within and beyond the EEZ.

Articles 64 and 67 concern highly migratory species, marine mammals, anadromous species (fish that live in salt water but spawn in fresh water, eg salmon), and catadromous species (fish that live in fresh water but spawn in salt water, eg eel). States primarily concerned with such species are to ensure their conservation and management.

Articles 69 to 72 describe the rights of land-locked and geographically disadvantaged States in the EEZ. Subject to the provisions of Articles 61 and 62, land-locked States have the non-transferable right to fish in the EEZs of adjoining coastal States under terms and conditions determined by agreement between the States concerned.

Article 69(3) permits regional arrangements granting equal or preferential treatment to land-locked States in the same region. Developing coastal States that cannot claim an EEZ and those geographically disadvantaged States that depend on fishing in neighbouring zones have the nontransferable right to fish in the EEZs of other States in a region or subregion. This right is to be exercised under terms and conditions determined by agreement, and is subject to the conservation and utilisation principles expressed in Article 61 and 62. Article 70(1) provides that such agreements shall take into account relevant economic and geographical circumstances including under Article 70(3)(d) the need to protect coastal fishing communities and industries. Further, under Article 71, coastal States whose economies depend overwhelmingly on fisheries in their EEZs are exempt from the provisions of Article 69 and 70.

Article 73 of the convention provides coastal States with various enforcement mechanisms – boarding, inspection, arrest, and judicial proceedings – but not imprisonment or corporal punishment.

Article 74 provides for the delimitation of the EEZ between adjacent and opposite States. Such delimitation shall be by agreement in accordance with international law as referred to in Article 38 of the Statute of the ICJ in order to achieve an equitable solution.

15.6 The high seas

Article 1 of the Geneva Convention on the High Seas 1958 provides:

> 'The term "high seas" means all parts of the sea that are not included in the territorial sea or in the internal waters of a State.'

Freedom of the high seas

The principle is stated in Article 2 of the Geneva Convention on the High Seas as follows:

> 'The high seas being open to all nations, no State may validly purport to subject any part of them to its sovereignty. Freedom of the high seas is exercised under the conditions laid down by these articles and by the other rules of international law. It comprises, *inter alia*, both for coastal and non-coastal States:
> 1) Freedom of navigation;
> 2) Freedom of fishing;
> 3) Freedom to lay submarine cables and pipelines;
> 4) Freedom to fly over the high seas.
> These freedoms, and others which are recognised by the general principles of international law, shall be exercised by all States with reasonable regard to the interests of other States in their exercise of the freedom of the high seas.'

Both Articles 1 and 2 of the Geneva Convention reflect customary international law.

The Law of the Sea Convention introduces some changes to the regime of the high seas.

Article 86 provides that the high seas comprises all parts of the sea that are not included in the EEZ, in the territorial sea or in the internal waters of a State, or in the archipelagic waters of an archipelagic State.

Article 87 sets forth the four freedoms stated in Article 2 of the Geneva Convention but the freedom of fishing is restricted by the new regime of the 200-mile EEZ.

This Article also lays down two additional freedoms of the high seas: Article 87(1)(d), freedom to construct artificial islands and other installations permitted under international law; and Article 87(1)(f), freedom of scientific research.

Customary law also recognises the freedom to use the high seas for naval exercises and weapons testing.

Nationality of ships

Article 90 of the 1982 Convention – reflecting Article 4 of the HSC – provides that 'every State whether coastal or land-locked, has the right to sail ships under its flag on the high seas'.

Under international law each State may determine for itself the conditions on which it will grant its nationality to a merchant ship, thereby accepting responsibility for it and acquiring legislative, administrative and judicial jurisdiction over the vessel on both the international and domestic plane which no other State can challenge.

Nationality is evidenced to the world by the ship's papers and its flag.

The nationality of the ship depends upon registration and registration is subject to conditions laid down by municipal law. These conditions vary from country to country and some States have less stringent conditions for registration than others.

The practice has therefore grown of shipowners registering their vessels under the so-called flags of convenience (Panama, Liberia, Honduras, etc), thereby avoiding paying taxes and statutory wage rates required under certain municipal laws, and also circumventing certain marine treaty obligations which do not bind those flag of convenience States which are not parties to them. Thus, it has become increasingly common for the nationality of a vessel to be divorced from its actual operation and control.

In an attempt to deal with this problem the 1958 Geneva Convention on the High Seas introduced into the law governing the nationality of ships the 'genuine link' principle which had been applied by the ICJ in the *Nottebohm Case*.

Article 5(1) of the Geneva Convention provides:

> 'Each State shall fix the conditions for the grant of its nationality to ships, for the registration of ships in its territory, and for the right to fly its flag. Ships have the nationality of the State whose flag they are entitled to fly. There must exist a genuine link between the State and the ship; in particular, the State must effectively exercise its jurisdiction and control in administrative, technical and social matters over ships flying its flag.'

Article 5(1) has had little effect on the practice of governments, many of which recognise the value of the flags of convenience. One major defect of Article 5(1) is that it does not state any consequences if there is an absence of any genuine link.

Article 91(1) of the Law of the Sea Convention nevertheless retains the requirement of the genuine link.

Article 6 of the Geneva Convention and Article 92 of the 1982 Convention provides that a ship shall sail under the flag of one State only and that, save in the case of a transfer of ownership or change in registry, a ship may not change its flag during a voyage or in a port of call. A ship sailing under the flags of two or more States may be assimilated to a ship without nationality.

Jurisdiction on the high seas

The basic principle under customary international law is that only the flag State may exercise jurisdiction over a ship on the high seas.

Article 92(1) of the 1982 Convention – embodying Article 6(1) of the HSC – affirms this principle by providing that:

> '... ships shall sail under the flag of one State only and, save in exceptional cases expressly provided for in international treaties or in this Convention, shall be subject to its exclusive jurisdiction on the high seas'.

Exceptions to this general principle

Piracy

Article 14 of the HSC and Article 100 of UNCLOS III provide:

> 'All States shall co-operate to the fullest possible extent in the repression of piracy on the high seas or in any other place outside the jurisdiction of any State.'

Article 101 of the 1982 Convention (Article 15, HSC) provides that piracy consists of any of the following acts:

> '1) Any illegal acts of violence, detention or any act of depredation; *committed for private ends* by the crew or the passengers of a *private* ship or a private aircraft, and directed:
> a) On the high seas, *against another ship* or aircraft, or against persons or property on board such ship or aircraft;
> b) Against a ship, aircraft, person or property in a place outside the jurisdiction of any State;
> 2) Any act of voluntary participation in the operation of a ship or of an aircraft with knowledge of facts making it a pirate ship or aircraft;
> 3) Any act of inciting or of intentionally facilitating an act described in sub-paragraph (a) or (b) of this article.'

Article 110 of the 1982 Convention (Article 22(1)(a), HSC) provides that a warship which encounters a foreign merchant ship on the high seas may board her where there is reasonable ground for suspecting that the ship is engaged in piracy.

If the vessel is so engaged then under Article 105 (1982) (Article 19, HSC):

> 'On the high seas, or in any other place outside the jurisdiction of any State, every State may seize a pirate ship or aircraft, or a ship taken by piracy and under the control of pirates, and arrest the persons and seize the property on board. The courts of the State which carried out the seizure may decide upon the penalties to be imposed, and may also determine the action to be taken with regard to the ships, aircraft or property, subject to the rights of third parties acting in good faith.'

Slave traders

Article 99 of UNCLOS III (Article 13, HSC) provides:

> 'Every State shall take effective measures to prevent and punish the transport of slaves in ships authorised to fly its flag, and to prevent the unlawful use of its flag for that purpose. Any slave taking refuge on board any ship, whatever its flag, shall *ipso facto* be free.'

Article 110 of the 1982 Convention (Article 22(1)(b), HSC) provides that a warship which encounters a foreign merchant ship on the high seas may board her where there is reasonable ground for suspecting that the ship is engaged in the slave trade.

The right of approach
Customary law recognises the right of approach by warships to verify the identity and nationality of any merchant ships they may meet on the high seas.

The right to board and search, and capture in time of peace
With the exception of known pirate vessels, customary law does not recognise the right of warships to visit and search foreign merchant ships on the high seas. Such a right could be abused and therefore the relevant provisions in the High Seas Convention are most strict.

Article 110 of the 1982 Convention (Article 22, HSC) provides:

'1. Except where acts of interference derive from powers conferred by treaty, a warship which encounters on the high seas a foreign merchant ship ... is not justified in boarding her unless there is reasonable ground for suspecting that:
  a) The ship is engaged in piracy;
  b) The ship is engaged in the slave trade;
  c) The ship is engaged in unauthorised broadcasting;
  d) The ship is without nationality; or
  e) Though flying a foreign flag or refusing to show its flag, the ship is, in reality, of the same nationality as the warship.
2. In the cases provided for in paragraph 1, the warship may proceed to verify the ship's right to fly its flag. To this end, it may send a boat under the command of an officer to the suspected ship. If suspicion remains after the documents have been checked, it may proceed to a further examination on board the ship, which must be carried out with all possible consideration.
3. If the suspicions prove to be unfounded, and provided that the ship boarded has not committed any act justifying them, it shall be compensated for any loss or damage that may have been sustained.'

Article 110 of the Convention also provides that the right of visit may be carried out by military aircraft and any other duly authorised ships or aircraft clearly marked and identifiable as being on government service.

The right of hot pursuit
The right of hot pursuit is a customary law right designed to prevent a ship avoiding arrest by escaping to the high seas. This is now regulated by Article 111 of the 1982 Convention (Article 23, HSC).

'1. The hot pursuit of a foreign ship may be undertaken when the competent authorities of the coastal State have good reason to believe that the ship has violated the laws and regulations of that State. Such pursuit must be commenced when the foreign ship or one of its boats is within the internal waters, the archipelagic waters, the territorial sea or the contiguous zone of the pursuing State, and may only be continued outside the territorial sea or the contiguous zone if the pursuit has not been interrupted. It is not necessary that, at the time when the foreign ship within the territorial sea or the contiguous zone receives the order to stop, the ship giving the order should likewise be within the territorial sea or the contiguous zone. If the foreign ship is within a contiguous zone, as defined in Article 33, the pursuit may only be undertaken if there has been a violation of the rights for the protection of which the zone was established.

2. The right of hot pursuit shall apply *mutatis mutandis* to violations in the exclusive economic zone or on the continental shelf, including safety zones around continental shelf installations, of the laws and regulations of the coastal State applicable in accordance with this Convention to the exclusive economic zone or the continental shelf, including such safety zones.

3. The right of hot pursuit ceases as soon as the ship pursued enters the territorial sea of its own country or of a third State.

4. Hot pursuit is not deemed to have begun unless the pursuing ship has satisfied itself by such practicable means as may be available that the ship pursued or one of its boats or other craft working as a team and using the ship pursued as a mother ship is within the limits of the territorial sea, or as the case may be, within the contiguous zone or the exclusive economic zone or above the continental shelf. The pursuit may only be commenced after a visual or auditory signal to stop has been given at a distance which enables it to be seen or heard by the foreign ship.

5. The right of hot pursuit may be exercised only by warships or military aircraft, or other ships or aircraft clearly marked and identified as being on government service and authorised to that effect.

6. Where hot pursuit is effected by an aircraft:

a) The provisions of paragraphs 1 to 4 of this article shall apply *mutatis mutandis*;

b) The aircraft giving the order to stop must itself actively pursue the ship until a ship or aircraft of the coastal State, summoned by the aircraft, arrives to take over the pursuit, unless the aircraft is itself able to arrest the ship. It does not suffice to justify an arrest outside the territorial sea that the ship was merely sighted by the aircraft as an offender or suspected offender, if it was not both ordered to stop and pursued by the aircraft itself, or other aircraft or ships which continued the pursuit without interruption.

7. The release of a ship arrested within the jurisdiction of a State and escorted to a port of that State for the purposes of an inquiry before the competent authorities, may not be claimed solely on the ground that the ship, in the course of its voyage, was escorted across a portion of the high seas, if the circumstances rendered this necessary.

8. Where a ship has been stopped or arrested outside the territorial sea in circumstances which do not justify the exercise of the right of hot pursuit, it shall be compensated for any loss or damage that may have been thereby sustained.'

The Law of the Sea Convention substantially reproduces Article 23 of the High Seas Convention.

Other exceptions to the principle of the freedom of the high seas

Self-defence

Although some States have asserted a right in peacetime to interfere with ships in the exercise of self-defence, the law on the point is uncertain.

The International Law Commission commentary on the Draft High Seas Convention states:

'The question arose whether the right to board a vessel should be recognised also in the event of a ship being suspected of committing acts hostile to the State to which the warship belongs, at a time of imminent danger to the security of that State. The Commission did not deem it advisable to include such a provision, mainly because of the vagueness of terms like "imminent danger" and "hostile acts" which leaves them open to abuse.'

Ships flying no flag

Ships which fly no flag or which refuse to show a flag when requested to do so may be boarded by the ships of any State.

Article 110(1)(d) of the Law of the Sea Convention provides that a warship may board a foreign ship on the high seas where there is reasonable grounds for suspecting that the ship is without nationality.

Right of belligerents

In time of war belligerent warships may impose blockades of the enemy's ports and coasts, seize enemy merchant ships and visit, search and capture neutral ships carrying contraband or engaged in unneutral acts.

Treaty restrictions

Treaties may confer upon contracting parties powers of visit and capture beyond those permitted by customary law. In the past such treaties have related to the prohibition of slave trading, fishery conservation, smuggling arms and contraband and the protection of submarine cables.

Penal jurisdiction in collisions at sea

Article 11 of the HSC – now Article 97 of the 1982 Convention – provides:

'1. In the event of a collision or of any other incident of navigation concerning a ship on the high seas, involving the penal or disciplinary responsibility of the master or of any other person in the service of the ship, no penal or disciplinary proceedings may be instituted against such persons except before the judicial or administrative authorities either of the flag State or of the State of which such person is a national ...

3. No arrest or detention of the ship, even as a measure of investigation shall be ordered by any authorities other than those of the flag State.'

This provision reverses the judgment of the Permanent Court of International Justice in the *Lotus Case: France* v *Turkey* (1927).

Unauthorised broadcasting from the high seas

Article 109 of the Law of the Sea Convention provides:

'1. All States shall co-operate in the suppression of unauthorised broadcasting from the high seas.

2. For the purposes of this Convention, "authorised broadcasting" means the transmission of sound radio or television broadcasts from a ship or installation on the high seas intended for reception by the general public contrary to international regulations, but excluding the transmission of distress calls.

3. Any person engaged in unauthorised broadcasting may be prosecuted before the court of:
   a) the flag State of the ship;
   b) the State of registry of the installation;

c) the State of which the person is a national;

d) any State where the transmissions can be received; or

e) any State where authorised radio communication is suffering interference.

4. On the high seas, a State having jurisdiction in accordance with paragraph 3 may, in conformity with article 110, arrest any person or ship engaged in unauthorised broadcasting and seize the broadcasting apparatus.'

Pollution of the high seas

Pollution may occur within internal waters or within territorial waters. Both these areas are subject to the coastal States exclusive jurisdiction and it may take all the measures deemed necessary to deal with the pollution at its discretion. The key question concerns the legal control of pollution on the high seas outside territorial jurisdiction. The high seas are open to all nations. Therefore, every State may be in a position to pollute the high seas. The problem is one of the need to protect the marine environment while at the same time ensuring freedom of navigation to shipping States.

The first international standard on prohibiting oil pollution on the high seas was set by the 1954 International Convention for the Prevention of Pollution of the Sea by Oil. The convention set up prohibited zones in which the discharge of oil and oily mixtures into the sea from tankers and, to a lesser extent, other ships, is proscribed except in special circumstances (leakages which are unavoidable, safety factors etc). The zone as a general rule extended to a distance of 50 miles from the coastline. The convention does not apply to naval ships, ships under 500 gross tons and discharges of not less than 1/10,000 of the mixture. Enforcement was left to the flag State rather than the coastal State.

The 1954 Convention was amended in 1962 when the gross tonnage of tankers excluded from the Convention was lowered from 500 to 150 tons and the prohibited zone was extended to 100 miles from the shoreline. In 1969 the Convention was further amended and the prohibition on discharging oil or an oily mixture was extended to cover any part of the sea. The amendment permits the spilling of oil by a non-tanker only when the following conditions are met:

1. it is proceeding en route;
2. the rates of discharge of oil do not exceed 60 litres per mile;
3. the oil content of the discharge is less than 1/10,000;
4. the discharge is made as far from land as is practicable.

Tankers must satisfy (1) and (2) above and also:

1. the total quantity of discharge oil must not exceed 1/15,000 of cargo carrying capacity; and
2. the tanker must be more than 50 miles from land.

The 1954 Convention as amended is soon to be replaced by the International Convention for the Prevention of Pollution from Ships 1973, which consolidates and updates the law contained in the previous convention and amendments. It will also cover other forms of pollution as well as oil.

The 1958 Convention on the High Seas, and now the 1982 Convention, also impose obligations upon States to prevent pollution of the high seas:

Under Article 24 of the 1958 Convention:

'Every State shall draw up regulations to prevent pollution of the seas by the discharge of oil from ships or pipelines or resulting from the exploitation or exploration of the seabed and its subsoil, taking account of existing treaty provisions on the subject.'

Under Article 25:

'1. Every State shall take measures to prevent pollution of the sea from the dumping of radioactive waste, taking into account any standards and regulations which may be formulated by the competent international organisations.

2. All States shall co-operate with the competent international organisations in taking measures for the prevention of pollution of the seas of air-space above, resulting from any activities with radioactive materials or other harmful agents.'

Intervention on the high seas in cases of oil pollution casualties

Under customary international law a coastal State had no right to intervene in respect of threats to its territory caused by casualties on the high seas. The problem was highlighted in 1967 by the *Torry Canyon* incident in which a Liberian supertanker became stranded, causing an escape of crude oil which seriously polluted the coasts of the UK and France. To prevent any further escape of oil the Royal Air Force bombed the tanker. However, it is doubtful that such action is justified under customary law, even in self-defence. The unsatisfactory state of the customary law prompted the introduction of the *International Convention Relating to Intervention on the High Seas in Cases of Oil Pollution Casualties 1969.*

Article I grants contracting parties the right to take such measures on the high seas as may be necessary to prevent, mitigate or eliminate grave and imminent danger to their coastline or related interests from pollution or threat of pollution of the sea by oil, following upon a maritime casualty or acts related to such a casualty, which may reasonably be expected to result in major harmful consequences. It does not apply in respect of warships or other State ships not used commercially.

Article II provides that 'maritime casualty' means a collision of ships, stranding or other incident of navigation, or other occurrence on board a ship or external to it resulting in material damage or imminent threat of damage to a ship or cargo.

Article III provides that before taking any measures, a coastal State shall consult with other States affected and also the flag State of the casualty and independent experts. However, measures may be taken without prior consultation in cases of extreme urgency.

Article V states that action taken by the coastal State must be proportionate to the actual or threatened damage.

Article VI authorises the payment of compensation by a party in respect of damage caused by measures which exceed those reasonably necessary to achieve the end mentioned in Article I.

Compensation in respect of oil pollution damage

The *International Convention on Civil Liability For Oil Pollution Damage 1969* assigns liability to ship owners where a maritime incident results in pollution damage caused by oil which escapes or is discharged. No liability is incurred in respect of acts of war, hostilities, civil war, insurrection or a natural phenomenon of an exceptional, inevitable and irresistible character. There is also no liability for acts or omissions with intent to cause damage by a third party or by negligence or wrongful acts of government or other authorities responsible for marine lights or other navigational aids.

The Convention applies to damage caused in the territory including the territorial sea of a contracting State and to preventive measures taken to prevent or minimise such damage.

In addition to the above Conventions the following Conventions have also been adopted:

The Oslo Convention for the Prevention of Marine Pollution by Dumping from Ships and Aircraft 1972.

The London Convention on the Prevention of Marine Pollution by Dumping of Wastes and Other Matter 1972.

The Paris Convention for the Prevention of Pollution from Land-based Sources 1974.

The Convention for the Protection of the Mediterranean Sea Against Pollution 1976.

High seas fisheries

The High Seas Convention 1958 restated in Article 2 the customary international law position that every State, coastal and non coastal has freedom to fish the high seas. However, the belief that the resources of the high seas are inexhaustible and that their exploitation should go unregulated is no longer supported by the facts, and attempts have been made to enforce conservation measures.

The first attempt came with the 1958 Geneva Conference on the Law of the Sea which adopted a Convention on Fishing and Conservation of the Living Resources of the High Seas. The Convention came into effect in 1966 but has been of little effect. Its provisions cover three main aspects of fishing conservation.

The duty of conservation

The Convention provides that a State whose nationals are engaged in fishing any stock of fish shall adopt, for its own nationals, measures for the conservation of such stock. Where the nationals of two or more States are engaged in fishing the same stock, those States shall enter into negotiations with a view to arriving at an agreement to prescribe for their respective nationals, the necessary measures for the conservation of the stock. Where an established conservation programme is in operation the Convention provides that any new State beginning fishing of the stocks is to apply to its nationals the existing measures which have been taken by the other fishing States. This is a revolutionary concept and is an obligation imposed upon all States ratifying the Convention.

Special interests of the coastal state

The coastal State, whose nationals need not even be engaged in fishing off its coasts, is entitled to participate with other fishing States in any conservation measures taken in respect of off-shore fisheries. Article 7 of the Convention provides that in relation to the special interests of the coastal State:

'(1) ... any coastal State may, with a view to the maintenance of the productivity of the living resources of the sea, adopt unilateral measures of conservation ... in any area of the high seas adjacent to its territorial sea, provided that negotiations to that effect with the other States concerned have not led to an agreement within six months.

(2) The measure ... shall be valid as to other States only if the following requirements are fulfilled:

a) That there is a need for urgent application of conservation measures in the light of the existing knowledge of the fishery:

b) That the measures adopted are based on appropriate scientific findings:

c) That such measures do not discriminate in form or in fact against foreign fishermen.'

Compulsory settlement of disputes

The Convention contains provisions for the compulsory settlement of disputes concerning the conservation of fishery resources. Under the Convention special commissions will be established on an *ad. hoc* basis. Resort to the special commissions is obligatory for parties to the Convention and their decisions are binding upon disputes.

High seas exclusive fishery zones

The Geneva Convention on Fishing and Conservation of the Living Resources of the High Seas has proved to be of limited practical value. It has been superseded in many respects by the fact that customary international law now permits coastal States to claim a 200-mile exclusive fishing zone. The regime of the EEZ under the Law of the Sea Treaty also contains detailed provisions for the conservation and management of the living resources of the EEZ.

The management and conservation of the living resources of the high seas under the Law of the Sea Convention

Article 116 of the Law of the Sea Convention provides that subject to their treaty obligations and the regime of the EEZ, all States have the right for their nationals to engage in fishing on the high seas.

Article 117 imposes a duty upon States to adopt with respect to their nationals measures for the conservation of the living resources of the high seas and Article 118 provides for the co-operation of States in the management and conservation of living resources in the areas of the high seas. In this respect States whose nationals exploit identical resources, or different resources in the same area, shall enter into negotiations with a view to adopting the means necessary for the conservation of the living resources concerned. They shall, as appropriate, co-operate to establish subregional or regional fisheries organisation to this end.

Article 119 provides that in determining the allowable catch and establishing other conservation measures for the living resources in the high seas, States shall:

'a) Take measures which are designed, on the best scientific evidence available to the States concerned, to maintain or restore populations of harvested species at levels which can produce the maximum sustainable yield, as qualified by relevant environmental and economic factors, including the special requirements of developing States, and taking into account fishing patterns, the interdependence of stocks and any generally recommended internationally minimum standards, whether subregional, regional or global.
b) Take into consideration the effects on species associated with or dependent upon harvested species with a view to maintaining or restoring populations of such associated or dependent species above levels at which their reproduction may become seriously threatened.
2. Available scientific information, catch and fishing effort statistics, and other data relevant to the conservation of fish stocks shall be contributed and exchanged on a regular basis through competent international organisations, whether subregional, regional or global, where appropriate and with participation by all States concerned.
3. States concerned shall ensure that conservation measures and their implementation do not discriminate in form or in fact against the fishermen of any State.'

15.7 The continental shelf

The continental shelf is the offshore part of the sea-bed covered by the shallow waters of the continental margin which separates the coastal land mass from the deep ocean floor. Some coasts have no continental shelf. Others have a shelf the width of which may extend for as little as one mile, to many hundreds of miles in some cases. The waters above the shelf may also vary in depth from as little as 50 metres to about 500 metres.

The evolution of continental shelf jurisdiction

The Truman Proclamation

The concept of national jurisdiction over the resources of the continental shelf springs from the Truman Proclamation of 28 September 1945 relating to the natural resources of the subsoil and sea-bed of the continental shelf:

'Having concern for the urgency of conserving and prudently utilising its natural resources, the Government of the United States regards the natural resources of the subsoil and sea-bed of the continental shelf beneath the high seas but contiguous to the coasts of the United States as appertaining to the United States, subject to its jurisdiction and control ... The character as high seas of the waters above the continental shelf and the right to their free and unimpeded navigation are in no way thus affected.'

The US Proclamation set a precedent which other States soon followed and the right to exploit the natural resources of the subsoil and sea-bed of the continental shelf by the coastal state rapidly crystallised into a rule of customary international law.

The Continental Shelf Convention 1958

The doctrine of the continental shelf grew in importance as new technology made possible greater exploitation of offshore deposits of minerals, oil and gas. However, State practice was not uniform and the 1958 Law of the Sea Conference therefore made an attempt to clarify the law in the Continental Shelf Convention 1958.

Article 1 of the Convention defines the continental shelf. For the purpose of these articles, the term 'continental shelf' is used as referring (1) to the sea-bed and subsoil of the submarine areas adjacent to the coast but outside the area of the territorial sea, to a depth of 200 metres or beyond that limit, to where the depth of the superjacent waters admits of the exploitation of the natural resources of the said areas; (2) to the sea-bed and subsoil of similar submarine areas adjacent to the coasts of islands.

As a result of technological developments, however, the definition embodied in the 1958 Convention proved unsatisfactory from the point of limiting the exploration for and exploitation of deep sea-bed resources. The 1982 Convention thus sets out to provide a more detailed definition of the continental shelf.

Article 76(1) of the Convention defines the Continental shelf as follows:

'The continental shelf of a coastal State comprises the sea-bed and subsoil of the submarine areas that extend beyond its territorial sea throughout the natural prolongation of its land territory to the outer edge of the continental margin, or to a distance of 200 nautical miles from the baselines from which the breadth of the territorial sea is measured where the outer edge of the continental margin does not extend up to that distance.'

The continental shelf thus extends to a distance of 200 nautical miles from the coast whether or not the geological shelf actually reaches that distance. In cases where the geological shelf exceeds that distance the continental shelf extends to the outer edge of the continental margin.

Article 76(3) defines the continental margin:

'The continental margin comprises the submerged prolongation of the land mass of the coastal State, and consists of the sea-bed and subsoil of the shelf, the slope and the rise. It does not include the deep ocean floor with its oceanic ridges or the subsoil thereof.'

The outer edge of the continental margin must be established by the coastal State in accordance with Article 76(4), wherever the margin extends beyond 200 nautical miles from the baselines from which the breadth of the territorial sea is measured. However, Article 76(5) provides that the outer limits of the continental shelf, drawn in accordance with Article 76(4):

'... either shall not exceed 350 nautical miles from the baselines from which the breadth of the territorial sea is measured or shall not exceed 100 nautical miles from the 2,500 metre isobath, which is a line connecting the depth of 2,500 metres.'

Article 76(8) provides that information on the limits of the continental shelf beyond the 200 nautical mile EEZ shall be submitted by the coastal State to the Commission on the limits of the continental shelf.

Article 77 of the 1982 Convention provides:

'1. The coastal State exercises over the continental shelf *sovereign* rights for the purpose of exploring it and exploiting its natural resources.

2. The rights referred to in paragraph 1 are exclusive in the sense that if the coastal State does not explore the continental shelf or exploit its natural resources, no-one may undertake these activities, or make a claim to the continental shelf, without the express consent of the coastal State.

3. The rights of the coastal State over the continental shelf do not depend on occupation, effective or notional, or on any express proclamation.

4. The natural resources referred to in this Part consist of the mineral and other non-living resources of the sea-bed and subsoil together with living organisms belonging to sedentary species, that is to say, organisms which, at the harvestable stage, either are immobile on or under the sea-bed or are unable to move except in constant physical contact with the sea-bed or the subsoil.'

Article 78 provides:

'The rights of the coastal State over the continental shelf do not affect the legal status of the superjacent waters as high seas, or that of the air-space above those waters.'

In the *North Sea Continental Shelf Cases* (1969), the ICJ stated that:

'The Court entertains no doubt [that] the most fundamental of all the rules of law relating to the continental shelf enshrined in Article 2 of the 1958 Geneva Convention (now Article 7 of the 1982 Convention), though quite independent of it, [is] that the rights of the coastal State in respect of the area of continental shelf that constitutes a natural prolongation of its land territory into and under the sea exists *ipso facto* and *ab initio*, by virtue of its sovereignty over the land, and as an extension of it in an exercise of sovereign rights for the purpose of exploring the sea-bed and exploiting its natural resources. In short, there is here an inherent right. In order to exercise it, no special legal process has to be gone through, nor have any special legal acts to be performed. Its existence can be declared (and many States have done this) but does not need to be constituted. Furthermore, the right does not depend on its being exercised.'

There can be no doubt that the doctrine of the continental shelf is now an accepted concept of customary international law and every State whether or not it has ratified the 1958 or 1982 Conventions is entitled to control, explore and exploit its shelf area.

Installations and other devices on the continental shelf

Article 80 of the 1982 Convention permits the construction of installations on the continental shelf necessary for its exploitation and the establishment of safety zones up to a distance of 500 metres around such installations. Such installations do not possess the status of islands, must not interfere with recognised sea lanes essential to international navigation and warnings of their presence must be maintained.

Natural resources of the continental shelf

Apart from minerals, the natural resources of the shelf for the purposes of the convention comprise 'living organisms belonging to sedentary species'. These include coral, sponges, oysters and pearl shell, etc, but exclude creatures which swim close to the sea-bed, such as shrimps, prawns, plaice and halibut. Problems have arisen regarding crabs and lobsters, certain States disputing whether or not they are sedentary species. The UK view is that crabs are sedentary but lobsters, because they swim, are not.

Delimitation of the continental shelf

Article 6 of the 1958 Convention provided that, failing agreement, the continental shelf boundary between adjacent or opposite states was to be determined by the median or equidistant line unless special circumstances justified the drawing of some other boundary.

Concern over the application of the equidistance principle led a number of States, eg Germany, not to ratify the Convention. In the *North Sea Continental Shelf Cases* (1969), the ICJ accepted that Germany was not bound by the rule of equidistance in the Convention and that the rule had not become part of customary international law.

The question therefore arises as to what rules are applicable to the drawing of lateral boundaries when one or both of the parties are not bound by that convention. In the *North Sea Continental Shelf Cases* (1969), the Court stated that there is no single method of delimitation which is obligatory and satisfactory in all circumstances and that:

'... delimitation is to be effected *by agreement in accordance with equitable principles*, and taking account of all the relevant circumstances in such a way as to leave as much as possible to each Party all those parts of the continental shelf that constitute a natural prolongation of its land territory into and under the sea, without encroachment on the natural prolongation of the land territory of the other.'

The ICJ stated that agreements delimiting the continental shelf should take into account all 'relevant circumstances'.

'In the course of negotiations, the factors to be taken into account are to include:
    the general *configuration of the coasts* of the Parties as well as the presence of any special or unusual features,
    so far as known or readily ascertainable, the *physical and geological structure*, and *natural resources*, of the continental shelf areas involved;
    the element of a *reasonable degree of proportionality* ... between the extent of the continental shelf areas appertaining to the coastal State and the length of its coast measured in the general direction of the coast line'.

In the *Anglo-French Continental Shelf Arbitration* (1977), the Court of Arbitration expressed the view that the rules of customary international law expressed in the *North Sea Continental Shelf Cases*, and the provisions of Article 6 of the Convention lead to the same result, ie a boundary of an equitable character.

'The Court found that Article 6 does not establish two rules – an equidistance rule and a special circumstance rule. Instead, the Court found that Article 6 provides a combined equidistance – special circumstances rule. Further, the role of special circumstances in Article 6 is to ensure an equitable delimitation and that the combined equidistance special circumstances rule in effect provides for the general norm of customary law that the continental shelf boundary is to be determined in accordance with equitable principles.'

The Court of Arbitration said:

'... the equidistance – special circumstances rule and the rules of customary law have the same object – the delimitation of the boundary in accordance with equitable principles. In the view of this Court, therefore, the rules of customary law are relevant and even essential means both for interpreting and completing the terms of Article 6.'

The 1982 Convention thus provided in Article 83(1) that:

'The delimitation of the continental shelf ... shall be affected by agreement ... in order to achieve an equitable solution.'

The vagueness of this provision has essentially left this matter to be determined by the Court. Little progress has, however, been made in defining what is meant by equitable principles. The Court has, nevertheless, indicated in a number of cases the *relevant factors* that will be taken into account in affecting any delimitation. These include:

1. The geography of the coastline, eg concavity (*NSCS*), broad equality of coastline (*UK/France*), change in direction of coastline (*Tunisia/Libya*), discrepancy in length of coastline (*Libya/Malta*).
2. The geological/geomorphological features of the area, ie the physical characteristics of the continental shelf itself. This was considered in the *NSCS Cases* but has virtually faded from use since then. In subsequent cases the court has held that the 200-mile minimum distance provision in Article 76, 1982 has effectively meant that geological features within this distance are irrelevant (*Libya/Malta*).
3. The conduct of the parties, eg consent or acquiescence by one party (*Tunisia/Libya*).
4. Security or other navigational interests – recognised but not decisive (*Tunisia/Libya*; *UK/France*).
5. Boundaries with or claims by third stages, eg in *UK/France* the Tribunal did not want to trespass on any delimitation involving Ireland. In *Tunisia/Libya* the Court indicated it would be careful about not damaging the interests of Malta. In *Libya/Malta* the court took Italian interests into consideration.
6. Proportionality – this was stressed in the *NSCS Cases*. The Court has since used proportionality to test the equity of the result. However, it has stressed that it is *not* a basis of entitlement, only a rough guide as to the fairness of the result.

As well as relevant factors, the cases indicate that a number of factors will *not* be taken into account:

1. Land mass: in *Libya/Malta* the Court indicated that it was the length of coastline that mattered, not the total land area of the party.
2. Location of natural resources: in *NSCS* the Court suggested that this would not apply. However, it is unlikely that the Court would not take into account, for example, existing oil installations, if for no other reason than they may be an indication of acquiescence by the other side.
3. The political status of the territory concerned, eg whether they are a long distance from the mainland of the State concerned, appears to be irrelevant, eg in

the *France/Canada* (French islands off Newfoundland) or *Denmark/Norway* (the island of Jan Mayen) cases pending.

15.8 The deep sea-bed

The question of the legal status of the sea-bed and ocean floor has assumed considerable significance. Exploitation of the vast mineral resources in and under the oceans is now a practicable proposition. These resources include petroleum, natural gas, sulphur, sand, gravel, tin, diamonds and the manganese nodules – rich in manganese, cobalt, copper and nickel, which are found in abundance on many parts of the deep ocean floor.

The legal regime of the deep sea-bed

In considering the nature of the legal regime of the deep sea-bed the question arises whether its resources are already subject to the regime of the continental shelf.

Article 1 'of the Geneva Continental Shelf Convention defines the limit of the continental shelf, over which, by Article 2, the coastal State has exclusive sovereign rights for the purpose of exploiting its natural resources, in dual terms – as the 200 metre isobath or beyond that limit, to where the depth of the superjacent waters admits of the exploitation of such resources. On this basis, it has been argued, that as new technology makes exploitation possible in the deep sea then the limits of coastal State jurisdiction are automatically extended up to the point where Article 6 of the Convention comes into play to delimit the boundaries with other coastal States whose sovereign rights have also been extended.

However, this proposition is unsound. The Geneva Convention refers to 'submarine areas adjacent to the coast' and while adjacency is not defined, the deep ocean floor cannot be regarded as adjacent to any coastal State. Also, in the *North Sea Continental Shelf Cases* (1969) the ICJ described the continental shelf as the natural prolongation of the land territory, and while the legal concept of the continental shelf is broader than its geological counterpart there is still a physical distinction between the shelf and the deep ocean floor.

As indicated above, the Law of the Sea Convention now also provides a clearer definition of the continental shelf and its delimitation, than that contained in the 1958 Geneva Convention.

If the continental shelf doctrine does not apply to the deep sea-bed its legal status must be determined by recourse to other principles of customary law. Some writers contend that the sea-bed is *res nullius* and capable of occupation and appropriation. Lauterpacht stated that on the basis of acquiescence and effective occupation and subject to non-interference with the freedom of the high seas, parts of the sea-bed could legitimately be appropriated. Other writers, however, adopt the principle that the sea-bed of the high seas is *res communis* and not susceptible of appropriation by States or private persons.

The general consensus among States has been that the deep ocean floor should be utilised for the benefit of mankind.

The Declaration of Principles Governing the Sea-Bed and the Ocean Floor, and the Subsoil Thereof, Beyond the Limits of National Jurisdiction, 1970

This resolution was passed by the General Assembly on 17 December 1970 by 104 votes to nil, with 14 abstentions.

'The General Assembly ...

Affirming that there is an area of the sea-bed and the ocean floor, and the subsoil thereof, beyond the limits of national jurisdiction, the precise limits of which are yet to be determined.

Recognising that the existing legal regime of the high seas does not provide substantive rules for regulating the exploration of the aforesaid area and the exploitation of its resources ...

Solemnly declares that:

1. The sea-bed and ocean floor and the subsoil thereof, beyond the limits of national jurisdiction (hereinafter referred to as the area), as well as the resources of the area, are the common heritage of mankind.

2. The area shall not be subject to appropriation by any means by States or persons, natural or judicial, and no State shall claim or exercise sovereignty or sovereign rights over any part thereof.

3. No State or person, natural or judicial, shall claim, exercise or acquire rights with respect to the area or its resources incompatible with the international regime to be established and the principles of this Declaration.

4. All activities regarding the exploration and exploitation of the resources of the area and other related activities shall be governed by the international regime to be established.

5. The area shall be open to use exclusively for peaceful purposes by all States whether coastal or land locked, without discrimination, in accordance with the international regime to be established.

6. States shall act in the area in accordance with the applicable principles and rules of international law ...

7. The exploration of the area and the exploitation of its resources shall be carried out for the benefit of mankind as a whole, irrespective of the geographical location of States, whether land locked or coastal, and taking into particular consideration the interests and needs of the developing countries.

8. The area shall be reserved exclusively for peaceful purposes ...

9. On the basis of the principles of this Declaration, an international regime applying to the area and its resources and including appropriate international machinery to give effect to its provisions shall be established by an international treaty of a universal character, generally agreed upon'.

The legal effect of this Declaration is uncertain. Its principles are now restated in greater detail in the Law of the Sea Convention.

The Law of the Sea Convention provisions relating to the area

The Convention attempts to establish the 'international regime' referred to in Paragraph 9 of the 1970 General Assembly Declaration.

Article 156 of the Convention establishes the International Sea-bed Authority as the organisation through which activities in the area are to be organised and controlled. All States parties to the convention are *ipso facto* members of the Authority.

Article 135 of the Convention declares that the provisions relating to the deep sea-bed shall not affect the legal status of the waters superjacent to the area (high seas) or that of the airspace above those waters.

Article 136 of the Convention declares that the area and its resources are the common heritage of mankind, and under Article 137(1):

'No State shall claim or exercise sovereign rights over any part of the Area or its resources, nor shall any state or natural or judicial person appropriate any part thereo'.

The principle that the area shall be used exclusively for peaceful purposes is reaffirmed in Article 141.

Financial and other economic benefits derived from activity in the area shall be applied by the Authority for the benefit of mankind as a whole, irrespective of the geographical location of States, whether coastal or land locked, taking into particular consideration the interests and needs of developing States (Article 140).

Problems arose during negotiations in establishing a system for exploiting the resources of the area which was acceptable to both the developed and the developing States. The developed States wished exploitation in the area to be conducted by national undertakings while the developing States demanded the establishment of an international body to control exploitation of the area's resources. The Convention represents a compromise. The International Sea-bed Authority will exploit the area but may grant licences to States or commercial undertakings for exploitation purposes.

The Convention also contains in Article 144 the controversial provisions for the transfer of technology relating to activities in the area, from the developed countries and their mining companies to the Authority and the developing States. Other controversial measures are contained in Articles 150 and 151 which seek to regulate the future development of the area so as to, *inter alia*, maintain stable mineral prices and protect the economies of those developing countries dependent on mineral exports. The developed States argue that such restrictions will deter international companies from committing the substantial investment that will be required to make deep-sea mining a feasible possibility.

The USA, Great Britain, Germany and certain other industrialised nations have refused to sign the convention unless changes are made to the provisions relating to the deep sea mining area. On 29 January 1982, the US President made a statement detailing the amendments which would have to be made to the Draft Convention before the USA would accept it:

'While most provisions of the Draft Convention are acceptable and consistent with United States interests, some major elements of the deep sea mining regime are not acceptable ...
In the deep-sea bed mining area, we will seek changes necessary to correct those unacceptable elements and to achieve the goal of a Treaty that:
  1. Will not deter development of any deep sea-bed mineral resources to meet national and world demand;

2. Will assure national access to these resources by current, and future qualified entities, to enhance US security of supply, to avoid monopolisation of the resources by the operating arm of the International Authority, and to promote the economic development of the resources;

3. Will provide a decision-making role in the deep sea-bed regime that fairly reflects and effectively protects the political and economic interests and financial contributions of participating States;

4. Will not allow for amendments to come into force without approval of the participating States, including in our case the advice and consent of the Senate;

5. Will not set other undesirable precedents for international organisations; and

6. Will be likely to receive the advice and consent of the Senate. In this regard, the convention should not contain provisions for the mandatory transfer of private technology and participation by and funding for national liberation movements.'

The USA, Great Britain and Germany have enacted domestic legislation authorising national companies to begin exploitation of the deep sea-bed.

16

The Use of Force by States

16.1   The right to wage war

The historical background

Until the late middle ages Western European attitudes towards war were based on the concept of just and unjust war, in accordance with the teachings of the Roman Catholic Church. St Augustine (354–430) said:

> 'Just wars are usually defined as those which avenge injuries, when the nation or city against which warlike action is to be directed has neglected either to punish wrongs committed by its own citizens or to restore what has been unjustly taken by it. Further, that kind of war is undoubtedly just which God Himself ordains.'

Towards the end of the sixteenth century this distinction between just and unjust war was breaking down. The modern State system was developing and the predominant view was that the right of a State to wage war was inherent in the concept of State sovereignty. By the end of the eighteenth century and throughout the nineteenth century the attitude that it was the right of every State to resort to war prevailed.

The institution of war fulfilled two functions in international law

1. In the absence of an international organ for enforcing the law, war was a means of self-help for giving effect to claims based or alleged to be based on international law.

277

2. War was recognised as a legally admissible instrument for attacking and altering existing rights of States independently of the objective merits of the attempted change. As Hyde, writing in 1922, said: 'It always lies within the power of a State ... to gain political or other advantages over another, not merely by the employment of force, but also by direct recourse to war.'

War had, therefore, become an instrument of national policy and customary law placed no limits on the right of States to resort to war. In 1880 Hall stated that:

> 'International law has no alternative but to accept war, independently of the justice of its origin, as a relation which the parties to it may set up, if they choose, and to busy itself only in regulating the effects of the relation ... Hence both parties to every war are regarded as being in an identical legal position, and consequently as being possessed of equal rights.'

Attempts to limit the right of war

The Hague Peace Conferences of 1899 and 1907 and the movement for the pacific settlement of international disputes marked the beginning of the attempts to limit the right of war both as an instrument of law and as a legally recognised means for changing legal rights. At the same time more direct attempts were made to limit the right of war.

The Hague Convention Respecting the Limitation of the Employment of Force for the Recovery of Contract Debts 1907

This Convention prohibited, subject to certain exceptions, recourse to force as a legal remedy for enforcing obligations in respect of such contracts.

The Covenant of The League of Nations 1919

The Covenant of the League, signed in 1919, radically changed the whole basis of the law in two important respects:

1. It created express obligations to employ pacific means of settling disputes and not to resort to war without first exhausting those means.

   Article 12(1) of the Convenant provided:

   > 'The Members of the League agree that, if there should arise between them any dispute likely to lead to a rupture, they will submit the matter either to arbitration or judicial settlement or to inquiry by the Council, and they agree in no case to resort to war until three months after the award by the arbitrators or the judicial decision, or the report by the Council.'

2. It established a central organisation of States empowered to pass judgment on the observance of those obligations by individual States and to apply sanctions in the event of the obligations being violated.

Therefore, although the Convenant did not prohibit war altogether, it did make it difficult for an aggressor State to resort to war without breaking its obligations under the Covenant. Also the three months 'cooling off' period was intended to prevent 'accidental' outbreaks of hostilities.

However, not all States were members of the League of Nations and its attempts to limit the right of war proved in practice to be ineffective. The Italian invasion of Abyssinia and the Japanese invasion of Manchuria illustrated the ineffectiveness of economic sanctions upon aggressor States, and the reluctance of the majority of League members to carry out their obligations under the Covenant.

The General Treaty for the Renunciation of War 1928

Although the Convenant of the League of Nations imposed some limitations upon the resort to war, it was not until the General Treaty for the Renunciation of War in 1928 that a comprehensive prohibition of war as an instrument of national policy was achieved. This Treaty, which came about largely owing to the initiative of France and the USA, was signed on 27 August 1928 in Paris by representatives of 15 governments who on the same day invited other governments to adhere to the Treaty. The Treaty, which is also referred to as the Pact of Paris, or the Kellogg-Briand Pact, or the Kellogg Pact, is still binding upon over 60 States including all the Great Powers. It is composed of a Preamble and two Articles:

Pact of Paris or Kellogg Briand Pact

> 'The Signatory States ...
>
> Persuaded that the time has come when a frank renunciation of war as an instrument of national policy should be made to the end that the peaceful and friendly relations now existing between their peoples may be perpetuated:
>
> Convinced that all changes in their relations with one another should be sought only by pacific means and be the result of a peaceful and orderly process, and that any signatory Power which shall hereafter seek to promote its national interests by resort to war should be denied the benefits furnished by this Treaty ...

renounces war

> Article I
> The High Contracting Parties solemnly declare in the names of their respective peoples that they condemn recourse to war for the solution of international controversies, and renounce it as an instrument of national policy in their relations with one another.

condemns

> Article II
> The High Contracting Parties agree that the settlement or solution of all disputes or conflicts of whatever nature or of whatever origin they may be, which may arise among them, shall never be sought except by pacific means.'

use of pacific means

The legal effect of the Paris Pact

The signatories of the Pact renounced the right of war both as a legal instrument of self-help against an international wrong and as an act of national sovereignty for the purpose of changing existing rights. However, the effect of the Pact is not to abolish the institution of war as such. The fact that the signatories renounced in their mutual relations recourse to war as an instrument of national policy means that resort to war still remains lawful:

1. as a means of legally permissible self-defence;
2. as a measure of collective action for the enforcement of international obligations by virtue of existing instruments such as the United Nations Charter;

3. as between signatories of the Pact and non-signatories;
4. as against a signatory who has broken the Pact by resorting to war in violation of its provisions.

The General Treaty for the Renunciation of War has never been terminated. For practical purposes it has, however, been superseded by Article 2(4) of the Charter of the United Nations.

16.2 The United Nations Charter

The fundamental law of the post Charter period is stated in the principles contained in paragraphs 3 and 4 of Article 2 of the Charter.

Article 2(3) of the Charter of the United Nations provides:

'All Members shall settle their international disputes by peaceful means, in such a manner that international peace and security, and justice, are not endangered.'

Article 2(4) provides:

'All Members shall refrain in their international relations from the *threat or use of force against the territorial integrity or political independence of any State*, or in any other manner inconsistent with the purposes of the United Nations.'

The purposes of the United Nations are laid down in Article 1 of the Charter. It may be argued, therefore, that the threat or use of force cannot be used if incompatible with Article 1. Therefore, as the purposes of the United Nations are so widely drawn, Article 2(4) places a very wide prohibition on the use of force by States. Any use of force by a State outside its own borders is likely to be inconsistent with the maintenance of international peace and security or of promoting friendly relations among nations.

The broad interpretation placed upon Article 2(4) is illustrated by the *Corfu Channel Case: United Kingdom v Albania* (1949).

Following an incident when two British warships had been struck by mines while exercising a right of innocent passage in Albanian territorial waters the UK carried out minesweeping operations (Operation Retail) in the Corfu Channel. The UK argued that its action was not contrary to Article 2(4):

'... our action ... threatened neither the territorial integrity nor the political independence of Albania. Albania suffered thereby neither territorial loss nor (loss to) any part of its political independence.'

The ICJ, however, rejected the British arguments:

'The Court can only regard the alleged right of intervention as the manifestation of a policy of force, such as has in the past given rise to more serious abuses and such as cannot, whatever be the present defects in international organisation, find a place in international law ...

... The United Kingdom Agent ... has further classified 'Operation Retail' among methods of self-protection or self-help. The Court cannot accept this defence either.

Between independent States respect for territorial sovereignty is an essential foundation of international relations.'

The following points regarding Article 2(4) should be noted: in the *Nicaragua Case* (1986) the ICJ accepted that Article 2(4) reflects a rule of customary international law applying to all States whether members of the United Nations or not, while, as a matter of strict law, the Article applies only to resort to force in international relations against another State and does not affect a State's legal right to use armed force in the suppression of internal disturbances, in practice the UN has interpreted a wide range of 'domestic' activities as falling within the purvey of the UN for these purposes.

The Article entirely prohibits the use or threat of armed force against another State except in self-defence (Article 51) or in execution of collective measures authorised by the Security Council or General Assembly. The force prohibited is *armed* force. The general view is that the Article does not preclude a State from taking unilateral economic or other reprisals not involving the threat or use of armed force, in retaliation for a breach of international law by another State.

The Article talks of the threat or use *of force* and not of war. Thus, all hostilities are covered even where no formal declaration of war has been issued and the parties have denied that a technical state of war exists.

The meaning of the phrase 'against the territorial integrity or political independence of any State'

The scope of this part of Article 2(4) is disputed by writers.

On the one hand Professor Bowett states:

'The phrase "against the territorial integrity or political independence of any State" may, on one construction, mean that the element of intent is introduced into the prohibition; namely, that the use or threat of force contravenes this obligation only where intended to jeopardise the political independence or territorial integrity of another State. Or, if specific intent is not required, it may mean that at least the use or threat of force must have this effect before being in contravention of Article 2(4).'

Professor Brownlie, on the other hand, argues:

'The conclusion warranted by the Travaux preparatoires is that the phrase under discussion was not intended to be restrictive but, on the contrary, to give more specific guarantees to small States and that it cannot be interpreted as having a qualifying effect.

... The phrase 'political independence and territorial integrity' has been used on many occasions to epitomise the total of legal rights which a State has. Moreover, it is difficult to accept a 'plain meaning' which permits evasion of obligations by means of a verbal profession that there is no intention to infringe territorial integrity and which was not intended by the many delegations which approved the text. Lastly, if there is any ambiguity the principle of effectiveness should be applied.'

The definition of aggression

As the organ having the primary responsibility for the maintenance of international peace and security, the United Nations Security Council has the power under Article 39 of the Charter to:

'... determine the existence of any threat to the peace, breach of the peace, or act of aggression and shall make recommendations, or decide what measures shall be taken in accordance with Article 41 and 42, to maintain or restore international peace and security.'

Article 1 of the Charter lists as one of the Purposes of the United Nations 'the suppression of acts of aggression'. Therefore if a State uses aggression this would be a breach of Article 2(4). What constitutes aggression is a question for the Security Council to determine in accordance with Article 39.

The problem is that a Member of the Security Council when called upon to decide whether or not a particular act is within the ambit of Article 39, may be motivated by its own political interests and ideology. Aggression is a subjective concept. In order to overcome this difficulty in deciding whether a particular use of force constitutes a breach of the Charter, the General Assembly in 1974 adopted Resolution 3314 on the Definition of Aggression.

Article 1:

'Aggression is the use of armed force by a State against the sovereignty, territorial integrity or political independence of another State, or in any other manner inconsistent with the Charter of the United Nations, as set out in this Definition.'

Article 2:

'The first use of armed force by a State in contravention of the Charter shall constitute prima facie evidence of an act of aggression although the Security Council may, in conformity with the Charter, conclude that a determination that an act of aggression has been committed would not be justified in the light of other relevant circumstances, including the fact that the acts concerned or their consequences are not of sufficient gravity.'

Article 3:

'Any of the following acts, regardless of a declaration of war, shall, subject to and in accordance with the provisions of Article 2, qualify as an act of aggression:
   a) The invasion or attack by the armed forces of a State of the territory of another State, or any military occupation however temporary, resulting from such invasion or attack, or any annexation by the use of force of the territory of another State or part thereof;
   b) Bombardment by the armed forces of a State against the territory of another State or the use of any weapons by a State against the territory of another State.
   c) The blockade of the ports or coasts of a State by the armed forces of another State; ...
   d) The use of armed forces of one State which are within the territory of another State, with the agreement of the receiving State, in contravention of the conditions provided for in the agreement or any extension of their presence in such territory beyond the termination of the agreement;
   e) The action of a State in allowing its territory, which it has placed at the disposal of another State, to be used by that other State for perpetrating an act of aggression against a third State;

f) The sending by or on behalf of a State of armed bands, groups, irregulars or mercenaries, which carry out acts of armed force against another State of such gravity as to amount to the acts listed above, or its substantial involvement therein.'

Article 4:

'The acts enumerated above are not exhaustive and the Security Council may determine that other acts constitute aggression under the provisions of the Charter.'

Article 5:

'1) No consideration of whatever nature, whether political, economic, military or otherwise, may serve as a justification for aggression.
2) A war of aggression is a crime against international peace. Aggression gives rise to international responsibility.
3) No territorial acquisition or special advantage resulting from aggression is or shall be recognised as lawful.'

Article 6:

'Nothing in this Definition shall be construed as in any way enlarging or diminishing the scope of the Charter, including its provisions concerning cases in which the use of force is lawful.'

Article 7:

'Nothing in this Definition, and in particular Article 3, could in any way prejudice the right to self-determination, freedom and independence, as derived from the Charter, of peoples forcibly deprived of that right and referred to in the Declaration on Principles of International Law concerning Friendly Relations and Co-operation among States in accordance with the Charter of the United Nations, particularly peoples under colonial and racist regimes or other forms of alien domination; nor the right of those peoples to struggle to that end and to seek and receive support, in accordance with the principles of the Charter and in conformity with the above mentioned Declaration.'

Article 8:

'In their interpretation and application the above provisions are inter-related and each provision should be construed in the context of the other provisions.'

There was great difficulty in formulating the Definition of Aggression and it represents a compromise between those States which favoured the enumerative approach, by which all of the acts that constitute aggression are listed, and those States which favour the general definition approach.

The Charter regime in review

Article 2(4) has had a pervasive influence on international law and politics. The total prohibition on the use of force is now regarded as the norm rather than the exception. The Charter restriction has, in addition, been reinforced by a number of important resolutions of the General Assembly which are widely regarded as reflecting the position at customary law. Chief amongst these have been GAR 2131

(1965) on the Prohibition of Intervention, which provides that 'armed intervention and all other forms of interference ... are to be condemned', and GAR 2625 (1970) on General Principles of International Law, which provides that 'every State has the duty to refrain from the threat or use of force' and that this would constitute 'a violation of international law'.

This prohibition has further been reinforced by decisions of the General Assembly and Security Council condemning specific acts of force as illegal – such as SC Resolution 660 (1990) with respect to the Iraqi invasion of Kuwait – and by a number of decisions of the ICJ, notably in the *Corfu Channel Case* (1949) and the *Nicaragua Case* (1986).

Nevertheless, there remains some room for doubt as to whether this norm should be considered as all-embracing as suggested. In particular, doubt has been expressed as to whether the prohibition on the use of force would apply in cases of a denial of self-determination or a manifest abuse of human rights. This doubt is reinforced by particular examples of State practice, eg the Indian invasion of Goa in 1961 in which India justified its use of force on the grounds of facilitating self-determination. The numerous examples of States disregarding the prohibition on the use of force also undermines the normative quality of the law.

16.3 The right of self-defence

Self-defence and self-protection under customary law

Perhaps the most important case on the law of self-defence is the *Caroline Case* which arose out of the Canadian Rebellion of 1837. The rebel leaders, despite steps taken by the US authorities to prevent assistance being given to them, managed on 13 December 1837 to enlist at Buffalo in the USA the support of a large number of American nationals. The resulting force established itself on Navy Island in Canadian waters from which it raided the Canadian shore and attacked British ships. The force was supplied from the USA by an America ship, the *Caroline*. On the night of 29–30 December a small Canadian force seized the *Caroline*, which was then in the American port of Schlosser, set her on fire and sent her drifting over Niagara Falls. Two US nationals were killed – Amos Durfee, whose body was found on the quay with a ball through his head, and a cabin boy known as 'little Billy', who was shot while attempting to leave the vessel. The USA claimed reparation to which Great Britain (as the colonial power) replied that the destruction of the *Caroline* had been a necessary act of self-defence.

Three years later a British subject, McLeod, who unwisely boasted in the US of his participation in the incident was arrested and tried for murder in New York State. Britain demanded his release on the ground that those who participated in the operation against the *Caroline* had been engaged in the execution of an act of State for which they were not answerable personally in a municipal court.

The US Government conceded that the public character of McLeod's acts relieved him of personal responsibility and sought to put an end to the proceedings against him in the New York courts. At the same time, it again disputed the British claim that the case was one of legitimate self-defence and the diplomatic correspondence contains the classical statement of the limits of self-defence.

The two Governments, although they disagreed about the facts of the particular case, were entirely agreed upon the principles applicable to armed intervention in self-defence. There must be a clear and absolute necessity for the intervention; that is to say:

1. there must, initially, be a necessity of self-defence, instant, overwhelming, leaving no choice of means and no moment for deliberation; and
2. the acts done in self-defence must *not be unreasonable* or excessive and the force used must be *proportionate* to the harm threatened.

On this basis, legitimate self-defence in customary international law has three main requirements:

1. an actual infringement or threat of infringement of the rights of the defending State;
2. a failure or inability on the part of the other State to use its own legal powers to stop or prevent the infringement; and
3. acts of self-defence strictly confined to the object of stopping or preventing the infringement and reasonably proportionate to what is required for achieving this object.

Self-defence under the Charter of the United Nations

Article 51 of the Charter of the United Nations provides:

> 'Nothing in the present Charter shall impair the inherent right of individual or collective self-defence if an armed attack occurs against a member of the United Nations, until the Security Council has taken the measures necessary to maintain international peace and security. Measures taken by members in the exercise of this right of self-defence shall be immediately reported to the Security Council and shall not in any way affect the authority and responsibility of the Security Council under the present Charter to take at any time such action as it deems necessary in order to maintain or restore international peace and security.'

Unlike the Covenant of the League, the right of self-defence under the Charter system is not left outside the collective system for maintaining peace. Self-defence is recognised to be a necessary exception to the fundamental principle in Article 2(4) that resort to force by an individual State is illegal without the prior authority of the United Nations. However, the exercise of the right of self-defence is made subject to the control of the international community – the individual State decides whether or not to use force in self-defence but the propriety of its decision is a matter for the United Nations.

The fact that resort to force in self-defence is lawful without the prior authority of the Security Council is of vital importance from the point of view of the veto. A State may begin action in self-defence without a prior recourse to the Security

Council and, therefore, no single Permanent Member may veto the action being initiated. Moreover, once the action in self-defence is being taken it requires an affirmative decision of the Security Council to order the cessation of that action. Therefore, action in self-defence under Article 51 cannot be barred by the veto and cannot be terminated except by the unanimous vote of the Permanent Members.

The inherent right of self-defence, as it existed in international law before the Charter, was a general right of protection against a forcible threat to a States legal rights. Article 51, however, speaks only of an inherent right of self-defence 'if an armed attack occurs'.

Does Article 51 cut down the customary right of self-defence and restrict it to cases involving resistance to an armed attack by another State?

There is some uncertainty as to the effect of Article 51 upon the customary international law right of self-defence. Kelson reads Article 51 as meaning that for United Nations members the right of self-defence 'has no other content than the one determined by Article 51'. Brownlie also argues that Article 51 says everything and that a State cannot be acting in self-defence unless within Article 51.

Bowett, however, argues that customary international law remains unless cut down by the Charter. If there is any ambiguity it is proper to look at customary international law:

> 'It is ... fallacious to assume that members have only those rights which the Charter accords them; on the contrary they have those rights which general international law accords to them except in so far as they have surrendered them under the Charter.'

Supporters of Bowett's view argue that the right of individual self-defence was regarded as automatically excepted in both the Covenant of the League and the Pact of Paris without any mention of it. The same would have been true of the Charter if there had been no Article 51. Indeed, the original Dumbarton Oaks proposals did not contain the Article 51 provisions. Committee 1 at the San Francisco Conference, commenting upon Article 2(4), reported that 'the use of arms in legitimate self-defence remains admitted and unimpaired'.

Article 51 was inserted in the Charter to clarify the position with respect to collective understandings for mutual self-defence and in particular the Pan-American treaty known as the Act of Chapultepec. The official British Government commentary on the Charter reads:

> 'It was considered at the Dumbarton Oaks Conference that the right of self-defence was inherent in the proposals and did not need explicit mention in the Charter. But self-defence may be undertaken by more than one State at a time, and the existence of regional organisations made this right of special importance to some States, while special treaties of defence made its explicit recognition important to others. Accordingly the right is given to individual States or to combinations of States to act until the Security Council itself has taken the necessary measures.'

Therefore, on the one hand it could be said that Article 51 of the Charter is exhaustive and says all there is to know about self-defence. On the other hand,

[handwritten margin notes: "customary + int'l law unless covered by the Charter"; "ie kelsen + Brownlie"]

however, it could be said that when Article 51 talks about the inherent right of self-defence it goes back to customary international law. Most writers accept the latter view, but there is a difference of emphasis as to how much of the customary law is still extant – and what it says.

The problem is that customary law clearly distinguishes between self-defence, self-preservation and self-help. Prior to the Pact of Paris there was no restriction on the right to wage war and, therefore, States did not always distinguish between self-defence and their other customary rights to use force. For example, in the *Caroline Case* it was unclear whether Great Britain was acting in self-defence or in self-preservation when she attacked the *Caroline*. The Charter, however, refers to the inherent right of *self-defence*. Therefore, when referring back to customary law does one consider the whole ambit of self-defence, self-preservation and self-help, which mean slightly different things, or are you restricted to clear and unambiguous examples of self-defence?

It must also be remembered that customary international law changes with the practice of States. It is, therefore, no use looking at the nineteenth century and before for the customary law of self-defence. It is argued that you have got to look at the practice of States just prior to the Charter.

Does Article 51 cut down the customary right by restricting forcible self-defence to cases where the attack provoking it has actually been launched? Article 51 refers solely to situations 'if an armed attack occurs'. The question arises, therefore, as to the legality of anticipatory self-defence. Is an imminent threat sufficient to create a right to resort to force in self-defence or must the victim wait until the aggressor has struck the first blow before it can resort to force in self-defence?

Some authorities have interpreted 'if an armed attack occurs' to mean 'after an armed attack has occurred'. However, this interpretation may be too restrictive. When the Article was drafted it is unlikely that there was any intention to cut down the right of self-defence beyond the already narrow doctrine of the *Caroline Case*. That doctrine allows a right of self-defence where there is an imminent threat of attack, and is recognised under Article 51 as being an *inherent* right which continues to exist. In the *Nicaragua Case* the ICJ accepted that the word 'inherent' in Article 51 was a reference to customary law. The Court declined, however, to rule one way or another on the question of anticipatory self-defence as this was not required by the case.

Before taking action in anticipatory self-defence the Charter of the United Nations imposes the obligation upon States to settle their disputes by peaceful means, and empowers the Security Council to take the steps necessary to ensure the maintenance of international peace and security. Members have, therefore, an imperative duty to invoke the jurisdiction of the United Nations whenever a grave menace to their security develops carrying the probability of armed attack. However, if the action of the United Nations is delayed or inadequate and the armed attack becomes imminent it would be contrary to the purposes of the Charter to compel the defending State to allow the aggressor to deliver the first and perhaps fatal blow.

This interpretation of the Charter accords with the practice of States and the generally accepted view of international law at the time when Article 51 was drafted. For example, it was argued before the International Military Tribunal at Nuremberg that the German invasion of Norway in 1941 was an act of self-defence in the face of an imminent Allied landing there. The Tribunal held that preventive action in foreign territory is justified only in the circumstances laid down in the *Caroline Case*, and that as there was no imminent threat of an Allied landing in Norway the argument must fail.

However, the International Military Tribunal for the Far East had no hesitation in deciding that the Dutch declaration of war upon Japan in December 1941 was justifiable on the grounds of self-defence. When considering the legality of Japan's invasion of Dutch territory in the Far East the Tribunal stated:

> 'The fact that the Netherlands, being fully appraised of the imminence of the attack, in self-defence declared war against Japan on 8 December and thus officially recognised the existence of a state of war which had been begun by Japan cannot change that war from a war of aggression on the part of Japan into something other than that.'

A recent example of anticipatory self-defence was the pre-emptive attack launched by Israel against the United Arab Republic in June 1967. Following Arab threats to liberate Israeli-occupied Palestine, the Israelis fearing imminent invasion launched an attack against Egypt destroying the Egyptian air force on the ground and cutting off the Egyptian army in Sinai. Israel claimed the action as necessary on the grounds of self-defence and that its pre-emptive strike had removed the threat of an Arab attack against its southern border.

The requirement of an 'armed attack'

An examination and comparison of Articles 2(4) and 51 indicate that the two provisions are not entirely compatible. Article 2(4) prohibits the threat or use of force. Article 51, in contrast, provides that there is a right of self-defence if an *armed attack* occurs. The question arises, therefore, as to whether the term 'force' in Article 2(4) equates with the term 'armed attack' in Article 51. More particularly, under the charter regime is there a right to use force in self-defence in response to a use of force by the other side that does not amount to an armed attack? This question presupposes that a distinction can usefully be drawn between a use of force amounting to an armed attack and one that does not.

Until the decision of the ICJ in the *Nicaragua Case* in 1986, most commentators accepted that a use of force or act of aggression by one State would give rise to a concomitant right of self-defence in the victim State. Any refinement that was required would then involve a discussion of the parameters of the phrase 'the territorial integrity or political independence' of a State. Thus, writers such as Bowett have consistently argued that a use of force against nationals abroad may give rise to a right of self-defence in protection of these nationals because a use of force against nationals abroad amounts to a use of force against the State itself. The ambit

of the action in self-defence would then fall to be determined in accordance with the principle of proportionality.

In contrast, writers such as Brownlie have argued that the use of force against nationals abroad will not give rise to a right of self-defence – and, therefore, of intervention – as the use of force against nationals abroad would not constitute a use of force against the territorial integrity or political independence of the State.

The approach of the majority of the Court in the *Nicaragua Case* throws much of this reasoning into doubt and casts a considerable shadow of uncertainty over the right to use force in self-defence. The case arose out of Nicaraguan allegations against the US in respect of a range of activities from the mining of the Nicaraguan ports to the arming, training and directing of the Contra rebels. To these allegations the US raised the defense, *inter alia*, that they were acting in the collective self-defence of El Salvador and Costa Rica against which, they alleged, Nicaragua had been involved in illegal uses of force.

Considering this argument the Court appeared to limit the right of self-defence to circumstances which amounted to an *armed attack*. This the Court defined as acts, *which because of their scale and effects*, would be classified as an armed attack rather than a mere frontier incident. Thus, to amount to an armed attack, the acts concerned must be of a particularly serious nature. While the Court appeared to accept that a use of force amounting to something less than an armed attack may give rise to a right to take counter-measures, they did not discuss this principle at any length.

Sir Robert Jennings, in his dissenting opinion in the case, argued that the Court's distinction between uses of force amounting to an armed attack and those which did not, was 'neither realistic nor just'. He continued:

> 'In this situation is seems dangerous to define unnecessarily strictly the conditions for lawful self-defence, so as to leave a large area where both a forcible response to force is forbidden, and yet the UN employment of force, which was intended to fill the gap, is absent.'

Given the difficulty in distinguishing sensibly between degrees of the use of force, the approach of the Court should be followed with caution and perhaps limited to the facts of the case in issue.

When does an armed attack begin?

To cut down the customary right of self-defence beyond the *Caroline* doctrine does not make sense in times when the speed and power of weapons of attack have greatly increased. For instance, in the case of nuclear missiles, when does an armed attack occur: when the missile lands, when it takes off or when there is the intention to fire it?

In its first Report in 1946 the United Nations Atomic Energy Commission stated:

> 'In consideration of the problem of violations of the terms of the Treaty or Convention (limiting the manufacture of nuclear weapons), it should also be borne in mind that a violation might be of so grave a character as to give rise to the inherent right of self-defence recognised in Article 51.'

Thus it may be argued that Article 51 is couched in 1946 terms and has not come to terms with nuclear weapons. Today weapons no longer depend on their being seen and clearly visible and therefore Article 51 is not specific enough for the commander in the field who must determine if an armed attack has occurred. Some writers, nevertheless, still argue that anticipatory self-defence is incompatible with the Charter.

against anticipatory self defence

They argue that Article 51 is an exception to Article 2(4) and that it is a general rule of interpretation that exceptions to a principle should be interpreted restrictively, so as not to undermine the principle. They also point out that some collective defence treaties such as the North Atlantic Treaty, based on Article 51, provide only for defence against armed attacks, and not for defence against imminent dangers of armed attacks.

A further argument against the right of anticipatory self-defence is that the question whether an attack is imminent is subjective and open to abuse. A State can never be absolutely certain about the other side's intentions and may mistakenly launch a pre-emptive strike in a moment of crisis when no actual threat in fact existed. Also, allowing an aggressor State to strike the first blow may not in practice result in military disadvantage to the innocent State as first strikes in inter-State hostilities are seldom conclusive.

Proportionality

The requirement of proportionality is not mentioned in Article 51. However, customary international law clearly states that force used in self-defence must be proportionate to the seriousness of the attack and justified by the seriousness of the danger. The Court in the *Nicaragua Case* accepted that the requirements of proportionality and necessity were fundamental to any exercise of the right of self-defence.

The question of proportionality may, however, be difficult to deal with in certain circumstances. For example, could a State counter a conventional armed attack with a nuclear attack in self-defence or would this be disproportionate?

The attack giving rise to the right of self-defence need not be directed against a State's territory

For example, Article 6 of the North Atlantic Treaty 1949 provides:

'For the purpose of Article 5 an armed attack on one or more of the Parties is deemed to include an armed attack on the territory of any of the Parties in Europe or North America, on the Algerian Departments of France, on the occupation forces of any Party in Europe, on the islands under the jurisdiction of any Party in the North Atlantic area north of the Tropic of Cancer or on the vessels or aircraft in this area of any of the Parties.'

In the *Corfu Channel Case* the ICJ held that the British warships attacked while exercising their right of innocent passage through Albanian territorial waters were entitled to be at action stations and to return fire if necessary.

16.4 Collective self-defence

Article 51 was introduced into the Charter primarily to safeguard the consistency of the Pan-American regional system of mutual defence with the new regime for maintaining peace established by the Charter. To these South American States the most significant aspect of self-defence was that it could justify collective action. In this respect the Colombian representative said at the San Francisco Conference in 1945:

'... an aggression against one American State constitutes an aggression against all the American States, and all of them exercise their right of legitimate defence by giving support to the State attacked, in order to repel aggression. This is what is meant by the right of collective self-defence.'

By referring to the 'inherent right of individual or collective self-defence' Article 51 has provided a legal basis upon which a number of regional security systems have been founded. However, Article 51 does *not* form part of Chapter VIII which regulates regional arrangements. This is important because Chapter VIII subordinates regional arrangements to the Security Council and specifically directs, in Article 53, that enforcement action should not be begun regionally without the Council's approval.

Article 51 was deliberately transferred at the San Francisco Conference from Chapter VIII to Chapter VII with the result that the right of collective self-defence is entirely independent of the existence of a regional arrangement, and is immune from the paralysing effect of the veto.

Mutual assistance treaties for collective self-defence

The North Atlantic Treaty 1949 provides under Article 5:

'The Parties agree that an armed attack against one or more of them in Europe or North America shall be considered an attack against them all; and consequently they agree that, if such an armed attack occurs, each of them, in exercise of the right of individual or collective self-defence recognised by Article 51 of the Charter of the United Nations, will assist the Party or Parties so attacked by taking forthwith, individually and in concert with the other Parties, such action as it deems necessary, including the use of armed force, to restore and maintain the security of the North Atlantic area.

Any such armed attack and all measures taken as a result thereof shall immediately be reported to the Security Council. Such measures shall be terminated when the Security Council has taken the measures necessary to restore and maintain international peace and security.'

The Warsaw Pact 1955 provides under Article 4:

'In the event of armed attack in Europe on one or more of the Parties to the Treaty by any State or group of States, each of the Parties to the Treaty, in the exercise of its rights to individual or collective self-defence in accordance with Article 51 of the Charter of the United Nations Organisation, shall immediately either individually or in agreement with other Parties to the Treaty, come to the assistance of the State or States attacked with all such means as it deems necessary, including armed force. The Parties to the Treaty shall immediately consult concerning the necessary measures to be taken by them jointly in order to restore and maintain international peace and security.

Measures taken on the basis of this Article shall be reported to the Security Council in conformity with the provisions of the Charter of the United Nations Organisation. These measures shall be discontinued immediately the Security Council adopts the necessary measures to restore and maintain international peace and security.'

The Inter-American Treaty of Reciprocal Assistance (Rio Treaty) 1947 provides under Article 3:

'1) The High Contracting Parties agree that an armed attack by any State against an American State shall be considered as an attack against all the American States and, consequently, each one of the said Contracting Parties undertakes to assist in meeting the attack in the exercise of the inherent right of individual or collective self-defence recognised by Article 51 of the Charter of the United Nations ...

4) Measures of self-defence provided for under this Article may be taken until the Security Council of the United Nations has taken the measures necessary to maintain international peace and security.'

These mutual assistance treaties must accord with the United Nations Charter. Article 103 of the Charter provides that:

'In the event of a conflict between the obligations of the Members of the United Nations under the present Charter and their obligations under any other international agreement, their obligations under the present Charter shall prevail.'

The scope of collective self-defence

Article 51 of the Charter refers to 'individual or collective self-defence': Professor Bowett has argued that this right of collective self-defence is merely a combination of individual rights of self-defence; 'States may exercise collectively a right which any of them might have exercised individually'. Thus, Bowett argues that no State may defend another State unless each State could have legally exercised a right of individual self-defence in the same circumstances. Thus, the USSR cannot defend Cuba against attack because an attack on Cuba does not affect the rights and interests of the USSR.

This view was based mainly on analogies drawn from English law. At the time when Bowett was writing English law did not allow one person to use force in defence of another person unless there was some close relationship between the two parties.

According to Bowett, therefore, if a State is not acting in its own self-defence it can only justify its involvement in the defence of another State if acting under Chapter VIII with the approval of the Security Council. Article 2(4) of the Charter is an attempt to limit conflicts and the maintenance of international peace and security should be in the hands of the Security Council.

State practice and the dicta of the ICJ do not support Bowett's view. Professor Brownlie, for example, argues that State practice shows that if any State asks for assistance, other States may go and help that State to defend itself. For example, the

USA in justifying its participation in the Vietnam conflict – or, more recently, justifying the sending of troops to Saudi Arabia – argued, *inter alia*, that international law permitted a right of collective self-defence even where one party (in this case, the USA) did not have an individual right of self-defence.

In the *Nicaragua Case*, the majority of the Court put forward a two-fold test regarding the exercise of collective self-defence. The State under attack must (1) have declared itself to be under attack, and (2) must *request* the assistance of the third State. This approach was contested by Jennings in his dissenting opinion:

> 'Whatever collective self-defence means, it does not mean vicarious defence; for that way the notion is indeed open to abuse ... The assisting State surely must, by going to the victim State's assistance, be also ... in some measure defending itself.'

Jennings, therefore, adopted Bowett's view of collective self-defence, ie that collective self-defence extends to the *collective exercise of individual rights of self-defence*.

Kelson in his *Law of the United Nations* has pointed out the dangers to world order which are involved in Article 51. Two groups of States centred on rival Great Powers may each decide that resort to force is justifiable in collective self-defence against the other and the exercise of the veto may prevent the Security Council from making a determination under Article 39. This may result in a war between two collective systems, each allegedly acting in self-defence, and the Security Council unable to make a determination even of a threat of the peace.

This difficulty has in some respects been overcome by the Uniting for Peace Resolution which is founded upon the principle that the General Assembly and individual Members have a secondary responsibility for the maintenance of international peace which comes into play when the Security Council has failed to discharge its primary responsibility. Under the Resolution the Assembly may investigate and pronounce upon any resort to force, including alleged acts of self-defence, provided that a two-thirds majority can be obtained.

For example, on 1 February 1951 the General Assembly, acting under the United for Peace Resolution, expressly found that Communist China had itself engaged in aggression in Korea by giving direct aid and assistance to those who were already committing aggression in Korea.

The practical effect of mutual assistance treaties for collective self-defence

Conflict in the world today is of a localised nature. The super powers do not directly confront one another for the simple reason that such States have the potential to create a nuclear holocaust; so in their power struggle, ideological and economic, the conflict is played by proxy through client-States. Dr Kissinger recognised the fact that conflict can further be contained if spheres of influence are recognised. If the USA recognised the fact that Eastern Europe was under Russian hegemony and equally the USSR admitted that the American continent was under US hegemony, tension in the respective spheres would be eased. These regional organisations thus created consolidate the power blocs and prevent intra-bloc disputes.

The basic point to understand is that the geographical factor which lies at the heart of Bowett's thesis – the need for a proximate relationship – is only one factor; the complexities of the world relations the Cubans to Angola, the USA to Vietnam, the Russians into Afghanistan. All these actions cannot be explained by a purely geographical criterion. Blocs such as have developed in South East Asia (ASEAN) and the Middle East (CENTO) represent a major trend of international politics of contemporary times. They are a new kind of political structure within which law has developed. They help to stabilise the polarised system and sustain the norms of that system.

16.5 Collective measures under the United Nations Charter

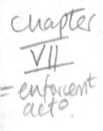

Under Article 24 of the UN Charter, the Security Council is invested with primary responsibility for the maintenance of international peace and security. This responsibility includes enforcement action in the case of threats to the peace, breaches of the peace or acts of aggression under Chapter VII of the Charter.

Under Article 39, the Security Council is required to determine the existence of a threat or breach of the peace or act of aggression. What constitutes a 'breach of the peace' is not, however, clearly defined and it is thus up to the Security Council to make a determination on a case-by-case basis. (This is done by a non-procedural vote.) As indicated above, General Assembly resolutions 3314 (1974) on the Definition of Aggression does, however, give some indication as to what is meant by the term 'aggression'. Even though the resolution was adopted by consensus, however, it remains controversial and it is open to question as to whether it reflects customary international law.

As a result of the veto, the Security Council has been able to make a determination under Article 39 on only three occasions, ie with respect to Korea, Rhodesia and, recently, following the Iraqi invasion of Kuwait on 2 August 1990.

The Korean question 1950

Korea became a part of Japan in 1910. In 1943, the Allied Powers agreed that it would become an independent State when the Second World War ended. In 1945, Japanese troops in Korea surrendered to the USSR north of the 38th Parallel and to the USA south of it. On 25 June 1950 North Korean armed forces crossed the 38th Parallel into South Korea and fighting broke out. The resulting crisis was immediately debated by the Security Council which (in the absence of the Russian representative) adopted the following series of resolutions:

Security Council Resolution of 25 June 1950:

The Security Council:

'... noting with grave concern the armed attack upon the Republic of Korea by forces from North Korea.

Determines that this action constitutes a breach of the peace.

I) Calls for the immediate cessation of hostilities; and calls upon the authorities of North Korea to withdraw forthwith their armed forces to the 38th Parallel ...

III) Calls upon all Members to render every assistance to the United Nations in the execution of this resolution and to refrain from giving assistance to the North Korean authorities.'

Security Council Resolution of 27 June 1950:
The Security Council:

'... recommends that the Members of the United Nations furnish such assistance to the Republic of Korea as may be necessary to repel the armed attack and to restore international peace and security in the area'.

Security Council Resolution of 7 July 1950:
The Security Council:

'3) Recommends that all Members providing military forces and other assistance pursuant to the aforesaid Security Council resolutions make such forces and other assistance available to a unified command under the United States;

4) Requests the United States to designate the commander of such forces;

5) Authorises the unified command at its discretion to use the United Nations Flag in the course of operations against North Korea forces concurrently with the flags of the various nations participating;

6) Requests the United States to provide the Security Council with reports as appropriate on the course of action taken under the unified command.'

In response to the Security Council Resolutions, 16 Member States sent armed forces to Korea.

Some writers are doubtful whether the forces in Korea constituted a United Nations Force. Although they were called a United Nations force, flew the United Nations flag and were awarded United Nations medals by the General Assembly, nevertheless all operational decisions concerning the force were taken by the USA. The Commander took his orders from the USA, not from the United Nations.

However, on the question whether the forces in Korea were United Nations Forces, Bowett concludes that: 'There can be no doubt that, in practice, the overwhelming majority of States involved in the Korean action were fully prepared to regard it as a United Nations action involving United Nations Forces.'

The Security Council ceased to play an active part in the conduct of the war after the USSR representative resumed his seat on 1 August 1950. In October China entered the war in support of North Korea. After the USSR had vetoed a draft resolution condemning the Chinese action on 30 November the General Assembly became the organ effectively seized of the question.

The Southern Rhodesia question 1965

On 12 November 1965, the day after Southern Rhodesia's unilateral declaration of independence, the Security Council by Resolution 216 decided 'to condemn the unilateral declaration of independence made by the racist minority in Southern Rhodesia' and 'to call upon all States not to recognise this illegal racist minority regime in Southern Rhodesia and to refrain from rendering any assistance to it'.

Security Council Resolution 221 (1966):

The Security Council:

'Gravely concerned at reports that substantial supplies of oil may reach Rhodesia as the result of an oil tanker having arrived at Beira and the approach of a further tanker which may lead to the resumption of pumping through the CPMR pipeline with the acquiescence of the Portuguese authorities;

... considering that such supplies will afford great assistance and encouragement to the illegal regime in Southern Rhodesia, thereby enabling it to remain longer in being;

1) Determines that the resulting situation constitutes a threat to the peace;

2) Calls upon the Portuguese Government not to permit oil to be pumped through the pipeline from Beira to Rhodesia;

3) Calls upon the Portuguese Government not to receive at Beira oil destined for Rhodesia;

4) Calls upon all States to ensure the diversion of any of their vessels reasonably believed to be carrying oil destined for Rhodesia which may be en route for Beira;

5) Calls upon the Government of the United Kingdom to prevent by the use of force if necessary the arrival at Beira of vessels reasonably believed to be carrying oil destined for Rhodesia, and empowers the United Kingdom to arrest and detain tanker known as the *Joanna V* upon her departure from Beira in the event her oil cargo is discharged there.'

At 07.20 hours GMT on 10 April, HMS *Berwick* made contact with the tanker *Manuela* which was then 180 miles south of Beira. A British naval officer with escort was put on board the tanker with written instructions to its master to divert from his course to Beira, and was followed by a British armed naval party. He was informed in writing that, in view of the United Nations resolution, the tanker could not be allowed to proceed to Beira and that the British Government had authority if necessary to use force to prevent this.

On 16 December 1966, the Security Council imposed selective mandatory economic sanctions on Southern Rhodesia under Article 41 of the Charter and reminded Members that failure to implement them would give rise to a violation of Article 24 of the Charter.

The Iraqi invasion of Kuwait

On 2 August 1990, Iraqi armed forces invaded the neighbouring sovereign state of Kuwait and ousted the incumbent Kuwaiti Government. The UN Security Council was immediately called into emergency session and on the same day passed Resolution 660 (1990) which condemned the Iraqi invasion of Kuwait, demanded the immediate and unconditional withdrawal of all Iraqi forces from Kuwait and called upon Iraq and Kuwait to settle their international differences by peaceful means.

After Iraq refused to withdraw its troops from Kuwait, the Security Council passed Resolution 661 (1990) of 6 August 1990. This Resolution imposed mandatory sanctions and an embargo on Iraq. Under the terms of the Resolution, all States (not just Members of the United Nations) were prohibited from permitting:

1. trade in commodities and products originating in either Iraq or Kuwait, other than medicine and humanitarian aid;
2. the transportation or transshipment of any Iraqi and Kuwaiti products, by land, air or sea, and the transfer of funds for payment of related transactions;
3. the supply of weapons or any other military equipment; and
4. the grant of financial assistance, credit, or any other economic resources to either Iraq or Kuwait.

In addition, all States were required to take 'appropriate measures' to protect the assets of the legitimate Government of Kuwait and the Resolution instructed all States to refrain from recognising any regime set up by the occupying power.

Iraq claimed that the Kuwaiti Government had been overthrown by an internal revolution and, on 5 August, a new Kuwaiti Government was announced by Iraq. Later, Iraq announced its intention to annex Kuwait, a move which was subsequently renounced by the Security Council in Resolution 662 (1990). Nevertheless, on 28 August, Iraq declared that Kuwait had become its nineteenth province and constitutional amendments were passed to that effect.

After numerous fruitless attempts to achieve a peaceful settlement, on 29 November, the Security Council passed Resolution 678 (1990) which demanded that Iraq 'comply fully with Resolution 660 (1990) and all subsequent relevant resolutions' and authorised 'Member States co-operating with the Government of Kuwait ... to use all necessary means to uphold and implement Security Council Resolution 660 (1990) and all subsequent relevant Resolutions and to restore international peace and security in the area'. 15 January 1990 was set as the deadline for Iraqi compliance with the Resolutions of the Security Council.

No Iraqi withdrawal was initiated before the deadline specified in Resolution 678 (1990) and on 16 January 1991, coalition forces from the multilateral forces stationed in Saudi Arabia commenced an aerial bombardment of military installations and strategic targets inside Iraq and Kuwait. After less than a month, the allied forces commenced ground operations to liberate Kuwait, and within four days the territory of Kuwait was surrendered to allied forces.

Resolution 678 (1990) is of particular significance because, for the first time in the history of the United Nations, the use of military force was authorised by the Security Council on the basis of a unanimous affirmative vote among the Permanent Members. However, the multilateral force was not a United Nations force in the sense of Chapter VII of the Charter, but rather a coalition of military forces organised under the command of the USA.

Once a determination under Article 39 has been made, the Security Council may proceed to adopt three types of measures:

Provisional measures

Article 40 of the Charter provides that:

> 'In order to prevent an aggravation of the situation, the Security Council may, before making the recommendations or deciding upon the measures provided for in Article 39, call upon the parties concerned to comply with such provisional measures as it deems necessary or desirable. Such provisional measures shall be without prejudice to the rights, claims, or position of the parties concerned. The Security Council shall duly take account of failure to comply with such provisional measures.'

For example, in the Palestine question, Article 40 was specifically invoked ordering a ceasefire and withdrawal. Such provisional measures may provide a basis for the settlement of the dispute without the need for further action by the Security Council. These provisional measures do not prejudice the rights of the parties. They are simply a means of preventing an aggravation of the situation.

One question arising under Article 40 is whether the adoption of a resolution providing for provisional measures creates an obligation upon the parties to whom the resolution is directed. In this respect it is generally agreed that the words 'called upon' when used in Article 40 mean 'order' and should be read in conjunction with Article 25. For this reason, to avoid having to take enforcement action against States, the powers under Article 40 are rarely used by the Security Council and most resolutions passed are phrased as recommendations and not orders.

The practice of the Security Council suggests that the power under Article 40 to call upon parties to comply with provisional measures does not depend upon a prior determination under Article 39.

(There is no measure under Chapter VI (Pacific Settlement of Disputes) corresponding to Article 40. Nevertheless, the absence of such authorisation has not prevented the Security Council from calling upon parties to cease conduct likely to aggravate a dispute.)

Enforcement action under Article 41 not involving the use of armed force

Article 41 provides:

> 'The Security Council may decide what measures *not involving the use of armed forces* are to be employed to give effect to its decision, and it may call upon the Members of the United Nations to apply such measures. These may include complete or partial interruption of economic relations and of rail, sea, air, postal, telegraphic, radio and other measures of communcation, and the severance of diplomatic relations.'

Action under Article 41 has been taken four times – with regard to Rhodesia, following the Unilateral Declaration of Independence of 1965, South Africa in 1977, Iraq in 1990, and Libya in 1992. In the case of Rhodesia the Security council called upon all States not to recognise the white minority regime established in Rhodesia following the Unilateral Declaration of Independence (UDI) and further called upon States to break economic and military relations with the country. These measures were strengthened in 1966 when the Council imposed selective economic sanctions on Rhodesia that were binding on all States. These measures were rendered comprehensive by SCR 253 (1968).

In the case of South Africa the measures imposed by the Security Council in 1977 were limited to an arms embargo. SCR 418 (1977) decided that:

'... all States shall cease forthwith any provision to South Africa of arms and related material of all types'.

In both of the above cases the measures imposed by the Security Council failed to have the effect envisaged. The inability to achieve consensus within the Security Council for comprehensive measures enforcing action taken under Article 41 has to a very large extent contributed to the perceived failure of the United Nations system in maintaining international peace and security.

failure of UN

Measures under Article 41 were also adopted by the Security Council in respect of the Iraqi invasion of Kuwait. The measures adopted by SCR 661 (1990) go considerably further and received greater support than measures previously adopted under Article 41. The text of the Resolution reads as follows:

'*The Security Council,*

Reaffirming its Resolution 660 (1990),

Deeply concerned that this Resolution has not been implemented and that the invasion by Iraq of Kuwait continues with further loss of human life and material destruction,

Determined to bring the invasion and occupation of Kuwait by Iraq to an end and to restore the sovereignty, independence and territorial integrity of Kuwait,

Noting that the legitimate Government of Kuwait has expressed its readiness to comply with Resolution 660 (1990),

Mindful of its responsibilities under the Charter for the maintenance of international peace and security,

Affirming the inherent right of individual or collective self-defence, in response to the armed attack by Iraq against Kuwait, in accordance with Article 51 of the Charter,

Acting under Chapter VII of the Charter of the United Nations,

1 *Determines* that Iraq so far has failed to comply with operative paragraph 2 of Resolution 660 (1990) and has usurped the authority of the legitimate Government of Kuwait;

2. *Decides*, as a consequence, to take the following measures to secure compliance of Iraq with operative paragraph 2 and to restore the authority of the legitimate Government of Kuwait;

3. *Decides* that all States shall prevent:

a) The import into their territories of all commodities and products originating in Iraq or Kuwait exported therefrom after the date of this Resolution;

b) Any activities by their nationals or in their territories which would promote or are calculated to promote the export or trans-shipment of any commodities or products from Iraq or Kuwait; and any dealings by their nationals or their flag vessels or in their territories in any commodities or products originating in Iraq or Kuwait and exported therefrom after the date of this Resolution, including, in particular, any transfer of funds to Iraq or Kuwait for the purposes of such activities or dealings;

c) The sale or supply by their nationals or from their territories or using their flag vessels of any commodities or products, including weapons or any other military equipment, whether or not originating in their territories but not including supplies intended strictly for medical purposes, and, in humanitarian circumstances, foodstuffs, to any person or body in Iraq or Kuwait or to any person or body for the purposes of any business carried on in or operated from Iraq or Kuwait, and any activities by their nationals or in their territories which promote or are calculated to promote such sale or supply of such commodities or products;

4. *Decides* that all States shall not make available to the Government of Iraq or to any commercial, industrial or public utility undertaking in Iraq or Kuwait, any funds or any other financial or economic resources and shall prevent their nationals and any persons within their territories from removing from their territories or otherwise making available to that Government or to any such undertaking any such funds or resources and from remitting any other funds to persons or bodies within Iraq or Kuwait, except payments exclusively for strictly medical or humanitarian purposes and, in special humanitarian circumstances, foodstuffs;

5. *Calls upon* all States, including States non-members of the United Nations, to act strictly in accordance with the provisions of this Resolution notwithstanding any contract entered into or licence granted before the date of this Resolution;

6. *Decides* to establish, in accordance with rule 28 of the provisional rules of procedure of the Security Council, a Committee of the Security Council consisting of all the members of the Council, to undertake the following tasks and to report on its work to the Council with its observations and recommendations:

   a) To examine the reports on the progress of the implementation of this Resolution which will be submitted by the Secretary-General;

   b) To seek from all States further information regarding the action taken by them concerning the effective implementation of the provisions laid down in this Resolution;

7. *Calls upon* all States to co-operate fully with the Committee in the fulfilment of its task, including supplying such information as may be sought by the Committee in pursuance of this Resolution;

8. *Requests* the Secretary-General to provide all necessary assistance to the Committee and to make the necessary arrangements in the Secretariat for the purpose;

9. *Decides* that, notwithstanding paragraphs 4 through 8, nothing in this Resolution shall prohibit assistance to the legitimate Government of Kuwait, and *calls upon* all States:

   a) To take appropriate measures to protect assets of the legitimate Government of Kuwait and its agencies; and

   b) Not to recognise any regime set up by the occupying power;

10. *Requests* the Secretary-General to report to the Council on the progress of the implementation of this resolution, the first report to be submitted within thirty days;

11. *Decides* to keep this item on its agenda and to continue its efforts to put an early end to the invasion by Iraq.'

The Security Council also adopted measures recently under Article 41 of the UN Charter against Libya for its refusal to extradite two accused persons suspected of planning and perpetrating the destruction of Pan Am Flight 103 over Lockerbie.

On 21 January 1992, the Security Council adopted Resolution 731 (1992) condemning Libya for failing to respond effectively to requests made to it for co-operation in establishing responsibility for the atrocity. The Resolution continued to urge Libya to provide 'a full and effective response to those requests so as to contribute to the elimination of international terrorism'.

In the absence of a satisfactory response for the Libyan Government, the Security Council adopted Resolution 748 (1992) which noted that Libya had failed to respond satisfactorily to the requests made in Resolution 731 and to renounce its involvement in international terrorism. The failure to do so amounted to a threat to international peace and security and accordingly the Security Council invoked Chapter VII of the Charter to impose mandatory sanctions on Libya.

These sanctions were threefold. First, flights to and from Libya from international destinations were prohibited. Second, an arms embargo was imposed. Third, States were required to reduce Libyan diplomatic and consular representation on their territories.

These measures were given effect in the UK by the Libya (United Nations Sanction) Order 1992 which prohibited all arms sales to Libya by British firms as well as payments to any persons connected with Libya under bonds relating to arms transactions. The effect of these measures was demonstrated in *Wahda Bank* v *Arab Bank* (1992), in which payment under a counter-guarantee was prohibited by an English court because to give effect to it would contravene the terms of the order.

Within the UK, sanctions under Chapter VII are not immediately effective and require a legislative measure such as an order-in-council. The authority to prohibit certain conduct lies in the national measure and not in the international sanction which is not automatically incorporated into UK law. Thus, in the case cited above, in the absence of the order, it was probably not illegal for the bank to make performance under the counter-guarantee.

Enforcement action under Article 42 involving the use of armed forces

Article 42 provides:

'Should the Security Council consider that measures provided for in Article 41 would be inadequate or have proved to be inadequate, it may take such action by air, sea or land forces as may be necessary to maintain or restore international peace and security. Such action may include demonstrations, blockade and other operations by air, sea or land forces of Members of the United Nations.'

To date, action under this provision has not been taken. (The United Nations forces in Korea arose following a *recommendation* by the Security Council following an Article 39 determination.) At time of writing, however, it appears likely that the Security Council will adopt a resolution to allow the multinational forces in the Gulf to take enforcement measures in support of SCR 661 (1990).

Agreements on the provision of armed forces by Member States

The basis of the scheme envisaged in Chapter VII lay in the provision to the Security Council of the armed forces necessary to enforce its decisions against recalcitrant States. This was to be effected by agreements between the Security Council and the Member States.

Article 43 of the Charter provides:

'1) All Members of the United Nations, in order to contribute to the maintenance of international peace and security, undertake to make available to the Security Council, on its call and in accordance with a special agreement or agreements, armed forces, assistance, and facilities, including rights of passage, necessary for the purpose of maintaining international peace and security.

2) Such agreement or agreements shall govern the number and types of forces, their degree of readiness and general location, and the nature of the facilities and assistance to be provided.

3) The agreement or agreements shall be negotiated as soon as possible on the initiative of the Security Council'.

Therefore, a State is not obliged to take part in military operations under Article 42 unless it has concluded a 'special agreement' under Article 43. No such agreements have been made. However, the absence of agreements under Article 43 does not prevent States agreeing *ad hoc* to place forces at the disposal of the Security Council in particular cases. For example, as with the United Nations Command in Korea 1950.

The Military Staff Committee

Article 46 of the Charter provides that:

'Plans for the application of armed force shall be made by the Security Council with the assistance of the Military Staff Committee.'

Article 47 provides:

'1) There shall be established a Military Staff Committee to advise and assist the Security Council on all questions relating to the Security Council's military requirements ...
2) The Military Staff Committee shall consist of the Chiefs of Staff of the permanent members of the Security Council or their representatives ...'

Although established in 1946 the Military Staff Committee has no real function. In practice the existence of this committee has been disregarded by the Security Council and responsibility for carrying out the Council's military requirements has been entrusted to the Secretary-General.

The failure of the Security Council to fulfil its primary purpose of maintaining international peace and security has led to three major developments:

1. The assumption by the General Assembly of the role of determining a breach of the peace, or act of aggression and of recommending action by members including the use of armed force.
2. The development of powerful regional systems outside the United Nations, eg NATO; Warsaw Pact.
3. The development of peacekeeping operations under either Chapter VI or VII of the Charter, using limited military forces, voluntarily contributed by Member States for: (1) observation and fact finding, eg UNMOGIP (Kashmir), UNYOM (Yemen), UNIFIL (Lebanon), UNDOF (Golan Heights); and (2) maintaining law and order in situations involving an actual threat to the peace, eg ONUC (Congo), UNFICYP (Cyprus).

This role falls between Chapter VI and Chapter VII and some writers have advocated a new Chapter VIA.

The Uniting for Peace Resolution

The creation of the Unified Command in Korea by the Security Council was only possible because of the fortuitous absence of the Soviet representative who had been boycotting the Security Council. As it was unlikely that Soviet boycotts would recur in the future the General Assembly, fearing that the veto would leave the Council powerless to act in a future case of the Korean type, examined methods whereby it could assume some of the responsibilities of the Security Council when the veto prevented it from acting.

As a result of its deliberations the Assembly on 3 November 1950 passed the Resolution on Uniting for Peace. By the first paragraph the General Assembly resolved that:

> '... if the Security Council because of lack of unanimity of the Permanent Members, fails to exercise its primary responsibility for the maintenance of international peace and security in any case where there appears to be a threat to the peace, breach of the peace, or act of aggression, the General Assembly shall consider the matter immediately with a view to making appropriate recommendations to members for collective measures, including in the case of a breach of the peace or act of aggression the use of armed force when necessary, to maintain or restore international peace and security. If not in session at the time, the General Assembly may meet in emergency special session ... Such emergency special session shall be called if requested by the Security Council on the vote of any seven Members, or by a majority of the Members of the United Nations.'

A Peace Observation commission of 14 Members was established which can be despatched to any troublespot so as to advise the Assembly of any necessary action, and a Collective Measures Committee of 14 Members was established to co-ordinate the action taken by Members on the Assembly's recommendations.

The justification for the Assembly assuming these powers was that generally the Assembly could do anything by recommendation that the Security Council could do by recommendation or decision. Article 24 of the Charter gave the Security Council *primary* responsibility for the maintenance of international peace and security. This did not preclude the General Assembly from exercising a secondary or residual responsibility. The foundation of this argument was the wide scope of Article 10 of the Charter which enables the General Assembly to discuss and make recommendations on any matter 'within the scope of the present Charter'.

The procedure has been used on several occasions. On 31 October 1956, following the UK and French vote against the resolution in the Security Council proposing measures for the cessation of the military action against Egypt, the Suez question was transferred to the Assembly.

On 4 November 1956, following a Soviet veto in the Security Council, the Hungarian question was referred to the Assembly.

On 17 September 1960, following a Soviet veto in the Security Council, the Congo question was referred by the Council to the Assembly.

On 6 December 1971, the Security Council referred the Bangladesh question to the General Assembly under the Uniting for Peace Resolution.

The United Nations Emergency Force in the Middle East (UNEF)

In October 1956 Israel, France and the UK attacked Egypt. On 5 November 1956, after a cease-fire had been agreed the General Assembly adopted a resolution by which it established a United Nations Emergency Force (UNEF) 'to secure and supervise the cessation of hostilities'. After the withdrawal of the Israeli, French and British troops UNEF was sent to patrol the Israeli-Egyptian armistice line, and to report troop movements near the line. The Force was authorised to fight in self-defence, but was not expected to resist any large scale invasion across the armistice line.

The Force was comprised of contingents of national armies and was founded on the principle of consent. No Member State was obliged to provide a contingent unless it consented to do so by means of an agreement between the State and the Secretary-General.

The General Assembly appointed the Commander of the Force, and authorised the Secretary-General to enact regulations essential to the effective functioning of the Force. The Force was paid by the United Nations and took its orders solely from the General Assembly and the Secretary-General.

The Force could not enter the territory of any State without that States consent. Israel refused to consent to its presence on Israeli territory and the Force therefore operated solely on Egyptian territory. The Force was withdrawn at the request of the United Arab Republic in May 1967.

The United Nations Force in the Congo (ONUC)

On 30 June 1960, the Republic of the Congo was granted independence by Belgium. Within a few days of independence the Congolese army mutinied and law and order broke down, resulting in injury to nationals, aliens, and property. On 10 July Belgian troops stationed in the Congo under a treaty of friendship between Belgium and the Congo intervened 'with the sole purpose of ensuring the safety of European and other members of the population and of protecting human lives in general'.

On 12 July the Congolese Government cabled the Secretary-General requesting 'urgent despatch by the United Nations of military assistance ... to protect the national territory of the Congo against the present external aggression which is a threat to international peace'. On 14 July the Security Council authorised the Secretary-General to provide the Congo with military assistance. In accordance with the Security Council resolution the Secretary-General established ONUC and the first troops entered the Congo in mid-July. The Force was not intended to take military action against Belgian troops but to help the Congolese Government maintain law and order. The Force was modelled on UNEF.

However, by 14 September 1960, the unanimity among the permanent members of the Security Council had disintegrated and disagreement over the extent and nature of ONUC's activities caused the USSR to veto a proposed resolution calling on States not to intervene unilaterally and to act through ONUC. An emergency session of the General Assembly was called under the Uniting for Peace Resolution on 17 September which adopted a resolution requesting:

'... the Secretary-General to continue to take vigorous action in accordance with the terms of the aforesaid Resolutions (of the Security Council) and to assist the Central Government of the Congo in the restoration and maintenance of law and order throughout the territory of the Republic of the Congo and to safeguard its unity, territorial integrity and political independence in the interests of international peace and security.'

Although the Force was originally intended to fight only in self-defence, following the disintegration of the Congolese Government the Force was authorised to fight in order to prevent civil war and to expel foreign mercenaries. In this respect the Force was engaged in extensive military operations against the secessionist movement in Katanga. By the end of 1961, Katangese resistance had been overcome.

ONUC left the Republic of the Congo on 30 June 1964.

The legal basis for the creation of ONUC is obscure and controversial. In the *Certain Expenses of the United Nations Case* (1962) the ICJ observed:

'It is not necessary for the Court to express an opinion as to which article or articles of the Charter were the basis for the resolutions of the Security Council, but it can be said that the operations of ONUC did not include a use of armed force against a State which the Security Council, under Article 39, determined to have committed an act of aggression or to have breached the peace. The armed forces which were utilised in the Congo were not authorised to take military action against any State. The operation did not involve "preventive or enforcement measures" against any State under Chapter VII and therefore did not constitute "action" as that term is used in Article 11.'

It has been suggested that the creation of ONUC constituted 'provisional measures' within the meaning of Article 40 of the Charter. This was the view expressed by the Secretary-General in the Security Council Debate of 13–14 December 1960.

Limitations upon the power of the General Assembly

In the *Certain Expenses of the United Nations Case* (1962) certain Members of the United Nations fell seriously behind in the payment of the financial contributions assessed to them by the General Assembly under Article 17 of the Charter because of their refusal to accept these assessments in so far as they related to the financing of UNEF and ONUC on the ground that both of these forces were unconstitutional and had been created illegally.

The General Assembly requested the advice of the ICJ as to whether the expenses of the two forces were expenses of the United Nations within the meaning of Article 17(2) of the Charter.

The main argument against the legality of the creation of UNEF by the General Assembly was that 'action' in the field of international peace and security was the sole prerogative of the Security Council. The General Assembly had argued that Article 24 of the Charter only gave the Security Council 'primary' responsibility for the maintenance of international peace and security. This did not therefore preclude the General Assembly from exercising a secondary or residual responsibility, in accordance with its wide general powers under Articles 10 and 14 of the Charter. However, it was contended that if the General Assembly did exercise such responsibility it would be in breach of that part of Article 11(2) of the Charter which states that any question relating to the maintenance of international peace and security upon which action is necessary must be referred to the Security Council.

The Court, in a majority opinion (nine votes to five) advised that the Security Council had 'primary' and not exclusive authority, and that whilst the taking of enforcement action was the exclusive prerogative of the Security Council under Chapter VII this did not prevent the Assembly from making recommendations under Articles 10 and 14. The limitation of Article 11(2) does not apply in such cases, since the 'action' referred to in that paragraph means only 'enforcement action' which is in the nature of coercive action directed against a State. The UNEF action was not, in the Court's view, enforcement action, but rather 'measures' recommended under Article 14.

(The validity of the Congo operation was not contested on the same grounds, because it was the Security Council and not the General Assembly which initiated them, therefore the Uniting for Peace Resolution was not in issue. The main argument relating to the Congo was that the Secretary-General had exceeded and abused the powers conferred on him. This allegation was rejected by the Court.)

A further problem arising from the Uniting for Peace Resolution is that of the procedure for convening an emergency session.

Article 20 of the Charter provides:

'The General Assembly shall meet in regular annual sessions and in such special sessions as occasions may require. Special sessions shall be convoked by the Secretary-General at the request of the Security Council or of a majority of the Members of the United Nations.'

However, the Uniting for Peace Resolution as amended provides that an emergency special session of the Assembly shall be called by a vote of 'any nine members of the Security Council'.

The Soviet Union contested the legality of this on the ground that Article 20 governs the convening of emergency sessions and the vote of the Security Council is a non-procedural one to which the veto applies. However, such arguments have not stopped the Assembly from convening to discuss matters, even where the protests of the permanent members have been raised.

16.6 Actions by regional agencies

Article 52 of the Charter of the United Nations provides:

'1) Nothing in the present Charter precludes the existence of regional arrangements or agencies for dealing with such matters relating to the maintenance of international peace and

security as are appropriate for regional action, provided that such arrangements or agencies and their activities are consistent with the Purposes and Principles of the United Nations.
2) The Members of the United Nations entering into such arrangements or constituting such agencies shall make every effort to achieve pacific settlement of local disputes through such regional arrangements or by such regional agencies before referring them to the Security Council.
3) The Security Council shall encourage the development of pacific settlement of local disputes through such regional arrangements or by such regional agencies either on the initiative of the States concerned or by reference from the Security Council.
4) This Article in no way impairs the application of Articles 34 and 35.'

Article 53 provides:

'1) The Security Council shall, where appropriate, utilise such regional arrangements or agencies for enforcement action under its authority. But no enforcement action shall be taken under regional arrangements or by regional agencies without the authorisation of the Security Council, with the exception of measures against any enemy State, as defined in paragraph 2 of this Article, provided for pursuant to Article 107 or in regional arrangements directed against renewal of aggressive policy on the part of any such State, until such time as the Organisation may, on request of the Government concerned, be charged with the responsibility for preventing further aggression by such a State.
2) The term enemy State as used in paragraph 1 of this Article applies to any State which during the Second World War has been an enemy of any signatory of the present Charter.'

Article 54 provides:

'The Security Council shall at all times be kept fully informed of activities undertaken or in contemplation under regional arrangements or by regional agencies for the maintenance of international peace and security.'

A regional arrangement or agency must therefore satisfy three conditions stipulated in Article 52:

1. It must be concerned with the maintenance of international peace and security.
2. It must be consistent with the Purposes and Principles of the United Nations.
3. It must in some way be regional.

[handwritten margin note: must satisfy criteria in art 52.]

Conflict between regional arrangements and the United Nations

The pacific settlement of disputes

Article 52(2) and (3) imposes upon the parties and the Security Council the obligation to utilise regional procedures for settlement. However, Article 52(4) states that 'this Article in no way impairs the application of Article 34 and 35'. Therefore it seems that the Security Council's own right to investigate a dispute or situation, and the Member States right to appeal to the Council are preserved.

[handwritten margin note: no conflict bt 34/35 and 52(2)/(3)]

This jurisdictional conflict has led some regional organisations to declare that so far as inter-regional disputes are concerned, the regional procedures have a 'priority' over the Security Council's procedures for settlement. In this way the regional organisations may take action without fear of a permanent member of the Security Council using the power of veto.

Bowett, in an attempt to rationalise the competing claims to jurisdiction places 'disputes' into three categories:

1) Disputes involving no actual or potential threat to international peace – here the priority of the regional procedures is undisputed, and the matter ought not to be referred to the Security Council.

2) Disputes involving a potential threat to international peace – here, the matter seems to fall squarely under Chapter VI of the Charter, so that the rights of the Council under Article 34, and of States under Article 35, are clear. Reference to a regional organisation's procedures becomes a matter of convenience, not of obligation, and much depends on the willingness of the parties to accept such a reference.

3) "Disputes" which involve an actual threat to peace – here the situation properly belongs in Chapter VII, not Chapter VI, and the "primary responsibility" of the Security Council to deal with the matter is clear: there can be no question of "priority" for regional procedures. Equally, clearly, there is nothing to prevent the Security Council utilising regional procedures to assist in any measures taken under Chapter VII, but they do this subject to the Council's primary responsibility.'

Enforcement action

Article 53 of the Charter provides that 'no enforcement action shall be taken ... by regional agencies without the authorisation of the Security Council'.

This provision constituted a serious obstacle to regional agencies and in particular to the Organisation of American States (OAS). The USA and its allies have attempted to overcome this in a number of ways.

Measures short of the use of force. In 1962 the OAS imposed economic sanctions against the Castro regime in Cuba. The USSR argued in the Security Council that such a measure constituted enforcement action which was illegal without the authorisation of the Security Council. However, the majority of Security Council Members considered that economic sanctions did not constitute enforcement action. The OAS was merely doing collectively what any of its members could have done individually – 'Under customary law, every State is at liberty to sever its economic relations with another State'.

Measures involving the use of force: the Cuban Missiles Crisis 1962. The USSR was sending to Cuba missiles and other weapons and materials which could be seen as a threat to US security. On 22 October 1962, President Kennedy announced America's intention to impose a 'strict quarantine on all offensive military equipment under shipment to Cuba'.

(This was essentially a blockade, but a blockade can only exist if there is a state of war and as the term 'war' was not politically acceptable they called it quarantine). There was a great deal of concern on the part of the USA to make what they were doing look to be consistent with international law. Two justifications were possible.

Self-defence under Article 51 of the Charter: the missiles in Cuba would pose a threat to America. But the action taken by the USA would be anticipatory self-defence. They were not only stopping the missiles being fired but were also stopping them being placed in Cuba. Even assuming that there is a right of anticipatory self-defence this must be exercised in accordance with the *Caroline* principle. There had to be an immediate threat and any action taken in self-defence had to be proportionate to the degree of harm threatened.

It would therefore have been a very dubious case of self-defence and it was argued that if the USA relied on self-defence it was not really genuine in showing a legal justification for the quarantine. The USA also had to consider the American missiles in Turkey aimed at Russia. Could Russia also attempt to remove these in self-defence? Reliance on Article 51 could therefore have created a precedent which could have been abused by many other States. So politically it was felt that self-defence was not the line to take.

Regional action under Chapter VIII of the Charter: the quarantine was contrary to Article 2(4) of the Charter and therefore it had to be justified. Self-defence could not seriously be used as a justification. The alternative was to ask the Security Council to act under Chapter VII, but Russia would veto. The General Assembly could, of course, then act in accordance with the Uniting for Peace Resolution but it was doubtful that the USA would receive the support of the General Assembly. The only alternative therefore was action under Chapter VIII of the Charter. This proved to be the best approach and it was followed.

On 23 October at the suggestion of the USA, the Security Council met and discussed the proposed quarantine but took no action. On the same day, the Council of the Organisation of American States adopted a resolution recommending that:

'Member States, in accordance with Articles 6 and 8 of the Inter-American Treaty of Reciprocal Assistance, take all measures, individually and collectively, including the use of armed force, which they may deem necessary to ensure that the Government of Cuba cannot continue to receive from the Sino-Soviet powers military material and related supplies which may threaten the peace and security of the Continent and to prevent the missiles in Cuba with offensive capability from ever becoming an active threat to the peace and security of the Continent.'

On 23 October the US President issued the following Proclamation:

'Any vessel or craft which may be proceeding towards Cuba may be intercepted and may be directed to identify itself, its cargo, equipment and stores and its ports of call, to stop, to lie to, to submit to visit and search, or to proceed as directed. Any vessel which fails or refuses to respond or to comply with directions shall be subject to being taken into custody.'

The US Deputy Legal Adviser, Meeker, justified the US action as follows:

'The quarantine was based on a collective judgment and recommendation of the American Republics made under the Rio Treaty. It was considered not to contravene Article 2, paragraph 4, because it was a measure adopted by a regional organisation in conformity with the provisions of Chapter VIII of the Charter. The purposes of the Organisation and its activities were considered to be consistent with the purposes and principles of the United Nations as provided in Article 52. This being the case, the quarantine would no more violate Article 2, paragraph 4, than measures voted for by the Council under Chapter VII, by the General Assembly under Articles 10 and 11, or taken by United Nations Members in conformity with Article 51.'

The problem was, however, that enforcement action under Article 53 could not be taken by regional agencies without the authorisation of the Security Council. The Soviet veto in the Security Council would have ensured that this authorisation was not given. The USA therefore argued that the concept of 'enforcement action' subject to prior authorisation by the Security Council does not embrace measures falling short of the use of armed force or taken voluntarily. Enforcement action – the term used in the Charter – meant enforcement action which was compulsory upon a State. If the enforcement action was not compulsory but merely voluntary it would not be enforcement action under the meaning of the Charter. The action taken by the OAS was not therefore enforcement action within the meaning of the Charter because it was only a recommendation to States which was not binding upon them and thus any action taken by them was purely voluntary.

OAS act⁰
≠ compulsory
∴ not w/in
Charter

The legal arguments put forward by the USA to justify their action are all very dubious in international law. Dean Acheson, a former US Secretary of State for Foreign Affairs commented:

dubious

> 'I must conclude that the propriety of the Cuban quarantine is not a legal issue. The power, position and prestige of the United States had been challenged by another State; and law simply does not deal with such questions of ultimate power – power that comes close to the sources of sovereignty. I cannot believe that there are principles of law that say we must accept destruction of our way of life ... The survival of States is not a matter of law.'

What is a regional arrangement?

Not all organisations with membership limited to States in a given geographical area are regarded as regional arrangements within the sense of Chapter VIII.

For example, the North Atlantic Treaty Organisation does not call itself a regional arrangement but is expressed in its Treaty as being an organisation for collective self-defence under Article 51 of the Charter. It therefore avoids the control of the Security Council and the Soviet power of veto.

BOWETT
what state
practice
perceives

No definition of regional arrangement is given in the Charter and there is controversy as to what the phrase actually means. Bowett argues that the real question is not whether a given organisation is a regional arrangement or not, but rather whether particular action is taken as a regional arrangement or not.

16.7 Controversial uses of force

Reprisals

A reprisal is an act which would normally be illegal but which is rendered lawful by a prior illegal act committed by the State against which the reprisal is directed. Reprisals have provided the main means of forcing States to obey international law and the laws of war in particular. However, the right of reprisal in retaliation against a prior illegal act was open to abuse especially by strong States against weaker

States. Certain conditions were therefore recognised as being necessary if such reprisals were to be valid.

In the *Naulilaa Case: Portugal v Germany* (1928) case, in October 1914, when Portugal was a neutral State during the First World War three members of a party of German soldiers lawfully in the Portuguese colony of Angola were killed by Portuguese soldiers. On the evidence it was clearly established that the incident arose out of a misunderstanding.

Germany, however, as a measure of reprisal sent a military force into Angola which attacked several frontier posts and destroyed property including the port at Naulilaa. Portugal claimed reparation for damage attributable to the German action. Germany argued that it was a case of legitimate reprisals.

The German plea was rejected by the Arbitrator who stated:

'Reprisals are acts of self-help by the injured State, acts in retaliation for acts contrary to international law on the part of the offending State, which have remained unredressed after a demand for amends. In consequence of such measures, the observance of this or that rule of international law is temporarily suspended in the relations between the two States. They are limited by considerations of humanity and the rules of good faith, applicable in the relations between States. They are illegal unless they are based upon a previous act contrary to international law. They seek to impose on the offending State reparation for the offence, the return to legality and the avoidance of new offences.'

The Arbitrator laid down three conditions for the legitimacy of reprisals:

1. there must have been an act contrary to international law on the part of the other State;
2. the reprisal must be preceded by an unsatisfied request for redress of the wrong committed;
3. the measures adopted as reprisals must not be excessive, in the sense of being out of all proportion to the wrong committed.

legality of reprisals

While traditional law did recognise that a State could engage in reprisals subject to the above conditions being satisfied, the Charter of the United Nations, in prohibiting the threat or use of force against the territorial integrity or political independence of any State, makes any use of force by a State, including reprisals, prima facie illegal. Article 51 of the Charter, however, preserves a States inherent right of self-defence. It is therefore necessary to distinguish between acts of self-defence which are permitted, and reprisals which are not.

The Harib Fort Incident 1964

In 1963 and 1964, the British Government had complained to the Security Council of a large number of shooting incidents on the Yemeni-South Arabian border and of aerial raids into South Arabian territory from the Yemen. In March 1964, three raids had taken place in which Bedouin and their flocks had been attacked from the air. Thereupon on 28 March 1964 British military aircraft bombed Harib Fort in the

Yemen after having first dropped leaflets advising people to leave the area. The Yemen brought the matter before the Security Council.

The British representative denied that the attack had been a reprisal. He argued that:

> '... there is, in existing law a clear distinction to be drawn between two forms of self-help. One, which is of a retributive or punitive nature – "retaliation" or "reprisals"; the other, which is expressly contemplated and authorised by the Charter – self-defence against an armed attack.
>
> ... it is clear that the use of armed force to repel or prevent an attack – that is, legitimate action of a defensive nature – may sometimes have to take the form of a counter attack.'

He pointed out that aggressive acts from the Yemen had resulted in loss of life and emphasised that the fort at Harib was not merely a military installation, but was known to be a centre for aggressive action against the Federation:

> 'To destroy the fort with the minimum use of force was therefore a defensive measure which was proportionate and confined to the necessities of the case.
>
> It has no parallel with acts of retaliation or reprisals, which have as an essential element the purposes of vengeance or retribution. It is this latter use of force which is condemned by the Charter, and not the use of force for defensive purposes such as warding off future attacks.'

The Security Council did not accept the UK view and adopted a resolution in which it:

1. condemns reprisals as incompatible with the purposes and principles of the United Nations;
2. deplores the British military action at Harib on 28 March 1964;
3. deplores all attacks and incidents which have occurred in the area.

The Security Council has generally taken a stand against reprisals, but recently it has tended to condemn only the more extreme examples. This development has led Bowett to suggest that 'the more relevant distinction today is not between self-defence and reprisals but between reprisals which are likely to be condemned and those which, because they satisfy some concept of reasonableness, are not'.

Bowett lists the following factors which the practice of the Security Council suggests are relevant to the question whether a reprisal is 'reasonable' and hence unlikely to be condemned.

1. The proportionality between the reprisal and the earlier illegal act that causes it.
2. Whether the reprisal is against civilians or the armed forces.
3. Whether the reprisal is one against human life or property.
4.) Whether the State against whom it is taken has provoked the reprisal.
5. Whether the reprisal jeopardises the changes of a peaceful settlement by its timing.
6. Whether, at least in the guerrilla context, the State taking the reprisal has exhausted all practical measures for the defence of its territory within its own borders.

Israel has relied less and less on a self-defence argument and has taken action which is openly admitted to be a reprisal. The Beirut raid of 28 December 1969 is the obvious example of an action not really defended on the basis of self-defence at all.

In the Beirut raid 13 civil airplanes valued at over $40 million were destroyed while on the ground at Beirut airport in Lebanon by Israeli commandos. There was no loss of life. The raid was in retaliation for an attack on 26 December of an El Al airplane at Athens airport by Palestine guerrillas. The airplane was damaged and a passenger – an Israeli – killed. Following the Beirut raid in retaliation for the Athens attack the Security Council condemned Israel 'for its premeditated military action in violation of its obligations under the Charter' and considered that Lebanon was entitled to 'appropriate redress for the destruction it has suffered'.

The Israeli Chief of Staff was reported to have stated the purpose as being 'to make it clear to the other side that the price they must pay for terrorist activities can be very high'.

Bowett states that:

'It cannot be expected that the Security Council will ever accept this justification. But there is clearly some evidence that certain reprisals will, even if not accepted as justified, at least avoid condemnation. This shift in argument from self-defence to reprisals may in part be due to the realisation that the self-defence argument is unlikely to be accepted in any event.

It may in larger part be due to a growing feeling that not only do reprisals offer a more effective means of checking military and strategic gains by the other party but also that they will meet with no more than a formal condemnation by the Council, and that effective sanctions under Chapter VII are not to be feared.

Obviously, if this trend continues, we shall achieve a position in which, while reprisals remain illegal *de jure*, they become accepted *de facto*. Indeed it may be that the more relevant distinction today is not between self-defence and reprisals but between reprisals which are likely to be condemned and those which, because they satisfy some concept of reasonableness, are not.'

Intervention

This is defined by Oppenheim as:

'Dictatorial interference by a State in the affairs of another State for the purpose of maintaining or altering the actual condition of things.'

In the nineteenth century intervention was usually associated with the armed intervention, usually on supposedly humanitarian grounds, by the powerful Western European States in the affairs of weaker, less civilised States.

Intervention to protect a State's own nationals and their property

Nineteenth-century jurists considered as lawful the use of force to protect lives and property of nationals. The theory behind this is that nationals of a State are an extension of the State itself. In this way intervention to protect the State's own nationals is reconcilable with the theory of self-defence – an injury to the national is an injury to the State. This thesis has, however, been the subject of much debate and controversy.

The Anglo-French Invasion of Suez 1956. In July 1956, Egypt nationalised the Suez Canal Company, a company in which there were considerable British and French interests. On 29 October 1956, Israel invaded Egyptian territory in the area of the Suez Canal Zone. France and the UK issued a joint ultimatum to Egypt and Israel demanding that they call a cease-fire, withdraw their troops from the Suez Canal area and allow British and French troops to be stationed along the Canal. The ultimatum was not complied with and on 31 October British and French troops invaded the Canal area.

The Lord Chancellor speaking in the House of Lords justified the British action:

'The position is that the combined effect of the Pact of Paris, the Charter of the United Nations and the General Assembly Uniting for Peace Resolution of 1951 is that force may lawfully be used or threatened only, first, with the express authority of the United Nations (that is, of the Security Council), and, secondly, in self-defence. But *self-defence undoubtedly includes a situation in which the lives of a States nationals abroad are threatened and it is necessary to intervene in that territory for their protection ...*
Now the tests of whether such intervention is necessary under customary international law are, first, whether there is an imminent danger of injury to nationals; secondly, whether there is a failure or inability on the part of the territorial Sovereign to protect the nationals in question; and thirdly, whether the measures of protection of the intervener are strictly confined to the object of protecting those nationals against injury.
It has been argued that there is a great distinction between the protection of human lives and the protection of property. That is not a proposition to which I would give absolute concurrence. I take the view that if really valuable and internationally important foreign property is in danger of irreparable injury, through the breakdown of order, entry by a foreign State for the sole purpose of securing the safety of that property is excusable. I take the view that, since we can show that the blocking of or interference with the Canal for a considerable period would cause ... irreparable damage and suffering to a number of nations, for which it would be difficult to see adequate compensation being afforded, our intervention is also justified by the danger to the Canal.
We have therefore three good grounds of intervention: the danger to our nationals; the danger to shipping in the Canal, which shipping carried many hundreds, at least, if not thousands, of people in their crews; and the danger to the enormously valuable installation of the Canal itself and the incalculable consequential effect on many nations if the Canal were blocked'.

Despite the arguments of the Lord Chancellor, the Suez invasion was regarded by the majority of the international community with such disfavour that its legality is difficult to justify.

The Entebbe Raid 1976. On 27 June 1976 an Air France airliner bound for Paris from Tel Aviv was hijacked over Greece. Two of the hijackers were West German nationals and the other two held Arab passports. The airliner was diverted to Entebbe airport in Uganda. The Jewish passengers, some 100 persons, were separated from the other passengers and the latter were released. The hijackers demanded the release of some 50 Palestinian terrorists imprisoned in various countries.

Following reports that Uganda was in fact helping the hijackers, on 2 July 1976, Israel flew soldiers to Entebbe and rescued the hostages by force. The hijackers were killed together with some Ugandan soldiers. Extensive damage was caused to Ugandan aircraft and the airport.

In the Security Council debate on the incident the US representative defended the action taken:

'Israel's action in rescuing the hostages necessarily involved a temporary breach of the territorial integrity of Uganda. Normally, such a breach would be impermissible under the Charter of the United Nations. *However, there is a well established right to use limited force for the protection of one's own nationals from an imminent threat of injury or death in a situation where the State in whose territory they are located is either unwilling or unable to protect them. The right, flowing from the right of self-defence, is limited to such use of force as is necessary and appropriate to protect threatened nationals from injury.*

The requirements of this right to protect nationals were clearly met in the Entebbe case. Israel had good reason to believe that at the time it acted Israeli nationals were in imminent danger of execution by the hijackers. Moreover, the action necessary to release the Israeli nationals or to prevent substantial loss of Israeli lives had not been taken by the Government of Uganda, nor was there reasonable expectation such action would be taken. In fact, there is substantial evidence that the Government of Uganda co-operated with and aided the hijackers ...

It should be emphasised that this assessment of the legality of Israeli action depends heavily on the unusual circumstances of this specific case. In particular, the evidence is strong that, given the attitude of the Ugandan authorities, co-operation with or reliance on them in rescuing the passengers and crew was impracticable.'

The right to intervene to protect nationals abroad has been advanced as an alternative ground for the intervention in a number of other cases. In December 1989, for example, following the intervention by 20,000 US troops in Panama, *one* of the grounds advanced by Secretary of State, James Baker justifying the action was that US nationals in Panama were under threat. The USA similarly advanced such arguments six years previously in justification of the landing of US troops in Grenada.

Amongst academic commentators, Professor Bowett has been the strongest proponent of the right to resort to measures of self-defence to protect nationals abroad. Not all writers, however, agree with his assessment. Professor Brownlie, for example, states:

'... it is very doubtful if the present form of intervention has any basis in the modern law. The instances in which States have purported to exercise it, and the terms in which it is delimited, show that it provides infinite opportunities for abuse. Forcible intervention is now unlawful. It is true that the protection of nationals presents particular difficulties and that a Government faced with a deliberate massacre of a considerable number of nationals in a foreign State would have cogent reasons of humanity for acting, and would also be under very great political pressure. The possible risks of denying the legality of action in a case of such urgency, an exceptional circumstance, must be weighed against the more calculable dangers of providing legal pretexts for the commission of breaches of the peace in the pursuit of national rather than humanitarian interests.'

These comments by Professor Brownlie notwithstanding, there is probably sufficient evidence in State practice to suggest that there is a limited right to use force to protect nationals abroad – at least in those circumstances in which the State in which the nationals are situated is unwilling or unable to acquit its responsibility to protect such nationals and the UN is unable to act.

Humanitarian intervention

Humanitarian intervention involves the intervention by one State on the territory of another in order to protect the nationals of a State other than the intervenor. This doctrine clearly cannot be justified by reference to self-defence for there is no direct and immediate nexus between the intervening State and the nationals to be protected. The existence of a right of humanitarian intervention is controversial. The most frequently quoted example of humanitarian intervention was India's intervention in Pakistan in 1971 in support of the Bangladeshis. More recent examples have included the Tanzanian intervention in Uganda which ultimately led to the downfall of Idi Amin. In all the examples apart from Bangladesh, however, the intervening State has justified its action by reference primarily to the doctrine of self-defence. These measures, therefore, are unsatisfactory examples of State practice which can be used to justify the existence of a right of humanitarian intervention.

Amongst academic commentators the majority opinion is clearly that international law does *not* allow humanitarian intervention.

Operation of the doctrine would be open to abuse since only powerful States could undertake police measures of this sort; and when military operations were justified as 'humanitarian intervention' this was only one of several characterisations offered and circumstances frequently indicated the presence of selfish motives. It was applied only against weak States and belongs to an era of unequal relations.

In the Declaration on the Inadmissibility of Intervention in the Domestic Affairs of States and the Protection of their Independence and Sovereignty 1965 (GAR 2131), Article 1 provides:

> 'No State has the right to intervene, directly or indirectly, for any reason whatever, in the internal or external affairs of any other State. Consequently, armed intervention and all other forms of interference or attempted threats against the personality of the State or against its political, economic and cultural elements, are condemned.'

Hot pursuit

In May/June 1977 Rhodesia entered Mozambique territory and attacked bases used by terrorists opposed to the Rhodesian Government, up to a distance of 60 miles from the border. It justified its action on grounds of 'hot pursuit'. The concept of hot pursuit exists under the law of the sea and Rhodesia argued that it applied to land offences as well.

The Security Council condemned the action. In the absence of a treaty between the States concerned permitting such action, there can be no right of 'hot pursuit' across land borders. However, such action may have been justified as a 'reasonable' reprisal or an act of anticipatory self-defence.

Annexation of territory

The proscription on the use of force contained in the Charter requires that annexation no longer be considered a basis for the acquisition of territory.

The General Assembly Resolution on Principles of International Law Concerning Friendly Relations and Co-operation Among States, etc (1970) provides, *inter alia*: the territory of a State shall not be the object of military occupation resulting from the use of force in contravention of the provisions of the Charter. The territory of a State shall not be the object of acquisition by another State resulting from the threat or use of force. No territorial acquisition resulting from the threat or use of force shall be recognised as legal. Nothing in the foregoing shall be construed as affecting:

'a) provisions of the Charter or any international agreement prior to the Charter regime and valid under international law; or
b) the powers of the Security Council under the Charter'.

The only possible justification for the temporary occupation of another State's territory would be self-defence, to create a buffer zone along the State's borders on the ground of self-defence against possible future attacks. For example, following the 'June War' of 1967 Israel was left in occupation of large areas of Egyptian and Jordanian territory which not only provided it with a strong bargaining counter but also strengthened its vulnerable boundaries between itself and its Arab neighbours. Nevertheless, self-defence could not justify a purported annexation of such territory and a State incorporating such territory permanently under its national sovereignty.

However, self-defence may be used to retake territory illegally occupied.

The invasion of Goa 1961

On 17–18 December 1961 India invaded the Portuguese territory of Goa, Danao and Dui on the Indian sub-continent. On 18 December Portugal asked the Security Council 'to put a stop to the contemptable act of aggression of the Indian Union, ordering an immediate cease-fire and the withdrawal of all the invading forces of the Indian Union'. A draft resolution recalling the terms of Articles 2(3) and (4) and calling both for an immediate cease-fire and for the withdrawal by India of its forces was vetoed by the USSR.

India argued that it was merely retaking a part of its country illegally occupied by the Portuguese.

'We are criticised here by various delegations which say "Why have you used force?" The Charter absolutely prohibits force, but the Charter itself does not completely eschew force, in the sense that force can be used in self-defence, for the protection of the people of a country – and the people of Goa are as much Indians as the people of any other part of India.'

17

Peaceful Settlement of Disputes Between States

17.1   Introduction

17.2   Arbitration

17.3   Judicial settlement: the ICJ

17.4   The role and future of the ICJ and international adjudication

17.1 Introduction

Article 33 of the Charter provides that parties to a dispute shall seek a solution by negotiation, mediation, enquiry, conciliation, arbitration, judicial settlement, the resort to regional agencies or by other peaceful means. The SC may attempt to achieve the peaceful settlement of a dispute in a number of ways:

1. it may investigate the dispute;
2. it may *call* upon parties to settle the dispute under Article 33 without specifying what means to use;
3. it may *recommend* a particular means of settlement;
4. it may *recommend* the actual terms of settlement;
5. it may set up machinery for settlement.

Diplomatic methods of dispute settlement

Diplomatic methods of dispute settlement, in contrast to legal means of dispute settlement, are not binding on the parties and place less emphasis on their formal positions under the law. Such methods include:

1. Negotiation – this is the most frequently used means of dispute settlement and is the normal method of diplomatic interchange. Negotiation can take place on an *ad hoc* basis, through semi-permanent missions (eg the Geneva arms negotiations) or via summit meetings. Negotiation may also be required as a first step before the parties to a dispute can have recourse to judicial settlement (eg the *SWA Case* (1962)).

318

2. Good offices – this arises when a state which is not a party to a dispute attempts to intervene between the parties to encourage negotiation. The role of the Secretary-General of the UN in facilitating dispute settlement is usually one of 'good offices'.
3. Mediation – this involves the active, though informal participation of a third party in the negotiating process. It may include the third party independently putting forward recommendations.
4. Inquiry – this involves third party investigation of the facts surrounding the dispute but does not include any formulation of proposals for a settlement (eg the *Dogger Bank* and *Red Crusader* Inquiries).
5. Conciliation – this occurs by agreement between the parties whereby a third party investigates the dispute and suggests terms for a settlement. The parties are not, however, bound by these recommendations.

17.2 Arbitration

Definition

The International Law Commission defined arbitration as: 'a procedure for the settlement of disputes between States by a binding award on the basis of law and as a result of an undertaking voluntarily accepted'.

Special features of arbitration

1. The selection of the arbitrator is made by the parties themselves, thus distinguishing arbitration from judicial settlement.
2. There is an implied duty on the parties to abide by the award that is made, unlike, for example, mediation or conciliation, which usually have no binding force upon the parties.
3. Arbitration tribunals are usually created to deal with a particular dispute or class of dispute.
4. The arbitration tribunal may consist of a single arbitrator or be a collegiate body, comprising two or more arbitrators appointed in equal numbers by each of the parties separately, plus an umpire appointed jointly by the parties or by the arbitrators appointed by them.

History of arbitration

Arbitration developed from a combination of negotiation and mediation and was originally a diplomatic procedure.

Modern 'judicial' arbitration dates from the mixed claims commission established under the *Jay Treaty* of 1794 between Great Britain and the USA to settle by arbitration issues outstanding after the War of Independence.

Arbitration increased in popularity following the successful *Alabama Arbitration* of 1871–72 between the USA and Great Britain concerning the dispute over the payment of compensation to the USA for losses caused to American shipping by Confederate cruisers built in neutral British shipyards. The success of the arbitration provided the impetus leading ultimately to the Hague Convention for the Pacific Settlement of International Disputes 1899 which created the Permanent Court of Arbitration.

The Permanent Court of Arbitration

This was established in 1900 under the Hague Convention for the Pacific Settlement of International Disputes, of 1899, revised in 1907.

The PCA consists not of a court, but of a panel of international lawyers nominated by States parties to the Convention and available to States wishing to select arbitrators.

Apart from the panel, the machinery of the Court comprises:

The International Bureau
Comprising a Secretary General and a small staff which acts as a secretariat or registry for the tribunals set up; and

The Permanent Administrative Council
Comprising the Foreign Minister of the Netherlands as President and the heads of the diplomatic missions at the Hague of States parties to the Convention.

As a result of the under-utilisation of this system, particularly after the Second World War, the PCA Rules were amended in 1962 to permit arbitration to take place under the machinery of the PCA between States and non-State parties. The amended rules have, however, only been used on one occasion in the case of *Turriff Construction* v *Sudan* (1970).

International commercial arbitration

Despite the lack of success of the PCA system, arbitration is today the most frequently used means of dispute settlement, with particular importance in the field of international commercial activity between states and corporations. A number of institutions exist to facilitate such settlement, notably the *International Chamber of Commerce*, under whose auspices the *International Court of Arbitration* is organised, and the *International Centre for the Settlement of Investment Disputes (ICSID)* set up by convention, under the auspices of the World Bank, in 1965. Both of these institutions have recommended rules and procedures to facilitate settlement between the parties.

As well as the ICC and ICSID rules, the UN Conference on International Trade Law has drawn up guidelines for use in arbitration proceedings. These rules also act as a Model Law for any State wishing to incorporate rules on arbitration into their domestic law. The *UNCITRAL* rules also formed the basis of the most extensive contemporary example of international arbitration, the *Iran–US Claims Tribunal*.

This Tribunal, set up by the Algiers Accord between the USA and Iran in 1980, was charged with assessing all the claims between the nationals of one State and the Government of the other arising out of the Iranian revolution. Around 2,500 claims have already been heard with a further 1,000 still to come.

Failure to appoint an arbitrator in accordance with the arbitration agreement

The appointment of the arbitrators, and in particular the appointment of neutral members of the arbitral tribunal or commission, is the key issue in any arbitration agreement. Such appointment was usually dependent on the good faith of the parties. It was possible therefore for arbitration agreements to become inoperative if one side resiled from its obligation to arbitrate, and deliberately failed to appoint its own member or members to the tribunal.

For example, the arbitral provisions of the Allies' peace treaties with the former enemy States of Bulgaria, Hungary and Romania of 1947 failed because the former enemy States deliberately failed to appoint their members of the arbitral tribunal, thereby rendering the arbitral provisions of the treaties inoperative.

To avoid this problem provisions have been adopted to provide for the appointment of arbitrators where one of the parties to the dispute fails to co-operate. For example, Article 21 of the European Convention for the Peaceful Settlement of Disputes 1957 provides:

> 'If the nomination of the members of the Arbitral Tribunal is not made within a period of three months from the date on which one of the parties requested the other party to constitute an Arbitral Tribunal, the task of making the necessary nomination shall be entrusted to the Government of a third State chosen by agreement between the parties, or, failing agreement within three months, to the President of the International Court of Justice. Should the latter be a national of one of the parties to the dispute, this task shall be entrusted to the Vice-President of the Court, or to the next senior judge of the Court who is not a national of the parties.'

The effect of the arbitral award

Normally arbitration between States is intended to be final and the award binding as a final settlement of a dispute. The general principle is that the decision of the arbitral tribunal should not be disturbed except in the event of a manifest error of law or fact.

Appeal of an arbitral award to the ICJ by a dissatisfied State has been permitted by the Court most recently in *Guinea-Bissau* v *Senegal* (1991), a decision which clarifies a number of points concerning the grounds on which such appeals may be made. There appear to be three separate grounds on which an appeal against the decision of a tribunal panel may be made:

1. *Exces de pouvoir* – if an arbitral body exceeds its competence, its decision is null and void. Arbitrators have only such powers as the parties have conferred on them in the document by which they refer the matter to the panel – the

compromis. If a tribunal fails to respect these limits, it exceeds its own competence and the decision can be declared void.

2. Failure to reach a decision by a true majority – if the vote passing the decision of the tribunal does not amount to a true majority the decision cannot be given legal effect.
3. Insufficiency of reasoning – the decision of the arbitral body must be supported by adequate legal arguments. However, a statement of reasoning, although relatively brief and succinct, if clear and precise, does not amount to an insufficiency of reasoning.

In the event that an arbitral decision is overturned on one of these grounds, the award of the tribunal is null and without binding force on the parties concerned. In some cases the question of nullity will itself be referred to further arbitration.

The role of arbitration

Arbitration has today been largely superseded by the judicial settlement of disputes. However, it does retain several distinct advantages:

1. it is well suited to the disposal of minor cases where an informal approach may be preferred by the parties in dispute;
2. only States may be parties to cases before the ICJ; therefore, if the dispute involves an international organisation, arbitration may be the only judicial proceedings a party may invoke to obtain a binding award;
3. arbitration is a convenient method of settling large numbers of outstanding claims between two States; for instance, a number of claims between the USA and Italy arising from the Second World War were settled in accordance with the arbitral provisions laid down in the 1947 Italian Peace Treaty;
4. it has been argued that arbitration may be a convenient method of deciding those inter-State disputes of a political rather than a legal nature; however, in view of the binding nature of arbitral awards, and the availability of alternative settlement procedure under the United Nations, this proposition seems rather dubious.

17.3 Judicial settlement: the ICJ

Introduction

The World Court is the name commonly applied to the PCIJ and the ICJ. The PCIJ was established in 1920 under the auspices of the League of Nations. In 1946, it was replaced by the International Court of Justice which is, in accordance with Article 92 of the Charter of the United Nations, 'the principal judicial organ of the United Nations'.

In most respects the Statute of the ICJ is identical to the Statute of its predecessor and there is continuity in the jurisprudence of the Court. The World Court has always had its seat at the Hague.

Organisation of the Court

The judges and their appointment

The present Court has 15 judges, five of whom are elected every three years to hold office for nine years, and no two of whom may be nationals of the same State.

Article 2 of the Statute of the ICJ:

> 'The Court shall be composed of a body of independent judges elected regardless of their nationality from among persons of high moral character, who possess the qualifications required in their respective countries for appointment to the highest judicial offices, or are jurisconsults of recognised competence in international law.'

The judges are elected by the General Assembly and by the Security Council from a list of persons nominated by the national groups in the Permanent Court of Arbitration. Members of the United Nations not represented in the Permanent Court of Arbitration may create national groups for this purpose.

In making their nominations each national group may nominate no more than four persons, not more than two of whom shall be of their own nationality.

Article 6 of the Statute of the Court provides that:

> 'Before making these nominations, each national group is recommended to consult its highest court of justice, its legal faculties and schools of law, and its national academies and national sections of international academies devoted to the study of law.'

The system of election involves independent, simultaneous, voting by the Security Council and the General Assembly. Those States which are parties to the Statute of the ICJ but not members of the United Nations are permitted to participate in the nomination and election procedures.

Article 10 of the Statute of the Court provides that to be elected, candidates must obtain an absolute majority in both the General Assembly and in the Security Council.

Article 9 of the Statute of the Court requires that:

> 'At every election, the electors shall bear in mind not only that the persons to be elected should individually possess the qualifications required, but also that in the body as a whole the representation of the main forms of civilisation and of the principal legal systems of the world should be assured.'

Independence

If the ICJ is to serve any effective purpose then it is vital that States have confidence in it. Therefore, the Statute of the Court reinforces the principle of impartiality and freedom from governmental influence.

Article 20 of the Statute of the Court provides:

> 'Every member of the Court shall, before taking up his duties, make a solemn declaration in open court that he will exercise his powers impartially and conscientiously.'

Article 16 of the Statute of the Court lays down that:

> 'No member of the Court may exercise any political or administrative function or engage in any other occupation of a professional nature.'

Article 17 of the Statute of the Court further provides:

'1) No member of the Court may act as agent, counsel, or advocate in any case.
2) No member may participate in the decision of any case in which he has previously taken part as agent, counsel, or advocate for one of the parties, or as a member of a national or international court, or of a commission of enquiry, or in any other capacity.'

South West Africa Cases, Second Phase (1966). Judge Zaffrula Khan was excluded from participating in the decision in this case apparently because he had played a major role as a member of the Pakistan delegation to the United Nations when matters pertaining to South West Africa had been under discussion.

Namibia Case (Advisory Opinion) (1971). South Africa opposed the participation of several members of the Court including Judge Zaffrula Khan of Pakistan, Judge Nervo of Mexico and Judge Morozov of the Soviet Union. These judges, when members of their national delegations to the United Nations had participated in activities directed against South Africa's presence in South West Africa.

These objections were overruled by the Court. The fact that a judge may have participated in his former capacity as representative of his government while the subject matter of the dispute was under discussion did not bring Article 17(2) of the Statute into application. Being a government spokesman in the area of dispute did not necessarily preclude an individual from later exercising judicial impartiality.

Further, Judge Zaffrula Khan, excluded from the 1966 case, was no longer prevented from sitting as the present advisory proceedings were entirely separate from the earlier contentious case.

However, some members of the Court were critical of this decision especially in relation to Judge Morozov who as a previous United Nations representative of the Soviet Union had played 'a spectacular role in the preparation of Security Council and General Assembly resolutions, the validity of which have had to be assessed by the Court in the present Advisory Opinion'.

Dismissal of members of the Court

Article 18(1) of the Statute of the Court lays down that:

'No member of the Court can be dismissed unless, in the unanimous opinion of the other members, he has ceased to fulfil the required conditions.'

Diplomatic status of members of the Court

Article 19 of the Statute of the Court provides that:

'The members of the Court, when engaged on the business of the Court, shall enjoy diplomatic privileges and immunities.'

The salaries of the members of the Court are fixed by the General Assembly of the United Nations and may not be decreased during their term of office and are free of all taxation.

Ad hoc judges

Article 31 of the Statute of the Court provides as follows:

'1) Judges of the nationality of each of the parties shall retain their right to sit in the case before the Court.

2) If the Court includes upon the Bench a judge of the nationality of one of the parties, any other party may choose a person to sit as judge ...

3) If the Court includes upon the Bench no judge of the nationality of the parties, each of these parties may proceed to choose a judge as provided in paragraph 2 of this Article'.

Thus, the fact that a judge is a national of one of the parties before the Court does not debar him from continuing to sit. Also in cases where a party has no national representative in the Court, it may appoint a national judge *ad hoc* for the purpose of the case.

Justification for the appointment of judges *ad hoc*

The appointment of *ad hoc* judges has been criticised as being incompatible with the notion of impartiality and independence of the judiciary.

The practice has been justified as being an incentive to States, who may submit more readily to the jurisdiction of the Court and have more confidence in it if there is a judge of their own choice sitting on the Bench. It has also been said that such judges 'fulfil a useful function in supplying local knowledge and a national point of view'.

Criticisms of the system of judges *ad hoc*

Fitzmaurice attacked the system on two main grounds:

1. those who argue that the presence of such judges increases confidence in the Court argue from an impermissible premise that judges, particularly *ad hoc* judges, will necessarily espouse the view of their government;
2. once a case has been decided, a judge *ad hoc* may feel himself free from any obligation of confidence and reveal to his government what was said in the deliberations of the Court.

In practice judges *ad hoc* usually give judgment in favour of the State which appointed them. Thus where two parties appoint judges *ad hoc* their votes will usually cancel each other out.

Access to the Court

Before any State may become a party to a case before the ICJ it must have access to the Court. In this respect there is a distinction between those States which are parties to the Statute of the ICJ and those States which are not.

Members of the United Nations

Article 93(1) of the Charter of the United Nations provides that:

'All Members of the United Nations are *ipso facto* parties to the Statute of the International Court of Justice.'

By becoming a Member of the United Nations, therefore, a State is bound by the provisions of the Statute of the Court.

Non-members of the United Nations

Non-members of the United Nations may become parties to the Statute under Article 93(2) of the Charter of the United Nations.

A number of States such as Nauru, Liechtenstein, San Marino and Switzerland, are currently parties to the Statute of the Court under Article 93(2) of the Charter of the United Nations which provides:

A State which is not a Member of the United Nations may become a party to the Statute of the ICJ on conditions to be determined in each case by the General Assembly upon the recommendation of the Security Council.

In 1946 the Swiss Government requested the Secretary General of the United Nations to state the conditions that would be laid down. The Security Council and the General Assembly replied as follows:

> 'a) Acceptance of the provisions of the Statute of the International Court of Justice;
> b) Acceptance of all the obligations of a Member of the United Nations under Article 94 of the Charter;
> c) An undertaking to contribute to the expenses of the Court such equitable amount as the General Assembly shall assess from time to time after consultation with the Swiss Government.'

States becoming parties in this way are entitled to nominate candidates for election to the Court and take part in the actual elections in the General Assembly.

Access for States not parties to the Statute

Under Article 35(2) of the Statute of the Court:

> 'The conditions under which the Court shall be open to other States shall, subject to the special provisions contained in treaties in force, be laid down by the Security Council, but in no case shall such conditions place the parties in a position of inequality before the Court.'

In respect of access to the Court by States not parties to the Statute, the Security Council, acting under Article 35(2) of the Statute, resolved in 1946 that:

> '1) The International Court of Justice shall be open to a State which is not a party to the Statute of the International Court of Justice upon the following conditions, namely, that such State shall previously have deposited with the Registrar of the Court a declaration by which it accepts the jurisdiction of the Court, in accordance with the Charter of the United Nations and with the terms and subject to the conditions of the Statute and Rules of the Court, and undertakes to comply in good faith with the decision or decisions of the Court and to accept all the obligations of a Member of the United Nations under Article 94 of the Charter.'

In the past, such declarations by non-parties were filed by Albania as respondent in the *Corfu Channel Case* (1954), Italy, as a claimant in the *Monetary Gold Case* (1954) and by a similar agreement, the Federal Republic of Germany as a party to the *North Sea Continental Shelf Cases*.

Article 94 of the Charter of the United Nations provides that:

'1) Each Member of the United Nations undertakes to comply with the decision of the International Court of Justice in any case to which it is a party.

2) If any party to a case fails to perform the obligation incumbent upon it under a judgment tendered by the Court, the other party may have recourse to the Security Council, which may, if it deems necessary, make recommendations or decide upon measures to be taken to give effect to the judgment.'

Jurisdiction of the Court in contentious litigation

The parties must consent

Jurisdiction in contentious proceedings is dependent upon the consent of the State parties.

In the *Eastern Carelia Case* (1923), the Permanent Court of International Justice stated in its Advisory Opinion:

'It is well established in international law that no State can, without its consent, be compelled to submit its disputes with other States either to mediation or to arbitration, or to any other kind of pacific settlement'.

Article 36(1) of the Statute of the Court provides that:

'The jurisdiction of the Court comprises all cases which the parties refer to it and all matters specially provided for in the Charter of the United Nations or in treaties and conventions in force.'

In the phrase, 'all cases which the parties refer to it', the word 'parties' implies that all the parties to the dispute must agree that the case should be referred to the Court.

However, a defendant State may accept the jurisdiction of the Court after proceedings have been instituted against it either:

1. by an express statement of acceptance; or
2. by implication where the State defends the case without challenging the jurisdiction of the Court.

The words, 'matters specially provided for in the Charter of the United Nations' (see Article 36(1) above), were included in the draft of the Statute in the belief that the Charter of the United Nations would provide for compulsory jurisdiction of the Court. But the proposals to provide for the compulsory jurisdiction of the Court in the Charter were rejected at the San Francisco Conference, but not deleted from the Statute. There are therefore no 'matters specially provided for in the Charter of the United Nations'.

The words, 'or in treaties and conventions in force', mean the treaty or convention must be in force on the date of the institution of proceedings.

Unilateral suspension of the treaty or convention

In the Appeal Relating to the Jurisdiction of the ICAO Council (1972) the ICJ was of opinion that a unilateral suspension of a treaty would not *per se* render jurisdictional clauses inoperative.

The Court's contentious jurisdiction may be conferred

1. by express agreement between the parties;
2. under the principle of *forum prorogatum*, ie by tacit agreement between the parties;
3. by compulsory jurisdiction.

Overlapping jurisdiction

Generally, where an applicant State alleges a number of alternative heads of jurisdiction the Court may proceed upon the one providing the wider basis for the exercise of its jurisdiction.

Jurisdiction by express agreement

There are several methods whereby States may grant jurisdiction by express agreement.

Special agreement

This is the classic method by which parties refer a case to the Court. It is an agreement whereby two or more States agree to refer a particular and defined matter to the Court for a decision. The jurisdiction of the Court is defined within the agreement itself and that jurisdiction is conferred and the Court is seized of the case by the mere notification to the Court of the agreement.

Article 40 of the Statute of the ICJ provides:

'1) Cases are brought before the Court, as the case may be, either by the notification of the special agreement or by a written application addressed to the Registrar'.

By a disputes clause contained in a treaty

Article 36(1) of the Statute of the ICJ provides:

'The jurisdiction of the Court comprises all ... matters specially provided for ... in treaties and conventions in force.'

Many multilateral and bilateral treaties contain clauses conferring jurisdiction over disputes arising from them to the ICJ or its predecessor the Permanent Court of International Justice.

Treaties for the general settlement of disputes

For example: Article 17 of the General Act of 1928 provides:

'All disputes with regard to which the parties are in conflict as to their respective rights shall, subject to any reservations which may be made under Article 39, be submitted for decision to the Permanent Court of International Justice, unless the parties agree, in the manner hereinafter provided, to have resort to an arbitral tribunal.'

In the *Nuclear Test Cases: Australia* v *France*; *New Zealand* v *France* (1974) the Government of Australia in its Application claimed *inter alia* to found the jurisdiction of the Court on Article 17 of the General Act of 1928 to which both Australia and France had acceded. Although the majority of the Court held that it lacked competence to hear the case the joint dissenting judgment was of opinion that Article 17 provided an adequate basis upon which to found the Court's jurisdiction.

Treaties primarily dealing with other matters, but including a provision for the settlement of disputes arising under the treaty

In the *Fisheries Jurisdiction Case: United Kingdom* v *Iceland* (1974), on 11 March 1961, Iceland and the UK concluded an agreement by exchange of notes regarding Icelandic fishing limits. The penultimate paragraph of the Exchange of Notes read:

'The Icelandic Government will continue to work for the implementation of the Althing Resolution of 5 May 1959, regarding the extension of fisheries jurisdiction around Iceland, but shall give to the United Kingdom Government six months' notice of such extension and, in case of a dispute in relation to such extension, the matter shall, at the request of either party, be referred to the International Court of Justice.'

In 1971 Iceland gave notice of its intention to claim a 50-mile exclusive fisheries zone. In 1972 the UK filed an application with the Court which held that it had jurisdiction to hear the case founded upon the above clause in the Exchange of Notes.

Treaties enabling a particular dispute to be referred to the Court

Jurisdiction may arise where an agreement, while not specifically providing for the case to be submitted to the Court, nevertheless enables a party to it to make an application to the Court.

Transferred jurisdiction in respect of treaties conferring jurisdiction on the PCIJ

Many treaties and conventions contain clauses conferring jurisdiction on the PCIJ. When the Statute was redrafted in 1945, in order to save such clauses, Article 37 of the new Statute of the ICJ provides:

'Whenever a treaty or convention in force provides for reference of a matter to a tribunal to have been instituted by the League of Nations, or to the Permanent Court of International Justice, the matter shall, as between the parties to the present Statute, be referred to the International Court of Justice.'

Therefore, in order for a treaty which conferred jurisdiction on the Permanent Court to bestow jurisdiction on the ICJ:

1. the treaty or convention must still be in force between the States;
2. all the parties to the treaty must also be parties to the new Statute.

The treaty must still be in force

In the *South West Africa Cases* (1950) the Court had to decide whether Article 37 could apply in respect of the Mandate between South Africa and the League of Nations by which South Africa administered South West Africa. It was argued that the Court had jurisdiction to hear the dispute under Article 7(2) of the Mandate which provided:

> 'The Mandatory agrees that, if any dispute whatever should arise between the Mandatory and another Member of the League of Nations relating to the interpretation or the application of the provisions of the Mandate, such dispute, if it cannot be settled by negotiation, shall be submitted to the Permanent Court of International Justice provided for by Article 14 of the Covenant of the League of Nations.'

The Court held that:

> 'Having regard to Article 37 of the Statute of the International Court of Justice, and Article 80(1) of the Charter, the Court is of opinion that this clause in the Mandate is still in force and that therefore, the Union of South Africa is under an obligation to accept the compulsory jurisdiction of the Court according to those provisions.'

A party to the new Statute

In *Barcelona Traction, Light and Power Company Case*: *Belgium* v *Spain* (1970) Belgium made application to the Court on the basis of Article 17 of the Spanish-Belgian Treaty of Conciliation, Judicial Settlement and Arbitration 1927, which provided that either party had an ultimate right to commence proceedings before the PCIJ.

Spain objected to the Court's jurisdiction *inter alia* on the ground that Spain only became a party to the Statute when admitted to the United Nations in 1955 and was not a party to the Statute before the dissolution of the Permanent Court in 1946. There had therefore been nine years in which this part of Article 17 of the 1927 treaty had ceased to operate.

The Court held that Article 37 of the Statute was not to be interpreted in this way and that the date on which Spain became a party to the Statute was irrelevant.

As the ICJ stated in its 1964 Report:

> 'States joining the United Nations or otherwise becoming parties to the Statute at whatever date, knew in advance (or must be taken to have known) that, by reason of Article 37, one of the results of doing so would, as between themselves and other parties to the Statute, be the reactivation in relation to the present Court, of any jurisdictional clauses referring to the Permanent Court, in treaties still in force, by which they were bound.'

Forum prorogatum

The Court may exercise jurisdiction in those cases where the respondent State *subsequently consents to submit to the jurisdiction.*

Lauterpacht stated that:

> '... exercise of jurisdiction by virtue of the principle of forum prorogatum takes place whenever, after the initiation of proceedings by joint or unilateral application, jurisdiction

is exercised with regard either to the entire dispute or to some aspects of it as the result of an agreement, express or implied'.

This *post hoc* acceptance by the parties of the Courts jurisdiction cures any defects which may have affected the Courts jurisdiction to hear the case originally.

The form of consent

Such consent may be granted by formal agreement, informal agreement, or agreement inferred from conduct. Consent may take the form of the respondent State refraining to contest the Court's jurisdiction once the proceedings have been instituted.

In the *Rights of Minorities in Polish Upper Silesia Case* (1928) the Permanent Court stated:

> 'And there seems to be no doubt that the consent of a State to the submission of a dispute to the Court may not only result from an express declaration, but may also be inferred from acts conclusively establishing it. It seems hard to deny that the submission of arguments on the merits, without making reservation in regard to the question of jurisdiction, must be regarded as an unequivocal indication of the desire of a State to obtain a decision on the merits of a suit'.

However, there must be something more than the negative fact that the State raises no objection to the Court's jurisdiction. The Court will not accept jurisdiction unless there has been real consent by the respondent State.

Consent may take the form of an agreement on the basis of successive acts of the parties.

In the *Corfu Channel Case (Preliminary Objections)*: *United Kingdom* v *Albania* (1948) the UK brought a claim against Albania before the Court by unilateral application. Albania in its reply declared that it:

> '... would be within its rights in holding that the Government of the United Kingdom was not entitled to bring the case before the International Court by unilateral application without first conducting a special agreement with the Albanian Government ... However ... it is prepared notwithstanding this irregularity in the action taken by the Government of the United Kingdom, to appear before the Court.'

The Court held that this reply:

> '... constitutes a voluntary and indisputable acceptance of the Court's jurisdiction ...
>
> While the consent of the parties confers jurisdiction on the Court, neither the Statute nor the Rules require that this consent should be expressed in any particular form. [There was] nothing to prevent the acceptance of jurisdiction, as in the present case, from being effected by two separate and successive acts, instead of jointly and beforehand by a special agreement.'

Compulsory jurisdiction of the Court

Acceptance of the compulsory jurisdiction of the Court is by means of a prior declaration in accordance with Article 36(2) of the Statute of the Court.

'The States parties to the present Statute may at any time declare that they recognise as compulsory *ipso facto* and without special agreement, in relation to any other State accepting the same obligation, the jurisdiction of the Court in all legal disputes concerning:
a) the interpretation of a treaty;
b) any question of international law;
c) the existence of any fact which, if established, would constitute a breach of an international obligation;
d) the nature or extent of the reparation to be made for the breach of an international obligation.'

This optional clause is a compromise between the advocates and the opponents of compulsory jurisdiction. Under the Article jurisdiction is only compulsory once the declaration is made and then only within the limits of that declaration. However, there is no obligation upon a State to make such a declaration and therefore jurisdiction cannot be regarded as compulsory in the true sense.

Currently, around 50 States have made declarations accepting the compulsory jurisdiction of the Court under Article 36(2).

Effects of the declaration

1. A State's declaration made under the Article creates bilateral relations with those other States which have also made declarations of acceptance.
2. A State may make a reservation to its acceptance permitting its withdrawal at any time. Unless such a reservation is made acceptance of the optional clause is irrevocable.
3. Declarations may be made indefinitely, for a fixed term of years, or may be terminable upon notice.
4. If a State withdraws its acceptance, in accordance with such a reservation, it prevents the Court trying future cases against it.
5. Once the Court is seized of a case on the basis of a declaration of acceptance of jurisdiction, the subsequent lapse or withdrawal of the acceptance cannot deprive the Court of jurisdiction.

   In the *Nottebohm Case (Preliminary Objections)* (1953) the declaration of the respondent Government, Guatemala, expired a few days after the applicant Government, Liechtenstein, had seized the Court. It was argued on behalf of Guatemala that upon the expiry of the Guatemalan declaration the Court no longer had jurisdiction to hear the dispute. The Court, in affirming its right to jurisdiction stated:

   'An extrinsic fact such as the subsequent lapse of the Declaration by reason of the expiry of the period or by denunciation, cannot deprive the Court of the jurisdiction already established.'

6. The contractual relations between the States concerned and the compulsory jurisdiction of the Court resulting therefrom comes into being on the day the new declarant State deposits with the Secretary General of the United Nations its Declaration of Acceptance.

Reciprocity

The principle of reciprocity

A State accepting the jurisdiction of the Court under the optional clause does so, according to Article 36(2) of the Statute of the Court only: 'in relation to any other State accepting the same obligation'.

According to this principle, a State accepts the Court's jurisdiction *vis-à-vis* any other State only in so far as that State has also accepted the Court's jurisdiction.

For example, if State A has accepted the optional clause and State B has not, State A cannot be sued before the Court by State B.

If State A makes a declaration subject to reservation Y and State B makes a declaration subject to reservation Z, the Court has jurisdiction to hear disputes between States A and B only in so far as they are not covered by reservations Y and Z.

Thus, a State cannot enjoy the benefits of the optional clause unless it is also prepared to accept the obligations of the optional clause.

The principle of reciprocity applies when a case is submitted to the Court and not before.

In the *Right of Passage Over Indian Territory Case (Preliminary Objections): Portugal* v *India* (1957) the Portuguese Declaration accepting the compulsory jurisdiction of the Court contained, *inter alia*, the following reservation:

> '3) The Portuguese Government reserves the right to exclude from the scope of the present declaration, at any time during its validity, any given category or categories of disputes, by notifying the Secretary General of the United Nations and with effect from the moment of such notification.'

The Court rejected India's contention that reciprocity applied thus allowing her to take advantage of the reservation in Portugal's Declaration. The reservation gave Portugal the right to reserve its position in respect of those categories of disputes notified by it to the Secretary General of the United Nations. But only when Portugal had notified the Secretary General pursuant to the condition, would the reservation become automatically operative against it, in relation to other Signatories of the Optional Clause.

The 'reciprocity' provision in Article 36(3) of the Statute

Article 36(3) of the Statute of the ICJ provides that:

> 'The declaration referred to above (Article 36(2)) may be made unconditionally or on condition of reciprocity on the part of several or certain States, or for a certain time.'

This condition of reciprocity is quite distinct from the principle of reciprocity contained in Article 36(2). Article 36(3) uses the word 'reciprocity' in a quite different sense.

The principle in Article 36(2) is part of the Statute itself and applies automatically. The condition in Article 36(3) is optional and is not a part of the Statute.

Article 36(3) was introduced to cover those cases where a State might only wish to be bound by the Court's jurisdiction if a worthwhile number of other States were also bound or if a State whose acceptance was particularly important to it was bound.

The effect of paragraph 3 therefore is that a State may add a reservation to its acceptance of the optional clause, to the effect that its acceptance is not to come into force until specified States have also accepted the optional clause. Until these named States have accepted the optional clause, the State making such a reservation cannot be sued by any State.

No reservations under Article 36(3) have in fact been made.

Reservations

Article 36(3) of the Statute of the Court provides that reservations may be made relating to reciprocity and relating to time.

In the early years of the PCIJ it was argued that only reservations in accordance with Article 36(3) were admissible. However, it is now accepted that, in practice, many other reservations may be made and the validity of such reservations is no longer questioned. Indeed at the San Francisco Conference during consideration of the Statute of the ICJ, the sub-committee, referring to the previous practice of the Permanent Court considered that, as Article 36(3) had been consistently interpreted as allowing reservations, there was no need to amend it to make express provision for them.

For example, the UK Declaration Accepting the Compulsory Jurisdiction of the Court (1969) confers jurisdiction on the Court in respect of:

'... all disputes arising after the 24th of October 1945, with regard to situations or facts subsequent to the same date, other than:
  i) any dispute which the United Kingdom
    a) has agreed with the other Party or Parties thereto to settle by some other method of peaceful settlement; or
    b) has already submitted to arbitration by agreement with any States which had not at the time of submission accepted the compulsory jurisdiction of the International Court of Justice;
  ii) disputes with the Government of any other country which is a member of the Commonwealth with regard to situations or facts existing before the 1st of January, 1969;
  iii) disputes in respect of which any other Party to the dispute has accepted the compulsory jurisdiction of the International Court of Justice only in relation to or for the purposes of the dispute; or where the acceptance of the Court's compulsory jurisdiction on behalf of any other Party to the dispute was deposited or ratified less than 12 months prior to the filing of the application bringing the dispute before the Court.
... The Government of the United Kingdom also reserve the right at any time, by means of a notification addressed to the Secretary General of the United Nations, and with effect as from the moment of such notifications, either to add to, amend or withdraw any of the foregoing reservations, or any that may hereafter be added'.

(Reservations (i) to (iii) in the Declaration of the UK are not reservations expressly permitted by Article 36(3) of the Statute of the Court.)

The 1963 UK Declaration also contained the following reservations which were omitted from its replacement in 1969:

'Disputes with regard to questions which by international law fall exclusively within the jurisdiction of the United Kingdom.

Disputes arising out of events occurring between the 3rd September 1939 and the 2nd of September 1945.

Disputes arising out of, or having reference to, any hostilities, war, state of war, or belligerent or military occupation in which the Government of the United Kingdom are or have been involved.'

Nevertheless, in spite of the general acceptance of reservations which are not expressly permitted by Article 36(3), certain reservations are subject to judicial criticism and controversy.

Automatic reservations

These are reservations the scope of which are left to be determined by the reserving State. For example, in 1946 the USA deposited what was known as the Connally reservation; this provided that the declaration accepting the jurisdiction of the Court would not apply to:

'... disputes with regard to matters which are essentially within the domestic jurisdiction of the United States of America as determined by the United States of America'.

Similarly, the UK Declaration of 1957 (now replaced) excluded, *inter alia*, disputes:

'... relating to any question which, in the opinion of the Government of the United Kingdom, affects the national security of the United Kingdom or of any of its dependent territories'.

The validity and application of such reservations come up for consideration in the *Norwegian Loans Case: France* v *Norway* (1957). France brought a claim against Norway under the 'optional clause' on behalf of French holders of Norwegian bonds. The French Declaration accepting the compulsory jurisdiction of the Court contained the following reservation:

'This Declaration does not apply to differences relating to matters which are essentially within the national jurisdiction as understood by the Government of the French Republic.'

Norway, in objecting to the Court's jurisdiction, presented, *inter alia*, the following argument:

'The Norwegian Government did not insert any such reservation in its own Declaration. But it has a right to rely upon the restrictions placed by France upon her own undertakings.

Convinced that the dispute which has been brought before the Court by the Application of 6 July 1955, is within the domestic jurisdiction, the Norwegian Government considers itself fully entitled to rely on this right. Accordingly, it requests the Court to decline, on the grounds that it lacks jurisdiction, the function which the French Government would have it assume.'

The Court, in its judgment, stated:

'France has limited her acceptance of the compulsory jurisdiction of the Court by excluding beforehand disputes "relating to matters which are essentially within the national jurisdiction as understood by the Government of the French Republic". In accordance with the condition of reciprocity to which acceptance of the compulsory jurisdiction is made subject in both Declarations and which is provided for in Article 36 paragraph 3 of the Statute, Norway, equally with France, is entitled to except from the compulsory jurisdiction of the Court disputes understood by Norway to be essentially within its national jurisdiction ...

The Court considers that the Norwegian Government is entitled, by virtue of the conditions of reciprocity, to invoke the reservation contained in the French Declaration of March 1st, 1949; that this reservation excludes from the jurisdiction of the Court the dispute which has been referred to it by the Application of the French Government; that consequently the Court is without jurisdiction to entertain the application'.

This successful application of the condition of reciprocity led several States which had previously inserted such reservations in their declarations of acceptance, to abandon them.

Judge Lauterpacht in the *Norwegian Loans Case*, however, took a different view about the validity of the automatic reservation.

'If that type of (automatic) reservation is valid, the Court is not in the position to exercise the power conferred upon it – in fact, the duty imposed upon it – under paragraph 6 of Article 36 of its Statute ... The French reservation lays down that if, with regard to that particular question, there is a dispute between the Parties as to whether the Court has jurisdiction, the matter shall be settled by a decision of the French Government. The French reservation is thus not only contrary to one of the most fundamental principles of international – and national – jurisprudence according to which it is within the inherent power of a tribunal to interpret the text establishing its jurisdiction. It is also contrary to a clear specific provision of the Statute of the Court as well as to the general Articles 1 and 92 of the Statute and of the Charter, respectively, which require the Court to function in accordance with its Statute.'

Lauterpacht further questioned the legality of the automatic reservation because it left:

'... to the party making the Declaration the right to determine the extent and the very existence of its obligation. The effect of the French reservation relating to domestic jurisdiction is that the French Government has, in this respect, undertaken an obligation to the extent to which it, and it alone, considers that it has done so. This means that it has undertaken no obligation. An instrument in which a party is entitled to determine the existence of its obligation is not a valid and enforceable legal instrument of which a court of law can take cognizance. It is not a legal instrument. It is a declaration of a political principle and purpose'.

Lauterpacht was the only member of the Court to take this view of the automatic reservation in the *Norwegian Loans Case*. He, together with other members of the Court, however, returned to consider the matter in the *Interhandel Case: US v Switzerland* (1959). In this case, Lauterpacht in his dissenting opinion argued that automatic reservations were invalid for the reasons he advanced in the *Norwegian*

Loans Case, namely that they purported to oust the jurisdiction of the ICJ to determine its own jurisdiction under Article 36(6) of the Statute and that such reservations lacked the essential conditions for the validity of a legal instrument. Lauterpacht further contended that any Declaration under Article 36(2) which included an automatic reservation would itself be void, ie it would be insufficient to establish the jurisdiction of the Court. The reasoning behind this conclusion was that the invalid reservations was to be regarded as an essential part of the optional clause declaration. As such, it could not be severable from the Declaration as a whole. The only result was, therefore, that the Declaration itself was to be regarded as void.

In his dissenting opinion in the *Nicaragua Case*, Judge Schwebel agreed that the effect of the automatic reservation would be to invalidate the entire declaration. At present, only five States of the 50 or so which have made Declarations, have included automatic reservations in their Declarations – Liberia, Malawi, Mexico, Philippines and Sudan.

Multilateral treaty reservations

The multilateral treaty reservation provides that the State in question accepts the compulsory jurisdiction of the Court except in so far that the parties to a multilateral treaty the subject of the dispute were not also before the Court. This arose as an issue before the Court in the *Nicaragua Case*. The USA had included in their Declaration under Article 36(2) a reservation known as the Vandenberg Reservation, otherwise known as a multilateral treaty reservation. The questions before the Court in this case involved, *inter alia*, questions of interpretation of the UN Charter, particularly Articles 2(4) and 51. The USA argued that as Costa Rica and El Salvador – parties to the UN Charter (and the Charter of the OAS) and involved in the dispute in question – were not also before the Court, the Court lacked jurisdiction to hear the dispute under the terms of the US Declaration. The Court accepted that the Vandenberg Reservation *did* have the effect of precluding the Court from exercising its jurisdiction in the context of the interpretation of these multilateral treaties. The Court went on to hold, however, that it did have jurisdiction to decide the issue on the basis of customary international law.

Time-limitations and reservations ratione temporis

Reservation of past disputes

These reservation clauses are worded in a variety of ways. They may comprise a single clause as for example that contained in the US Declaration, which applies to disputes 'hereafter arising', ie after 14 August 1946, the date on which the Declaration was made, or they may be double clauses.

The UK Declaration Accepting The Compulsory Jurisdiction of the Court states that the UK accepts the jurisdiction of the ICJ under Article 36(2):

'... until such time as notice may be given to terminate the acceptance, over all disputes arising after the 24th of October, 1945, with regard to situations of facts subsequent to the same date, other than: disputes with the Government of any other Country which is a member of the Commonwealth with regard to situations or facts existing before the 1st of January 1969'.

Objections to the Court's jurisdiction *ratione temporis*

If the Declaration of a State contains a time reservation then it may in appropriate circumstances object to the Court's jurisdiction *ratione temporis*, ie it may allege that the dispute or the facts upon which it is based occurred outside the period common to both declarations.

In its jurisprudence the Court has taken the view that for the limitation to be effective the situation or the facts which are the source of the real cause of the dispute must occur outside the period of acceptance.

In the *Phosphates in Morocco Case* (1938) T, an Italian national, was assigned in 1918–19 various phosphate prospecting licences in French Morocco. In 1920 France, allegedly in contravention of French treaty obligations, established a monopoly over phosphate mining, and T's rights were denied recognition by the French Moroccan Mines Department. In 1931 France made a Declaration accepting jurisdiction of the PCIJ over: 'any disputes which may arise after the ratification of the present declaration with regard to situations or facts subsequent to such ratification'.

The Court found that the facts and situations giving rise to the dispute were earlier than the 1931 exclusion date. Although the alleged illegality continued after the French Declaration of 1931 the operative event was the creation of the monopoly in 1920. The dispute and the facts and situation out of which it had arisen preceded the period covered by the French Declaration of Acceptance and thus fell outside the Court's jurisdiction.

Limitation periods for international actions

The Statute of the Court contains no express provision relating to a period within which a case must be brought to its attention. However, this is not to say that such a period of limitation does not exist, for clearly the Court would be reluctant to adjudicate disputes that have their origins other than in the recent past.

The issue of a limitation period arose in the *Certain Phosphate Lands in Nauru Case (Preliminary Objections)* (1992) where, in a dispute between Australia and Nauru concerning compensation for the rehabilitation of certain mines, the question arose whether or not the action was time barred. Australia challenged the admissibility of the application on the ground, *inter alia*, that Nauru had achieved independence in 1968 and had had ample opportunity to initiate proceedings on this matter but had chosen not to do so until 1988.

The Court acknowledged that a delay in initiating proceedings might render an application inadmissible if the delay prejudiced the rights of the other party. But the overriding principle was that it was for the Court to decide 'in the light of the circumstances of each case whether the passage of time renders an application inadmissible'.

A number of factors have to be taken into consideration in assessing whether the circumstances of the case render the application inadmissible, including the relationship between the parties and the steps that had been taken prior to litigation to resolve the matter.

On the other hand, the Court has a responsibility to ensure that any future delay in proceedings does not prejudice the rights of the defending state with regard to both the establishment of the facts and the determination of the content of the applicable law.

It should be noted that, if an action is time-barred, the underlying rights of the parties do not cease to exist. Rather, it is the right of the party raising the action to bring proceedings that is affected. In other words, the rights of the parties under international law do not expire, only their right to vindicate these rights before the Court.

Transfer of jurisdiction from the PCIJ

Article 37 of the Statute of the court provides that:

'Whenever a treaty or convention in force provides for reference of a matter to a tribunal to have been instituted by the League of Nations, or to the Permanent Court of International Justice, the matter shall, as between the parties to the present Statute be referred to the International Court of Justice.'

Article 36(5) of the Statute of the ICJ, drafted in 1945, provides:

'Declarations made under Article 36 of the Statute of the Permanent Court of International Justice and which are still in force shall be deemed, as between the parties to the present Statute, to be acceptances of the compulsory jurisdiction of the International Court of Justice for the period which they still have to run and in accordance with their terms.'

In the *Aerial Incident Case (Preliminary Objections)* (1959) Israel sought damages from Bulgaria for the shooting down of an Israeli airliner. Bulgaria contested the Court's jurisdiction.

Bulgaria had made a declaration accepting the jurisdiction of the old PCIJ in 1921. This declaration ceased to be in force on the dissolution of that Court in April 1946. In 1955 Bulgaria was admitted to Membership of the United Nations and thereby became a party to the Statute of the new ICJ.

The Government of Israel argued that the effect of the declaration of 1921 was revived in accordance with Article 36(5) when Bulgaria once again became a party to the Statute when it joined the United Nations in 1955.

The Court upheld the Bulgarian objection:

1. Article 36(5) applies only to States which were signatories of the new Statute;
2. Article 36(5) applied to declarations still in force and did not have the effect of suspending declarations until a State had become a party to the new Statute;
3. if Bulgaria's admission to Membership of the United Nations reactivated its previous declaration of acceptance, it would run counter to the principle that the

Court's jurisdiction is founded on the consent of States and that Bulgaria's admission would be subject to legal consequences different from those of other States on admission.

However, Judges Lauterpacht, Spender and Wellington Koo delivered a strong Joint Dissenting Opinion. They argued that: declarations in regard to Article 36(5) and treaties and conventions in regard to Article 37, did not lose their validity when the Permanent Court was dissolved in 1946:

> '... having regard both to the ordinary meaning of their language and their context, the words "which are still in force" refer to the declarations themselves, namely to a period of time, limited or unlimited, which has not expired, regardless of any prospective or actual date of the dissolution of the Permanent Court. So long as the period of time of declarations made under Article 36 of the Statute of the Permanent Court still has to run at the time when the declarant State concerned becomes a party to the Statute of the International Court of Justice, those declarations fall within the purview of Article 36(5).'

The relationship between Article 36(5) and Article 37: if, in the opinion of the dissenting judges in the *Aerial Incident Case*, Article 36(5) and Article 37 are to be treated alike, then the decision of the majority in that Case could be used to reduce the effect of Article 37.

The question of Article 37 was considered by the Court in the *Barcelona Traction Case*: *Belgium* v *Spain* (1970), where the approach of the dissenting judges in the *Aerial Incident Case* was adopted.

In the *Barcelona Traction Case* Spain raised the objection, *inter alia*, that it was not a party to the Statute before the dissolution of the Permanent Court in 1946.

The Court held that Article 37 was not to be interpreted in this way and that the date on which Spain became a party to the Statute was irrelevant. The decision in the *Aerial Incident Case* was distinguished as being 'confined entirely' to the matter of the applicability of Article 36(5).

There would seem, however, to be no logical reason to distinguish between Article 36(5) and Article 37 and it has been argued that the better view would be to adopt the decision in the *Barcelona Traction Case* in respect of both Articles 36(5) and 37.

> 'By becoming a member of the United Nations and a party to the Statute, a State is clearly accepting obligations under Article 36 and Article 37 of the Statute if it had once granted jurisdiction to the Permanent Court in an instrument which still had a period of time to run. If it was not prepared to accept the transfer of obligations, it should take appropriate steps to terminate its earlier declaration or treaty obligation accepting the compulsory jurisdiction of the Court.'

Incidental jurisdiction

Other important aspects of the Court's jurisdiction include the following:

Interim measures of protection

Article 41(1) of the Statute of the ICJ provides that:

'The Court shall have the power to indicate, if it considers that circumstances so require, any provisional measures which ought to be taken to preserve the respective rights of either party.'

Circumstances in which interim measures may be granted pending the decision as to the Court's jurisdiction to hear the merits of the case

The difficulty facing the Court when deciding the question of interim measures is that of reconciling the fact that the Court may ultimately decide that it lacks jurisdiction to hear the case with the fact that the party's rights may be irreparably damaged before the decision as to jurisdiction is taken.

The degree of likelihood necessary that the Court will have jurisdiction over the merits of the case

In the *Anglo-Iranian Oil Company Case (Interim Measures)* (1951) the UK brought a claim against Iran in respect of the nationalisation by Iran of the Anglo-Iranian Oil Company. Before the Court ruled on Iran's objection to the Court's jurisdiction to hear the case, the UK asked the Court to grant interim measures of protection.

The Court by ten votes to two granted the interim measures saying that:

'Whereas the complaint made in the Application is one of an alleged violation of international law by the breach of the agreement for a concession of 29 April 1933, and by a denial of justice which, according to the Government of the United Kingdom, would follow from the refusal of the Iranian Government to accept arbitration in accordance with that agreement, and whereas it cannot be accepted a priori that a claim based on such a complaint falls completely outside the scope of international jurisdiction.

Whereas the considerations stated in the preceding paragraph suffice to empower the Court to entertain the Request for interim measures of protection the indication of such measures in no way prejudices the question of the jurisdiction of the Court to deal with the merits of the case and leaves unaffected the right of the Respondent to submit arguments against such jurisdiction ... the object of interim measures of protection provided for in the Statute is to preserve the respective rights of the Parties pending the decision of the Courts.'

However, Judges Wincarski and Badawi Pasha in their Dissenting Opinion stated that:

'The power given to the Court by Article 41 is not unconditional; it is given for the purposes of the proceedings and is limited to those proceedings. If there is no jurisdiction as to the merits, there can be no jurisdiction to indicate interim measures of protection. Measures of this kind in international law are exceptional in character to an even greater extent than they are in municipal law; they may easily be considered a scarcely tolerable interference in the affairs of a Sovereign State. For this reason, too, the Court ought not to indicate interim measures of protection unless its competence, in the event of this being challenged, appears to the Court to be nevertheless reasonably probable. Its opinion on this point should be reached after a summary consideration; it can only be provisional and cannot prejudge its final decision, after the detailed consideration to which the Court will proceed in the course of adjudicating on the question in conformity with all the Rules laid down for its procedure.'

In the *Fisheries Jurisdiction Cases (Interim Protection)*: *United Kingdom* v *Iceland*: *Federal Republic of Germany* v *Iceland* (1972), there was a shift away from the majority opinion expressed in the *Anglo-Iranian Case* as to the degree of likelihood necessary that the Court would have jurisdiction over the claim on its merits.

The Court in its judgment said:

'Whereas in a request for provisional measures the Court need not, before indicating them, finally satisfy itself that it has jurisdiction on the merits of the case, yet it ought not to act under Article 41 of the Statute if the absence of jurisdiction on the merits is manifest.'

The Court referring to a provision in the Exchange of Notes between the Governments of Iceland and the UK then went on to say that:

'... the above cited provision in an instrument emanating from both Parties to the dispute appears, *prima facie*, to afford a possible basis on which the jurisdiction of the Court might be founded'.

The shift in opinion was even more pronounced in the *Nuclear Test Cases (Interim Protection)*: *Australia* v *France*; *New Zealand* v *France* (1973) where the Court stated that:

'Whereas the material submitted to the Court leads it to the conclusion, at the present stage of the proceedings, that the provisions invoked by the Applicant appears, *prima facie* to afford a basis on which the jurisdiction of the Court might be founded, and whereas the Court will accordingly proceed to examine the Applicant's request for the indication of interim measures of protection'.

The accepted test now appears to be that put forward by Lauterpacht in the *Interhandel Case* (1959), namely, that the Court may only award interim measures if it is prima facie satisfied that it will have jurisdiction to hear the merits of the dispute. This test has most recently been accepted by the Court in March 1990 in the *Guinea-Bissau* v *Senegal* case. This case also establishes that a request for interim measures will only be considered if it relates to the subject matter of the dispute before the Court.

In another recent case, the requirements for obtaining interim protection were again discussed at length by the Court. In the Case Concerning Questions of Interpretation and Application of the 1971 Montreal Convention Arising from the Aerial Incident of Lockerbie (1992), the Court appears to confirm its earlier jurisprudence.

The Court confirmed that two pre-conditions were required for the grant of interim protection, namely, the existence of a prima facie case for the exercise of jurisdiction by the Court over the merits of the dispute and the existence of a risk of imminent and irreparable damage to the rights of the party seeking protection.

Libya alleged that the interpretation of Security Council Resolution 748 (1992) imposing certain sanctions in response to Libya's refusal to hand over two terrorists suspecting of destroying Pan Am Flight 103 over Lockerbie amounted to a prima facie case over which the Court exercised exclusive jurisdiction.

The Court declined to find the existence of such a dispute and continued to declare that the rights of the parties to contest the relevant issues at the merit stage of the proceedings must be unaffected by the Court's decision granting or refusing interim protection.

Neither did the Court find the existence of a risk of imminent and irreparable damage to the rights of Libya. In fact, the Court found quite the reverse. The refusal of Libya to comply with the terms of the Security Council Resolution was more likely to impair the rights enjoyed by the UK than the rights of Libya.

In the circumstances, the application for interim protection was rejected and the grant of interim measures refused. The decision of the Court was, however, adopted by a majority with five votes against and strong dissenting opinions were submitted by the minority.

Preliminary objections

Usually, before it can examine the merits of a particular case the Court has to consider preliminary objections to the Court's jurisdiction. Such objections are usually dealt with in a separate preliminary judgment but in some cases the objection is 'joined to the merits' and dealt with together with the merits in a single judgment. This will occur, for example, in cases where it is not possible to decide the jurisdictional issue without hearing the parties' evidence in full.

Objections to the admissibility of the claim

The respondent State may submit that a case is not admissible on the following grounds: that although the claim is of an international character, it is not admissible before the Court.

For example:

1. where there has been a failure to exhaust local remedies;
2. where there has been a failure to comply with the procedures required by the treaty or other instrument which confers jurisdiction upon the Court.

   Or the respondent State may submit that a case is not admissible on the grounds that the claimant State is not entitled to bring the claim.
3. Where the claimant State lacks the necessary *locus standi*:

   failure to comply with the nationality of claims rule;

   failure to establish any legal right or interest on the part of the Applicant.

In the *South West Africa Cases, Second Phase: Ethiopia* v *South Africa; Liberia* v *South Africa* (1966) Ethiopia and Liberia, two former Members of the League of Nations, in 1960 instituted proceedings against South Africa before the ICJ claiming that South Africa had failed to carry out the obligations imposed upon it by the Mandate under which it had agreed with the League of Nations to administer the territory.

In its 1966 Judgment the Court ruled that South Africa's obligations under the Mandate, in so far as they concerned the treatment of the inhabitants of South West Africa, had been owed to the League of Nations and not to individual members of the League. The Court held that Ethiopia and Liberia had therefore failed to establish any legal right or interest appertaining to them in the subject matter of the claims. Ethiopia and Liberia were not entitled to enforce rights which did not belong to them and the Court rejected their claims.

Where the claim is not within the court's competence:

1. Where the dispute is of a political rather than a legal nature.

    Although the Court has never denied its jurisdiction in this respect, it has been recognised by certain judges of the Court that political matters should be non-justicable.

    In the *Nuclear Test Cases* (1974) the political nature of the dispute was referred to by several of the judges.

2. Where the objective of the applicant has been accomplished or where adjudication on the merits would be devoid of purpose.

    In the *Northern Cameroons Case* (1963) the Republic of the Cameroons asked the Court to declare that the United Kingdom had failed to carry out its duties as laid down in the Trusteeship Agreement under which it had formerly administered the Northern Cameroons.

    The Northern Cameroons had, under a United Nations supervised plebiscite, voted for incorporation into Nigeria and this was effected by a General Assembly resolution which brought the Trusteeship Agreement to an end. The applicant State sought neither to have the plebiscite declared invalid nor the resolution void.

    The Court refused to hear the case as the decision requested by the Applicant would be pointless.

    > 'The function of the Court is to state the law, but it may pronounce judgment only in connection with concrete cases where there exists at the time of the adjudication an actual controversy involving a conflict of legal interests between the parties. The Court's judgment must have some practical consequence in the sense that it can affect existing legal rights or obligations of the parties, thus removing uncertainty from their legal relations. No judgment on the merits in this case could satisfy these essentials of the judicial function.'

    Nuclear Test Cases (1974): following France's declaration of intention not to hold any further tests in the atmosphere in the South Pacific after 1974 the Court found that the claim of Australia no longer had any object and that the Court was not therefore called upon to give a decision thereon.

The position where the parties enter into an interim agreement

In the *Fisheries Jurisdiction Case* (1974) the UK and Iceland entered into 'an interim agreement ... relating to fishing in the disputed area, pending a settlement of the substantive dispute and without prejudice to the legal position or rights of either Government in relation thereto'. The agreement was valid for two years.

The Court observed that this agreement did not constitute a settlement and that as the dispute still continued the Court retained its primary duty to discharge its judicial function. It was qualified therefore to deal with the matter notwithstanding the fact that its decision may only regulate the parties relations when the interim agreement expired, ie in the future.

Intervention

The Statute provides for two forms of third-State intervention in cases already before the Court:

1. *Article 63*: in cases where the main issue in dispute is the construction of a multi-lateral treaty of which the intervening State is a party. In such cases intervention is *as of right* (although it remains for the Court to determine admissibility – El Salvador's declaration to intervene in *Nicaragua*). Intervention of this nature has only taken place on two occasions: Poland's intervention in the *Wimbledon Case* (1923) and Cuba's intervention in the *Haya de la Torre Case* (1951).

2. *Article 62*: this provides that a State may request to intervene in a case in which it has an interest of a legal nature which may be affected by the decision. In such cases there is *no* right to intervene; this is to be decided by the Court. As well as the requirements of (1) a legal interest and (2) one that may be affected by the decision in issue, there is some debate as to whether the State seeking to intervene needs to show an independent basis of jurisdiction between itself and the parties to the dispute. This question arose, but was not decided, in both the *Tunisia/Libya* (Malta seeking to intervene) and *Libya/Malta* (Italy seeking to intervene) cases. It would appear that some jurisdictional link will be required if the notion of the consent of States to proceedings before the Court is not to be undermined.

   Both the Maltese and Italian requests to intervene in the above cases were denied by the Court on the grounds that they could not show a sufficient legal interest likely to be affected by the decision in question. There has been no case to date in which a request to intervene under Article 62 has been granted.

Interpretation of a judgment

Article 60 of the Statute of the Court provides:

> 'The judgment is final and without appeal. In the event of a dispute as to the meaning or scope of the judgment the Court shall construe it upon the request of any party.'

The Court cannot go beyond the scope of its original judgment.

Revision of a judgment

Article 61 of the Statute of the Court provides:

> '1) An application for revision of a judgment may be made only when it is based upon the discovery of some fact of such a nature as to be a decisive factor, which fact was, when the judgment was given, unknown to the Court and also to the party claiming revision, always provided that such ignorance was not due to negligence ...
> 4) The application for revision must be made at latest within six months of the discovery of the new fact.

5) No application for revision may be made after the lapse of ten years from the date of the judgment.'

Chambers of the Court

Article 26 provides that the Court may form a Chamber composed of three or more judges either to hear a particular category of disputes or to hear a particular case. Four such Chambers have been formed since 1984 to hear specific cases:

1. *Gulf of Maine*
2. *Burkina Faso* v *Mali*
3. *ELSI*
4. *El Salvador* v *Honduras*.

Following the *Gulf of Maine Case*, the practice has arisen whereby the parties may, by agreement between them, influence the composition of the Chamber by indicating a preference from amongst the judges on the Court. *Note*: under Article 27, a judgment of a Chamber is to be considered as a judgment of the Court.

The advisory jurisdiction of the Court

The right to request an advisory opinion
In addition to its jurisdiction to decide cases brought by States under Article 36 of its Statute, Article 65(1) of the Statute of the ICJ provides that:

'The Court may give a advisory opinion on any legal question at the request of whatever body may be authorised by or in accordance with the Charter of the United Nations to make such a request.'

The Charter of the United Nations in Article 96 provides:

'1) The General Assembly or the Security Council may request the International Court of Justice to give an advisory opinion on any legal question.
2) Other organs of the United Nations and specialised agencies, which may at any time be so authorised by the General Assembly, may also request advisory opinions of the Courts on legal questions arising within the scope of their activities.'

The following United Nations organs have been authorised to request opinions: ECOSOC, The Trusteeship Council, 13 of the 14 United Nations Specialised Agencies (the exception being the Universal Postal Union), the International Atomic Energy Authority, The Interim Committee of the General Assembly, and the Committee on Applications for Review of Administrative Tribunal Judgments.

Jurisdiction in advisory cases
The object of the advisory role of the Court is to assist the political organs of the United Nations in settling disputes and to provide guidance on points of law arising from the operations of the organs and specialised agencies of the Organisation.

Article 65(1) of the Statute of the Court places two limitations upon the Court's advisory jurisdiction:

'1. An advisory opinion may only be given on a legal question;
2. The Court may decline to give an opinion – it has a discretion.

In exercising this discretion the Court, in accordance with Article 68 of the Statute shall:

'In the exercise of its advisory functions ... be guided by the provisions of the present Statute which apply in contentious cases to the extent to which it recognises them to be applicable.'

The exercise of the Court's discretion to hear requests for advisory opinions

The Court may refuse to hear in its advisory capacity a dispute over which it would have no jurisdiction as a contentious case.

In the *Eastern Carelia Case* (1923) the Court, in the exercise of its discretion, refused jurisdiction.

The request for an Advisory Opinion arose out of a dispute between Finland and Russia over Russian government of Eastern Carelia. The Council of the League of Nations referred the matter to the Permanent Court and requested an opinion as to the effect of the relevant article of the Treaty of Peace between Finland and Russia, signed at Dorpat on 14 October 1920. Russia, which was not a member of the League, refused to participate in the proceedings in the case.

The Court decided not to give an Opinion.

'It is well established in international law that no State can without its consent be compelled to submit its disputes with other States either to mediation or to arbitration, or to any other kind of pacific settlement.'

The Court may exercise its jurisdiction where the Advisory Opinion requested does not relate to the merits of the dispute

Interpretation of Peace Treaties Case (1950): this dispute arose out of the refusal of Bulgaria, Hungary and Roumania to appoint members to the Commissions established under the 1947 Peace Treaties, thereby preventing the settlement of a dispute regarding the human rights guarantees in the treaties. The General Assembly asked the Court whether the Secretary General could appoint the member of the Commission where one party had failed to appoint its member.

It was argued before the Court that it cannot:

'... give the Advisory Opinion requested without violating the well established principle of international law according to which no judicial proceedings relating to a legal question pending between States can take place without their consent'.

However, in its Opinion the Court stated that:

'... the circumstances of the present case are profoundly different from those ... in the *Eastern Carelia Case* ... where that Court declined to give an Opinion because it found that the question put to it was directly related to the main point of a dispute actually pending between two States, so that answering the question would be substantially equivalent to deciding the dispute between the parties, and that at the same time it raised a question of fact which could not be elucidated without hearing both parties.

... the present Request for an Opinion is solely concerned with the applicability to certain disputes of the procedure for settlement instituted by the Peace Treaties, and it is justifiable to conclude that it in no way touches the merits of those disputes'.

The Court went on to suggest that, in so far as its advisory functions were concerned, the question of consent is now irrelevant.

'... even where the Request for an Opinion relates to a legal question actually pending between States. The Court's reply is only of an advisory character; as such, it has no binding force. It follows that no State, whether a Member of the United Nations or not, can prevent the giving of an Advisory Opinion which the United Nations considers to be desirable in order to obtain enlightenment as to the course of action it should take. The Court's Opinion is given not to States, but to the organ which is entitled to request it: the reply of the Court, itself an "Organ of the United Nations", represents its participation in the activities of the Organisation, and, in principle, should not be refused.'

The Court may in the exercise of its advisory jurisdiction determine questions of fact

In the *Namibia Case* (1971) the Court rejected South Africa's argument that the Court could only answer the question submitted to it by considering the factual issues relating to South Africa's conduct in the disputed territory, and that the Court had no more competence to decide such disputes as to the facts than it had jurisdiction over legal disputes between States.

'In the view of the Court, the contingency that there may be factual issues underlying the question posed does not alter its character as a "legal question" as envisaged in Article 96 of the Charter ...'

The Court may in the exercise of its advisory jurisdiction deal with questions involving a political element

Since the creation of the United Nations its members have sought to interpret the provisions of the charter in accordance with their own political philosophy. Inevitably, therefore, Opinions are sought of the Court which are essentially political in their nature.

In the *Conditions of Admission of a State to Membership in the United Nations Case* (1948) the argument that the question before the Court was a political one and thus fell outside the Court's jurisdiction was rejected.

In the Opinion of the Court:

'It has nevertheless been contended that the question put must be regarded as a political one and that, for this reason, it falls outside the jurisdiction of the Court. The Court cannot attribute a political character to a request which, framed in abstract terms, invites it to undertake an essentially judicial task, the interpretations of a treaty provision. It is not concerned with the motives which may have inspired this request, nor with the considerations which, in the concrete cases submitted for examination to the Security

Council, formed the subject of the exchange of views which took place in that body. It is the duty of the Court to envisage the question submitted to it only in the abstract form which has been given to it; nothing which is said in the present opinion refers, either directly or indirectly, to concrete cases or to particular circumstances.'

In the *Certain Expenses of the United Nations Case* (1962) the Court was asked to advise whether the costs of the United Nations operation in the Congo and the operation of the United Nations Emergency Force in the Middle East, constituted expenses of the Organisation that could be apportioned between Members of the United Nations.

The legal issues regarding the interpretation of the Charter were bound up with the differing political views of members as to the United Nations peacekeeping role. It was argued that the matter was of a political nature and therefore incapable of solution by legal measure.

The Court acknowledged that it had a discretion and could refuse to give an Opinion. Nevertheless such a refusal would only be used where there were 'compelling reasons', and in the Court's opinion political factors did not constitute a sufficiently compelling reason to refuse an Opinion.

'It is true that most interpretations of the Charter of the United Nations will have political significance, great or small. In the nature of things it could not be otherwise. The Court, however, cannot attribute a political character to a request which invites it to undertake an essentially judicial task, namely, the interpretation of a treaty provision.'

In the *Namibia Case* (1971) South Africa objected, *inter alia*, that political pressures on the Court and its members were so great as to make it 'impossible for the Court to exercise its judicial function properly'.

The Court rejected the allegation stating that it would not be:

'... proper for the Court to entertain these observations, bearing as they do on the very nature of the Court as the principal judicial organ of the United Nations, an organ which, in that capacity, acts only on the basis of the law, independently of all outside influence or interventions whatsoever, in the exercise of the judicial function entrusted to it alone by the Charter and its Statute.'

In practice, in such cases where political considerations of the Member States predominate, the Court's Opinion is usually disregarded by those Member States who are unwilling to accept a legal solution to their political problems.

17.4 The role and future of the ICJ and international adjudication

Reasons for decline

Since the advisory jurisdiction of the ICJ is limited to non-contentious issues, the contentious jurisdiction which depends on the acceptance of the optional clause is of great significance. However, only around one-third of the States parties to the Statute of the Court have accepted the optional clause.

Moreover, most of the States which have accepted the optional clause have inserted reservations in their acceptances restricting their liability under the clause. In addition States have shown a tendency not to appear before the Court if they disagree with it having jurisdiction. In the *Nuclear Test Cases*, France did not appear. In the *Icelandic Fisheries Case*, Iceland did not appear. In the *Aegean Sea* dispute, Turkey not only failed to appear, she ignored the interlocutory orders. Similarly, in the *Hostages Case* Iran failed to appear and in the *Nicaragua Case* the US withdrew from proceedings following the jurisdictional phase. The degree of compliance with the judgments of the Court has dropped dramatically over the years.

It is necessary to distinguish between two sorts of difficulty: an absolute difficulty associated with any form of international adjudication and the difficulties peculiar to the ICJ as an institution.

Difficulties of international adjudication

The absolute difficulty is represented as the distrust States feel for any form of international adjudication. Despite cynical views to the contrary, this reluctance is seldom caused by a desire to breach international law with impunity, although the absence of an adjudicatory system is a sore temptation. However, international law does not rely on a sanctions mechanism for obedience. International law worked before the existence of international courts. Indeed, the former Communist States remained opposed to international courts although they did not deny the binding force of international law.

This distrust of States of international adjudication arises from three separate fears:

States believe that judicial decisions are often unpredictable

It is not that international law is uncertain; but since most States have legal advisers and a settlement can in most cases be effected, the fact that the particular dispute is not capable of settlement indicates that the relevant law or facts are uncertain.

States also point to the number of dissenting judgments given as evidence of judicial unpredictability. If different judges come to different conclusions, it is surely evident that the outcome of litigation is pure chance! Also where the law is uncertain, a judge may be influenced by political considerations. However, the fears about the unpredictable nature of international law may be a mere excuse. As Rosenne points out, the notion that international law is vague is arguable in view of the predominance of multilateral conventions and treaty law; agreements which are chosen for their precision.

There must be a loser

In any international adjudication there must be a 'losing' party. Thus, to expose serious political issues to the unpredictability of adjudication is a risk not many

States wish to take. This explains why a State like the USA which has engaged in many 'specific' commitments feels unable to make a 'general commitment' to appear before the international courts, even though its refusal takes the disguised form of an automatic reservation.

The effects of a court's decision are not limited to the facts of the particular case

A decision of the Court may form a precedent for future cases. It is the practice of judges to look to the past for authority. Some States distrust the ICJ because they think its decisions have been too innovative. States generate law for themselves through treaties and custom and are therefore jealous of rival sources. If changes are required, States prefer to retain the competence to decide what those changes will involve.

The basic problem in any adjudicating process is that it cannot satisfy everyone. In municipal law judges are accused of class bias in comparatively stable and homogeneous liberal societies. What hope is there of an adjudicating process being accorded respect in a world divided by ideology, poverty and race? The Third World countries distrust international courts because they are wary of taking immediate cognisance of new customary rules.

A psychological factor of some importance is that States do not like taking other States to court: it may be construed as an unfriendly act. Moreover, if a State loses, an inevitable loss of prestige is incurred.

Special problems of the ICJ

Faced with the problem of being an institution modelled from and sustained by essentially Western ideals of justice and process in a world which, for most part, identified those ideals with the colonial powers, the Court blotted its copybook very badly in the *South West Africa Case*. In that case Ethiopia and Liberia sought a declaration from the Court to the effect that the Mandate for South West Africa was still in effect; and that South Africa remained under obligations placed upon it under the Mandate and was subject to the supervision of the United Nations. South Africa raised a preliminary objection on the basis of the *locus standi* of the applicants. The Court rejected this, and ordered the parties to plead to the merits.

After four years of dispute, the Court then said that the applicants did not have *locus standi*. The composition of the Court had changed. In the previous vote a narrow majority had prevailed in favour of a plea to the merits. In the latter vote, Sir Percy Spender (Australia) was given the casting vote. The volte-face was effected by the Court by recourse to the most specious legal reasoning. It has been suggested that the *South West Africa Case* marked the beginning of the disillusionment of the Third World countries with the Court, and so put it on the defensive.

Outlook for the future

The aforegoing comments notwithstanding, the ICJ at present appears to be going through something of a renaissance. It currently has eight cases pending, more than at any other time in the history. This revival can probably be traced to four main factors:

1. the general political rapprochment. For example, on 28 February 1989 the Soviet Union proposed that all states accept the compulsory jurisdiction of the ICJ with respect to human rights instruments. The Soviet Union then proceeded to recognise the Court's jurisdiction with respect to six human rights treaties including the 1984 Convention Against Torture;
2. a change in the composition of the Court to reflect a greater presence of judges from developing States. There are currently, for example, three judges from Africa represented on the Court, a greater number than at any other time in the history of the Court;
3. linked to this, there has been an increase in the use of the Court by developing States, for example, the *Burkina Faso* v *Mali* case and the case of *Guinea-Bissau* v *Senegal*; and
4. the development of the use of Chambers since 1984.

18

The United Nations

18.1 Purposes and principles

The purposes of the United Nations are stated in Article 1 of the Charter as follows:

'1) To maintain international peace and security, and to that end: to take effective collective measures for the prevention and removal of threats to the peace, and for the suppression of acts of aggression or other breaches of the peace, and to bring about by peaceful means, and in conformity with the principles of justice and international law, adjustment or settlement of international disputes or situations which might lead to a breach of the peace;
2) To develop friendly relations among nations based on respect for the principle of equal rights and self-determination of peoples, and to take other appropriate measures to strengthen universal peace;
3) To achieve international co-operation in solving international problems of an economic, social, cultural or humanitarian character, and in promoting and encouraging respect for human rights and for fundamental freedoms for all without distinction as to race, sex, language, or religion; and
4) To be a centre for harmonising the actions of nations in the attainment of these common ends.'

Article 2 of the Charter provides:

'The Organisation and its Members, in pursuit of the Purposes stated in Article 1, shall act in accordance with the following Principles:

1) The Organisation is based on the principle of the sovereign equality of all its Members.

2) All Members, in order to ensure to all of them the rights and benefits resulting from membership, shall fulfil in good faith the obligations assumed by them in accordance with the present Charter.

3) All Members shall settle their international disputes by peaceful means in such a manner that international peace and security, and justice, are not endangered.

4) All Members shall refrain in their international relations from the threat or use of force against the territorial integrity or political independence of any State, or in any other manner inconsistent with the Purposes of the United Nations.

5) All Members shall give the United Nations every assistance in any action it takes in accordance with the present Charter, and shall refrain from giving assistance to any State against which the United Nations is taking preventive or enforcement action.

6) The Organisation shall ensure that States which are not Members of the United Nations act in accordance with these Principles so far as may be necessary for the maintenance of international peace and security.

7) Nothing contained in the present Charter shall authorise the United Nations to intervene in matters which are essentially within the domestic jurisdiction of any State or shall require the Members to submit such matters to settlement under the present Charter; but this principle shall not prejudice the application of enforcement measures under Chapter VII.'

The Charter is, therefore, a multilateral treaty establishing the rights and duties of the signatory States. It is not subject to reservation or denunciation.

Each Member remains sovereign

Article 2(7) provides that the Organisation has no competence in matters within the domestic jurisdiction of a State.

For example, the discussion in the United Nations of questions regarding the then French colonies of Tunisia, Morocco and Algeria, brought strong protest from the French Government and on occasion the French delegates to the United Nations withdrew in protest.

A matter is *unlikely* to be regarded as within a State's domestic jurisdiction if it amounts to an infringement of the interests of other States, a breach of international law, or a gross violation of human rights. During the 1960s it became apparent that the Assembly would refuse to regard any colonial situations as a matter of domestic jurisdiction. Any matter which threatens international peace and security also ceases to be domestic.

It has been said that the application of Article 2(7) is a matter for political judgment rather than legal interpretations.

Non-members

The Charter as a treaty cannot bind non-members. Charter obligations therefore which go beyond the obligations of general international law, do not bind non-members. However, Article 2(6) states the principle that the Organisation shall ensure that non-members act in accordance with the Principles of the Charter.

For example, Resolution 232 (1966) of the Security Council, imposing economic sanctions against Rhodesia invoked Article 2(6) in urging non-members to act in accordance with it.

18.2 The organs of the United Nations

The United Nations has six principal organs:

1. The General Assembly.
2. The Security Council.
3. The Economic and Social Council.
4. The Trusteeship Council.
5. The Secretariat.
6. The ICJ.

18.3 The Security Council

The Dumbarton Oaks proposals envisaged the need for an executive organ of limited membership to be entrusted with primary responsibility for the maintenance of international peace and security.

Composition

Article 23 of the Charter, as amended, provides that:

'1) The Security Council shall consist of fifteen Members of the United Nations. The Republic of China, France, The Union of Soviet Socialist Republics, the United Kingdom of Great Britain and Northern Ireland, and the United States of America shall be permanent members of the Security Council. The General Assembly shall elect ten other Members of the United Nations to be non-permanent members of the Security Council, due regard being specially paid, in the first instance to the contribution of Members of the United Nations to the maintenance of international peace and security and to the other purposes of the Organisation, and also to equitable geographical distribution.

2) The non-permanent members of the Security Council shall be elected for a term of two years ... A retiring member shall not be eligible for immediate re-election.

3) Each member of the Security Council shall have one representative.'

The permanent members

The five permanent members enjoy an exceptional status. This is justified on the basis of the 'inescapable fact of power differentials'. It is upon these 'Great Powers' that the responsibility for maintaining international peace and security will fall. They must, therefore, have the final vote in determining how that responsibility should be exercised.

The non-permanent members

The ten non-permanent members of the Security Council are elected for two years by the General Assembly. To ensure continuity the elections are staggered. They are chosen on the basis of 'equitable geographical distribution'. Five from Afro-Asian States, two from Latin-American States, one from Eastern European States and two from Western European and other States.

Voting procedure

Voting procedure in the Security Council is regulated by Article 27 of the Charter:

'1) Each member of the Security Council shall have one vote.
2) Decisions of the Security Council on procedural matters shall be made by an affirmative vote of nine members.
3) Decisions of the Security Council on all other matters shall be made by an *affirmative vote of nine members including the concurring votes of the permanent members*; provided that, in decisions under Chapter VI, and under paragraph 3 of Article 52, a party to a dispute shall abstain from voting.'

The permanent members, therefore, have a privileged position with regard to voting and may use their power of veto in respect of non-procedural questions. The power of veto does not, however, apply to procedural questions.

The double veto

There is a distinction between 'procedural matters' and 'all other matters'. The Security Council is thus faced with the problem of determining into which category any particular decision falls. This is a preliminary question. Where a dispute arises, the permanent members have relied on the statement of the Four Sponsoring Powers at San Francisco:

'1) In the opinion of the Delegations of the Sponsoring Governments, the Draft Charter itself contains an indication of the application of the voting procedures to the various functions of the Council.
2) In this case, it will be unlikely that there will arise in the future any matters of great importance on which a decision will have to be made as to whether a procedural vote would apply. Should, however, such a matter arise, the decision regarding the preliminary question as to whether or not such a matter is procedural, must be taken by vote of seven members of the Security Council, including the concurring votes of the permanent members.'

The USSR in reliance upon the second paragraph insisted that the question as to whether or not a particular question was procedural and therefore not subject to the veto was itself a non-procedural question subject to the veto. A permanent member of the Security Council could therefore veto an attempt to classify a question as procedural and then veto any draft resolution dealing with that question. In this way, by using the double veto, procedural questions may be converted into non-procedural questions and vetoed.

However, the abuse of the double veto may be prevented by the President of the Security Council making a ruling under rule 30 of the Rules of Procedure on whether or not the draft resolution before the Council is procedural. Under the Rules of Procedure of the Court the President's ruling is final unless reversed by a majority of nine members of the Council.

Abstention

Article 27(3) of the Charter provides that a member of the Council must abstain in decisions under Chapter VI and Article 52(3), if that member is a party to the dispute.

Chapter VI deals with disputes, or any situation which might lead to international friction or give rise to a dispute. The distinction between a 'dispute' and a 'situation' is therefore imprecise. Article 27(3) refers only to members who are 'a party to the *dispute*'.

If a 'dispute' as opposed to a 'situation' does exist it may also be difficult to ascertain who the parties to the dispute are as many States may have some degree of interest in the dispute. In effect Article 27(3) is largely ignored by States who continue to vote in respect of disputes to which they are parties.

The abstention of a permanent member: if Article 27(3) were given a literal interpretation all the permanent members would have to vote for a draft resolution in order for it to be passed, and an abstention would constitute a veto. However, the practice has become established of not regarding the abstention of a permanent member as a veto and such an abstention will not affect the validity of a resolution which otherwise satisfies the requirements of Article 27.

This practice was upheld as lawful by the ICJ in the *Namibia Case* (1971).

> '... the proceedings of the Security Council extending over a long period supply abundant evidence that presidential rulings and the positions taken by members of the Council, in particular its permanent members, have consistently and uniformly interpreted the practice of voluntary abstention by a permanent member as not constituting a bar to the adoption of resolutions ... This procedure followed by the Security Council ... has been generally accepted by Members of the United Nations and evidences a general practice of that Organisation.'

Absence

The question as to the effect of the absence of a permanent member was raised in 1950 when the Security Council, in the absence of the Soviet Union who were boycotting the proceedings, passed a resolution creating a force to operate under US control to help South Korea repel the Communist invasion from the North. The Soviet Union questioned the validity of this resolution on the grounds that it had been passed in its absence.

The Soviet Union was itself in breach of Article 28(1) of the Charter which provides: 'The Security Council shall be so organised as to be able to function continuously. Each member of the Security Council shall for this purpose be represented at all times at the seat of the Organisation.'

If the Soviet protest were upheld it would have meant that one State, by breaching Article 28(1), could bring the work of the Security Council to a halt.

Although practice does not make the point clear, Judge Nervo stated in the *Namibia Case* (1971) that it is: 'generally recognised that the absence of a permanent member from a meeting of the Security Council does not prevent the taking of decisions which are valid even if they relate to questions of substance'.

Functions and powers

Article 24 of the Charter provides that:

'1) In order to ensure prompt and effective action by the United Nations, its Members confer on the Security Council primary responsibility for the maintenance of international peace and security, and agree that in carrying out its duties under this responsibility the Security Council acts on their behalf.
2) In discharging these duties the Security Council shall act in accordance with the Purposes and Principles of the United Nations. The specific powers granted to the Security Council for the discharge of these duties are laid down in Chapters VI, VII, VIII and XII.
3) The Security Council shall submit annual and, when necessary, special reports to the General Assembly for its consideration.'

The Security Council therefore acts as agent of all the Members and not independently of their wishes. It is bound by the purposes and principles of the Organisation. But if it acts *ultra vires* the Members of the Organisation are bound by its action.

Article 25 of the Charter provides:

'The Members of the United Nations agree to accept and carry out the decisions of the Security Council in accordance with the present Charter.'

Article 24(2) refers to specific powers granted in Chapters VI, VII, VIII and XII. This enumeration is not exhaustive. Other implied powers exist as may be required.

The Security Council's primary function of maintaining international peace and security is exercised by two means:

1. Pacific settlement of such international disputes as are likely to endanger international peace and security.
2. The taking of enforcement action.

Pacific settlement of disputes

Chapter VI of the Charter sets out the various means which the Security Council may use to assist in the settlement of a dispute. The Council is not concerned with all disputes – only those likely to endanger international peace and security.

Article 33 of the Charter makes clear that Chapter VI supplements the traditional measures of settlement which the parties must use first:

'1) The parties to any dispute, the continuance of which is likely to endanger the maintenance of international peace and security, shall, first of all, seek a solution by negotiation, enquiry, mediation, conciliation, arbitration, judicial settlement, resort to regional agencies or arrangements, or other peaceful means of their own choice.
2) The Security Council shall, when it deems necessary, call upon the parties to settle their dispute by such means.'

If the parties to a dispute fail to settle it by the traditional means indicated in Article 33(1) then they must refer it to the Security Council.

Article 37(1) provides:

'Should the parties to a dispute of the nature referred to in Article 33 fail to settle it by the means indicated in that Article, they shall refer it to the Security Council.'

The following have a right to submit disputes to the Security Council:

The General Assembly: Article 11(2) of the Charter provides:

'The General Assembly may discuss any questions relating to the maintenance of international peace and security brought before it by any Member of the United Nations, or by the Security Council, or by a State which is not a Member of the United Nations in accordance with Article 35, paragraph 2, and, except as provided in Article 12, may make recommendations with regard to any such questions to the State or States concerned or to the Security Council or both. Any such question on which action is necessary shall be referred to the Security Council by the General Assembly either before or after discussion.'

Article 11(3) provides:

'The General Assembly may call the attention of the Security Council to situations which are likely to endanger international peace and security.'

The Secretary General: Article 99 of the Charter provides:

'The Secretary General may bring to the attention of the Security Council any matter which in his opinion may threaten the maintenance of international peace and security.'

Member States: Article 35(1) of the Charter provides:

'Any Member of the United Nations may bring any dispute, or any situation of the nature referred to in Article 34, to the attention of the Security Council or of the General Assembly.'

Non-member States: Article 35(2) of the Charter provides:

'A State which is not a Member of the United Nations may bring to the attention of the Security Council or of the General Assembly any dispute to which it is a party if it accepts in advance, for the purposes of the dispute, the obligations of pacific settlement provided in the present Charter.'

Placing the matter on the agenda

It is for the Council to decide as a procedural matter whether or not to place a particular matter on its agenda. If a matter is placed upon the agenda then the procedure to be adopted in respect of any party to the dispute who is not a member of the Security Council is laid down in Article 31 and 32 of the Charter.

Article 31 provides that:

'Any Member of the United Nations which is not a member of the Security Council may participate, without vote, in the discussion of any question brought before the Security Council whenever the latter considers that the interests of that Member are specially affected.'

Once seized of a 'dispute' the Council is bound under Article 32 to invite the parties to participate in discussions:

'Any Member of the United Nations which is not a member of the Security Council or any State which is not a Member of the United Nations, if it is a party to a dispute under consideration by the Security Council, shall be invited to participate, without vote, in the discussion relating to the dispute. The Security Council shall lay down such conditions as it deems just for the participation of a State which is not a Member of the United Nations.'

The duty imposed upon the Security Council under Article 32 is dependent upon a prior determination that the matter under consideration is in the nature of a dispute.

In the *Namibia Case* (1971) South Africa argued that the Security Council had failed to comply with its duty under Article 32 to invite South Africa to participate in its deliberations.

The Court stated that the duty under Article 32 depended upon a prior determination that the matter under consideration was in the nature of a dispute and pointed out that:

'The question of Namibia was placed on the agenda of the Security Council as a "situation" and not as a "dispute".'

In dealing with a dispute the Security Council has a number of alternative procedures open to it:

Powers of investigation
Article 34 of the Charter provides:

'The Security Council may investigate any dispute, or any situation which might lead to international friction or give rise to a dispute, in order to determine whether the continuance of the dispute or situation is likely to endanger the maintenance of international peace and security.'

The Security Council may therefore set up an investigation under Article 34, using a subsidiary organ.

Further, Article 29 provides that:

'The Security Council may establish such subsidiary organs as it deems necessary for the performance of its functions.'

For example, in 1958 the Council established an observer group to investigate a complaint by the Lebanon that the United Arab Republic was infiltrating men and materials into the Lebanon in order to subvert the Lebanese Government.

However, the Charter imposes no legal obligation on a State to permit a commission of investigation to have access to its territory. But it has been argued that such an obligation exists by virtue of the general term of Article 25.

The Council may also appoint special representatives to act on behalf of the Council in various world trouble spots. For example, Count Bernadotte was appointed United Nations Mediator in Palestine in 1948.

Power to call upon the parties to utilise the traditional means of settlement in accordance with Article 33(2), leaving the choice of such means to the parties

Power to recommend a particular means of settlement
Article 36 of the Charter provides:

> '1) The Security Council may, at any stage of a dispute of the nature referred to in Article 33 or of a situation of like nature, recommend appropriate procedures or methods of adjustment.
> 2) The Security Council should take into consideration any procedures for the settlement of the dispute which have already been adopted by the parties.
> 3) In making recommendations under this Article the Security Council should also take into consideration that legal disputes should as a general rule be referred by the parties to the International Court of Justice in accordance with the provisions of the Statute of the Court.'

Power to recommend actual terms of settlement: Article 37(2) of the Charter provides:

> 'If the Security Council deems that the continuance of the dispute is in fact likely to endanger the maintenance of international peace and security, it shall decide whether or take action under Article 36 or to recommend such terms of settlement as it may consider appropriate.'

It has been argued that this is tantamount to the Council assuming a quasi-judicial function where the dispute affects the legal rights of the parties.

This procedure is available only where the dispute is considered by the Security Council to endanger international peace and security. Otherwise the Security Council can only act, under Article 38, with the consent of all the parties.

> 'Without prejudice to the provisions of Article 33 to 37, the Security Council may, if all the parties to any dispute so request, make recommendations to the parties with a view to a pacific settlement of the dispute.'

Power to set up machinery for settlement
The Council may set up machinery for the settlement of a dispute, within the United Nations. For example, in 1947 the Council established the Committee of Good Offices in Indonesia. It may also refer a dispute to an existing organ, for example the General Assembly.

Whatever course of action is adopted by the Security Council under Chapter VI, it must be adopted by a non-procedural decision, thus giving the permanent members the opportunity to exercise their power to veto.

The powers of the Security Council in such matters are to make 'recommendations'. These are not binding on the States to whom they are addressed. Article 25 of the Charter relates only to 'decisions'.

For example, the recommendation by the Security Council to the parties in the Corfu Channel dispute that they submit their dispute to the Court, was not regarded by the majority of the Court as creating a legal obligation to submit to the Court's jurisdiction.

Enforcement action

(see Chapter 16 The Use of Force by States, above.)

18.4 The General Assembly

Composition

The General Assembly is the plenary organ of the United Nations comprising all Member States, each with one vote but entitled to five representatives.

The original Members
Article 3 of the Charter of the United Nations provides that:

> 'The original Members of the United Nations shall be the States which, having participated in the United Nations Conference on International Organisation at San Francisco, or having previously signed the Declaration by United Nations of 1 January 1942, sign the present Charter and ratify it in accordance with Article 110.'

Subsequent membership
Admission to membership is dependent on the fulfilment of certain conditions specified in Article 4 of the Charter.

> '1) Membership in the United Nations is open to all other peace-loving States which accept the obligation contained in the present Charter and, in the judgment of the Organisation, are able and willing to carry out these obligations.
> 2) The admission of any such State to membership in the United Nations will be effected by a decision of the General Assembly upon the recommendation of the Security Council.'

Statehood alone is, therefore, not sufficient. A prospective Member must satisfy the Organisation that it is 'peace-loving', 'accepts' the Charter obligations and is both 'able and willing' to carry them out.

Refusal of membership
During the 'cold war' between the Soviet Union and the Western Powers many applications for membership of the United Nations were rejected for reasons of political strategy, each side seeking to keep out States politically sympathetic to the other. The following were among the reasons given for rejection:

Legal reasons: (1) The State was not truly independent (Ceylon, Jordan). (2) The State was not a peace-loving State (Albania, Bulgaria, Hungary, Roumania). (3) The State would be unable to carry out its obligations under the Charter (Mongolia).

Political reasons: (1) The State had remained neutral in the war with Germany (Ireland, Portugal). (2) The States (Finland, Italy) would have their admission vetoed unless Bulgaria, Hungary and Romania were also admitted at the same time.

The *Admissions Case* (1948). In order to prevent the Security Council misusing its powers in this way the General Assembly requested an advisory opinion of the ICJ as to the legal effects of Article 4 of the Charter.

The Court declared that the conditions stipulated in Article 4(1) that 'an applicant must (1) be a State; (2) be peace-loving; (3) accept the obligations of the Charter; (4) be able to carry out these obligations; and (5) be willing to do so' were exhaustive and therefore it was not permissible for a Member to attach other conditions to the casting of its affirmative vote.

Nevertheless, in 1955 16 States were admitted to membership at the United Nations in a political 'package deal' which openly flouted the Court's interpretation of Article 4(1).

Voting

Voting procedure in the General Assembly is regulated by Article 18 of the Charter:

'1) Each member of the General Assembly shall have one vote.

2) Decisions of the General Assembly on important questions shall be made by a two-thirds majority of the Members present and voting. These questions shall include: recommendations with respect to the maintenance of international peace and security, the election of the non-permanent members of the Security Council, the election of members of the Economic and Social Council, the election of members of the Trusteeship Council in accordance with paragraph 1(c) of Article 86, the admission of new Members to the United Nations, the suspension of the rights and privileges of membership, the expulsion of Members, questions relating to the operation of the trusteeship system and budgetary questions.

3) Decisions on other questions, including the determination of additional categories of questions to be decided by a two-thirds majority, shall be made by a majority of the Members present and voting.'

The vote can be by 'acclamation' (an expression of unanimity without resort to vote) or by show of hands, roll call or secret ballot.

Functions and powers

Article 10 of the Charter provides:

'The General Assembly may discuss any questions or any matters within the scope of the present Charter or relating to the powers and functions of any organs provided for in the present Charter, and, except as provided in Article 12, may make recommendations to the Members of the United Nations or to the Security Council or to both on any such questions or matters.'

This Article provides the basis for the overall authority of the Assembly over the various organs of the United Nations. Its authority over the Security Council and the ICJ is, however, limited.

The basis of the Assembly's political power lies in Article 11 of the Charter which provides:

'1) The General Assembly may consider the general principles of co-operation in the maintenance of international peace and security, including the principles governing disarmament and the regulation of armaments, and may make recommendations with regard to such principles to the Members or to the Security Council or to both.

2) The General Assembly may discuss any questions relating to the maintenance of international peace and security brought before it by any Member of the United Nations in accordance with Article 35, paragraph 2, and, except as provided in Article 12, may make recommendations with regard to any such questions to the State or States concerned or to the Security Council or to both. Any such question on which action is necessary shall be referred to the Security Council by the General Assembly either before or after discussion.

3) The General Assembly may call the attention of the Security Council to situations which are likely to endanger international peace and security.

4) The powers of the General Assembly set forth in this Article shall not limit the general scope of Article 10.'

Further Article 14 provides:

'Subject to the provisions of Article 12, the General Assembly may recommend measures for the peaceful adjustment of any situation, regardless of origin, which it deems likely to impair the general welfare or friendly relations among nations, including situations resulting from a violation of the provisions of the present Charter setting forth the Purposes and Principles of the United Nations.'

These powers of the General Assembly overlap with those of the Security Council. However, whilst a concurrent jurisdiction may exist in these spheres, a conflict is sought to be avoided. For example, the last sentence of Article 11(2) stresses the fact that if 'action' is necessary, it is the Council and not the Assembly which is competent.

Further Article 12 of the Charter provides:

'1) While the Security Council is exercising in respect of any dispute or situation the functions assigned to it in the present Charter, the General Assembly shall not make any recommendation with regard to that dispute or situation unless the Security Council so requests.

2) The Secretary-General, with the consent of the Security Council, shall notify the General Assembly at each session of any matters relative to the maintenance of international peace and security which are being dealt with by the Security Council and shall similarly notify the General Assembly, or the Members of the United Nations if the General Assembly is not in session, immediately the Security Council ceases to deal with such matters.'

In practice, when the Security Council wishes the General Assembly to deal with a matter it removes the question from its agenda, in order to leave the General Assembly free to deal with the question.

However, in some cases, where the Security Council has been unable or unwilling to act due to the veto being exercised, the General Assembly has placed a matter on its own agenda whilst it still remains on the agenda of the Security Council. There has therefore been a tendency for the General Assembly to assume a much more important role than that originally intended by those who drafted the Charter.

The additional and specific powers of the Assembly

Article 13 of the Charter permits the General Assembly to initiate studies and make recommendations for the purpose of:

'a) promoting international co-operation in the political field and encouraging the progressive development of international law and its codification;
b) promoting international co-operation in the economic, social, cultural, educational, and health fields and assisting in the realisation of human rights and fundamental freedoms for all without distinction as to race, sex, language, or religion.'

Article 15 of the Charter gives power to receive reports from other organs:

'1) The General Assembly shall receive and consider annual and special reports from the Security Council; these reports shall include an account of the measures that the Security Council has decided upon or taken to maintain international peace and security.
2) The General Assembly shall receive and consider reports from the other organs of the United Nations.'

Article 16 refers to its functions relating to the trusteeship system.

'The General Assembly shall perform such functions with respect to the international trusteeship system as are assigned to it under Chapters XII and XIII, including the approval of the trusteeship agreements for areas not designated as strategic.'

Article 17 confers on the Assembly the power to consider and approve the budget of the Organisation.

'1) The General Assembly shall consider and approve the budget of the Organisation.
2) The expenses of the Organisation shall be borne by the Members as apportioned by the General Assembly.
3) The General Assembly shall consider and approve any financial and budgetary arrangements with specialised agencies referred to in Article 57 and shall examine the administrative budgets of such specialised agencies with a view to making recommendations to the agencies concerned.'

Article 19 provides that:

'A Member of the United Nations which is in arrears in the payment of its financial contributions to the Organisation shall have no vote in the General Assembly if the amount of its arrears equals or exceeds the amount of the contributions due from it for the preceding two full years. The General Assembly may, nevertheless, permit such a Member to vote if it is satisfied that the failure to pay is due to conditions beyond the control of the Member.'

Article 22 of the Charter provides that 'The General Assembly may establish such subsidiary organs as it deems necessary for the performance of its functions.'

The effect of resolutions of the General Assembly

The General Assembly cannot directly legislate for the Member States and as a general rule its recommendations have no legally binding effect on the Members. However, there are some circumstances in which a recommendation may create direct legal obligations for Members.

For example, in relation to membership of the United Nations, it is the Assembly which makes the decision albeit on the recommendation of the Security Council. It is the Assembly's approval of the budget which creates an obligation on a State to pay its contribution.

The General Assembly also has a variety of powers, the exercise of which creates situations which are binding within the internal structure of the Organisation.

For example, under Article 61 the Assembly elects members to the Economic and Social Council. By Article 86(1)(c) it elects members to the Trusteeship Council. It also participates in the election of judges to the ICJ.

General Assembly resolutions as evidence of international law

Certain resolutions of the General Assembly have assumed a quasi-legislative role and while they cannot create direct legal obligations for Member States they can embody a consensus of opinion about what the law is so that, indirectly, they become evidence of international law.

For example, the repeated affirmation of the right of self-determination has probably given normative status to what was originally regarded as a political doctrine, at least in the colonial context.

However, if many States vote against the resolution or if it fails to gain the support of those States principally concerned, then its value as evidence of customary law is correspondingly reduced.

18.5 The Economic and Social Council

Composition

The Economic and Social Council comprises 54 members, 18 of which are elected by the General Assembly each year to service for three years. There are no permanent members but in practice the 'five powers' are always elected. An attempt is made to represent a variety of social, economic, cultural and geographical interests. Fourteen members are elected from African States, 11 members from Asian States, 10 members from Latin America States, 13 from Western European and other States and six members from Eastern European States.

Voting procedure

Each member has one vote and decisions are made by a simple majority of the members present and voting.

Functions and powers

The Council operates under the authority of the General Assembly. Its terms of reference are wide, but its powers are limited. It cannot take decisions which are binding on Member States and has only the power to recommend to States, the General Assembly and to the specialised agencies.

Functions and powers under Article 62

'1) The Economic and Social Council may make or initiate studies and reports with respect to international economic, social, cultural, educational, health and related matters and may make recommendations with respect to any such matters to the General Assembly, to the Members of the United Nations, and to the specialised agencies concerned.

2) It may make recommendations for the purpose of promoting respect for, and observance of human rights and fundamental freedoms for all.

3) It may prepare draft conventions for submission to the General Assembly, with respect to matters falling within its competence.

4) It may call, in accordance with the rules prescribed by the United Nations, international conferences on matters falling within its competence.'

Assistance to other organs, States and specialised agencies

The Council acts as an organ of assistance to the Security Council. Under Article 65 'The Economic and Social Council may furnish information to the Security Council and shall assist the Security Council upon its request.'

Under Article 66(1) and (3) the Council may also assist the General Assembly:

'The Economic and Social Council shall perform such functions as fall within its competence in connection with the carrying out of the recommendations of the General Assembly. It shall perform such other functions as are specified elsewhere in the present Charter or as may be assigned to it by the General Assembly.'

Article 66(2) also provides that 'It may, with the approval of the General Assembly, perform services at the request of Members of the United Nations and at the request of specialised agencies.'

Co-ordination of work with and between the specialised agencies

One of the main tasks envisaged for the council was the co-ordination of the work of the various specialised agencies to be established under the United Nations.

Article 57 defines specialised agencies as those 'established by intergovernmental agreement and having wide international responsibilities, as defined in their basic instruments, in economic, social, cultural, education, health, and related fields'.

Such an organisation becomes a specialised agency when it is:

'... brought into relationship with the United Nations by means of an agreement made by the agency with the Economic and Social Council and approved by the General Assembly in accordance with Article 63(1)'.

The Economic and Social Council is empowered by Article 63(2) of the Charter to:

'... co-ordinate the activities of the specialised agencies through consultation with and recommendations to such agencies and through recommendations to the General Assembly and to the Members of the United Nations'.

So far, the following international organisations have become specialised agencies of the United Nations: The Food and Agricultural Organisation (FAO), the Inter-Governmental Maritime Consultative Organisation (IMCO), the International Civil Aviation Organisation (ICAO), the International Labour Organisation (ILO), the International Bank for Reconstruction and Development (World Bank), the International Fund for Agricultural Development (IFAD), the International Monetary Fund (IMF), the International Telecommunications Union (ITU), the United Nations Educational Scientific and Cultural Organisation (UNESCO), the Universal Postal Union (UPU), the World Health Organisation (WHO), the World Intellectual Property Organisation (WIPO), and the World Meteorological Organisation (WMO).

The committee structure of ECOSOC

There are three plenary committees (economic, social, programme and co-operation) together with several standing committees. Article 68 of the Charter permits the Council to 'set up commissions in economic and social fields and for the promotion of human rights, and such other commissions as may be required for the performance of its functions'. These commissions may be grouped into three classes.

Functional commissions
These are established and defined by subject matter and include the Commission on Human Rights, the Commission for Social Development, the Population Commission, the Statistical Commission, the Commission on Narcotic Drugs, and the Commission on the Status of Women.

Regional commissions
Five such commissions now exist: The Economic Commission for Europe (ECE), the Economic and Social Commission for Asia and the Pacific (ESCAP), the Economic Commission for Latin America (ECLA), the Economic Commission for Africa (ECA), and the Economic Commission for Western Asia (ECWA).

Other bodies
These include the United Nations High Commissioner for Refugees, the Permanent Central Narcotics Board, the Drug Supervisory Body, United Nations Development Programme and UNICEF.

18.6 The Trusteeship Council

The Trusteeship Council operates under the control of the General Assembly. Article 85 of the Charter providing that:

'1) The functions of the United Nations with regard to trusteeship agreements for all areas not designated as strategic, including the approval of the terms of the trusteeship agreement and of their alteration or amendment, shall be exercised by the General Assembly.
2) The Trusteeship Council, operating under the authority of the General Assembly, shall assist the General Assembly in carrying out these functions.'

The objects of the trusteeship system are provided in Article 76 of the Charter which emphasises the duties of the administering authority to promote self-government or independence and to encourage respect for human rights and fundamental freedoms.

Composition and voting

The composition of the Trusteeship Council is based upon the principle that administering and non-administering Member States shall be equally represented.
Article 86 provides that:

'1) The Trusteeship Council shall consist of the following Members of the United Nations:
a) those Members administering trust territories;
b) such of those Members mentioned by name in Article 23 (the permanent Members of the Security Council) as are not administering trust territories; and
c) as many other Members elected for three year terms by the General Assembly as may be necessary to ensure that the total number of members of the Trusteeship Council is equally divided between those Members of the United Nations which administer trust territories and those which do not.'

Members of the Council are represented by governmental representatives who are 'specially qualified.' Each Member has one vote and decisions are taken by a majority of the Members present and voting.

Functions and powers

The Trusteeship Council was given the power to receive and consider petitions from the inhabitants of the territories. It also has power to send periodic visiting missions to trust territories. The Council considers the reports submitted by the administering authorities, on the basis of the Councils Questionnaire (Article 88) and then reports to the General Assembly or the Security Council, depending upon whether the territory is 'strategic' or 'non-strategic'. The Council may also make recommendations to the Security Council, the General Assembly, or to Member States.

Although mainly of historic interest the trusteeship system remains available for further use in the future.

18.7 The Secretariat

Article 7 of the Charter describes the Secretariat as one of the 'principal organs' of the Organisation. Article 97 provides that 'The Secretariat shall comprise a Secretary-General and such staff as the Organisation may require.' The Secretary-General is an integral part of the Secretariat and assumes final responsibility for its conduct.

The Secretary-General

Appointment of the Secretary-General

Article 97 of the Charter provides that the Secretary-General shall be appointed by the General Assembly upon the recommendation of the Security Council.

In practice the permanent members of the Security Council agree upon a candidate who is recommended to the General Assembly. Upon receiving the recommendation of the Security Council, the Assembly holds a private meeting and then holds a vote by secret ballot but in public session. The decision is by a simple majority vote.

No term of office is set down in the Charter but in 1946 a General Assembly resolution fixed a five-year term which can be renewed or extended.

The functions and powers of the Secretary-General

The functions of the Secretary-General may be divided into two categories:

Administrative functions

Article 97 refers to the Secretary-General as the 'Chief Administrative Officer' of the Organisation. He is responsible for the organisation of the meetings of the organs and committees and of the special United Nations Conferences. In this connection he will draft the agenda, provide staff and facilities and prepare a report for the organ concerned. He will also dispense legal and technical advice.

Other duties include the co-ordination of the work of the Secretariat, the specialised agencies and other inter-governmental organisations. The Secretary-General also assumes responsibility for the preparation of studies and reports extending over all aspects of the Organisation's work.

His financial responsibilities include the preparation of the annual budget of the Organisation, and he also has custody of all United Nations funds and responsibility for their expenditure.

Under Article 102 of the Charter every treaty entered into by Members is registered with the Secretariat and must be published by it. There are also more than 60 multilateral treaties which entrust the Secretary-General with such functions as the notification of signatures, accessions and reservations to the States concerned.

Article 98 of the Charter also requires the Secretary-General to make an annual report to the General Assembly on the work of the Organisation.

Executive functions
Article 99 of the Charter provides that:

> 'The Secretary-General may bring to the attention of the Security Council any matter which in his opinion may threaten the maintenance of international peace and security.'

It has been said that Article 99 conferred upon the Secretary-General 'world political responsibilities which no individual, no representative or a single nation, ever had before'.

However, the power under Article 99 has very rarely been invoked. In June 1950 the Secretary-General brought to the attention of the Security Council the aggression upon the Republic of Korea and in July 1960 the Secretary-General convened the Council to deal with the Congo crisis.

Implied power of investigation
The power of the Secretary-General to bring matters to the attention of the Security Council carries with it the power of investigation and inquiry to ascertain the necessary facts.

Article 98 of the Charter further provides that:

> 'The Secretary-General shall act in that capacity in all meetings of the General Assembly, of the Security Council, of the Economic and Social Council, and of the Trusteeship Council, and shall perform such other functions as are entrusted to him by those organs'.

The Secretary-General may therefore exercise considerable political influence in these organs. He may place items of their provisional agenda, submit proposals or draft resolutions, make statements and submit amendments to proposals.

Implied authority to act in the interests of international peace and security
The Secretary-General has claimed a general power to act on his own initiative whenever such action seemed necessary in the interests of international peace and security. In 1957 Secretary-General Hammarskjold claimed the right to act to fill 'any vacuum that may appear in the systems which the Charter and traditional diplomacy provide for the safeguarding of peace and security'.

In the Lebanon crises of 1958, the Security Council created an observer group (UNOGIL) to investigate the Lebanese complaint of intervention by the United Arab Republic in its internal affairs. Following increasing UAR infiltration a force of US marines were landed in Lebanon. The Security Council was unable to agree on how to deal with the crisis. Hammarskjold on his own initiative therefore increased the size of UNOGIL thereby bringing about a normalisation of the situation and the withdrawal of US troops.

In 1960 the Secretary-General entered into discussions with the Government of South Africa on the segregation issue. In 1966 and 1968 the Secretary-General put forward proposals on Vietnam. In all such cases the Secretary-General, guided by the purposes and principles of the Charter, was acting within the legal limits of his political discretion.

In the Congo crisis the Security Council gave the Secretary-General considerable power to take action. When faced with the absence of guidance of the Security Council as to the question of Katanga he declared to the Council, 'I have the right to expect guidance. But ... if the Security Council says nothing I have no other choice than to follow my conviction.'

The Secretary-General as mediator

The Secretary-General may act 'as a mediator and as an informal adviser of many governments'. Through 'quiet diplomacy' he may mediate between governments outside the full glare and publicity of an open debate in the Council or Assembly. An example of the Secretary-General's role as mediator can be seen in the function performed by Perez de-Cuellior in the context of the Iran-Iraq war.

The Secretariat

Its international character

Article 100 of the Charter provides:

> '1) In the performance of their duties the Secretary-General and the staff shall not seek to receive instructions from any government or from any other authority external to the organisation. They shall refrain from any action which might reflect on their position as international officials responsible only to the organisation.
> 2) Each Member of the United Nations undertakes to respect the exclusively international character of the responsibilities of the Secretary-General and the staff and not seek to influence them in the discharge of their responsibilities.'

This article is supplemented by Staff Regulations and Rules regulating such matters as outside employment, public statements, honours, gifts and awards and the right to engage in political activities.

Recruitment, appointment and conditions of service

Regulation 4, 2 of the Staff Regulations provides:

> 'The paramount consideration in the appointment, transfer or promotion of the staff shall be the necessity for securing the highest standards of efficiency, competence and integrity. Due regard shall be paid to the importance of recruiting the staff on as wide a geographical base as possible.'

Article 101 of the Charter provides that the staff shall be appointed by the Secretary-General under regulations established by the General Assembly.

There are at present some 20,000-odd staff in the Secretariat, recruited in accordance with rules about national quotas thus ensuring international representation. However, the quota rule may result in candidates who are poorly qualified having to be appointed.

Appointments may be permanent, temporary or regular. Any allegations of infringement of terms of service are heard by an Administrative Tribunal established by the General Assembly.

18.8 Termination of membership and suspension of the rights of membership

Express provision

When provision is made, the Member wishing to withdraw, or the organisation wishing to expel or suspend, shall act in accordance with the rules laid down.

Withdrawal

Some organisations have no withdrawal clause in their constitutions, eg World Health Organisation. However, withdrawal is expressly provided for in the treaties establishing most international organisations. In such cases there will probably be a period of compulsory membership before withdrawal is permitted.

Method of withdrawal

Usually notice is required in writing, or formal notice must be given to the Secretary-General of the Organisation. Notice may also be required to be given to the Secretary-General of the United Nations or to the depository government.

Period of notice

The notice may be effective on receipt. However, many constitutions provide for 12 months' or one year's notice. The ILO requires two years' notice. In some cases withdrawal may be dependent upon the Member having fulfilled all its financial obligations to the Organisation.

Suspension

Suspension is a sanction designed to secure compliance with the various obligations of membership of the Organisation. It may be discretionary or mandatory.

For example, Article 5 of the Charter of the United Nations provides for discretionary suspension:

> 'A Member of the United Nations against which preventive or enforcement action has been taken by the Security Council may be suspended from the exercise of the rights and privileges of membership by the General Assembly upon the recommendation of the Security Council. The exercise of these rights and privileges may be restored by the Security Council.'

However, Article 19 of the Charter provides for mandatory suspension in certain cases:

'A Member of the United Nations which is in arrears in the payment of its financial contributions to the Organisation shall have no vote in the General Assembly if the amount of its arrears equals or exceeds the amount of the contributions due from it for the preceding two full years. The General Assembly may, nevertheless, permit such a Member to vote if it is satisfied that the failure to pay is due to conditions beyond the control of the Member.'

Expulsion

The constitutions of several international organisations contain an exclusion clause enabling a State to be expelled from membership.

For example, Article 6 of the United Nations Charter provides:

'A Member of the United Nations which has persistently violated the Principles contained in the present Charter may be expelled from the Organisation by the General Assembly upon the recommendation of the Security Council.'

Where no provision is made

Withdrawal

Some Organisations have no specific provisions governing the right of a Member State to withdraw. For example, at the San Francisco Conference on the drafting of the United Nations Charter, the committee stated that 'the Charter should not make express provision either to permit or prohibit withdrawal from the Organisation'.

Purported withdrawal from the United Nations has only been in issue in relation to one State. In 1965 the Indonesian Government informed the Secretary-General that it was withdrawing from the Organisation following the election of Malaysia to a non-permanent seat on the Security Council. In September 1966, following a change of government, Indonesia notified the Secretary-General that it had 'decided to resume full co-operation with the United Nations and to resume participation in its activities'.

Indonesia argued that its absence from the United Nations was not based upon a withdrawal but upon a cessation of co-operation. This was apparently accepted as Indonesia simply 'resumed' its place and was not formally readmitted in accordance with Article 4.

Suspension and expulsion

In the absence of an express provision enabling suspension or exclusion it would seem that such action has no legal effect. Within the United Nations there have been attempts to expel both South Africa and Israel. However, in such cases, while retaining membership of the Organisation, diplomatic pressure has been brought to bear on these States by excluding them from participation in the activities of the Organisation.

Index